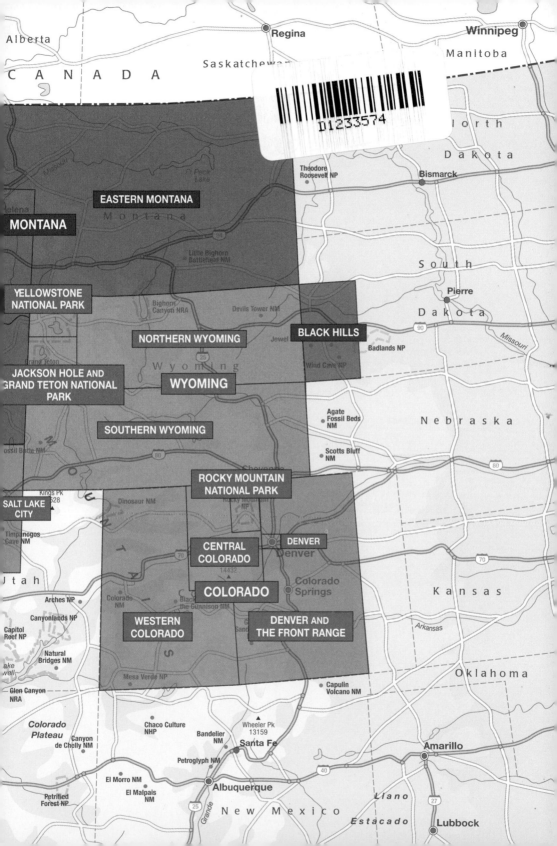

INSIGHT ⊙ GUIDES

USA: THE ROCKIES

PLAN & BOOK
YOUR TAILOR-MADE TRIP

BRAZIL

CHILE

ECUADOR

TAILOR-MADE TRIPS & UNIQUE EXPERIENCES CREATED BY LOCAL TRAVEL EXPERTS AT INSIGHTGUIDES.COM/HOLIDAYS

Insight Guides has been inspiring travellers with high-quality travel content for over 45 years. As well as our popular guidebooks, we now offer the opportunity to book tailor-made private trips completely personalised to your needs and interests. By connecting with one of our local experts, you will directly benefit from their expertise and local know-how, helping you create memories that will last a lifetime.

HOW INSIGHTGUIDES.COM/HOLIDAYS WORKS

STEP 1

Pick your dream destination and submit an enquiry, or modify an existing itinerary if you prefer.

STEP 2

Fill in a short form, sharing details of your travel plans and preferences with a local expert.

STEP 3

Your local expert will create your personalised itinerary, which you can amend until you are completely satisfied.

STEP 4

Book securely online. Pack your bags and enjoy your holiday! Your local expert will be available to answer questions during your trip.

BENEFITS OF PLANNING & BOOKING AT
INSIGHTGUIDES.COM/HOLIDAYS

PLANNED BY LOCAL EXPERTS

The Insight Guides local experts are hand-picked, based on their experience in the travel industry and their impeccable standards of customer service.

SAVE TIME & MONEY

When a local expert plans your trip, you save time and money when you book, even during high season. You won't be charged for using a credit card either.

TAILOR-MADE TRIPS

Book with Insight Guides, and you will be in complete control of the planning process, from the initial selections to amending your final itinerary.

BOOK & TRAVEL STRESS-FREE

Enjoy stress-free travel when you use the Insight Guides secure online booking platform. All bookings come with a money-back guarantee.

WHAT OTHER TRAVELLERS THINK ABOUT TRIPS BOOKED AT
INSIGHTGUIDES.COM/HOLIDAYS

Trip to Portugal

Every step of the planning process and the trip itself was effortless and exceptional. Our special interests, preferences and requests were accommodated resulting in a trip that exceeded our expectations.

Corinne, USA ★★★★★

Trip to Vietnam

The organization was superb, the drivers professional, and accommodation quite comfortable. I was well taken care of! My thanks to your colleagues who helped make my trip to Vietnam such a great experience. My only regret is that I couldn't spend more time in the country.

Heather ★★★★★

DON'T MISS OUT
BOOK NOW AT
INSIGHTGUIDES.COM/HOLIDAYS

CONTENTS

LEGEND
🔍 Insight on
📷 Photo story

⊘ A NOTE TO READERS

At Insight Guides, we always strive to bring you the most up-to-date information. This book was produced during a period of continuing uncertainty caused by the Covid-19 pandemic, so please note that content is more subject to change than usual. We recommend checking the latest restrictions and official guidance.

THE BEST OF USA: THE ROCKIES: TOP ATTRACTIONS

△ **Durango & Silverton Narrow Gauge Railroad, CO.** This steam-train ride corkscrews through spectacular mountains from historic Durango to the old mining town of Silverton, set beneath the tall peaks of Colorado's San Juan Mountains. See page 164.

△ **Grand Teton National Park, WY.** This spectacular chain of saw-toothed mountains, rising abruptly to tower 7000ft (2134 meters) above the Jackson Hole valley floor, is prime territory for hiking and biking, and elk, bison, and moose viewing. See page 198.

▽ **Glacier National Park, MT.** Montana's most spectacular park holds not only 25 glaciers, but also 2,000 lakes, 1,000 miles of rivers, and the exhilarating 50-mile (80km) Going-to-the-Sun highway. See page 243.

△ **Mesa Verde National Park, CO.** Explore extraordinary cliffside dwellings, giant stone palaces, towers, storerooms, and mystical circular *kivas* abandoned by the Ancestral Puebloans in southwest Colorado 800 years ago. See page 164.

△ **Sawtooth Mountains, ID.** Of all Idaho's numerous mountain ranges, the Sawtooth summits make for the most awe-inspiring scenic drive, with Red Fish Lake offering some of the most mesmerizing scenery in the Rockies. See page 270.

△ **Yellowstone National Park, WY.** The national park that started it all has everything, from steaming fluorescent hot springs and spouting geysers to sheer canyons and meadows filled with wild flowers and assorted fauna. See page 203.

△ **Skiing in the Rocky Mountains.** The Rockies boast some of the best skiing anywhere in the world, with their glitzy resorts and atmospheric former mining towns such as Aspen, Vail, Telluride, Park City, Sun Valley, and Jackson Hole. See page 100.

△ **Buffalo Bill Center of the West, WY.** This vast complex in the Old West town of Cody comprises five museums, covering Native American culture, Western art, the life of Buffalo Bill himself, and more. See page 213.

▽ **Black Hills, SD.** This cluster of forest-smothered peaks rising from the Great Plains features Mount Rushmore, the Crazy Horse Memorial, Deadwood, and an incredible amount of wildlife. See page 221.

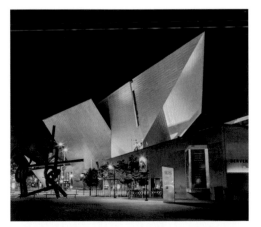

△ **Denver, CO.** The de facto capital of the Rockies is crammed with world-class museums, restaurants, and craft breweries, including the unique Clyfford Still Museum and the home of the "unsinkable Molly Brown." See page 123.

THE BEST OF USA: THE ROCKIES: EDITOR'S CHOICE

Grand Teton National Park.

BEST WINTER SPORTS

Big Sky Resort, MT. Montana's largest ski resort envelopes the steep, beautiful slopes of the Madison range. See page 255.

Crested Butte, CO. Skiers and especially snowboarders flock to Crested Butte to enjoy its challenging terrain, remote bowls, and steep faces. See page 153.

Grand Targhee Resort, WY. Famed for its "three-inch day" snow, this remote ski resort attracts hardcore snowboarders and skiers. See page 200.

Ogden Valley, UT. The three ski resorts east of Ogden are relatively uncrowded, with Nordic Valley best known for its beginner slopes and night skiing. See page 169.

Park City, UT. This vast ski area has something for everyone, with its three major resorts of Park City Mountains, The Canyons, and Deer Valley. See page 182.

Steamboat Springs, CO. Famed for its airy "champagne powder," Steamboat is Colorado's oldest ski resort and one of America's best all-round winter sports venues. See page 146.

Winter Park, CO. One of the oldest of Colorado's ski resorts combines three interconnected mountain peaks and exceptional facilities for kids and disabled skiers. See page 145.

BEST VIEWS

Alpine Loop Scenic Drive, UT. Scintillating route through the Wasatch Range, offering stupendous views of Mount Timpanogos and other forest-smothered peaks. See page 180.

Beartooth Highway, MT/WY. The mountain highway between Red Lodge and Yellowstone is truly majestic, snaking through untouched plateaus and high passes. See page 235.

Black Canyon of the Gunnison, CO. Hike or drive the rim roads taking in the views of this spectacular mountain gorge. See page 161.

Million Dollar Highway, CO. Traverse this 25-mile (40km) scenic highway between Silverton and Ouray for sensational mountain, valley and gorge views. See page 163.

Pikes Peak, CO. Hike, drive or take a train ride to the towering summit of Colorado's most famous summit. See page 135.

Rim Rock Drive, CO. This 23-mile (37km) scenic road twists through the Colorado National Monument, passing redrock canyons and towering sandstone outcrops. See page 156.

Trail Ridge Road, CO. Drive across pristine Rocky Mountain National Park on this high-altitude highway, with alpine panoramas at every turn. See page 137.

A skiier at Big Sky resort in Montana.

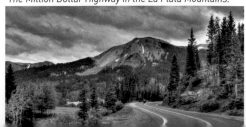

The Million Dollar Highway in the La Plata Mountains.

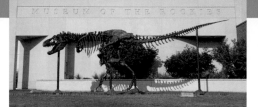
The Museum of the Rockies, Montana State University.

BEST MUSEUMS AND GALLERIES

C.M. Russell Museum, MT. Great Falls institution that celebrates "cowboy artist" Charles Marion Russell, incorporating his former studio and home. See page 237.

Denver Art Museum, CO. The region's foremost cache of art comprises over 70,000 works, from rare Native American pieces to paintings by Picasso and Georgia O'Keeffe. See page 126.

Idaho State Museum, ID. This fun and interactive museum in Boise is the best place to learn about Idaho history, nature and culture. See page 265.

Museum of the Rockies, MT. Huge museum in Bozeman known for its exceptional dinosaur collection and Native American art. See page 255.

US Olympic & Paralympic Museum, CO. Stunning building opened in 2020 outside Colorado Springs, dedicated to the story of America's Olympic and Paralympic athletes. See page 133.

Wyoming Dinosaur Center, WY. Located in tiny Thermopolis, this enlightening museum displays 58 dinosaur skeletons, most found nearby. See page 216.

BEST HIKES

Bear Lake & Emerald Lake, CO. The Rocky Mountain National Park is laced with trails, but the hikes around these two alpine lakes are truly breathtaking. See page 141.

Jenny Lake, WY. You can spend days enjoying the trails around this Grand Teton landmark, with glorious waterfalls and views of the magnificent Tetons themselves. See page 199.

Maroon Bells, CO. Gorgeous recreation area south of Aspen, with trails revealing one of the most extraordinary lake-and-mountains vistas anywhere in the world. See page 152.

Mickelson Trail, SD. This long-distance rail trail cuts through the spruce and ponderosa pine forests of the Black Hills, shared by bicyclists, hikers and horseback riders. See page 229.

The historic mining town of Leadville, Colorado.

BEST OLD TOWNS

Butte, MT. One of the most fascinating towns in Montana, Butte is crammed with remnants of its once flourishing copper industry, from old mines to grand Victorian mansions. See page 255.

Deadwood, SD. Classic Western town, the home of Wild Bill and Calamity Jane, with beautifully restored saloons and hotels in the heart of the Black Hills. See page 226.

Leadville, CO. Colorado is crammed with once booming Victorian mining towns, but this is one of the most atmospheric, with a stock of grand architecture to match. See page 149.

Ouray, CO. Thanks to silver and gold mining, Ouray remains one of the prettiest small towns in the West, enhanced by its famed hot springs. See page 162.

South Pass City, WY. This historic town site preserves over 30 historic structures dating from the gold boom of the 1860s and 1870s. See page 191.

Wallace, ID. Few Old West towns are as authentic as this former silver mining hub in the Idaho Panhandle. See page 269.

Boating on Jenny Lake, Grand Teton National Park.

Tunnels in Craters of the Moon National Monument.

Bison in Custer State Park.

OFF THE BEATEN TRACK

Black American West Museum, CO. One of Denver's most intriguing small museums chronicles the lesser-known history of African Americans in the Old West. See page 127.

Boulder Dushanbe Teahouse, CO. An exquisite Tajikistan-style teahouse in the heart of Boulder, a unique gift from the city of Dushanbe, offering premium teas and snacks. See page 130.

Craters of the Moon National Monument, ID. This weird volcanic landscape of lava cones, tubes, craters and caverns really does look like an alien world. See page 271.

Little Bighorn, MT. One of the most famous battlefields in America, where Custer faced Sitting Bull and Crazy Horse. See page 232.

Garnet Ghost Town, MT. The Rockies are littered with abandoned mining towns, but this is one of the best preserved. See page 260.

Shooting Star Saloon, UT. Located in quiet Huntsville, Utah, the Shooting Star has been serving cowboys since 1879. See page 168.

Spiral Jetty, UT. Robert Smithson created this unique spiraling earthwork on a remote section of Great Salt Lake coastline in 1970. See page 180.

BEST FOR FAMILIES

Big Dipper Ice Cream, MT. Delicious handcrafted ice cream from Missoula, available via several branches in Montana and always a big hit in summer. See page 258.

Downtown Aquarium, CO. One of Denver's top family-friendly attractions, featuring underwater exhibits, a 4-D Theater, restaurant and a Mermaids show. See page 126.

Clark Planetarium, UT. Budding astronomers will love Salt Lake City's excellent planetarium and space museum, with moon rock samples and more on display. See page 178.

Custer State Park, SD. Wildlife is virtually guaranteed at this huge Black Hills preserve: herds of buffalo, elk, prairie dog towns, bighorn sheep, burros and more. See page 225.

Elitch Gardens Theme and Water Park, CO. Denver's beloved summer-only theme park features all sorts of thrill rides, waterslides and entertainment for children (and grown-up children). See page 126.

Leadville, Colorado & Southern Railroad, CO. Kids love this scenic train ride through the Colorado Rockies and Arkansas River Valley. See page 150.

Town Square Shootout, Jackson WY. Evening gunfights held for tourists – with music, food and dancing thrown in – are an annual summer tradition in Jackson's Town Square. See page 196.

The Spiral Jetty.

BEST FESTIVALS AND EVENTS

Aspen Music Festival Aspen, CO. Highly respected classical music festival founded in 1949, featuring over 400 concerts from some of the world's most celebrated musicians. See page 104.

Cheyenne Frontier Days, WY. Huge rodeo and celebration of cowboy culture that takes place over 10 days every July and draws massive crows. See page 186.

Colorado State Fair, CO. The region's biggest state fair runs from August into September in Pueblo, featuring concerts, carnival rides and lots of food. See page 105.

Crow Fair, MT. One of the biggest Native American powwows in the region, a dynamic celebration of Crow and Plains Indian culture. See page 232.

Lionel Hampton Jazz Festival, ID. This extremely popular festival held at Moscow's University of Idaho showcases the top names in jazz every February. See page 268.

Telluride Bluegrass Festival, CO. Running over four days in late June, performances of bluegrass and all sorts of other country and folk music genres feature at this mountain town festival. See page 162.

Whitewater rafting on the Salmon River.

BEST OUTDOOR ACTIVITIES

Float trips on the Snake River, WY. This is an incredibly fun thing to do on a summer's day out in the Grand Tetons, floating (or rafting or kayaking) gently along crystal-clear waters. See page 97.

Jet-boating in Hells Canyon, ID. America's deepest river gorge is best experienced on a thrilling jet-boat ride from Riggins or White Bird. See page 267.

Mountain biking in Durango, CO. Mountain bikers will love Durango, an off-road biking hotspot known for the Haflin Creek Trail and Hermosa Creek Trail. See page 163.

Mountain biking in Grand Junction, CO. Grand Junction's rugged deserts offer excellent mountain biking, with a network of local trails here and in nearby Fruita. See page 156.

Rafting the Salmon River, ID. It's one of the ultimate Rockies adventures; a five-day rafting trip down the Middle Fork of the rushing Salmon River. See page 271.

Snowboarding at Park City, UT. Utah's biggest ski resort is a paradise for snowboarders, with world-class terrain parks and Olympic half-pipes. See page 182.

Rock climbing at Vedauwoo, WY. The piled-up and mushroomed rock formations of southern Wyoming offer rock climbing for beginner through to expert climbers. See page 187.

Whitewater rafting on the Animas River, CO. Everything from family-friendly excursions on the Lower Animas to Class IV and V thrills on the Upper Animas. See page 163.

Competing in the Cheyenne Frontier Days rodeo.

The Garden of the Gods Park in Colorado Springs.

St. Mary Lake and Wild Goose
island in Glacier National Park.

A munching bull moose in Grand Teton National Park.

AN OPEN INVITATION

Only when you traverse the Rocky Mountain states does the immense size of the American West really hit home.

Male mountain bluebird.

Stretching over 1,000 miles (1609km) from the virgin forests on the Canadian border to the deserts of New Mexico, America's rugged spine encompasses an astonishing array of landscapes – geyser basins, lava flows, arid valleys, and huge sand dunes – each in its own way as dramatic as the region's magnificent snow-capped peaks. All that geological grandeur is enhanced by wildlife such as bison, bear, moose, and elk, and the conspicuous legacy of the miners, cowboys, outlaws, and Native Americans who struggled over the area's rich resources during the 19th century.

Theodore Roosevelt called these shimmering blue lakes, scenic roadways, parks, forests, recreation areas, and wondrous rock formations "scenery that bankrupts the English language." Then there are the thrills of going to see a real life rodeo, of skiing over powdery snow on choice mountain slopes, and of whitewater rafting down an exhilaratingly rushing river, not to mention the abundance of opportunities for fishing, sailing, camping, and backpacking.

A wild coyote.

The air somehow just feels fresher here, the water clearer, the sky bigger than just about any place you'll ever get to visit. In all the states covered in this book (Colorado, Idaho, Montana, South Dakota, Utah, and Wyoming) you'll find a combination of adventure, natural beauty, wildlife, sports, history, and art, and all against a crisp, wholesome backdrop.

Today you'll find the Rockies as compelling as when Lewis and Clark first came this way early in the 19th century on their famous expedition to unlock the American West. Coming on the heels of that pair of explorers were the fabled mountain men, prospectors in search of gold and silver, fur traders, cattle and land barons, cowboys, ranchers, copper kings, and prophets and visionaries of one sort or another.

Given the vast distances involved, you are unlikely to cover everything the Rockies has to offer in one trip; but even picking a few highlights will give you a deeper insight into the Rockies' natural and historic wonders. And while there is no such thing as a typical Rockies experience, there can be few places in the world where strangers can feel so confident of a warm reception.

A professional cowgirl riding a horse at a rodeo.

ROCKY MOUNTAIN PEOPLE

Most folks who live in the Rockies feel that they are a breed apart, whether their families have been here for generations, or they arrived for a visit and never left.

The mountain men who ventured into the nearly impenetrable wilderness of these mountains were the first whites to come under the spell of the Rockies; Native Americans have been here for at least 10,000 years. These mountain men made their living primarily from hunting beaver, but when the demand for beaver pelts died out in the 1840s, the mountain men became guides and scouts for the wagon trains heading west. A relatively small handful of pioneers stopped at the eastern plains and foothills of the Rockies, becoming small time farmers and cattle ranchers, some of whose descendants still live here today.

EARLY DAYS: MINERS AND PIONEERS

The first big group to invade the Rockies in the 19th century, though, was the miners. Beginning in the late 1850s, most of them followed the siren call of big strikes and easy riches from valley to valley or mountain range to mountain range, but many stayed even after the silver had played out. Though the 100,000 people who headed west for Colorado in 1859 were ostensibly on their way to make a fortune panning for gold in the mountains, they were spurred on by an economic depression and by the promise of a new beginning. Only half of them made it, and few stayed long; the 5,000 or so that were left a year later were a determined, hardy bunch.

There was also "Uncle Dick" Wooton, who opened the first tent saloon in Denver. He arrived on Christmas Eve with a wagon full of groceries and 10 kegs of whiskey, one of which he cracked open with an axe, handing out free drinks.

Mining ore in a mine at Eagle River Canyon in 1905.

In Colorado, the first European-Americans to settle in the lush and spectacularly beautiful Estes Park area were Joel Estes and his son Milton, who built a cabin in the grassy meadows at the bottom of the valley in 1859. They later sold their property to the Earl of Dunraven, who wanted to turn it into a game preserve. Joe Shipler was among the first to stake out claims in the Never Summer Mountains at the headwaters of the Colorado River in 1879. Though he never got much silver out of Shipler Mountain, he and his family lived in the Kawuneeche Valley until 1914.

Another notable pioneer, "Uncle Dick" Wooton was a Virginian who made his fortune by hacking out a 27-mile (43km) road over Raton Pass on the New Mexico border, then charging a hefty toll to

> *Today there are towns that exist solely because of their ski mountains – Vail and Beaver Creek are two prime examples. Aspen was almost a ghost town before the skiing craze revived it, as were Steamboat Springs and Breckenridge.*

those who wanted to cross it. He wisely let Native Americans pass without charging them, probably to save his own skin, but also perhaps out of a

A Mormon vigilante aiming his gun at a pioneer wagon.

sense of justice, considering that they had been using the route long before Europeans appeared on the scene. When the Santa Fe railroad wanted to use the pass, Wooton sold his rights to the company, and helped build the graded track.

As you might expect, it could be tough to be a woman in the Old West; they were often divided into two categories, "good" and "bad". However, those that fell into the latter category (saloon waitresses and sex workers known as "hurdy gurdy" girls) often ended up marrying well despite their supposed "badness", and due to the scarcity of women in the West, they were usually in a strong position to be choosy. The "good" girls were almost by definition already married or had parents who were wealthy

enough to support them until they found an appropriate husband. Nevertheless, plenty of women managed to carve out successful, independent careers in the Old West, though their stories are rarely told (see page 46).

While most mining towns established law and order within a matter of months, there were also those that remained lawless, spawning legends of gunfighters and outlaws. Henry Plummer was one of the "baddest" of the Montana outlaws but, handsome and charismatic as he was, he literally got away with murder for years. At the height of his checkered career, Plummer led a band of more than 100 men who called themselves "The Innocents". They robbed stagecoaches and mines in Montana and killed anyone who got in their way. Plummer somehow managed to get himself elected sheriff of Bannack and Virginia City. After years of being terrorized by "The Innocents", a group of citizens calling themselves "The Vigilantes," led by John X. Beidler, took matters into their own hands. Eventually Sheriff Plummer was given away by one of his men, exposed as the leader of the notorious band and hanged in 1864.

Mining is still a major industry in the Rockies, from the massive open-pit copper mines of Montana and the Climax molybdenum mine near Leadville, Colorado, to small gold and silver mines that are privately owned. Mining is very much a way of life in the Rockies. Hours are long, the work hard and dirty, but for some it's the only life they know, and the life they choose.

FROM MINERS TO MORMONS

Throughout the Rockies, the pattern of settlement from the 1860s onwards remained consistent. Mining towns sprang up overnight and disappeared just as quickly when the silver or gold failed to live up to its promise. Those towns that survived and grew, such as Helena, Montana, and Boise, Idaho, were favorably located along roads or railways. Nearly every town in the Rockies has its origins in mining – the ranchers, farmers and merchants followed the miners. Some towns continued to flourish because minerals such as copper, coal and uranium were discovered, while others such as Glenwood Springs, Colorado Springs and Idaho Springs became health spas. Jackson, Wyoming, grew because of its proximity to Yellowstone National Park.

The promise of wide open spaces, freedom and opportunity also inspired a variety of religious and utopian groups to settle in the Rockies, of which the Mormons were the largest and most successful – today they account for over 55 percent of residents in Utah, 23 percent in Idaho, and 9 percent in Wyoming.

Though not Mormon, the town of Greeley, Colorado was founded as a cooperative agricultural colony that sold its goods to the mining towns. The original members were religious and conservative, banning drinking and gambling,

mines and hunt grizzlies. Susan B. Anthony and Elizabeth Cady Stanton spent months among the women of the Rockies, lobbying furiously for women's rights. In the late 1800s and early 1900s, celebrities flocked to the health spas and hot springs of the Rockies in much the same way as they flock to the ski slopes today.

SKI RESORTS AND THE TOURIST INDUSTRY

Within a few decades after the miners arrived, tourists began flocking to the Rockies to gaze

The handcart pioneers struggle through a blizzard while crossing the Rocky Mountains on the Mormon Trail.

encouraging church socials and setting up libraries and schools. Other towns along the Front Range of Colorado, such as Longmont, Fort Collins and Colorado Springs, became thriving towns in the same manner. Though they soon ceased to be communally owned, the settlements were very successful and established a tradition of conservatism that survives to this day.

There was a great fascination with the early West not only back in the eastern states but in Europe as well. Oscar Wilde toured the mining camps of the Rockies in the 1880s and said the miners were the best audience he'd ever had. Silver bricks were laid in Leadville for the visit of President Grant. Dukes, lords, barons and other dignitaries from Europe came to invest in the

at the splendor of the snow-capped peaks, to hunt for elk, bear and mountain lions, to fish for trout in the streams, to cure illness in the hot springs, or to play cowboys at dude ranches. One narrow-gauge railway that followed a creek bed survived by catering to trout fishermen, who were dropped off at likely-looking spots along the way. Colorado Springs became a famous health resort for the wealthy, beginning a tradition of sumptuous grande dame hotels in the middle of nowhere, many of which still stand.

Nevertheless, throughout the early and mid-20th century, the Rockies remained somewhat obscure. Denver, Cheyenne and Helena were little more than sprawling cow towns, hanging on for their economic life to mining, agriculture and

It was skiing that finally made the Rockies a year-round tourist attraction. What began after World War II as a somewhat eccentric industry catering to a select group of wealthy clients become an established sport, and continues to grow in popularity.

ranching through booms and busts, droughts and depressions. Tourists continued to trek west in the summers, but the winters found

towns, but even today there are still plenty of holdouts who live in log cabins with no electricity or running water and lead a largely self-sufficient way of life. Bearded and long-haired mountain men and their female counterparts are still a relatively common sight in the mountain towns of the Rockies. For these people, the Rockies represent the same things they did to the first immigrants – space, freedom and an opportunity to live their lives as they choose.

The ski bums who came and never left are a similar group in ski towns. They came on vaca-

Members of Indigenous communities taking part in a march protesting a Colorado Detention Facility.

most towns semi deserted and economically impoverished.

The birth of the ski industry created a mini-boom of immigrants to the mountain towns; people who were willing to forgo the convenience and job opportunities of the cities for the easygoing lifestyle and beauty of the ski resorts – not to mention the chance to spend a good part of each winter's day on downhill skis.

The growth of the ski industry in the 1960s coincided with the era of hippies, the so-called "flower children" who, at least for a while, rejected the values of their parents in favor of a simpler, less ambitious lifestyle. Of the thousands who moved to the mountains, most were eventually absorbed into the mainstream mining, ranching and resort

tions or during a year off from college and fell in love with the thrill and adrenalin of downhill skiing and the mountains. When the idyllic summers came, they couldn't bear to leave, so they put down roots instead. Their first few years in town are usually spent washing dishes, cleaning hotel rooms, running ski lifts, waiting on tables, and performing all the other services so vital to a resort town. An equal number stay only for a season. Most ski resorts have an ample supply of young transients who are willing to do menial labor in exchange for the chance to hit the slopes.

Today winter visitors to the Rockies are more than likely to meet ski instructors and the ski patrol. Competition is stiff for these jobs and those who make it are highly qualified and certified. On any given day, a member of the ski patrol may have set off an avalanche with dynamite, marked a dangerous spot on the ski slope, put a broken leq in a temporary splint and hauled the injured party off the mountain on a sled, and then gone on an out-of-bounds search for a missing skier.

THE ROCKIES MELTING POT

The Rockies have always been an Anglo melting pot, with heavy German and Slavic populations in the mountains. Other ethnic groups, such as African Americans, Chinese and Latinos, tend

group, accounting for over half of the population of Denver's public schools. The Latino community is also playing an increasingly important role in local politics.

Another unusual and disappearing group of people in the Rockies are the Basque sheepherders and ranchers. Beginning in the 1870s, Basque herders established communities from Colorado to Boise, Idaho. Overgrazing, legislation limiting transient grazing in the 1930s, and competition between large ranches spelled the demise of the independent Basque sheepherder, but many

A mariachi band playing to celebrate the Day of the Dead.

to be concentrated in urban settings along the Front Range. African Americans played a large part in the settling of the West – the Black American West Museum in Denver covers this history in fascinating detail. The Chinese came to build the railroads in the late 1800s, and many settled in Denver. Southern Colorado is a part of the Southwest that has been settled by Spanish settlers and Mexicans for centuries. In fact, English is a second language in some of the small isolated Hispanic villages in the San Juan Mountains of southern Colorado, and the cultural milieu has changed little over the centuries. Adobe houses, strings of red chilis hanging in the sun, and the cadence of the Spanish language mark these villages. In Denver, Latinos are by far the dominant ethnic

⊘ NATIVE AMERICANS

In contrast to the large reservations in the Southwest, there are relatively small Ute, Cheyenne, Crow, Shoshone, Bannock and Arapaho reservations scattered about the Rockies. Each tribe has its own celebrations and ceremonies, but they aren't widely publicized outside of the reservation. The Plains and Mountain tribes tended to be more warlike than their Pueblo neighbors to the south, and their land was more valuable to white settlers. As a result, they were nearly wiped out by the late 1900s, but have slowly made a comeback both in terms of population and in preserving their cultural heritage.

of their descendants can still be found working for large ranches, living a simple life in modest trailers.

NEW ARRIVALS

The late 20th century saw an even larger wave of young immigrants to the cities and the mountain towns. Typical were the successful New York City advertising executives who made a lot of money, got fed up with the frenetic lifestyle, took their life savings out of the bank, moved to a resort town and opened up a shop, a real estate office or a

of the big cities and ski resorts – the idyllic summers attract artists of every kind, from the orchestras of the Aspen Festival to the top-notch musicians of the Telluride Bluegrass Festival. Acting troupes, film-makers, classical musicians, craftspeople, painters and sculptors flock to the mountains where, it seems, their creative juices flow like nowhere else. To celebrate these artists, every resort town has its own concerts, festivals, fairs and shows.

Every town also has its part-time resident celebrities – some of them come for the ski-

A quiet mountain lake at Rocky Mountain National Park.

lodge. Many of these immigrants also brought with them a firm commitment to preserving the beauty of the mountains. Thousands of young people have moved to the Front Range of Colorado where, they believe, they have the best of both worlds – the sophistication and excitement of a metropolis, combined with the recreational playground and pristine wilderness of the mountains only a few miles away. The Front Range has attracted many high-tech industries in the past few decades, creating its own Silicon Valley and lucrative jobs for young professionals.

ARTISTS AND CELEBRITIES

Though the Rockies can be something of a cultural desert in the winter – with the exception

ing, some for the cultural events, some simply for peace, quiet and mountain air. Aspen and Jackson Hole are particularly popular with celebrities, although Vail, Park City, Steamboat Springs, Sun Valley and Telluride aren't far behind. A virtual invasion of wealthy out-of-towners has moved into these areas. Sometimes it seems movie stars outnumber local residents. Writers seek the solitude and big horizons of Montana and Wyoming, while painters look for Victorian towns, weather-beaten cowboys and snowcapped peaks.

OUTDOOR PEOPLE

If there is one easy generalization to make about those who live in the Rockies today, it's that they love the outdoors. Health and physical fitness are virtually a regional obsession. It often seems that everyone under the age of 40 is involved in jogging, bicycling, aerobics, athletic clubs or exercise classes of some sort. The goal is not only staying fit and slim but excelling in one or more of the many mountain sports, from riding mountain bikes over rocky passes to skiing, hiking, rock climbing, kayaking and backpacking. If those sports are too taxing, there is always trout fishing, ice fishing, bird watching, gardening, horseback riding, snowmobiling, ballooning – there's always one more run to make, or one more turn to carve out of the powder.

PARK RANGERS

Travelers who venture into the national parks, forests and wilderness areas of the Rockies are very likely to meet a ranger working for one of the numerous government agencies that maintain, regulate and watch over them – these dedicated people perhaps best sum up what being a Rocky Mountain person is all about. Most have degrees that make them experts in the conservation,

A peaceful flight during the annual balloon festival in Colorado Springs.

and golf – the point is getting outside to enjoy the wilderness, the scenery, the crisp air and the blue skies.

For every sport in the Rockies, there are races, contests, celebrations and festivals, from marathons to rodeos that are enthusiastically attended by crowds of people. Summers are all too fleeting in the Rockies, so they are approached with gusto; a sense of now or never, take-it-while-you-can. When the hunting season arrives in the fall, hunters flock to the mountains by the thousands – many say it's as much an excuse to get out into the wilderness before winter sets in as it is a desire to shoot a deer or an elk. And even with the long winters, there never seems to be time to get in enough skiing

management, identification and preservation of the plants and animals of the Rockies. Their job description may include giving nature talks and walks, keeping the peace at crowded campgrounds, picking up litter and looking for lost backpackers. It can also include spending weeks at a time alone in the wilderness on foot or horseback, maintaining trails and signs and cataloging flora and fauna.

Though the people of the Rockies are Americans through and through, but there is a certain exuberance, a joie de vivre, and a keen appreciation among those who have fallen under the spell of the blue skies and snowcapped peaks that sets them apart. It's an outlook that is apparent in the eyes and the minds of the locals, and visitor to the Rockies should watch out: it can be contagious.

Custer's Last Stand at the Battle of Little Bighorn, 1876.

DECISIVE DATES

THE FIRST PEOPLES

15,000 BC
First nomadic peoples from Asia reach Alaska.

9,000 BC
Almost all North America's large mammals become extinct, possibly due to over-hunting.

700–1130 AD
Ancestral Puebloan culture blossoms at Mesa Verde, Colorado.

1400
Oral histories of the Kiowa place their ancestors in the Yellowstone area from this period.

EUROPEAN EXPLORATION

1540
Spanish explorer Francisco Vázquez de Coronado traverses the southern end of the Rockies (New Mexico).

1610
Santa Fe is founded as the Spanish capital of New Mexico; horses begin to spread across the West, leading to a new Native American "horse culture."

1682
France claims the "Louisiana Territory," which encompasses much of Montana, Wyoming and Colorado – the rest of the West is nominally Spanish.

1741
Pierre Antoine and Paul Mallet, Canadian *voyageurs* (fur traders), become the first Europeans to report the existence of the Rocky Mountains.

1793
Scottish explorer Alexander MacKenzie becomes the first European to cross the Rocky Mountains.

THE WESTERN FRONTIER

1803
President Thomas Jefferson buys French Louisiana for $15 million; Montana, Wyoming, and parts of Colorado are incorporated into the USA.

1804
The Lewis and Clark Expedition explores the Rockies through to 1806.

1812
South Pass in Wyoming is discovered – wagon trains on the Oregon Trail subsequently follow this route, beginning in 1832.

1846
The Oregon Treaty between the US and Great Britain officially adds Idaho to the United States.

1847
Fort Benton established as a fur trading post in Montana; the Mormons begin settling near the Great Salt Lake in Utah.

1848
Mexico cedes California, the rest of Colorado and New Mexico to the United States of America, after defeat in the Mexican-American War.

1850
Utah Territory created, with the capital at Fillmore; Salt Lake City replaces Fillmore in 1856.

1858
Pike's Peak Gold Rush in Colorado; Denver founded.

1861
The start of the US Civil War; Territory of Colorado established.

1863
Creation of Idaho Territory.

1864
Montana Territory is created; John Bozeman helps found the town named after him.

1865
End of the US Civil War.

1866
Red Cloud's War between the Lakota, Northern Cheyenne, Northern Arapaho, and the United States rages until 1868.

The aftermath of the Ludlow Massacre.

1868
Territory of Wyoming is organized.

1869
Wyoming becomes first US territory to grant women the right to vote; the transcontinental railroad is completed.

1870
Colorado becomes the 38th US state.

1872
Yellowstone becomes the world's first National Park.

1876
Native tribes defeat the 7th Cavalry, and kill General George Custer, at Little Bighorn.

1877
The flight of the Nez Percé from the Pacific Northwest to Montana.

1889
Montana becomes the 41st state.

1890
Idaho becomes 43rd US state; Wyoming becomes the 44th state.

1896
Utah becomes 45th state on condition that a ban on Mormon polygamy be written into the state constitution.

1893
Women win the right to vote in Colorado.

THE 20TH CENTURY

1914
Ludlow Massacre: 21 people (striking coal miners and family members) killed during the Colorado Coalfield War.

1914
Howelsen Hill in Colorado founded as America's first ski area.

1919
Jack Dempsey of Colorado becomes world heavyweight boxing champion – he holds the title until 1926 and becomes a cultural icon.

1961
Author Ernest Hemingway commits suicide at his home in Ketchum, Idaho.

1966
Cheyenne Mountain Complex in Colorado is completed as United States Space Command and NORAD.

1981
The iconic soap series *Dynasty*, set in Denver, debuts on US television.

1991
Wellington Webb becomes the first African-American mayor of Denver.

1996
Ted Kaczynski, aka the Unabomber, is arrested at his cabin in Lincoln, Montana.

1999
The Columbine High School massacre in Colorado; 12 students and one teacher murdered

THE 21ST CENTURY

2000
Wyoming's Dick Cheney becomes Vice President.

2001
Judy Martz becomes the first (and so far only) female governor of Montana.

2002
Salt Lake City hosts the XIX Olympic Winter Games; Mitt Romney leads the organizing committee.

2012
Aurora, Colorado shooting: 12 people are killed and 70 more injured; Colorado is the first US state to legalize marijuana for recreational use.

2014
Colorado, Idaho, Montana, Utah, and Wyoming all legalize same-sex marriage.

2018
Former presidential candidate – and devout Mormon – Mitt Romney is elected US Senator for Utah.

2020
Montana legalizes marijuana. The COVID-19 pandemic hits the Rockies, as it does America and the rest of the world.

2022
The COVID-19 Pandemic eases. In Colorado, over 11,000 people have died; in Idaho over 4,000; in Montana over 3,000, and in Wyoming over 1,600.

Former Governor Mitt Romney.

Mesa Verde is the largest archeological preserve in the United States.

ANCIENT INHABITANTS

The Rockies were thrust up from the bottom of the sea over 135 million years ago. Worn down and uplifted two more times since then, the present range rose up about 50 million years ago.

The upheaval was accompanied by volcanic activity, showering the region with deep layers of ash and sending waves of liquid rock bubbling up to the surface like oatmeal. Glaciers finished the job.

In Colorado, these mountains take up an area more than six times the size of the Swiss Alps – with 53 snowy peaks towering more than 14,000ft (4,260 meters) above sea level and a total of 1,143 mountains rising to 10,000ft (3,040 meters) or more.

In Idaho, the gaps between mountains were depressed and filled by lava flows and carved by the violent Snake River. The lava plains here are second in size only to the Columbia River Plateau of Oregon and Washington. The Craters of the Moon National Monument at the northern edge of these lava fields preserves breathtaking volcanic features.

Evidence of the ancient rock layers bending and turning upward can be found everywhere in the Rocky Mountains. Lifted, folded, mangled, crushed, and broken rock formations created today's magnificent scenic features. The vast mineral wealth, concentrated deep in the earth's cracks and crevices, has challenged miners for hundreds of years to make a living from the natural resources before them.

Most geological processes happen far too slowly to be perceived by humans. They usually

Native American petroglyphs in Mesa Verde.

occur on a time scale of thousands or millions of years. However, there is occasionally a particularly dramatic geologic event that reminds us that these seemingly timeless, unchanging mountains are constantly evolving. In 1925 near Jackson Hole, for example, a cowboy outran a rain-soaked avalanche more than a mile wide while six of his cattle died.

Great shields of ice flowed from the north at least three times in the last several hundred thousand years, widening valleys, sheering off mountain tops, polishing bedrock, and depositing great mounds of debris.

FIRST PEOPLES

Paleo-Indians entered the region at least 15,000 years ago. Although their weapons were primitive, they were clever hunters able to take down the largest and most ferocious game. Mammoths were chased into swamps where they were mired in mud and easily killed. Herds

The sides of these mountains often reveal ancient marine fossils, fascinating dinosaur remains, and rocks that were formed in the hot interior of the earth – invaluable links to our planet's history.

of giant bison were stampeded over cliffs or into corrals. Some archeologists believe that prehistoric hunters may have contributed to the wide-

cultivating maize, beans and squash on the mesa tops and canyon floors as well as hunting game and harvesting wild foods in the forests. There are several major Anasazi sites in this corner of Colorado, but the most impressive are the cliff dwellings of Mesa Verde National Park. Tucked into alcoves in the canyon walls, the pueblos were abandoned in the 14th century. After around 800 years of habitation in the region, the Ancestral Puebloans seem to have moved away suddenly. Quite why this happened is one of the most enduring questions in Ameri-

Square Tower House in Mesa Verde National Park.

spread extinction of giant Ice Age mammals.

Evidence of these nomadic cultures has been pieced together from various archeological finds, including piles of bones from slaughtered mammoths and basic quartzite quarries in Wyoming. Additionally, records of ancient societies are supplemented by petroglyphs (rock etchings) and pictographs (rock paintings), scattered in pockets of former settlement throughout the region – though most are estimated to date from no earlier than about 2,000 BC.

About 2,000 years ago a farming and hunting people known as the Ancestral Puebloans or Anasazi moved into the canyon country of what is now southwestern Colorado. The Anasazi occupied the region for more than 1,000 years

can archeology; one theory posits a possible period of drought in the 14th century that made farming in the area impossible.

Much less is known about the early history of the rest of the Rocky Mountain region. To the north, the Rocky Mountains provided a bounty of game and wild foods to a variety of nomadic tribes. The Shoshone and Ute made forays into the mountains from the west. The Kootenai,

The first Europeans to penetrate the region were members of a Spanish expedition led by Francisco Coronado in 1540.

Kalispel, Nez Percé (Nimiipuu) and powerful Blackfeet dominated present-day Idaho and western Montana. The Apache migrated into the region about 600 years ago and became a major force in the southern Rockies. The Arapaho, Cheyenne and Sioux were among the last to arrive, traveling east across the plains from the Great Lakes region.

The number of people living in the mountains themselves was tiny by today's standards.

With so much space to roam, it's not surprising that relations between tribes were punctuated by friction only occasionally. The harmonious balance seems to have been upset by the first contact with Europeans, which occurred south of the Rockies, between the Pueblo tribes and the Spanish.

Coronado set out from Mexico City in search of the fabled Seven Cities of Cibola to the north. Rumors were rampant that the seven cities were filled with gold and gems. The Spaniards were so angry when they discovered that Cibola consisted of nothing more than a collection of pueblos and caves that they ransacked the place from kiva to kiva, providing Native Americans with a sample of what was to come for the next 300 years.

Coronado continued north through Colorado and into Kansas but nothing resembling the legendary cities of gold was found. He returned to Mexico City having accomplished two things: he destroyed the myth of great golden cities to the north, and engendered a bitter hatred of the Spanish in the Native Americans.

Nevertheless, expeditions to the north continued for various reasons. Some of the explorers were devout men who wanted to convert the Native Americans to Christianity, while others were interested in elevating their family's social status and gaining land.

However, the Spanish did introduce something that would prove extremely precious: horses. Spanish ponies moved quickly from tribe to tribe and within only a few generations revolutionized the Native American way of life. Mounted tribes could easily roam over vast

Pipe Shrine Houses in Mesa Verde National Park.

stretches of territory and hunt from the massive herds of buffalo that blackened the plains. By the time the first Anglo pioneers came from the east, the horse-and-buffalo culture of the powerful Sioux, Cheyenne, Crow, and Blackfeet were in full bloom and presented a formidable barrier to western settlement.

Alone on the frontier and fiercely resisted by Native American tribes, the Spanish were unable to establish settlements much farther north than the San Luis valley, in what is now southern Colorado.

⊘ MESA VERDE

European-Americans first saw Mesa Verde in 1888, when two cowboys stopped to rest their ponies and discovered a group of ancient dwellings in a huge cave about 50 feet (15 meters) below the rim of the mesa. They found what is now called Cliff Palace. This structure, with its 150 rooms, is thought to be the largest group of dwellings of its kind. The four-story rooms are decorated with red and white designs, and there is a 30-foot (9-meter) tower, of which each stone was shaped with the crudest tools. Grinding bowls and storage bins for corn were also found, which would have been invaluable to the survival of the population, estimated to have been about 100.

Lewis and Clark as well as Sacagawea with her baby and husband, Toussaint Charbonneau.

PATHFINDERS

Most of the Rocky Mountains came under nominal American ownership in 1803, though they were inhabited almost exclusively by independent Native American tribes for the next 60 years.

After Coronado, the early 18th-century Old World powers divvied up the Rocky Mountain territory between them, despite their having little or no knowledge of the lands or natives who inhabited them. The Spanish had the most significant foothold close to the region; the French also made major claims on the territory, though by 1762 had ceded all land west of the Mississippi to the Spanish. In a spate of political wrangling that followed the wilting of British power on the continent after the War of Independence (1775–76), the bulk of the Rockies reverted again to French ownership as part of territory attached to Louisiana. Nevertheless, the Spanish maintained a small toehold in the Rockies, in fact sending the first expedition that deliberately set out to explore a portion of the region.

French interest, on the other hand, was minimal. The only French influx came in the form of a small number of mountain men – estimated at around 150 – who, having ventured in to trap beaver from their bases in French Canada, mostly found homes among the indigenous people, and never left the region. While the French also contributed names to some features in the northern half of the territory – like the Grand Tetons (large breasts) – French possession was to be short-lived.

THE LOUISIANA PURCHASE

The Louisiana Purchase took in some 827,987 sq. miles (2 million sq. km) of land between the Mississippi and the Rockies, stretching from the Gulf of Mexico to the Canadian border. The purchase took place in 1803 during President Thomas Jefferson's first administration. The price was $15 million, which made it the greatest land bargain in the history of the United

Sacagawea on a USA postage stamp.

States – it doubled the size of the nation overnight. Though this was land that had nominally belonged to France (and some of it still contested by Spain), in reality it was roamed almost exclusively by Native Americans, who had no

The 1775–76 Domínguez–Escalante expedition visited parts of both Colorado and Utah, providing the first written accounts of the area, in search of a useful overland route to connect the Missions in New Mexico with those in California.

part in the deal and indeed no knowledge of it. Small French settlements and trading posts dotted the banks of the Mississippi River and the Plains, but apart from a few hardy mountain men and French-Canadian voyageurs, this was land mostly devoid of European Americans.

THE CORPS OF DISCOVERY

Within weeks of the purchase, President Jefferson sent his private secretary, Captain Meriwether Lewis, and Lewis' friend William Clark, on a mission to gather information about this

they recruited and trained themselves. The journals of Lewis and Clark tell of a remarkable 8,000-mile (13,000-km) round trip to the Pacific Ocean. Between them, the explorers named around three hundred plants and animals, including the grizzly bear.

A French-Canadian trapper named Toussaint Charbonneau and his family joined the group in North Dakota. He and his Native American wife, Sacagawea, were to serve as interpreters and horse traders for the party as they traveled through Shoshone country.

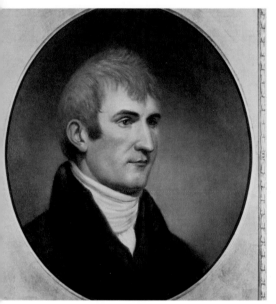

Meriwether Lewis.

William Clark.

newly acquired territory. They were to investigate the plants and animals, Native American cultures and trade, and the possibility of discovering a route over the mighty mountains to the Pacific. As a 29-year-old schizophrenic alcoholic with no expertise in cartography, native languages or botany, Meriwether Lewis was a strange choice to head an expedition across the country. Thankfully, the 33-year-old William Clark was already an army veteran and experienced frontiersman, and within a year they had assembled an expedition.

Known officially as the Corps of Discovery, the Lewis and Clark expedition set out from a spot near St Louis on May 14, 1804, with a party of 45 men, most of them rugged frontier types whom

The Lewis and Clark expedition set out from Fort Mandan for the west in the spring of 1805. They fought the currents of the Missouri River, struggled through deep canyons, and learned from the native people as they went. Across the Continental Divide and down the Columbia River they traveled until they finally saw the Pacific Ocean on November 17, 1805. They spent the winter and started back the way they had come. The party divided, Lewis going north and Clark following the Yellowstone River east. In August of 1806 they were reunited and the expedition was complete, having brought to the nation a real sense of pride and the first glimpse of understanding about the western reaches of its territory. Lewis died three years later from what was thought to have been a self-inflicted gunshot wound, most likely due to either a bout of schizophrenia or a drunken accident.

Before Lewis and Clark returned, Jefferson sent Thomas Freeman with a second party to the southern portion of the Louisiana Territory. Although Freeman's expedition didn't cause quite the stir that the Lewis and Clark trek did, it nevertheless provided valuable information about the extent of Spanish military operations in the area and the appropriate waterway to the

Clark went on to be an agent of Indian Affairs in the Louisiana Territory, then governor of the Missouri Territory, and finally US Superintendent of Indian Affairs until his death in 1838.

In 1818, Congress ordered an expedition to continue Pike's work and to investigate animal, vegetable and mineral life and trade with the

John C. Fremont.

Zebulon Montgomery Pike.

Rocky Mountain country.

That waterway was the Arkansas River, and Captain Zebulon Pike was selected to explore it. In 1806, while making a map of the Arkansas and Red rivers east of the Rockies, he followed the Arkansas into Colorado and discovered the peak that eventually made his name famous. He noted it on his map as Highest Peak and it was originally named James Peak after the first man who scaled it. However, trappers and hunters persisted in calling it Pike's Peak and, in 1835, the name was officially changed. Zebulon Pike's notes on his exploration were of a military intelligence nature – he was an army officer at heart and not so concerned with the possibilities of the development of the territory.

Native Americans. Military man Stephen H. Long was to be in charge of the expedition. Like Pike, Long named the first mountain he observed in the Front Range of the Rockies "Highest Peak". That peak is the highest summit in Rocky Mountain National Park and is now known as Long's Peak.

By 1841, proof of the riches of the West were filtering back and exploration began anew. Always the travelers were at the mercy of Native Americans and the weather. John C. Fremont made five expeditions across the mountains mainly for the purpose of publicizing the West. Until this time, an artist had been sent along with each expedition to sketch significant scenery, but Fremont was the first explorer to make use of a new invention, the camera. In addition, he was distinguished by his determination to find a central route to California as there was increasing talk of a rail line that would unite east and west.

Fremont's attempts to find the central route proved futile, and instead the discovery was made by John Gunnison, tragically killed by an arrow while trying to explain to a Native American that he was an explorer and not a settler. The Gunnison expedition brought the United States government to the decision that any fur-

sense of direction, they carried a more complete map of the Rocky Mountain country in their heads than any expedition hired by the government was able to put down on paper.

Beaver was the fur that lured men to the West. The skins were used for hats, muffs, coats, linings, and collars. Two hundred thousand pelts a year were sent to China alone during this period for the Emperor's garments. The demand for the pelts nearly killed off the beaver, but a change in fashion saved them from extinction in the nick of time.

Lewis and Clark holding a council with Native American people at what became known as Council Bluffs.

ther explorations would have to be conducted by military men.

THE FUR TRADE

The history of the real pathfinders can be traced in the story of the Rocky Mountain fur traders. From the Lewis and Clark expedition until the middle 1840s, commerce in the West was controlled by the fur trade. The employees of the fur trading companies and the free trappers (who sold furs they trapped themselves) were the first people to explorer the West as outsiders. Unfortunately, they left behind few records of their discoveries. Many mountain men were illiterate, but they could instead read trails, tracks, and weather signs. Trusting their instincts and

The trappers in their buckskin suits and coonskin caps lived entirely in the open with their Native American wives and families. They met other trappers at the annual "rendezvous" where white men and Native Americans gathered to drink, trade, and gamble. The heads of fur companies met their employees, paid them for their furs and gave them supplies for the year. The free trappers brought their furs, and the Native Americans came to gamble and trade. Business transactions at a rendezvous usually took about a week, followed by two to three weeks of carousing. Gunpowder and whiskey were the medium of exchange, and more than one trapper went back to the wilds with nothing to show for a year's work but a wicked hangover, while the owners of the fur-trading companies often made large profits.

William H. Ashley and Andrew Henry founded the Rocky Mountain Fur Company in St Louis, a rival to the British Hudson's Bay Company and John Jacob Astor's American Fur Company, in 1822. They employed some of the West's most famous mountain men: Jedediah Smith, a tough Methodist who went West with a gun in one hand and a Bible in the other, David Jackson, who gave his name to Jackson Hole in Wyoming, William Sublette, one of two brothers who made

grueling journey to the Oregon Country or California. In addition to supplies, the wagon trains brought tourists and journalists who talked and wrote about the Rocky Mountain country and its wonders, one of which was the warm and versatile buffalo robe. This, in turn, produced increased demands on the fur business and necessitated the cooperation of the Native Americans who could slaughter great herds of buffalo.

Forts and trading posts started to replace the annual rendezvous. Fort Laramie, the midway

Fort Laramie National Historic Site.

their living as trappers, Thomas Fitzpatrick, or "Broken Hand" as he was called by the Native Americans who seemed to both fear and admire him, and Old Jim Bridger, whose prowess as a storyteller was almost as great as his skill with a rifle. All of the mountain men in one way or another had a profound influence on the history of the Rockies.

PIONEERS AND TRAILS

Following on the heels of the mountain men were pioneers seeking a way west on the Oregon, Mormon, or Santa Fe trails. William Sublette proved that wagon wheels could negotiate mountain passes and other mountain men often worked as guides, leading immigrants on a

point between the Missouri and Salt Lake on the Overland Trail, was built on the site of a rendezvous in 1834. It operated as a private trading establishment until 1849 when the government bought it to use as a holding place for the troops that protected gold-rush caravans. There were 12 buildings surrounded by a 4ft (120cm) -thick adobe wall that was 20ft (6 meters) high. It could corral 200 animals if necessary and 40 men were employed there as traders, tailors, and buffalo hunters. Fort Laramie was the capital of the Rocky Mountain country until the discovery of gold.

Fifty-five thousand travelers were said to have stopped at Fort Laramie in the summer of 1850 alone. The Oregon Trail was the longest of the

> *The discovery of gold in California in 1848 turned a trickle of immigrants into a flood. One observer in the spring of 1849 estimated that there were 12,000 wagons in the Rocky Mountain country headed for California.*

overland routes used in westward expansion; ruts left by wagon wheels can still be seen today along the trail. Families traveled up the Platte

Participant in the annual Fort Bridger Rendezvous.

River to Fort Laramie, Wyoming and along the North Platte to its Sweetwater branch; across the South Pass in the Rocky Mountains to the Green River Valley at Fort Bridger, Wyoming; through the Snake River area and on to Idaho; across the Blue Mountains to Marcus Whitman's mission and down the Columbia River to Fort Vancouver, Oregon. Settlers dealt with flooded rivers, Native American attacks on their wagons, outbreaks of cholera, and scarcity of food, wood, and drinking water. The journey took six months and was a severe test of endurance and strength.

An estimated one in 17 emigrants died along the way, with on average 10 graves for every mile (1.6km) of trail. Women had a particularly

bad lot, an estimated one in five of them being pregnant, with many dying during childbirth, and nearly all having small children in their care. In turn, the children were particularly susceptible to disease and accidents, like falling out of the wagons or becoming lost and crushed among livestock. Not surprisingly perhaps, emigrants were not overly impressed by the Wyoming they passed through; one wrote "this is a country that may captivate mad poets, but I swear I see nothing but big rocks ... high mountains and wild sage. It is a miserable country."

MEXICAN-AMERICAN WAR (1846–48)

Exploration of the Rockies was interrupted by the Mexican-American War of 1846. The squabbles between Mexico and the United States were 20 years old. Idle mountain men were harassing Mexican wagon trains, and the United States was worried about the Mexicans' relationship with the Utes and Apaches. At Taos in 1847, Mexicans and Pueblo Indians raged into the home of Charles Bent, the military governor of New Mexico, scalped him in front of his family and rode off with his scalp tacked to a board. To achieve peace and extend its frontiers, the United States became involved in what many historians feel was an unnecessary attack on a weaker nation, and the war ended in total defeat for Mexico. By the treaty of Guadalupe Hidalgo in 1848, the United States acquired California, Nevada, Utah, and parts of Arizona, New Mexico, Colorado, and Wyoming.

William Gilpin was appointed the first governor of the new Colorado Territory in 1861. Having visited the Rocky Mountain country in the days of the Mexican War, he must have been astonished as he rode into Denver on a stagecoach. What had once been a favorite camping ground had turned into a bustling city of several thousand people with hotels and restaurants.

There was a method to President Lincoln's madness when he offered Gilpin the post of governor of the territory. Colorado, with its gold rush, was important to the economy of the Union. But Colorado and New Mexico had an inordinate number of secessionists in their midst. So Gilpin, a Southerner on the side of the Union, didn't waste any time squashing the secessionist movement before it had a chance to take hold.

THE MOUNTAIN MEN

The history of the Rockies echoes with legends of the "Mountain Men", fiercely independent fur traders and explorers who had close and complex relations with Native Americans.

In 1826 Jedediah Smith, Sublette, and Jackson bought the Rocky Mountain Fur Company from William H. Ashley and began trapping. Smith met a grizzly bear in the Black Hills and was so badly chewed that he nearly died; he was sewn up with a needle and trapped on. It wasn't the danger of his work that led Smith to eventually give up the trade but the fact that the beaver population was dying out and fashions had changed. The pack of furs he delivered to St Louis in 1830 was his last; he sold his holdings in the company and set his sights on the Sante Fe trade, though he was killed in 1831 by a band of Comanches before he could reach Sante Fe.

Kit Carson was another hunter and trapper with a vast knowledge of the Rocky Mountain country. He spent eight years as a buffalo hunter and later served as an Army scout, leading punishing campaigns against the Navajo and Mescalero Apache. Later he became a prominent citizen of Taos, New Mexico, which he helped defend against Confederate attack during the Civil War. Carson's second wife was Josepha Jamarillo, the sister-in-law of Charles Bent, military governor of New Mexico. Josepha had witnessed the murder of Bent by Mexican and Native American rebels in 1847, and with the chaos created by his death and the start of the gold rush, the mountain man era was drawing to a close. Kit Carson died in 1868 having outlived the last act of the mountain man drama.

BROKEN HAND

Thomas Fitzpatrick, dubbed "Broken Hand" (after his new rifle exploded, maiming several of his fingers), was a trapper and hunter who became the first federal Native American agent in the Rocky Mountains. The practical experience he gained with Native Americans while he was trapping was to come in handy 20 years later when the government was formulating a policy for Native American relations. With the buffalo disappearing and the hunting grounds of the native inhabitants being overrun, Fitzpatrick urged the Native Americans to turn to agriculture and tried to persuade the government to start a program to equip them for a farming life. Under his leadership, the first treaty between whites and Native Americans was drawn up, with 10,000 Native Americans present

Kit Carson with his horse, Apache.

at the meetings at Fort Laramie in 1851. Though Fitzpatrick tried to set a foundation of trust and understanding, the United States government never lived up to its obligations.

Jim Bridger, hunter, trapper, fur trader, and guide, was another of the mountain men who bought into the Rocky Mountain Fur Company in 1830. In 1843, when the fur trade declined, he built Fort Bridger in southwest Wyoming, a way station to supply immigrants on the Oregon Trail. By 1850, the fort had been taken over by the Mormons and Jim Bridger was among many old mountain men who went to live at Fort Laramie. Many of the tales he told there are still repeated in the West; one such story is that that he'd come West so long ago that "Pike's Peak" was nothing but a hole in the ground when he arrived.

In 1868, Red Cloud signed the Treaty of Fort Laramie with the US government, guaranteeing the region to Native Americans, but peace was short-lived.

The Confederates swept north up the Rio Grande intending to seize the Colorado gold fields in 1862 but were forced to retreat. Even as the Civil War was won in the Rockies for the Union, another war was started, this one involving Native Americans.

and overtook anything from stage routes to isolated settlers.

War parties on the rampage in 1863 and 1864 continued their destruction despite vigorous United States military operations. Colonel John Chivington, who had won the Civil War for the Union in the Rockies, took over the handling of the war. Governor Evans, who had replaced Gilpin, felt that things were headed for a truce until in 1864, Chivington and his 600 men marched into a camp at Sand Creek and brutally slaughtered more than 200 Cheyenne and

Information boards in Eads, Colorado.

THE AMERICAN-INDIAN WARS

The War Department had withdrawn most of the weapons and regulars from the Rocky Mountains and sent them east to fight Southerners during the US Civil War (1861–65). Native American tribes throughout the western mountains were tired of being confined to various uninhabitable reservations. For 10 years they had suffered in silence, and now they were intent on moving to more bountiful hunting grounds as once had been their custom. Their revenge was swift as they realized that the white man was at a disadvantage,

Arapaho people (the exact figure is disputed), most of them women and children. The soldiers returned to Denver with scalps and other trophies taken from their victims.

The Sand Creek Massacre served only to intensify the wars. In the northern Rockies, Sioux Chief Red Cloud led a campaign to eject white soldiers and settlers from the rich Powder River country of Montana. After two years of hard fighting, the Army relented.

Violence broke out yet again when gold was discovered in the Sioux's sacred Black Hills. The conflict came to a bloody climax in 1876 when Lt. Colonel George Armstrong Custer and his elite 7th Cavalry were wiped out by Sioux and Cheyenne warriors at the Battle of Little Bighorn, also known as Custer's Last Stand. The wars raged on for another 14 years, with predictable results. By 1890, the year of the Wounded Knee Massacre, the last of the free-living Native Americans were confined to reservations.

MISSIONARIES AND MORMONS

Religion was one of the reasons that settlers first undertook the trip west across the Rocky Mountain country. Once William Sublette proved that wagon trains could cross the mountains in 1830, missionaries felt sure that they possessed West for a place of refuge. After the murder of their founder, Joseph Smith, in Illinois, the Mormons searched for a new home far from the disapproval of outsiders; a place that, in Brigham Young's words, "nobody else wanted." In 1847, Young led the first party of Mormon pioneers on a westward journey to the Promised Land. There was nothing haphazard about the Mormon migration – they knew exactly where they were going. Wagons, crop seeds, cows, oxen, men, women, and children traveled west in military formation and rarely came to

New Mormon settlement buildings in Salt Lake City, around 1849.

the time, energy, and courage to move their households West. Marcus Whitman was such a missionary.

Commissioned in 1835 by the Presbyterian and Congregational churches, Whitman was to go West and report back to them on the feasibility of setting up a mission. He reported that not only could women and wagons cross the Rockies but that milk cows could be herded, guaranteeing a solid agricultural foundation. In 1836, a missionary party of six set out to make the overland journey through the Rocky Mountain country and on to the Pacific; two of the six were the first women to make such a trip.

While Whitman and his party were settling in Oregon, another group was looking to the blows with Native Americans. They ran across mountain men in the Rockies who scoffed at the idea that they could grow corn in the desert; they didn't know Brigham Young had studied irrigation.

In July 1847, they reached the valley of the Great Salt Lake and immediately went to work planting crops, building irrigation ditches, and planning their city. Some of the original 150 settlers went east for their families, and soon there was a long line of Mormons winding through the Platte Valley, over the sand hills, past Fort Laramie, and across South Pass down to the Great Salt Lake. By October, they were 4,000 strong, and it seemed that they had indeed found their new Zion.

📷 PIONEERING WOMEN OF THE OLD WEST

Contrary to the standard history of the Old West, it wasn't all about cowboys, lawmen, and mountain men – women were crucial to the taming of the frontier, though these trailblazers are rarely lauded like their male counterparts.

GUNSLINGERS, SOLDIERS AND STAGECOACHES

Thanks to the movies, almost everyone has heard of Annie Oakley (1860–1926) and Calamity Jane (1852–1903), both very real characters despite the legends – and both highly proficient with a gun. Both performed in Buffalo Bill's Wild West show, though Jane also worked as an army scout, even skirmishing with Native Americans. Pearl Hart (1871–1955) took things one step further and robbed stagecoaches, while "Bandit Queen" Belle Starr (1848–89) was one of the most notorious female outlaws in the Wild West, associated with the Jesse James–Younger Gang. The remarkable Cathy Williams (1844–93) – born into slavery – remains the only known African American woman to have served as a Buffalo Soldier in the Indian Wars, while Mary Fields (1832–1914), also known as "Stagecoach Mary," was the first African American woman to carry mail, and delivered across Montana in the 1890s. Unable to find a "respectable" way to make a living, "Poker Alice" (aka Eva Ivers, 1851–1930) took a job dealing cards in a saloon and found that she had a talent for gambling, later opening a bordello in the Black Hills.

Annie Oakley in 1885, the year she and husband Frank Butler joined Buffalo Bill's Wild West. At five feet tall, Oakley was given the nickname of "Watanya Cecilla" by fellow performer Sitting Bull, meaning "Little Sure Shot"

Calamity Jane gained fame in the 1870s and later toured in Wild West shows.

Belle Starr with her manacled lover, Blue Duck, after his arrest for the murder of a farmer.

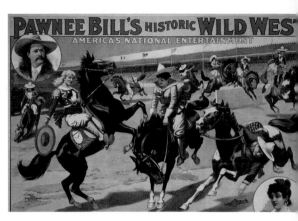

Pawnee Bill's Historic Wild West poster, 1898.

Entrepreneurs and trail pioneers

A former enslaved woman, Clara Brown (c.1800–1885) became known as the "Angel of the Rockies" during Colorado's Gold Rush, aiding other African Americans seeking freedom. Settling in Central City, Colorado, she slowly invested her earnings from work as a laundress, cook, and midwife into mines and land, becoming rich in the process.

Missionary Narcissa Whitman (1808–47) was the first white woman to cross the Rocky Mountains, in 1836, on her way to found the Whitman Mission among the Cayuse in modern-day Washington state. Many others followed. Tabitha Moffatt Brown (1780–1858) traveled the Oregon Trail in 1846, going on to found schools and universities in Oregon Country. Amelia Stewart Knight (1817–96) successfully traversed the Oregon Trail in 1853, with her husband and seven children, while pregnant. Her diary of the journey is an important and moving record. Susan Shelby Magoffin (1827–55) was an early pioneer on the Santa Fe Trail in the 1840s, and also recorded her experiences in a diary, which was later published.

elle Starr riding side saddle, dressed in velvet.

eplica covered wagons on the Oregon Trail at Scotts luff National Monument, Nebraska.

Official Scenic Historic Marker, Women of the Santa Fe Trail.

Central Pacific Railroad construction workers at Promontory Point in Salt Lake Valley.

RAILROADS AND ROUNDUPS

The settling of the West and Rockies accelerated with the coming of the railroads in the 1860s, with mining and railroad camps transforming into towns and cities soon after.

Transportation to the West improved with the emergence of the stagecoach in the mid-1850s, 10 years before the first transcontinental railway was finished. Stagecoaches – four-wheeled covered coaches, usually pulled by four horses – were to travel in the 1800s what the airplane is to travel today, and stage drivers solved the problem of the need for speedy mail and passenger service. Ben Holladay, a well-known character in the saga of the lusty stagecoach days, was a driver-turned-boss of his own firm. He knew firsthand that the success of the coach company lay in the hands of the drivers, and he is credited with immortalizing their role. Ben Holladay sold out to Wells Fargo & Company in 1865 after a series of disasters, including several attacks by Native Americans. The stagecoach disappeared almost completely when railroads arrived, being relegated to freighting over the back roads of the Rocky Mountain country that the railroads couldn't reach.

An even faster method of transportation was the Pony Express, whose primary purpose was speed and the express delivery of mail. Riders galloped through the central Rockies and had to change ponies frequently to keep their speed up. Though it was only in operation for 18 months between 1860 and 1861, some of the greatest stories of the old West come from the courage and endurance of the Pony Express riders.

The opening of the Rocky Mountain country really began with the Transcontinental Railroad, the 1,911-mile (3,075km) rail line constructed between 1863 and 1869.

XPRESS.—[Photographed by Savage, Salt Lake City, from a Painting by George M

A Pony Express rider and a telegraph construction crew.

THE TRANSCONTINENTAL RAILROAD

Grenville Dodge, nominated by President Lincoln, was to decide what route the railroad should take from Julesburg over the Continental Divide. Trappers and traders had told Dodge of a way through the Continental Divide below South Pass, but it wasn't until he was accidentally led by a group of Native Americans through an outlet to the West that the Granite Canyon route was finally chosen. Dodge went to work recruiting thousands of young men recently discharged from the Union and Confederate armies to lay tracks, build trestles, and blast a path through the mountains. By 1867, a total of 250 miles (310km) had already been laid and the Continental Divide had been crossed. On May 10, 1869, the Union Pacific track-layers met the Central Pacific track-layers and drove a golden spike into the ground to mark the railroad's completion at Promontory Summit near the Great Salt Lake in Utah. Bound to both east and west by steel, the Rocky Mountains were at last a real part of the United States.

RANCHES AND CATTLE WARS

The coming of the railroad encouraged ranchers, who – with the buffalo gone – would not only have access to endless free grazing, but also to the all-important eastern markets. Vast herds came into

Most ranchmen held two roundups each year. In the fall, cowboys gathered the cattle together, separated them according to their brands, and selected the marketable beef to be driven to the nearest shipping center. In spring, another roundup was held to brand the calves. Early roundups were great social occasions that included bronco busting, horse racing, and all kinds of contests, much like a modern-day rodeo.

Beginning in 1862, many settlers took advantage of the Homestead Acts, which essentially

Cattle on a ranch.

the region, often owned by absentee business-men and kept by huge teams of cowboys. Alexander Swan, who controlled around half a million acres (2023 sq km) in Wyoming, ran herds under so many brands that he had to publish a reference book for his cowboys. The dominance of the plains by the large ranchers and their manner of riding roughshod over the interests of home-steaders precipitated a number of cattle wars.

The sheep and cattlemen were in real competition for the best range on the government-owned lands. Each group felt that the other was making life impossible for them and their families. Many a gun battle was fought between rivals until the government established national forests and assigned pastures to various ranchmen.

gave away public land for free (with some conditions), to start farming the mountain country. They selected green places where water was plentiful, near flowing streams or in fertile valleys.

GOLD AND SILVER

When gold was discovered in California in 1848, adventurers started scurrying through the Rockies on their way to the Pacific Coast. Some camped alongside promising-looking streams on their way West and decided to stay. Others remembered them and returned when they failed to make their fortune in California. By 1860, there were hundreds of men seeking "pay dirt" in mountain streams. They were soon followed by thousands more prospectors, all in search of the mother lode.

The gold camps in the region provided the first good reason for settlement there, and so heralded the start of the modern-day Rockies. It also marked the beginning of the end for the traditional lives of the Native American people. Not only were the sheer numbers of new arrivals offensive to local populations, but the settlers' complete ignorance of local culture and disrespect for Native American practices caused frictions and triggered a more aggressive role

Peak. These nine men did indeed find a decent little deposit, but it was nothing compared to the rumor that spread like wildfire of the quantity of gold around the area. Thousands of people loaded up wagons and headed West with "Pike's Peak or bust" painted garishly on the side. Some were lucky, but most were disappointed. They went limping back a few months later with "Busted" on their wagons.

The finds in Denver actually proved to be tiny, but by the following year gold had been found around the Clear Creek Valley, a short trek to the west,

A lithograph of the Gold Rush in around 1849.

on the part of the indigenous peoples.

The gold rush is also the subject of countless myths and legends. One of them is the story of the "lost-cabin-mine." There are several versions of this story, but the basics are these: a Spanish explorer found gold in the Rockies, built a cabin and carried away all that he could along with a map to show where his claim was. After he died, one of his descendants searched for the cabin and the mine and when he couldn't find it, he sold the map to an American prospector. The map is likely to have changed hands many times, as prospectors were either gullible or optimistic and usually believed the story.

A party of men in 1858 heard that some Cherokees had found gold in the streams near Pike's

⊘ BUILDING UTOPIA

With the success of irrigation and the beginnings of the cattle industry in the late 1860s, Ohio-born farmer Nathan Meeker was consumed with the idea of establishing a model farming community in the West. In 1870 he established the Utopian-like Union Colony in Greeley, Colorado, with some 700 settlers. When the colonists turned toward capitalism, Meeker reapplied his puritan agrarian ideas to the Utes on a reservation in northwestern Colorado. His insistence that the Ute give up their way of life won him neither respect nor confidence, and Meeker and 10 of his employees were killed by the Utes in the Meeker Massacre in 1879.

and the towns of Central City, Idaho Springs and Georgetown sprung up as a result. At around the same time major finds occurred in both Idaho – the 1862 Boise Basin strikes – and Montana, where incredible finds at Grasshopper Creek in the same year created Bannack, a camp that produced $5 million of gold in its first year. Soon railroad spurs fed into the mountainous parts of the region, prompting miners to pour in and ore to flow out.

Cripple Creek appeared on the mining maps upon the discovery of the Independence Lode by W.S. Stratton in 1891. Stratton found a pre-

veins of silver and gold. Ethan and Hosea Grosh discovered silver at the site in 1857 but died before they could develop their claim. It was rediscovered in 1859, setting off a stampede of prospectors eager to strike it rich.

Perhaps the mining city with the most sensational career was Leadville. In 1877, there were 200 people in the whole Leadville region; a scant three years later there were over 14,000 in the city alone. The story was a familiar one: two relatively inexperienced fellows struck it rich and a roaring mining camp took off. Saloons, dance

"The Last Spike", an 1881 painting by Thomas Hill depicting the completion of the transcontinental railroad in 1869.

viously unknown, gold- and silver-bearing mineral called telluride. The strange new ore made Cripple Creek one of the richest mining centers in the world. The problem, however, was extracting the precious metals from the otherwise worthless rock. Mills needed to be built so the ore could be processed and the concentrates shipped to smelters in Denver and Pueblo.

Fortunes were made by men like Swiss-born entrepreneur Meyer Guggenheim who set up a highly lucrative smelting and refining business in Colorado with his seven sons in the 1880s. The family later established the Guggenheim Foundation to support academic research and the arts.

Virginia City, Nevada, grew up on the site of the Comstock Lode, made up of several rich

halls, and gambling halls sprung up like mushrooms, and fortunes in gold and silver were made and lost overnight.

The Crystal Castle was a ballroom, skating rink, dining hall, and riding gallery in one, and was composed almost entirely of blocks of ice. The rooms were heated and lit by electricity with massive pillars and towers throughout the building.

The story of Horace Tabor is at least as fantastic as that of the Crystal Castle. Tabor backed the two men responsible for the claim that set Leadville awhirl, and the mines he bought and sold made him a great fortune. He was easy with his money, building a bank and an opera house and giving freely to philanthropic institutions.

Tabor kept his mistress, Elizabeth McCourt Doe, well-situated in a suite at the Clarendon Hotel in Leadville. Once he set his sights on becoming the US Senator for Colorado, he divorced his wife. He wanted to marry Elizabeth "Baby Doe" in Washington, so he bought himself a seat in the US Senate, a maneuver that did little to win over his colleagues in Washington or his constituency at home.

Tabor and his new wife were never really accepted in "polite" society, and when the silver market collapsed, Tabor's debts mounted faster than he could add them up; he died a pauper

> Of all the fantastic things that happened in Leadville at this time, one of the most spectacular was the opening of the Crystal Castle in 1895.

Yet dependence on agriculture and the extractive industries provided a fickle economic base. The brutal winter of 1887–88 – which included a single blizzard that dumped enough snow to bury

Jesse and Frank James, and Cole, John, and Bob Younger robbing the Hot Springs Stagecoach in 1874.

in 1899. "Baby Doe" lived another 35 years and never gave up hope that the price of silver would turn up again and rehabilitate her own fortunes.

STATEHOOD

Towards the second half of the nineteenth century, the region had built up a formidable economy based on the extractive industries that helped earn the Rocky Mountain territories statehood; Colorado in 1876; Montana in 1889; Idaho and Wyoming in 1890; and Utah in 1896. Wyoming, intriguingly, was the first state to offer full suffrage to women, more the result of a desperate shortage of women in the state – they were outnumbered by men six to one – than a deeply held belief in the equality of the sexes.

cattle – saw around 400,000 cattle perish and both small holders and wealthy ranchers go bankrupt. Similarly, mining provided at best a precarious way to make a living. The early gold mines were quickly played out, particularly those in Colorado, where silver mining became the main source of income until the dramatic silver crash of 1893, when overnight the US moved off the silver standard, making almost all mines worthless.

Ups and downs in the mining business were common, and nowadays ghost towns exist in all the old mining districts. When the streams were emptied of gold, one by one the miners and their families moved away. The last to leave was usually an old prospector whose hopes were not easily crushed, but who had finally been forced to give up.

THE 20TH AND 21ST CENTURIES

During the 20th century the Rockies transformed from mining hub to tourist paradise, but even today the Rocky Mountain states remain important producers of agricultural products, oil, and minerals.

Though it remained prosperous, the mining industry was fraught with tensions in the early 20th century. Workers in large mines were often severely exploited, forced to live in company housing and paid in coupons valid at company stores. Morale was low, and as mines became less profitable, the actions of mine owners often made pay and conditions even worse. Tensions escalated into clashes at many mines. Perhaps the worst conflict of all occurred in Colorado, when the National Guard was called in to keep the peace in Cripple Creek, Telluride, and Trinidad during the Ludlow Massacre of 1914.

BETWEEN THE WARS

For the Rockies, the years between the two world wars brought much change and uncertainty. The Great Depression that had spelled death for stock investors as well as the railroads brought a flicker of life back to the mining industry; the clean-up operations in the mines were boosted in 1934 when President Franklin Roosevelt devalued the dollar. Gold prices leaped from $20.67 to $36 an ounce. It wasn't a true resurgence, though; mining, in fact, just shifted course to copper, lead, zinc, and other minerals. Improvements attributed to the war turned surviving mines into economic giants.

POST-WORLD WAR II

The rise in enthusiasm for outdoors activities was mirrored by an increasingly active environmental movement in the Rockies after World War II, which steadily gained momentum throughout the second half of the 20th century. Encouraged by a spate of successful protests – including voting down an initiative to attract the 1976 Olympic Games to Colorado on the basis of ecological

Bison statue, painted for the Winter Olympics.

concerns – the Rockies became known for a brand of hippie-activism centered on university towns like Boulder, even though most of the region outside Colorado has been solid Republican country for the past 30 years or so.

Thus it comes as no real surprise that the region has also continued to harbor maverick individualists with beliefs much further to the right than those political activists. Idaho in particular developed a reputation as a militia hotbed, based partly on an incident near Bonners Ferry in 1992, in which alleged white separatist Randy Weaver spent 11 days under siege from the FBI, his wife and child dying before his surrender. Though compensated for this heavy-handed treatment (a 1995 judge awarded

Weaver $3.1 million) by the justice system, the siege later became rallying cry for militants across the US.

The greatest change over the last few decades, though, has been economic. Not only did towns like Durango become fashionable among teleworkers in the 1990s, but Denver, too, embarked on an explosion of expansion, doubling its population in that decade alone. Such is the rate of economic development that today a major debate in Colorado is how to halt or control its growth – particularly in old mountain

Union Station in downtown Denver.

towns, where deluxe second homes are pricing locals out of the market. Urban centers like Denver, Bozeman and Boise are experiencing similar issues as expensive homes encroach on the adjacent mountains, forcing new roads and consequently encouraging more traffic in those areas. In Utah, both Salt Lake City and Park City

As a knock-on effect of the closeness of so many splendid recreation opportunities, most major towns in the Rocky Mountains have experienced rapid growth since the 1990s, thanks in part to the growth of footloose hi-tech industries.

experienced extraordinary construction spurts and expansion in the run up to the 2002 Winter Olympics. Though the development and growth of the other Rocky Mountain states is still less impressive than Colorado's, developments may well be pointing to a similar future for the rest of the region.

THE ROCKIES IN THE 21ST CENTURY

Colorado became one of the first US states to legalize marijuana in 2012 (Montana followed in 2020), though it's only liberal to a point; some parts are still very conservative. It was also here that horrific mass shootings took place in Columbine (1999) and Aurora (2012).

In Montana, a series of oil discoveries have led to an unlikely commodities boom, though the state remains primarily rural and agricultural. Like Wyoming and Idaho, it has a become a bastion of the Republican party in presidential elections, though Steve Bullock served as the Democratic Governor of Montana from 2013 to 2021. Indeed, only one of the eight current US senators from Utah, Wyoming, Montana, and Idaho is a Democrat (John Tester of Montana), and each state's legislature is more or less dominated by Republicans. Wyoming is so thinly populated that it gets just one member of the House of Representatives (Liz Cheney since 2017), though it gets the mandatory two senators; Montana also gets just one member in the House of Representatives, while Idaho gets two (all reliably conservative Republican). In contrast, Colorado is now considered a fairly safe Democratic state.

When dealing with the COVID-19 pandemic (2020–22), like much of conservative America, the Rocky Mountain states responded first with a degree of cynicism then a patchwork of only moderate restrictions on its citizens, keen to avoid criticism of government over-reach. With their primarily rural and therefore more widely dispersed populations making it more difficult to transmit the disease, they faired much better than urban America in terms of deaths from COVID-19, but the statistics remain grim. By 2022 there had been over 11,000 deaths in Colorado, over 4,000 in Idaho, over 3,000 in Montana, and over 1,600 in Wyoming, the nation's least populous state (for comparison, only around 115 people die annually in Wyoming from flu or pneumonia).

TOURISM AND CONSERVATION

With the advent of the family vacation in the 20th century, the Rocky Mountains became known to millions of people, and today it still exerts a strong pull on tourists.

Tourism began tentatively in spa towns like Colorado Springs and Glenwood Springs, which had been attracting the elite since the 1890s, and in Yellowstone, which had been made a national park in 1872; but with dawn of the motorcar age in the 1920s, the Rocky Mountains began to lure large numbers of ordinary vacationers.

Every grade of accommodation was available, from campgrounds in the national parks, where only water was provided, to chateaux in the mountains with every modern convenience. Dude camps with pack animals and old-fashioned ranches took in boarders from the east who wanted a peek at life in the Wild West. Providing recreation and inspiration, the tourist business probably brought more money into the Rocky Mountain country than all the mineral wealth taken out of it.

During Theodore "Teddy" Roosevelt's presidency (1901–09), preservation of the national parks, monuments, and primitive areas was encouraged. That meant alienating the ranchers who had been grazing their livestock on public lands and would no longer be afforded this privilege. The fight was bitter and long but the fireworks were confined to Congress – not a massive shootout as might have occurred in the old days. Wind Cave (1903), Mesa Verde (1906), Glacier (1910), Rocky Mountain (1915) and Grand Teton (1929) all became national parks.

THE MODERN ERA

Tourism particularly bloomed after World War II, when gasoline rationing had ended and tourists withdrew money from bulging savings accounts to converge on the Rockies in record numbers. In the mid-1950s, Yellowstone National Park attracted four times the population of Wyoming in annual visitor numbers. Several towns in the regions were quick off the mark to court this new economic opportunity as well: Colorado Springs, for example, built an auto route up Pike's Peak (1915) and the Royal Gorge Bridge (1929), both specially designed to give motorists splendid views.

The post-depression era also saw the first ski resorts evolve, at first primarily as entertainment for locals. In Idaho, though, the Sun Valley resort,

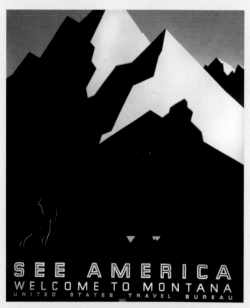

Poster encouraging visitors to Montana, 1939.

opened in the late 1930s, became the vogue winter destination for Hollywood film stars. Curiously, it was World War II that acted as a catalyst for the development of ski resorts. Chosen as the location of a large training camp for the 10th Mountain Division, the Sawatch and Elk Mountains of Colorado would see veterans' return from fighting become a major postwar impetus behind the development of resorts like Vail and Aspen. These resorts especially took off in the late 1960s, and by the 1970s winter had begun to overtake summer as the main tourist season. With so much new infrastructure in place, ski resorts have subsequently concentrated on developing off-season tourism based on conferences, golfers, hikers, and, more recently, mountain bikers.

A cowboy gathering Texas Longhorn cattle.

COWBOYS AND FARMERS

Cowboy culture is quintessential to the West and the Rockies, and what's known as the "Code of the West" remains an integral part of daily life.

Locals take pride in offering a friendly welcome to strangers, while neighbors offer to lend a helping hand and everyone has a deep respect for the land. Visitors can experience contemporary cowboy culture at dude and guest ranches with horseback riding and fishing, or watch a thrilling rodeo in Denver, Cody, or Cheyenne. Cattle ranching remains big business in Montana, while Wyoming especially is still known as the Cowboy State, its license plate embossed with a cowboy on a bucking bronco. It's here that you'll still see hitching posts at local watering holes.

ORIGINS

The early cowboy was a hybrid creature. He drew some of his gear and many of his skills, notably roping, from the *vaqueros* of Mexico. Traces of Spain echoed in his cowboy palaver (itself a term derived from the Spanish, *palabra*, meaning word). *Cincha* became cinch, *la reata* lariat, *rancho* ranch; the *vaquero* himself became the buckaroo. Yet other aspects of the cowboy world has roots deep in the United States itself. The roundup, for example, can be traced back to the Appalachian Mountains.

Who were these cowboys? They were not great in number – historians estimate that between 1866 and 1896 some 35,000 men rode the cattle trails between Texas and Kansas, or worked on ranches elsewhere on the plains. They were young, generally in their teens or twenties. And, according to Montana cowboy E.C. "Teddy Blue" Abbott, they tended to be "medium-sized men, as a heavy man was hard on horses, quick and wiry, and as a rule good-natured: in fact it didn't pay to be anything else." Chiefly Texans at first, they were eventually joined by men from other regions including Midwestern boys seeking

A cowboy in Sturgis, South Dakota.

better pay than could be found on the farm and East Coast remittance men seeking excitement. And although decades of dime novels and Western movies have popularized a whitewashed portrayal of cowboys with Anglo-Saxon features, some historians estimate that as many as one-third of cowboys were Black or Hispanic.

TEXAS LONGHORNS

Christopher Columbus brought Spanish cattle to the Americas in 1493. Two hundred years later, descendants of those animals were grazing the Mexican range. In 1690, about 200 head of cattle were driven north to a mission near the Sabine River, land that would soon be known as Texas. By the Civil War, nearly 300 years after the first cattle

> *The cattle these buckaroos tended were Texas longhorns. Without them, all the romantic legends about cowboys and their wild and wicked adventures would not have been possible.*

set hoof in America, millions of longhorn ranged the southwestern plains. In the next quarter century, 10 million head were herded north as far as the plains of Colorado, Wyoming, and Montana.

Unfortunately, however, longhorns had some major failings as a consumer product. "Eight pounds of hamburger on 800 pounds of bone and horn," one critic carped. Longhorns produced beef that was stringy and tough – a far cry from the marbled, tender steaks for which easterners paid top dollar. By the late 1870s, longhorns had mainly been abandoned for "American" cattle like Herefords and Shorthorn bulls.

CONTEMPORARY COWBOYS

Today, cowboys still wear their well-known tra-

A cowboy clinging onto his bucking horse.

The "Fordson" was powered by an internal engine.

In 1860 Charles Goodnight and Oliver Loving created the famous Goodnight-Loving Trail, driving several hundred longhorns into Denver City for hungry Colorado gold miners. Around the same time, Lovell and Reed, a well-known firm of Texas cattlemen, brought in another herd, thereby starting the Colorado range cattle industry.

Longhorns were well suited to the Rockies. They could travel nearly 100 miles (160km) without water, surviving on prairie or mountain grasses that no other animal would even look at. Their calves stood up right after birth and traveled side-by-side with the mother. Longhorns were feisty, rangy animals, adept at protecting their young from natural predators, such as coyotes.

ditional outfits: broad-brimmed hats, pointed, high-heeled boots, rawhide belts with fancy buckles, denim jeans, shirts that snap all the way down, and sometimes neckerchiefs that protect them from dust and wind when pulled up "bank-robber style." You'll be sure to hear a cowboy at a distance because his spurs "jingle-jangle" as he walks.

Some have skin that's as weathered and wrinkled as the clothes they wear, some sport shirts of flashing, bright colors and wear smiles that are just as "shiny." But these days you won't see many of them whirling a rope or with a "chaw" of tobacco tucked inside a cheek.

There are cowboys working daily with machinery over acres and acres of crops. Some are seen on horseback "moseying along" with their herd of cows or flock of sheep, while others will be found caring for fruit orchards. A cowboy's life is a lonely one; his best friend is sometimes his horse or his own company, a fact that hasn't changed much over the past hundred years.

The old cowboy lifestyle may be a dying out as a way of life today. Modernization has moved in and though fence lines didn't even exist 100 years ago, present-day prairies are full of barbed wire, electric fences, truck power, and modern equipment. The cowboy may soon be

Originally known as "cow country," Wyoming became a major wool-producing state in the late 19th century.

maybe even a hawk or an eagle. You won't have to look hard to find jack rabbits, but you may strain yourself in an attempt to avoid hitting one: they frequently insist on jumping out in front of unsuspecting drivers, especially at night when mesmerized by the headlights of oncoming cars.

A cowboy with a lamb.

A cowboy throwing a lasso in 1898.

put on the endangered species list.

A cattle rancher used to be called a cattle baron or a cattle king, depending upon the number of cattle he owned. It wasn't unusual to own a ranch covering more than 1,000 sq miles (2,500 sq km) teeming with cattle and a few cowboys employed to tend the herds. Cattle ranches today are few and far between compared to those operating in years past, but traveling across the golden plains of Montana, Colorado, and Wyoming into the mountain regions, you can see a little history come vividly to life.

From Herefords to Texas Longhorns, every breed with beef on its sides can be found grazing the endless grasslands. If you keep your eyes open, you may also notice antelope or deer,

SHEEP COUNTRY

Heading north from colorful Colorado into the great Wyoming range area, you'll notice that numbers of cattle start to decline, to be replaced by sheep.

Range wars between sheep and cattle ranchers during the 19th century became a major theme in Wyoming's history. It was the cattlemen in Wyoming who claimed first-come, first-served rights to the land. However, as sheep vied for space, the conflict grew violent. In one skirmish, more than 150 masked men attacked a sheep ranch, killing at least 2,000 sheep and a number of shepherds who tried in vain to protect their valuable woolly charges.

These range wars, otherwise known as sheep slaughters, continued until the Wyoming Wool

Growers' Association was organized in 1905. The organization attracted many members who eventually put a stop to the bloodshed. In reality, sheep were more profitable than cattle, and, sensing this, many cattlemen became sheepherders. The feuding ground to a halt, and wool was soon to become one of the state's leading industries. By 1900, Wyoming had more than 5 million sheep at pasture, and by 1910 revenues had far surpassed those of the cattle industry.

With the rapid reduction of free grazing land after World War I, Wyoming's wool industry drawn by federal land grants, and pioneers guided by their own particular star. Sheep ranchers followed, giving the farmers one more reason to cultivate crops.

When the miners and traders moved on, the farmers and ranchers stayed behind to settle the states of Idaho, Wyoming, Montana, and Colorado. These hardworking men and women, standing firm against adverse weather conditions, possessed an undying love for the land that nurtured the Rocky Mountain cowboy farmer of the 20th century. You'll find those

Planting potatoes in the fertile farm fields of Idaho.

declined as fast as it had appeared, and despite a minor boom during World War II, Wyoming's sheep population fell below one million in 1984. The current population is thought to be around 360,000.

WHEAT AND POTATOES

Pioneers made their way west in the 19th century, blazing trails for the crowds who followed them. Those same pioneers soon became farmers, miners, ranchers, cowpunchers, or gunmen. "Go West Young Man," said Horace Greeley, a New York newspaper editor – and go they did, by the thousands.

Farmers flocked into populated areas to feed miners attracted by the gold rush, cattlemen farmers today cultivating everything from potatoes to wheat to fruit orchards.

Ask any American where potatoes are grown and chances are he'll say Idaho. Although potatoes are grown right across the United States, the largest crop yields are cultivated in Idaho, mainly in the irrigated Snake River area.

Luther Burbank accidentally found a seed pod in his New England garden and transferred it to Idaho. Then Joe Marshall, the legendary "Idaho Potato King," developed the potato to its present status. Marshall had such a love for "his" potatoes that any employee he observed handling them carelessly or bruising them was instantly fired. Thanks to the tireless efforts of Joe Marshall, Idaho is the leading producer of potatoes in the United States.

The tall, amber-colored wheat grain seen all over Colorado's Rocky Mountain plains is one of the state's chief field crops. Successful wheat farming in Colorado began in 1876, the same year Colorado reached statehood. Cowboy pioneers learned to cultivate their land for this golden crop, opening the door for the wheat-raising families of today. Long, hard hours are spent planting, tending and harvesting wheat. Fields are planted alternately. A crop is raised in one field one year and another the next year, enabling the fallow fields to rest to enhance

> Horticulturist Luther Burbank is known as the "father of the russet burbank potato," developed in 1872 and still the leading potato variety grown in Idaho.

thousands of pounds of the juicy fruit are produced in the area each year. Peach trees are scattered over thousands of acres, bearing fruit from July through September, and in April the western

Organic yellow peaches, fresh from the orchard.

the quality of future crops. Wheat farmers are always gambling on weather conditions, losing when a hailstorm or drought ruins the crop and waiting until the next year for another chance to win. Two-thirds of Colorado wheat is shipped to other countries, a surplus that feeds hundreds of millions abroad. In turn, income from the fields feeds the farmers' families and their state taxes pay for schools, roads, parks, and other systems – a boon to the state's economy.

FRUIT GROWERS

Peaches, peaches and more peaches are produced each year in Colorado, mostly in the Grand Valley. In fact, the town of Fruita is named for the massive amount of peaches grown in its vicinity;

slopes of the Rockies are covered with the beautiful colors and aroma of peach blossom.

The soil of the western mountain valleys is the most fertile in the nation, and the land west of the Continental Divide gets more than two-thirds of the state's surface water from rain and snow run-off. The dry, warm summers are ideal for growing fruit. In addition to peach trees, orchards full of cherries, pears and apricots dot the countryside.

Local roadside stands, farmers' markets, and grocery stores make fruit easily available to tourists at very reasonable prices. If you plan your Colorado vacation during the summer months, you should take a drive through this fruit-filled area for sights, scents, and tastes that you'll never forget.

📷 RODEOS

Bad-tempered bulls and bucking broncos ridden by lean, laconic, tobacco-spitting types clad in tight blue Wrangler jeans and plaid shirts; happily, the rodeo is one sporting spectacle that has changed very little over the years, and it remains a true cultural bastion in the Rocky Mountains.

BRONCS, BULLS AND BARRELS

The main rodeo events are the spectacular bull-riding and bronc-riding competitions. Each ride is scored according to how hard the animal bucks and how well the cowboy rides – while keeping one hand swinging free in the air at all times. A minimum eight seconds is the time required to earn a score. Calf-roping is another crowd favorite, for its combination of daring, skill, and speed. A cowboy pursues the calf on horseback, hurls a lasso around its neck, dismounts at a full run, then tackles the animal to the ground before trussing three of its legs together, thus rendering it immobile. It may sound like an afternoon's work, but in fact squashing all this into under 10 seconds is considered a good effort. Cowgirls often feature in the barrel-riding, which demands great riding skill as competitors turn tight figure-eights around barrels at a full gallop. Among other events are races for the kids, the grand tradition of the rodeo being that everyone can get involved.

Cowboy riding a bull in the College rodeo in Missoula.

Participant riding two horses in the 111th Annual Trinida Round-Up Rodeo.

A cowboy waits to compete in the roping competition.

Calf roping at Jefferson County Fair and Rodeo.

Regional rodeos

In January, cowboys flock to Denver for the National Western Stock Show and Rodeo, but in summer, you'll find foot-stompin' rodeos up and down the Rockies. In Wyoming the family-friendly Jackson Hole Rodeo runs from late May to early September on Wednesdays and Saturdays, with additional rodeos every Friday in July and August. Over in Cody, the annual Cody Stampede in July features parades, rodeos, and fireworks, while the College National Finals Rodeo is held in Casper (June). In Montana, there's the Wild Horse Stampede in Wolf Point (July).

The Daddy of 'em all

As far as rodeos go, the Daddy of 'em all is Cheyenne Frontier Days, which began in 1897 when 15,000 people cheered cow-pony races, pitching and bucking broncos, a pony express demonstration and a mock battle between Sioux warriors and US cavalrymen. It was so successful, that it carried on for two days. Today, Frontier Days lasts for 10 days during the final full week of July. The world's largest outdoor rodeo is combined with a fabulous mile-long (1.6km) parade, superstar entertainers, country music concerts, free pancake breakfasts, square dancing, and a Native American Village.

...aying a prayer before a bull-riding competition.

...cowgirl racing during San Miguel Basin Rodeo.

Cowboy boots, famous for their spurred heels.

NATIVE AMERICANS

For thousands of years, the Rocky Mountains were inhabited exclusively by Native Americans, who came here to live, hunt and pray.

Several tribes once roamed the Rockies, including the Arapaho, Bannock, Bitterroot Salish, (Flathead), Blackfeet, Cheyenne, Cree, Crow, Nez Percé (Nimiipuu), Shoshone, Sioux and Ute. Some were Plains tribes that moved west to escape the encroachment of white settlers. Others came from the west to take advantage of abundant game and wild foods on the slopes of the mountains. Although their ways of life were similar in some respects, there were significant differences too, not the least of which were the many languages they spoke. The tribes also had their own strengths: the Utes were known for their horsemanship, the Comanches had a reputation for their skill in war, the Blackfeet for their smarts in dealing with white aggressors.

PRE-COLUMBIAN ERA

Before the arrival of Europeans, the tribes learned from each other. The Utes learned the Sun Dance from the Shoshone, who in turn seem to have learned it from either the Arapaho or Cheyenne. The Sun Dance is the most sacred religious observance of Plains Native Americans. It includes fasting and dancing in an enclosed area, always facing the sun or another sacred object such as a buffalo head on a pole in the center of the lodge. The object is spiritual growth through a personal sacrifice. Some tribes pierced their flesh to signify that they would fulfill their

Three Cheyenne men with an interpreter in 1887.

vows. The US government banned the Sun Dance in 1904, but it has been making a comeback since the 1960s as tribes try to restore their culture; the Sun Dance has been a protected right since the 1978 American Indian Religious Freedom Act.

The Shoshone followed the game to high country in the summer and to the valleys in winter. Before the introduction of horses they relied heavily on buffalo products, using different parts of the buffalo for food, shelter, clothing, tools, and ceremony. They knew the ways of both animals and plants and respected them highly. Their respect for animals stemmed from the belief that animals, like humans, had souls that survived after death. They believed that animal souls reported how they were killed, butchered,

> *The Shoshone call themselves "the people," and if asked where they came from, they might say they've been in the Rockies forever. Ancient rock art indicates a very long tenure indeed.*

and consumed back to living animals. This could lead to living game refusing to allow their bodies to be slain by an unkind hunter, who would thereafter find hunting more and more difficult.

Natural phenomena were often incorporated into tribal mythology; for example, an eclipse was thought to be caused by an animal trying to swallow the sun or moon. These stories often lend human attributes to animals such as bears, mountain lions, eagles, and snakes. The coyote, one of the cleverest critters in the West, often appears in Native American legends as a trick-

Native Americans made beautiful works of art, such as beadwork, tanned leather, bone and teeth breastplates, jewelry, and other adornments. Furs were worn not only for warmth but as hair ornaments or as a decorative part of their clothing.

COLONIZATION

Native American tribes were highly functioning societies, a far cry from the "savage nomad" image promoted by white aggressors. With the arrival of white Europeans, many Native Ameri-

Three members of the Sioux Nation entering the Badlands on horseback.

ster, creating havoc wherever he goes.

Most tribes had taboos concerning pregnancy, birth, menstruation, and going to war. Some tribes isolated expectant mothers immediately before birth and for 30 days afterwards. Isolation from the tribe was common for women who were menstruating and such women were also barred from tribal rites such as the sweat lodge. In some tribes, preparation for war included dancing, fasting, and isolation to ensure abstinence from sex. Their medicine and treatment of sickness consisted of a mixture of religion, magic, and herbalism. Marriage was a contract between kin rather than between two individuals, and was widely celebrated and served as a way to regulate sexual activity.

can tribes were made to trade the lands they called home for the most uninhabitable acreage their white oppressors could force upon them. They were beaten back by unfamiliar diseases brought from Europe, such as smallpox, to which they had little immunity, by harsh and unethical military attacks, and by a federal government that did not honor its treaties.

Peter and Paul Mallet are credited with being the first European-Americans to have reached the Rockies by crossing the plains in 1739. The Spanish priests Dominguez and Escalante, exploring for Spain, came across the Rocky Mountains as they searched for a trail from New Mexico to California. When Lewis and Clark came West in an attempt to find a route across the continent in 1804, their contact with the Rocky Mountain tribes included the Shoshone, who had by that time acquired Spanish horses from the Utes and Comanches.

The introduction of the horse into tribal society brought drastic change. Mounted, Native Americans could pursue both game and enemies over far greater areas. In their increased contact and exchanges with neighboring tribes, they picked up new ways of warring and celebrating.

From 1795 to 1822, the US government operated trading posts in the West. Native American

Native Americans in the southern Rockies probably encountered their first Europeans when the Spanish colonization of the Pueblos began in around 1600. Contact with Spanish invaders and Mexican explorers is reflected in the Ute language.

Native Americans to the fact that white invaders had little respect for land or animals, and that the resources on which they depended were

A Lakota Sioux camp at White Clay Creek watering hole near Pine Ridge, South Dakota in 1891.

contact with traders was mostly friendly; traders wanted the beaver and buffalo pelts that Native Americans could supply, while native tribes wanted the utensils, firearms, fabric, and liquor that traders could offer them in exchange.

The first treaty the US signed was with the East Coast Delaware tribe in 1778. From then until 1849, when the Bureau of Indian Affairs was moved out of the US War Department to the Department of the Interior, all Native American agents were military officers charged with protecting the interests of the fur traders, missionaries, miners, and finally the settlers. No one was charged with protecting the interests of the Native tribes. It was the California gold rush in the middle of the 19th century that alerted

finite. Tribes began to fight back with attacks on forts, wagon trains and settlements, leading the white invaders to annihilate those they thought of as "the savages" once and for all.

The miners who poured into the area after the discovery of gold not only drove out buffalo and other game but wantonly killed animals without eating the meat. That practice was an affront to Native Americans and showed huge disrespect; it also made it harder and harder to supply meat to their hungry people. On the heels of the miners came the Transcontinental Railroad. The venture not only appropriated vast amounts of land, but destroyed forests and buffalo herds. Twenty-five hundred railroad ties per mile stripped timberlands. Feeding railroad

> *More than half the Native Americans killed at Sand Creek were women and children; soldiers committed unspeakable atrocities. The event has since been termed "the foulest and most unjustifiable crime in the annals of America."*

workmen further reduced the buffalo herds, and for the majority of whites, who favored massacring the Native Americans, killing buffalo became a means to that end as they realized the tribes' dependence on the shaggy beasts.

As Native Americans fought back in an attempt to protect their resources, the government shored up its resolve to conquer by force. Weakened by a plague of smallpox, the Shoshone and Bannock gathered on the Bear River in 1863; a military attack took the lives of 400 people. By 1864, 20,000 whites had entered Idaho's richest mining area.

In 1854, the Utes were called to a peace conference in Taos, New Mexico. Blankets were given

Portrait of an Araphoe woman, 1899.

UTAH INDIAN PRISONERS UNDER THE COMMON PLAT

Ute prisoners at Fort Utah.

⊘ THE GREAT SIOUX NATION

Some 62,000 Native Americans today call South Dakota home (10 percent of the total population of the state), almost all of them Sioux; it is no surprise that the movie *Dances With Wolves* was filmed here in the late 1980s. Known to themselves as the Oceti Sakowin ("seven council fires"), the Great Sioux Nation can be loosely divided into three linguistically distinct dialect groups (Santee-Dakota, Yankton-Nakota and Teton-Lakota), and further divided into bands such as the Oglala and Hunkpapa (both Lakota), though there are nine official tribes (each with a reservation) in the state today.

For decades after Wounded Knee (when, in 1890, the US Army massacred more than Sioux men, women, and children during a tribal round-up, most of whom were unarmed as they had had their weapons confiscated), Sioux history and culture were outlawed; until the 1940s, it was illegal to teach or even speak their language. Today, more Sioux live on South Dakota's six reservations than dwelled in the whole state during pioneer days, but their prospects are often grim. Native American traditions are still celebrated, however, at powwows, held in summer on or near the reservations (especially large in Rapid City); local tourism offices offer annual dates and locations. Check also www.sdtribalrelations.com.

to the Native Americans as gifts and every person who received a blanket contracted smallpox. Many Utes still believe that the disease was deliberately introduced by the whites who came to talk peace. With more and more settlers coming into their territory, the Utes joined the Apaches to drive the whites from Colorado. Kit Carson led the defensive action against the Apache and the Utes, eventually defeating them; he also led a brutal campaign against the Navajo in 1863.

Colorado Governor John Evans ordered the Cheyenne and Arapaho who were refusing to live

> In 2021 Representative Deb Haaland of New Mexico and a member of the Laguna Pueblo tribe, became Secretary of the Interior, the first Native American to lead a cabinet post.

to meet the soldiers alone, carrying a sign of peace. He was shot, the first of many Blackfeet killed that day in the Marias (or Baker) Massacre.

A battle between the Sioux and Blackfeet Nations.

Oglala chiefs American Horse and Red Cloud.

in reservations to lay down their arms and report to Fort Lyon. Native American agent Colonel John Chivington believed that only a harsh lesson would persuade the two bands to "behave." Shortly after, in 1864, Chivington attacked a peaceful camp of Cheyenne on Sand Creek with 900 men, most of whom were miners who had enlisted in the cause of exterminating the "savages."

It plunged Colorado into a state of emergency, martial law, and economic crisis because of the surprising number of whites who protested against such brutality.

The Blackfeet, too, were suffering from a smallpox epidemic in 1870. When they saw soldiers approaching their encampment on the Marias River, Chief Heavy Runner went out

Weakened by disease, beaten in battle, dogged by hunger, tribe after tribe signed a treaty with the US government. Not only were Native Americans without options, it is doubtful that they were able to fully understand what they were signing, as the concepts they were grappling with (such as ownership) were so culturally alien. In a United States Supreme Court Case in 1945, US versus Shoshone, Chief Justice Black wrote: "Ownership meant no more to them than to roam the land as a great common and to possess and enjoy it the same way they possessed and enjoyed the sunlight, the west wind and the feel of spring in the air."

The treaties with the Utes are typical examples of the misunderstanding. The second treaty was signed in 1868 by Chief Ouray and Kit Carson. It designated the land on which the Utes could live without intrusion by whites; but almost immediately, both gold and silver were discovered in the San Juan Mountains and the mountains were filled with miners. Ouray was considered a great mediator by the US government, but some Utes considered him a traitor. Ouray felt that Native Americans had to change their ways to survive and he joined the white effort to assimilate the Utes into white society. In 1873, Ouray signed the Brunot Treaty with the US government that gave

Cheyenne Sun Dance pledgers in Oklahoma.

6,000 sq. miles (15,540 sq. km) of Ute land to miners – almost one-quarter of the reservation agreement of 1868. In an attempt to demonstrate to Native Americans that they could succeed in an agrarian civilization, Ouray and his wife, Chippeta, lived on a farm near Montrose, Colorado, cultivating their lands and raising crops, sheep, and cattle. But after repeated contact with the Great White Father in Washington, Ouray died, realizing that his life's work had failed. Chippeta remarried and lived in a traditional teepee until her death in 1924.

By 1871, the US had stopped treaty-making with Native Americans. Through a series of government programs, attempts were made to force Native Americans to adopt white people's ways. First they were assigned to agencies where food and goods were to be distributed and natives were forced to learn farming. The Dawes Act of 1887 gave Native American heads of families 160-acre (64 hectare) allotments, opening the rest of the reservation lands to white settlers.

Native Americans were (and continue to be) highly spiritual peoples. Because the "superior" whites had no concept of any religion except their brand of Christianity, the move to "Christianize" the tribes diluted their native faith with an often demoralizing result. Many Native American spiritual leaders see a direct result of that spiritual destruction in the high suicide rates among the population today.

Attempts to "educate" Native Americans were even less successful. Teachers spoke English in boarding schools at which any use of a tribal language was punished. Not only did children not understand the subject matter, but they were separated from their families and tribes and experienced severe trauma.

All the government's attempts to assimilate Native Americans were marked by a paternalism that encouraged dependence. In 1924, the US government finally bestowed citizenship on Native Americans, but it was not until 1948 that they could vote in every state in the Union.

POLICIES AND PROGRAMS

In 1934, the Indian Reorganization Act reversed the Dawes Act, stipulating that no tribal lands should be parceled out in individual allotments. Annual authorizations of $2 million for the purchase of tribal land were established. Credit funds for incorporated tribes were set up. Loans for vocational training and academic study were provided.

The power of tribes as self-governing units was established. Although funds to enact many of these provisions were never fully approved by Congress, the policies of the Indian Reorganization Act were theoretically much better than the federal government's next idea.

In 1953, the United States Congress officially announced a new "termination" policy with regards to Federal relations with Native Americans – the idea was to assimilate Native Americans into mainstream American society once and for all, and to abolish tribes as legal entities (a process which had begun in the 1940s). Between 1953 and 1964, the government terminated recognition of more than 100 tribes. Termination was only formally abandoned in 1988, and it took many years of legal challenges for tribes to regain their status. Concurrent with the termination policy was the Relocation Program; the Indian Relocation Act of 1956 encouraged Native Americans to relocate to urban areas, and proved to be just a new form of disaster.

Rattling away in the background was another legal brouhaha; in 1946, a Claims Commission had been established to settle all grievances with Native Americans by cash payments with the objective of cutting off financial aid. By 1951, 852 land claims had been filed – a legal nightmare that defied resolution since many claims overlapped each other.

In 1961, most tribes were represented at a government-called conference where a declaration of Native American purpose was drafted. "Indians ask for assistance, technical and financial, for the time needed, however long that may be, to regain in the America of the space age, some measure of the life they enjoyed as original possessors of the land."

Native Americans played a large role in the civil rights movements of the 1960s. In 1964 they staged a fish-in in Washington State where they had been denied the right to fish. They took over Alcatraz Prison in San Francisco Bay in 1969. In 1968, the American Indian Movement (AIM) was founded. Leaders said they formed AIM because they were tired of not being allowed a say in their own destiny, and AIM stormed the Bureau of Indian Affairs (BIA) office in 1972.

When they left the BIA's offices, they took with them an estimated $750,000 worth of art objects that missionaries had reputedly stolen from Native Americans many years previously. They left behind a statement which read: "Gentlemen: I do not apologize for the ruin nor the so-called destruction of the mausoleum. For in building anew, one must first destroy the old. This is the beginning of a new era for the North American native people. When history recalls our efforts here, our descendants will stand with pride, knowing their people were the only ones responsible for the stand taken against tyranny, injustice, and the gross inefficiencies of this branch of

a corrupt and decadent government." AIM activists also took over the village of Wounded Knee in 1973, and the siege lasted 71 days. It is seen by many as poetic justice that the arid lands on which many tribes were forced to live were later discovered to be rich in mineral resources.

President Johnson was against the termination policy, and in 1968 the Indian Civil Rights Act finally granted Native American tribes most of the benefits included in the Bill of Rights.

Today, the situation on many reservations in the Rocky Mountain region has improved, but rates of

A portrait of members of the Sioux Nation.

unemployment and alcoholism are still well above the national averages. The cultural renaissance of more recent years seems to have had a positive impact, however; participation of young people in a variety of traditional arts and ceremonies bodes well for the future of tribal cultures.

Meanwhile, the tribes of the Rocky Mountains and elsewhere in the United States continue to work toward a vision articulated by Chief Joseph of the Nez Perce more than a century ago: "Let me be a free man – free to travel, free to stop, free to work, free to trade where I choose, free to choose my own teachers, free to follow the religion of my fathers, free to think and act and talk for myself... for this, the Indian race is waiting and praying."

God and Jesus appear before Joseph Smith in a vision.

MORMONS

The Mormon experience and the American experience have much in common, yet for more than the first half-century of their history, Mormons confronted fellow citizens across a gulf of seemingly endless hostility.

Mormonism, the most American of the world's major religions, has always had an ambivalent relationship with the rest of the nation. Officially known as the Church of Jesus Christ of Latter-day Saints, "Mormon" is the name given to the largest branch of followers of founder Joseph Smith. From the start they were considered a peculiar people with odd, un-American attitudes, and for a while Mormons toyed with the idea of building a separate nation. On the other hand, it is hard to imagine how Mormonism could have spread anywhere but on the intellectually and socially turbulent North American frontier.

The Western frontier was the prime source of America's symbolic identity and national character. Mormon culture, born and nurtured on the frontier, selected from the available components of that identity, choosing from the Puritan sense of mission and divine selection, freemasonry's cult of secrecy and brotherhood, pseudo-intellectual attempts to explain Native American origins, and the swirl of social, religious, and economic experimentation that gripped a young nation in the romantic era of the early 19th century. Mormons saw danger and excess in the wilderness, and they, like other Americans, tried to subdue it, pursuing an orderly, civilized ideal of neat farms and great cities – an ideal made possible by a steady, strengthening flow

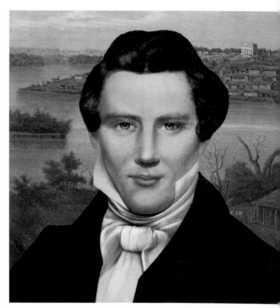
A portrait of Joseph Smith.

of immigrant converts to new orthodoxies like American ideology and Mormon theology.

The parallels between the religion's and the nation's experiences became more apparent in the 20th century after the Latter-day Saints, under duress, abandoned their more idiosyncratic ways – polygamy, theocracy, and communalism – and re-embraced middle-class America. More recent parallels could be observed in the 1980s as a Mormon vanguard led the national shift to the political right in government.

ORIGINS

Frontier New York in the first three decades of the 19th century underwent cycles of religious

---

In 1820, Joseph Smith, a 14-year-old in a state of religious confusion, sought answers in prayer and had the first of a series of visions in which God and others told him that true Christianity had been lost from the earth.

revivalism that historians call the Second Great Awakening. In hectic camp meetings, wandering evangelists competed for the souls of tradition-ally irreligious frontiersmen. The "burned-over district," as upstate New York was known because of the fervor that swept across it, had been peopled largely by descendants of New England's fervent Calvinist settlers, people like Joseph Smith's Vermont parents.

Between 1823 and 1827 the Angel Moroni, the last survivor of a chosen people who had inhabited pre-Columbian America, revealed to

banking scheme in 1837 led to widespread apos-tasy and the leadership's retreat to a town called Far West, Missouri. Devout Mormons expected to await the imminent second coming of Christ here, but instead they were violently attacked by Missouri mobs; 18 were massacred at the Mor-mon settlement at Haun's Mill, and Governor L. W. Boggs issued an order that the Mormons "must be exterminated or driven from the State."

After retreating to other parts of Missouri, the Mormons arrived in Illinois. Here Mormon culture truly blossomed, as the harassed people seemed

In October 1838, Missouri Governor Boggs authorized the state militia to drive all Mormons from the state.

Smith in a vision the location of a buried set of gold plates that told the story of Moroni's people, the Nephites, and the ancestors of Native Ameri-cans, known as the Lamanites. Smith reported uncovering the plates and translating what was transcribed on them using a special instrument buried with the plates. The translation formed the basis of the Book of Mormon, the sacred text for the church he founded, with six members, in 1830.

From the moment he began to tell the story of Angel Moroni, the vision and the gold plates, Joseph Smith and his followers were criticized, ostracized, and attacked by neighbors who con-sidered him a charlatan. As the number of his followers slowly grew, Smith had to move the church, first to Kirtland, Ohio, where failure of a

to have found their "City on a Hill" on the swampy banks of the Mississippi, where they built the com-munity of Nauvoo in the 1840s. Nauvoo was the largest city in Illinois of its time, and it benefited from a liberal state charter that gave its govern-ment – that is to say, Smith and fellow church leaders – almost independent powers, including its own army, the Nauvoo Legion. However, the problems that had repeatedly alienated neigh-bors arose again: the Mormons asserted that as a divinely chosen people they would inherit the earth, and with their industrious accumulation of property and military potential, they seemed poised to do just that – by force. They also tended to vote as a bloc, giving them the potential to control close elections. Then there were their unorthodox beliefs, which by the 1840s were rumored to include polygamy. A breaking point came when Smith ordered a Nauvoo newspaper run by critical ex-Mormons to be closed down and its presses smashed. Joseph and his brother Hyrum were arrested and taken to the jail in Carthage, Illinois, in June 1844, then killed by a mob.

BRIGHAM YOUNG AND THE GREAT SALT LAKE

Rather than disbanding after Joseph Smith's death, Mormons rallied around Brigham Young,

other Mormon settlements, and from overseas, where missionaries were at work. The Saints in Salt Lake City supported migration through donations to the Perpetual Emigrating Fund, which the migrants were expected to reimburse after establishing themselves. Some walked to Zion, pulling handcarts behind them, but in 1856 the Martin and Willie handcart companies started late and were trapped by snow in central Wyoming. In the worst tragedy of America's overland migration, between 200 and 225 people died before relief arrived.

Polygamy was once a Mormon institution; here, a Latter-day saint is pictured with his mother, five wives and child.

the head of their preeminent governing body, the Council of Twelve Apostles. In an unparalleled organizational feat, Young led his people West in search of a new haven. Migrants were divided into companies of 100, support farms were established along the way, and crews constructed trails and river ferries. Twelve thousand people moved across Iowa in 1846, to Winter Quarters near present-day Council Bluffs. This was the jumping-off point for the journey to the isolated and barren valley of the Great Salt Lake, the place that Young, as head of the first 148-person migration, chose as their refuge. Between 1847 and 1869, the year of the railroad's arrival, Mormon parties annually crossed the plains from Winter Quarters, from

Meanwhile, Brigham Young sought to build Joseph Smith's dream of the kingdom of God on earth. His visions of the new Mormon homeland were imperial: he proposed a new state of Deseret (a word from the Book of Mormon meaning beehive) encompassing all of present-day Utah, Nevada and Arizona and parts of Idaho, Wyoming, Colorado and southern California. Young sent out parties, carefully composed of men with varied and useful occupations, to begin occupying this vast expanse. By 1855, a corridor of settlements stretched from Idaho down the west slope of the mountains to San Bernardino, California. Mormons now had the chance for uninhibited open practice of their experimental social philosophy. After years of

Utah was, in effect, a theocracy where absolute obedience to a hierarchy was the norm.

persecution, the Mormons had found an isolated home away from the rest of the United States.

During their first years in the West, there was no clear line between ecclesiastical and secular government in Utah. Young was a territorial governor, and church leaders held most government offices.

blocks. Each individual village strived toward its own self-sufficiency within the overall general economic and political independence of the kingdom of Zion.

Manufacturing or raising specific products, especially those which otherwise would be imported, was encouraged and supported by the hierarchy. In the 1860s, the first of many local cooperative merchandising stores was opened; the modern ZCMI department store chain is a free-enterprise descendant of these co-ops. Many of these operations included

A Mormon preacher delivering a sermon.

Brigham Young's design for the "Deseret Costume".

That hierarchy pursued its goals of economic cooperation and self-sufficiency through careful planning. Living on the edge of the desert, the Mormons first needed to find a different way of watering their crops than that used in the well-watered East. They hit upon the idea of extensive irrigation systems, the first widespread non-Native American use of irrigation in the United States. These systems were built by cooperative labor, and local church leaders allocated the water. They also distributed land for homes and farm fields according to members' perceived needs. The fields typically surrounded a small village, the focus of Mormon life, where the houses, farm buildings and stock corrals were situated in the middle of carefully laid out

communally owned factories producing items such as clothing, furniture, textiles, and dairy products. In the 1870s, Young encouraged the creation of United Orders in Mormon villages. In this most extreme Mormon communal experiment, members gave up private ownership of all property other than clothing and personal goods. Everything else was communally owned and managed. Most of these experiments, especially the United Orders, failed to achieve their ends, mainly because of growing Mormon connections with the outside world and economy. That process began with the 1849 gold rush, which brought the Mormons a windfall in abandoned or traded goods as passing forty-niners lightened their loads in exchange for badly needed Mormon farm products and livestock. The outside world connections accelerated again after the arrival of the transcontinental railroad in 1869.

CONFLICT WITH THE USA

The most notorious Mormon institution was polygamy, the practice of having more than one spouse at the same time, though in the Mormon context it generally only applied to men having several wives. Joseph Smith, whose own marriages are still debated, first announced

Knocked out of the limelight by these tense events was the tragic massacre of 120 immigrants by Mormons and Native Americans at Mount Meadows on the south California trail.

several federally appointed territorial officials who felt thwarted by Utah's theocracy. Probably seeking to divert national attention away

Mormon Temple in Nauvoo, Illinois.

Smith was killed by a mob whilst inside Carthage Jail.

the concept to a small group of church leaders at Nauvoo. In the promised land of the Rocky Mountains, polygamy came out into the open, although only a small minority – those with enough wealth and influence to support several wives – practiced it. Before long, however, it became the rallying point for national anti-Mormon forces, who looked down upon the custom. The early Republican party, for example, campaigned fiercely against what were known as the "twin relics of barbarism:" slavery, and polygamy.

There were other reasons why Mormons, by the mid-1850s, found themselves in a state of renewed conflict with other Americans. Foremost amongst these were the complaints of

from sectional conflicts over slavery, President Buchanan in 1857 sent Colonel Albert Sidney Johnston, 2,500 soldiers, and a new territorial governor to enforce federal authority over the rebellious Mormons. In response, Brigham Young sent out guerrilla soldiers to harass the army, ordered his people to abandon Salt Lake City and retreat south, and prepared armed resistance. The bogged-down army, after spending a winter in camp at Fort Bridger, accepted a settlement negotiated by an intermediary and marched through Salt Lake City without incident to establish Camp Floyd far south of the city. The Mormons, in return, accepted their new governor, although Brigham Young continued to be the real authority.

> *Today, thousands of missionaries effectively spread a message first spoken by the son of an itinerant family in the primitive backcountry villages of upstate New York.*

Southern Utah Mormons, in the midst of a religious revival, were expecting a US military invasion. They knew that some members of the immigrant group were from hated Missouri and

United States senator Mitt Romney is Mormon.

had insulted other Mormon communities along the way. Many years later, John D. Lee, the only Mormon ever brought to justice for the crime, was executed at the massacre site.

During the Civil War, volunteer troops from California occupied Salt Lake City to insure Mormon loyalty to the Union cause. Their commander, Colonel Patrick Connor, was eventually known as the father of mining in Utah because he encouraged his soldiers to prospect in their spare time and helped develop some of Utah's earliest strikes. He was virulently anti-Mormon and hoped that mining would encourage immigration of Gentiles to Utah. He was correct, and mining in places like Alta, Park City and the Oquirrh Mountains eventually

created a second, non-Mormon economy in the state.

After the Civil War, Congress stepped up its crusade against polygamy. In a series of acts culminating in the Edmunds-Tucker Act of 1887, stiff penalties were imposed for its practice. Polygamists were disenfranchised and prohibited from public office and jury duty, test oaths were introduced, the church was excommunicated and its property confiscated, the Perpetual Emigrating Fund was dissolved, and women's suffrage was abolished. Federal marshals hounded polygamists throughout the state while church leaders went underground. In 1890 Mormon president Wilford Woodruff (Brigham Young had died in 1877) publicly advised members "to refrain from conducting any marriage forbidden by the law of the land," thereby surrendering to overwhelming federal powder. With the Woodruff Manifesto, as it was known, and the admission of Utah to statehood in 1896 after 50 years of waiting, church members took their first steps toward reconciliation with the rest of the nation.

THE 20TH CENTURY

Mormons in the 20th century moved further and further from their early attempts to build a perfect community and embraced the more traditional social ideals of middle-class America. Members at first entered the Democratic and Republican parties in roughly equal numbers, ceasing to be a solid voting bloc, but in more recent years, most of them have adopted the predominant Republican business ideology. The church's own economic strength rebounded gradually until after World War II, when the Latter-day Saints grew into one of the country's wealthiest religions, with major investments in real estate, communications, and insurance among other things. Mormon leaders keep in touch with members through an organized network so intricate, it would make most federal bureaucracies jealous. Members pay not only a tithe of 10 percent of their income but also contribute to a building fund, a missionary fund, and a welfare fund.

THE MORMONS TODAY

Throughout much of their history, the Mormons always sought to organize their society along different lines to those extolled by the State. Today, their culture's uniqueness is still in part due to what remains of that distinct social order: the insulating sense that they are a people apart, their rigid adherence to a set of values that they feel the modern world threatens, and an institutional framework that permeates their lives. Of course, they are no longer just an American people; they have achieved an international presence for which they worked hard. They are emerging as a major religion, certainly not yet on the scale of the world's largest religions – their membership is quite modest compared with 50 million American Catholics, for example – but their influence exceeds their numbers and they are one of the world's fastest-growing churches.

LATTER-DAY SAINTS (LDS) ORGANIZATION AND CULTURE

The organizational framework for Mormonism was the lay priesthood held by all adult males in the church. It was a patriarchal order that reached from priesthood-holding fathers in the family through bishops of neighborhood wards (similar to parishes) through other ascending levels to Brigham Young, the prophet, at the top. The overland migration had strengthened organizational ties; in the mountainous West these were refined and institutionalized. Young's charisma built up member loyalty and willingness to obey, but so did their sense of shared hardship and group destiny. Jedediah Grant, Mormon leader and first mayor of Salt Lake City, once said that Mormon faith and testimony were different and much stronger than that of other religions because the Latter-day Saints were asked to believe in so much more – including in God's appearance to men in modern times – in the face of great challenges.

There are other distinctive cultural attributes of the Mormons, such as abstinence from alcohol and tobacco, the wearing of specially designed, sanctified undergarments, dedication to genealogical research, and a high value placed on education and the arts. But it was the increasingly conservative politics of many members, an attribute shared with many other Americans, that brought them much attention in the 1980s and 1990s. Patriotism and traditional family values were suddenly popular;

Ronald Reagan received his largest margins in the presidential elections in Utah (almost 75 percent). He considered the Mormon West one of his prime constituencies and brought a number of prominent Mormons to Washington, DC, to enter national government. Ever since then, Utah has been an extremely safe Republican state, George W. Bush receiving 71.54 percent of the vote in the 2004 presidential election. Mormon Mitt Romney won 73 percent in 2012 and Donald Trump won 58 percent in 2020, despite both candidates losing the election overall.

Temple Square in Salt Lake City, Utah.

Mormons are fiercely partisan, and they take great pride in celebrities of their faith. They loyally follow the careers of well-known members like entertainers Donny and Marie Osmond, and politician Mitt Romney. While there are many kinds of Mormons with different attitudes – political columnist Jack Anderson, for example, did not fit the Mormon stereotype and his religious persuasion was hence less well-known – there is still a striking uniformity among most Mormons. They remain, after all, a tightly unified people who largely conform to the wishes of their church leaders. As such, they are a people apart, one subculture in the endlessly fascinating hodgepodge of American society.

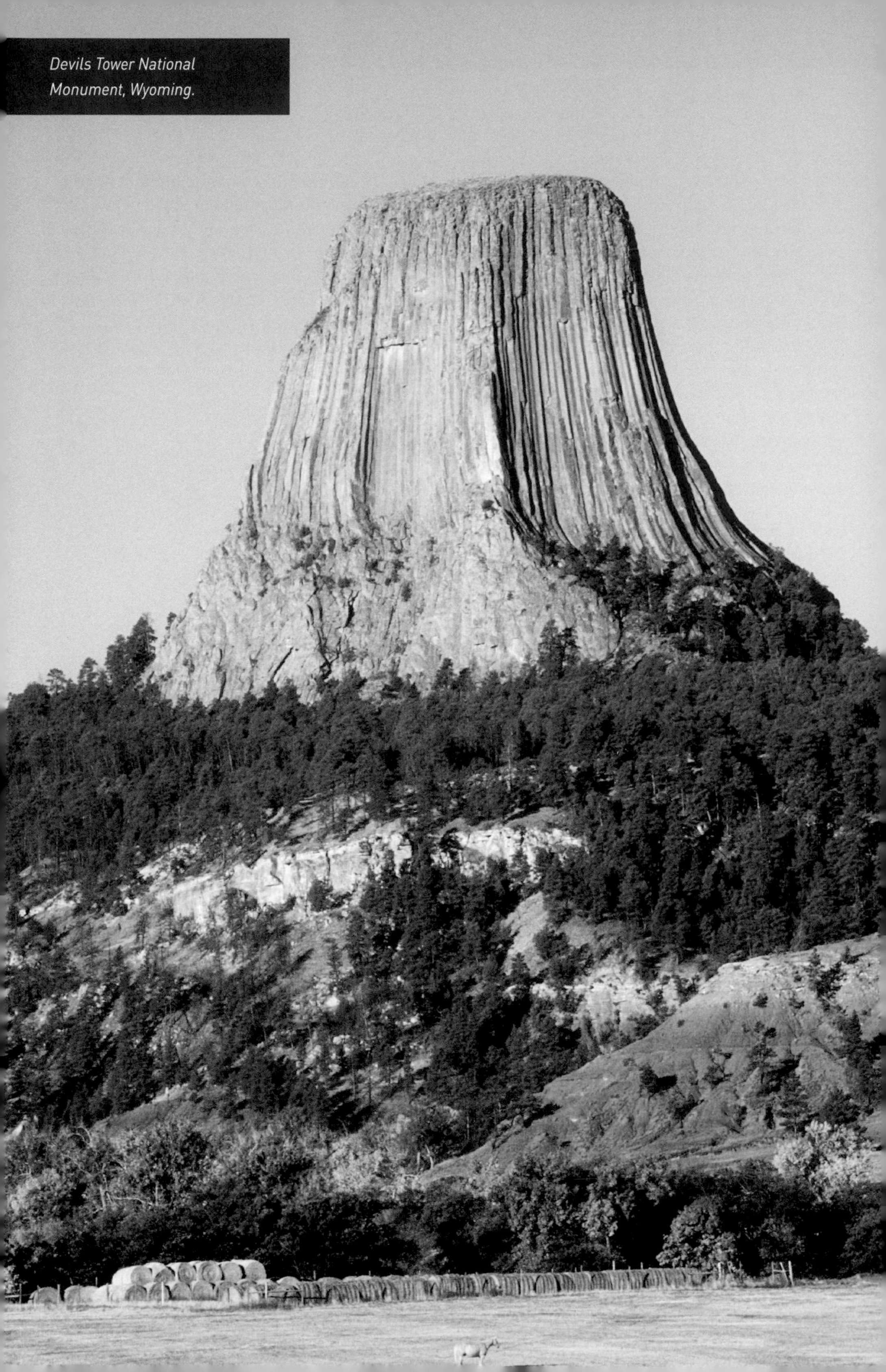

Devils Tower National Monument, Wyoming.

NATURAL WONDERS

Because of their many snowcapped peaks, the Rocky Mountains were called the "Shining Mountains" by the Native Americans who lived or traveled within sight of them.

This poetic name was recorded in 1742 by the Verendrye brothers, French explorers who were among the first Europeans to see the Rockies in the states now known as Montana and Wyoming. Plains tribes, such as the Cheyenne, who lived east of the Rockies in the flat country of the High Plains, considered the mountains a place where only spirits could safely go and humans dared not venture – a place to hold in awe, but not to explore.

When Europeans began to come into the area, they pragmatically called the range filled with bare-rock crests the Stony Mountains, and later

The entire Rocky Mountain chain extends 3,000 miles (4,800 km) from Alberta and British Columbia in Canada to Mexico and at most points is several hundred miles wide.

An open road leads to the Grand Teton's mountain range.

the Rocky Mountains. To them, these ranges were not a forbidden place but a barrier to be overcome.

The mountains slowed but could not stop the westward push of the United States population. The first whites to appear in this area were fur trappers who lived in isolation; then, wagon trains heading for the lush Pacific Northwest forests and the California gold fields found advantageous passes that let them through the barrier.

The highest peak in this entire cordillera is Mount Elbert in Colorado, which stands at 14,431ft (4,400 meters). Because of their size, the Rockies are generally divided into four regions: Canadian (outside the scope of this book), Northern, Central, and Southern.

The Northern Rockies comprise northern Idaho and western Montana, and include the peaks of the Sawtooth, Salmon River, Bitterroot, Clearwater, Selkirk, and Cabinet mountains, as well as Glacier National Park. The highest point in this region is Borah Peak (12,622ft/3,847 meters) in Idaho's Lost River Range.

The Central Rockies take in southern Montana, eastern Idaho, western Wyoming and northeastern Utah, encompassing the Absaroka, Beartooth, Big Horn, Teton, Snake River, Wind River, Wasatch, Salt River, and Uinta mountains, the last of these unusual in that they are the only mountains in the Rockies to run east–west – every other range trends north–south. Grand Teton and Yellowstone

Today much of the land in the five Rocky Mountain states is owned by state or federal government. In Montana, for example, the federal government owns about 29 percent of the land, while in Utah and Idaho it owns about 63 to 66 percent.

national parks are within the Central Rockies, so it's no surprise that this is one of the most geologically active regions of the entire range.

Mount Elbert, Colorado.

High points here include rugged Granite Peak (12,799ft/3,901 meters), Montana's highest mountain, and Wyoming's magnificent Grand Teton (13,770ft/4,197 meters).

The Southern Rockies extend from the Wyoming Basin in the south of the state – the desert-like "hole in the mountains" used as a wagon-train passage by the Mormon, Overland, and Oregon Trails of the 19th century – through Colorado to central New Mexico, and have the highest peaks in all the Rocky Mountains (including Mount Elbert, and those of Rocky Mountain National Park). The region is made up of two separate north–south belts of mountains separated by lower lying basins – the main ranges in the west are the Park, Sawatch, and

San Juan, and in the east are the Front Range, Laramie, and Sangre de Cristo.

NATURAL RESOURCES

To this day, the land of the Rockies still hasn't been conquered. Populations in the five Rocky Mountain states are among the lowest in density in the whole United States. For example, the western half of Colorado is in the mountainous portion of the state, and of the 34 counties there, 11 have between five and 20 residents per sq. mile (2 sq. km), 12 have between two and five, and the remaining 11 have fewer than two people per square mile of land.

The rugged land and climate have always dictated which major industries can flourish. After the native people, who lived off the land's wildlife and its natural crops, those who came and stayed participated in what are known as extractive industries; they harvested the pelts of fur-bearing animals, mined precious and then basic metals (and, more recently, radioactive ores), and cut the forests (originally "clear-cutting," or removing all trees without replanting).

Agriculture began as mining camps sprang into being, but given that the land was so dry, cattle and sheep ranching prevailed over crops. In "open range" days, this meant letting the herds of cattle or flocks of sheep graze where they chose. It was only in the 20th century that tourism became a major "industry" for the Rockies, affecting delicate ecosystems in some locations but not permanently removing resources.

Because this region is difficult to travel across and lacking in water and arable land, few major cities have developed in the Rockies. The two metropolitan centers of the Middle Rockies, Denver and Salt Lake City, are much like cities of their size elsewhere in the US, but are not representative of the smaller settlements in the region.

Mineral extraction and logging, as well as recreational uses of such land, are carefully controlled by the federal government. Among these publicly owned lands are "wilderness areas," portions protected even more completely where, by law, humans may only visit temporarily.

The concept of a "wilderness area" continues to be hotly debated in the United States. At one extreme are those who believe that the mineral and timber resources "locked away" there should be fully utilized, while at the other extreme are those who believe that the level of protection and the amount of protected land should be expanded. Environmentalist groups engage in endless battles with developers, ranchers and the extractive industries over uses – or alleged misuses – of federal lands. Naturally, most US citizens fall between these two viewpoints and seek a compromise. While acknowledging both the nation's and the world's need for the resources located in the Rocky Mountains, they believe that preserving these surviving true wilderness areas is a worthy goal. They are aware that, besides providing a home for wildlife, these pristine mountain forests also benefit human ecology and supply one of the West's most precious resources, the same resource that has been the cause of fierce battles, broken friendships, and dirty political scams: water.

Today's Rocky Mountains are no longer the abode of mysterious spirits, or a great wall separating one part of the nation from the other. They are settled lands – if lightly populated – clustered around wilderness. Their future is a point of national concern, but for now people who come to live or vacation in this area seek spiritual and physical refreshment in the beauty of the Shining Mountains.

GEOLOGICAL WONDERS

The Rocky Mountain chain is comprised of a complex series of individual mountain ranges whose hills vary from jagged, incised peaks to flat-topped crags. The Rockies are young compared with other North American ranges, formed mainly by the Laramide Revolution, a period of tectonic uplifts that took place in the late Cretaceous Period, around 65 million years ago. This was followed by volcanic activity and the folding and faulting that continued into the early Tertiary Period. The result of this powerful but gradual collision of tectonic plates was the upward thrust of the Rockies, as land that had previously been at sea level was pushed skyward. Today, the base of the Rockies is about 1 mile (1.6 km) above sea level. The Rockies were later reshaped by heavy glaciation during the Pleistocene era, when a sizeable portion of the earth was covered in ice. This process ground

> On an August night at Hebgen Lake in Yellowstone National Park, the lake bottom tipped 20ft (six meters) toward the northeast and a massive landslide buried 50 campers before they could flee.

down mountains, smoothed out valleys, and also left a series of mountain lakes when the glaciers receded. Glacial activity continues to affect the

Snowy Borah Peak, Idaho.

landscape of the area's higher mountain ranges – Glacier National Park in northern Montana, for instance, has good examples of these processes in action. Major volcanic action further shaped some of these mountains, building upon the upthrust rock masses, as clearly seen in the San Juan Mountains of Colorado. By contrast, the Blue Ridge Mountains in the eastern United States are thought to have formed some 200 million years ago, with the first great tectonic collision.

Although most geological changes occur far too slowly for humans to witness with the naked eye, a disaster in 1959 demonstrated that the block faulting which built the Rockies does indeed continue to this day.

Earthquakes are common throughout the Rockies, but most are small tremors causing little or no damage, and usually go unnoticed by most people. In 1935, however, a series of particularly powerful earthquakes damaged buildings throughout Wyoming and Utah.

Traveling through the Rockies today still gives a sense of seeing earth's geology at work, as a wide range of conditions vividly illustrates the forces that shape our planet. In Wyoming, the Grand Teton Mountains abruptly rise up to 13,737ft (4,100 meters), towering 7,000ft (2,100

spring emptying into icy snowmelt. Indeed, what is bubbling down below may appear in the more docile form of hot springs rather than the visual eye-candy of erupting geysers.

Mighty rivers rising in these mountains leave their mark, too. North America's deepest gorge is Hell's Canyon in Idaho: it is 1 mile (1.6 km) deep, cut through rock by the coiling, well-named Snake River. In Colorado, the Arkansas River has cut more than 1,100ft (335 meters) through granite to form Royal Gorge; from its headwaters, the Arkansas drops 6,600ft

A great grey owl watches from a branch in Wyoming.

A spot of lunch for a bull moose.

meters) above the fertile valley named Jackson Hole; likewise, the Wasatch Range rises 6,000ft (1,800 meters) above Salt Lake City in Utah. These mountains don't have foothills, illustrating the way in which the tremendous forces of colliding continental plates quickly uplifted the Rocky Mountains.

Although mountains may seem to be proof of the thickness of the earth's crust, Yellowstone National Park in Wyoming demonstrates how comparatively thin the surface is here; geysers periodically spout boiling water from the depths. "Mudpots" – or rock basins filled with constantly boiling mud – spew their sulfurous smells into the otherwise sweet air. A plume of steam at the edge of a cold stream alerts the visitor to a hot

(2,000 meters) in elevation within only 150 miles (240km) before reaching flat land.

CLIMATE

The climate throughout the Rockies remains generally dry, making for clear skies that enhance visibility over long distances. Nights are much cooler than days in summer (and much colder winter). Because snow forms a greater proportion of annual precipitation than rain, "snowpack" throughout the area is carefully monitored. Snowpack is each winter's accumulation of snow and snowdrifts; when it melts, it feeds rivers supplying the region's comparatively scarce water supply. Where the coolness of altitude is too great for snowpack to melt in the warm summer sun, glaciers form instead.

From April into June each year, springtime in the Rockies means the flooding "runoff" season as snow melt runs into streams, forming the headwaters of several major rivers. The Arkansas River, the North and South Platte rivers, the Rio Grande, the Missouri, and the Colorado rivers all rise in the Rocky Mountains. The Continental Divide, which generally follows the crest of the mountains, is the great watershed of North America. Precipitation, when it

In general, the western side of the mountains receives more moisture than the eastern side, as clouds cool when rising over the land mass and their moisture condenses into rain – or, in greater quantity, into snow.

years old) that runs roughly parallel on the East Coast. As a consequence, the region's flora remains fairly uniform, at least as far as

The bald eagle is the national bird of the United States.

A huge bison in Grand Teton National Park.

falls or melts on the east side of the Continental Divide ultimately flows into the Atlantic Ocean; any precipitation falling on the west of the Continental Divide flows to the Pacific Ocean. Of the major rivers found in these awesome mountains, only the Colorado River flows to the Pacific Ocean.

FLORA OF THE ROCKIES

The landscape of the Rockies further demonstrates the youth of these ranges. Its soil is thin and stony because fewer eons of erosion have gone into its creation. In this shorter time period (60 million years), fewer species of trees have evolved to survive here than in the ancient Appalachian chain (225 million

geography goes; the types of forests, plants, and flowers you will find depend much more on the altitude you're at than the state you're in. Thus, whether you're in Idaho or Colorado, you will find similar trees and flowers at an altitude of, say, 10,000ft (3,048 meters). Tall and dense fir woods characterize the lower elevations on the wetter western side of the Rockies, with pine forests on the drier east, and spruces braving the higher slopes heading toward the "timber line", the point at which trees can no longer grow.

The mountain environment consists of three essential ecosystems: these are the montane (6,000–9,000ft/1,829–2,743 meters), sub-alpine (9,000–11,500ft/2,743–3,505 meters) and alpine (above 3,505 meters). The montane is where you'll find forests of lodgepole and ponderosa pine as well as stands of aspen and blue spruce. Like its eastern counterpart, the jack pine, the lodgepole requires intense heat before opening and releasing its seeds, and huge stands of these trees grew in the aftermath of the forest fires which accompanied the building and running of the railways. The Engelmann spruce, sub-alpine fir, and Douglas fir take over as the predominant tree above 9,000ft/2,743 meters, where the temperatures get a bit cooler, and wildflowers start to appear in meadows, while alpine tundra supports only slow-growing plants such as mosses, lichens, and a variety of delicate wildflowers, all of which can survive on the thinnest soil and air and with a minimal supply of water. The various species of wildflower that you might come across are numerous; among their huge number are the columbine, alpine sunflower, elephant's head, alpine buttercup, and alpine phlox. Because they grow so slowly – the tiniest wildflower may take many years to reach maturity – any

Salt Lake City skyline on an early spring evening, with the snow-capped Wasatch Mountains in the distance.

⊘ PARK PASSES

Most parks and monuments charge admission fees, usually somewhere in the range of $5 to $35, which tend to cover a vehicle and all its occupants for up to a week. For anyone on a touring vacation, it may well make more sense to buy the Inter-agency Annual Pass, also known as the "America the Beautiful Pass". Sold for $80 at all federal parks and monuments, or online at https://store.usgs.gov/pass/index.html, this pass entitles the bearer (who must be 16 or older - children under 16 enter the parks for free) and any accompanying passengers in one vehicle to a year's unrestricted access to over 2,000 recreational areas including all national parks and monuments, as well as sites managed by such agencies as the US Fish and Wildlife Service, the Forest Service and the Bureau of Land Management. It is also useful to note that each pass can have up to two "owners".

While hotel-style lodges are found only in major parks, every park or monument tends to have at least one well-organized campground with all the usual amenities. Often, a cluster of fairly standard motels can be found not far outside the park boundaries. With the appropriate permits – and subject to restrictions in popular parks – backpackers can also usually camp in the backcountry (a general term for areas inaccessible by road).

damage done to these plants impacts dramatically on the alpine ecosystem, so hikers have a special duty of care in while exploring these areas.

NATIONAL PARKS AND MONUMENTS

The US National Park Service administers both national parks and national monuments throughout the Rockies. Its rangers do a superb job of providing information and advice to visitors, maintaining trails, and organizing such

National parks and monuments are often surrounded by tracts of national forest – also federally administered but much less protected. These too usually hold appealing rural campgrounds but, in the words of the slogan, each is a "Land Of Many Uses," and usually allows logging and other land-based industry – though more often ski resorts than strip mines.

Other government departments administer wildlife refuges, national scenic rivers, recreation areas, and the like. The Bureau of Land Management (BLM) has the largest holdings

Castle Geyser erupts with hot water and steam in Yellowstone National Park, Wyoming.

activities as free guided hikes and campfire talks. In principle, a national park preserves an area of outstanding natural beauty, encompassing a wide range of terrain and prime examples of particular landforms and wildlife. Thus Yellowstone has boiling geysers and herds of elk and bison, while Rocky Mountain offers towering granite walls and cascading waterfalls.

A national monument is usually much smaller, focusing perhaps on just one archeological site or geological phenomenon, such as Devil's Tower in Wyoming. Altogether, the national park system in the four Rockies states comprises around 48 national park units, 104 National Historic sites, and 47 National Natural sites.

of all, most of it open rangeland, such as in Utah, but also including some enticingly out-of-the-way areas. While state parks and state monuments preserve sites of more limited, local significance, many are explicitly intended for recreational use, and thus can often hold better quality campgrounds than their federal equivalents.

Visiting the Rockies means enjoying a great variety of spectacular scenery, having opportunities to view many types of flora and fauna from the tiny to the huge, and being warmly welcomed by the locals. It is a land of extremes in climate and geography, but the hardness of the land has bred a robust people who are happy to share the rugged beauty of their home.

Taking in the view over a mountain valley in Grand Teton National Park.

THE OUTDOORS EXPERIENCE

The Rocky Mountains' trails, lakes, rivers, and forests offer the opportunity to indulge in a vast range of outdoor pursuits, from rafting and hiking to skiing and mountain biking.

For more than 200 years, the spectacular scenery alongside the opportunity for adventure and personal fulfilment have been what draw people to the Rocky Mountains. Only minutes from the door of many Rocky Mountain communities, you can find the peaceful solace in nature that helps to replenish the mind and soul. The only sounds are of the wind in the trees, the rushing stream at the bottom of the valley, and the scurrying wildlife that goes about its daily business uninterrupted by outsiders.

> *Mountain weather can change frequently and rapidly, and what starts out as a sunny day can be punctuated by a snowstorm even at the height of summer.*

East Rim Arch at Rattlesnake Canyon.

HIKING

In the Rockies, hiking into unique wilderness spots can occupy whole days, weekends, or even entire summers. The region is laced with hiking trails that are maintained primarily by the US Forest Service, and you will find maps available through the Forest Service and at many information centers. Colorado alone has 11 national forests that encourage camping in the numerous campgrounds as well as even more rugged backcountry experiences. Once again mountain guides and outfitters can help with equipment, advice, booklets, and routes if visitors are backpacking novices, as it is very dangerous to strike off into the wilderness without first becoming properly equipped and instructed in the correct use of the equipment.

Many Rocky Mountain states boast – or caution – that somewhere in the high country, it snows every month of the year. It's worth keeping in mind that the well-known national parks such as Yellowstone are not automatically the best places for hikes; if solitude is your goal, you may be better off heading for a less-visited wilderness area or national forest – several of which offer superb hiking without the crowds. An excellent example of this is Wyoming's stunning Wind River region; overshadowed by two famous national parks nearby (Yellowstone and Grand Teton), the Wind River, which is the name given to the upper reaches of the Bighorn River, is nevertheless widely considered to be the state's best for backcountry hiking. However, it may be that the facilities available at established parks – which include visitor centers, well-marked and maintained trails, and ranger-led activities – suit you best.

Colorado's Rocky Mountain National Park features forested trails, plenty of wildlife, and seemingly endless stretches of wild alpine tundra, while the huge rock arches of Rattlesnake Canyon in the Colorado National Monument seem tailor-made to be explored on foot. In Idaho, the Sawtooth National Recreation Area contains easily accessible trails beneath some

Sawtooth Mountains Wilderness near Sun Valley, Idaho.

of the most rugged peaks in the Rockies, while the Frank Church-River of No Return Wilderness is crisscrossed with 2,600 miles (4,184km) of trails through impeccable, wildlife-rich backcountry. In Montana, Glacier National Park boasts spectacular mountain peaks and glaciers in the heart of grizzly and black bear country, and Utah's Logan Canyon offers family-friendly hikes to alpine lakes, past explosions of spring and summer wildflowers.

The region is also packed with long-distance hiking trails that could easily be the focus of an entire trip. The staggering Colorado Trail (https://coloradotrail.org) cuts across the heart of the Rocky Mountains from Denver to Durango (486 miles/782km), usually taking 4–6 weeks

> *The Rocky Mountain region is the US's pre-eminent backcountry camping location.*

to complete. The mammoth Continental Divide Trail (3,028 miles/4,873km; https://continentaldividetrail.org) runs the entire length of the Rockies, from the Mexican to Canadian border. The Pacific Northwest Trail (1,200 miles/1,900km; www.pnt.org) connects the Continental Divide in Montana (Glacier National Park), with Washington's Olympic Coast.

SAFETY IN THE MOUNTAINS

Safety issues regarding hiking in the Rockies have much to do with altitude; dehydration occurs quickly in the thin, dry air of the mountains, and altitude sickness is an ever-present danger. Mountain weather is notoriously unpredictable, and snowstorms can appear suddenly at any time of the year. When hiking above the treeline you'll be completely exposed to the sun – in which case a lightweight long-sleeve shirt and a hat are essential to protect you from its rays. If lightning is a potential threat, you should head back down below the treeline; if you're stuck in the open, crouch between a couple of boulders, or hunker down on top of a small one, preferably on some insulating material such as a foam sleeping mat. Hiking alone is not recommended, and you should ideally let someone know your plans and when you expect to return.

BACKCOUNTRY CAMPING

Nearly every national park and forest, wilderness and recreation area allows for camping at minimal or no cost – though a permit is often required. Check with the local ranger office for detailed maps and regulations on camping grounds, and for weather forecasts and any potential hazards along the way, such as wildlife, avalanches areas or rivers that may need to be forded.

ROCK CLIMBING

With an abundance of peaks in the 12,000–14,000ft (3,658–4,267-meter) range, plus clusters of huge boulders and hundreds of precipitous walls of granite, limestone, and ice, the Rocky Mountains serve up abundant climbing and mountaineering opportunities. Whether your preference is for summiting a mighty peak, scaling a granite wall or sheer sheet of ice, or undertaking some unfettered free-climbing or bouldering, you'll find plenty of routes to choose from.

For beginners, there are numerous rock-climbing schools throughout the area where, under the watchful eye of guides and well-trained instructors, students spend a few days or even weeks learning the art of rock climbing, just as they learn to respect the technical knowledge needed to complete exercises and journeys successfully and smoothly.

Top climbing spots include Ouray in Colorado, home of the Ouray Ice Park, one of the premier ice climbing destinations in the US, as well as the City of Rocks National Reserve in Idaho, east of Pocatello, where amazing granite pinnacles thrusting out of the desert provide a challenge for climbers of all abilities. Chimney Rock near Priest Lake is the Idaho Panhandle's top vertical challenge. Some of the best ice climbing in the Rockies is to be found in Hyalite Canyon, Montana, within easy reach of Bozeman, while Wyoming's Grand Teton National Park is peppered with technical and non-technical climbs. The Vedauwoo Recreation Area, east of Laramie, Wyoming, offers several free-standing granite formations with challenges to suit every proficiency level.

CYCLING

Even the thoroughly active person will find bicycling in the Rockies a challenge. Steep climbs and exhilarating descents are the rule in all but a few mountain locations. In many communities and counties, a good system of bike trails links cities and towns some 20 miles (32km) apart. Some trails climb mountain passes or meander along mountain streams where the refreshing sights, sounds and smells of the outdoors take much of the effort out of the climb. Being in good physical shape before tackling one of the mountain passes is imperative.

Renting a bicycle and pedaling around the villages and into the surrounding valleys is a pleasure that can be enjoyed by almost anyone.

An ice climber ascending at Ouray Ice Park, Colorado.

☉ FALL FOLIAGE

While summer overflows with adventures and activities, in fall the already spectacular scenery takes on new beauty as aspen trees turn to burnished gold, striking a contrast with the deep green pine forests and bright blue skies. A weekend jaunt into the mountains is a regular fall activity for Front Range residents and is a must for visitors in September and October. Warm days invite hiking before the snow begins to fall. While it rains or snows frequently in October, extended summers are more generally the rule in Colorado. In Montana, Glacier National Park and the Bitterroot Valley are top spots for leaf peepers, while fall is a wonderful time to visit Yellowstone in Wyoming.

Many winter-time ski rental stores switch to mountain bikes and fishing tackle in summer. They can recommend trails that are a joy to those who want fresh air and light exercise or can point out the more challenging rides.

Colorado has an extensive network of dedicated bike trails: the Peaks to Plains Trail runs 65 miles (105km) along Clear Creek, while the Cherry Creek Regional Trail runs for 40 miles (64km) through suburban Denver. The scenic Rio Grande Trail stretches 42 miles (68km) between Aspen and Glenwood Springs (mostly downhill).

In Montana the paved Bitterroot Trail (https://bitterroottrail.com) gains just 400ft (122 meters) over 51 miles (82km), making it ideal for cyclists. In Idaho there's the Trail of the Coeur

> *Almost every good-sized mountain town in the Rockies will have a bike shop offering rentals to visitors.*

d'Alenes (a paved 73-mile/117-km route across the Panhandle), and the spectacular Route of the Hiawatha (www.ridethehiawatha.com), a 15-mile/24-km gravel trail that features 10 tunnels, including the 1.66-mile/2.6-km-long St. Paul Tunnel. In Utah you can cycle 28 miles

Biking a snodgrass trail in Mount Crested Butte.

(45km) from Park City to Echo Reservoir through the Wasatch Mountains on the Historic Union Pacific Rail Trail. Websites such as www.rails-totrails.org can help with planning. The national non-profit Adventure Cycling Association, based in Missoula, Montana (www.adventurecycling.org), publishes maps of several lengthy routes, detailing campgrounds, motels, restaurants, bike shops, and places of interest.

MOUNTAIN BIKING

Though all wilderness areas and national park trails are out of bounds to mountain bikes, fat tires are welcome on almost all national forest and BLM trails. These include thousands of miles of single track and many more miles of old logging and mining roads. Whether you are a skilled mountain biker after technical challenges or a more leisurely cyclist looking to explore the countryside on traffic-free trails, it's hard to think of a place better suited to exploration by mountain bike. The mountainous topography and high altitude of course mean that it pays to be fit, particularly if you have a longer multi-day tour in mind. For those looking for more thrills with less climbing, many resorts open their ski-lifts to bikes in the summer.

The quality of the bikes available to rent is reliably good – almost all have good front suspension and if you want to rent a full suspension rig, it's usually not too hard to find one. Local bike stores are also the best source of advice and information about nearby trails.

Mountain biking hubs include Crested Butte in Colorado, one of the birthplaces of mountain biking, with several world-class trails to choose from, and Grand Junction and Fruita, where the "Lunch Loops" are challenging but lots of fun. The best ski resorts to hit up for lift-serviced trails are Winter Park, Keystone, Vail, and Breckenridge in Colorado. Winter Park in particular has a huge network, while all the trails in Keystone are fairly challenging – a couple of sections are the most technical lift-serviced sections in the state – while at Vail you can ride the remnants of past years' World Cup cross-country and downhill courses.

The entire Idaho Sun Valley has worthwhile trails, one of the finest (with plenty of steep single track downhill action) being the Fisher Creek-Williams Creek Trail. Wyoming's Medicine Bow National Forest is also popular, with trails including the incredible Rock Creek Trail along a granite ledge high above forests of lodgepole, pines, spruces, and aspens.

WHITEWATER RAFTING

You'd be hard pressed to find many other regions in the world with as many whitewater rafting opportunities as the Rockies. There are several fast-moving rivers throughout the mountains for everyone from first timers to experienced pros; first-timers will need a river guide. The whitewater season runs from late April through September, though the early part of this season is for hardened paddlers only as the waters tend to be very fast and very cold. The months of May and June typically see rivers at their highest as a result of spring runoff, making for a faster ride and bigger rapids. Though the water flow decreases in the second half of the season, trips can be just as enjoyable as the warmer waters make for more pleasant swimming and splashing about. The most popular method of floating down is on a raft; kayaks and canoes are also available. Regardless of the craft, just getting out onto the water is a thrill, and one that allows you to take in a great deal of natural beauty, spy on wildlife, and often cast a line or two.

Classifications identify the rivers' ruggedness – from Class I, an easy river with small waves and generally sandy, accessible beaches, and Class III with medium-sized or high irregular waves and passages dotted with boulders and rocks, to Classes V and VI where only the most experienced boatmen dare to travel.

It's not unusual for even novice rafters, after a short riverside safety course, to bash through Class III or even occasionally Class IV rapids in the hands of a good river guide. It's highly advisable to use a well-established company as their guides will know the river well and are trained in first aid skills in the rare event that they are required.

Various types of craft are used for rafting. Paddle rafts are up to 14ft (4.3 meters) long, hold six to eight paddlers and a guide, and are great fun in rapids. One- or two-person inflatable kayaks, known as "rubber duckies," may also be available for more adventurous paddlers who want to take on the rapids independently. Oar rafts are up to 22ft (6.7 meters) long, controlled and paddled with a rear oar and used to transport camping gear and equipment downriver, and are often manned only by a guide and partner. Some companies also use traditional wooden or steel-hulled dories that are also controlled by paddles, but are less mobile than modern rafts. Occasionally, motorized jet boats are used as well.

Some of the standout locations for rafting in Colorado include the Cache la Poudre River, a designated "wild and scenic river" with Class III–V rapids, and the Arkansas River, which traverses four states including Arkansas – hence its name! – and is the busiest stretch of whitewater in the country. It owes its popularity to long runs of continuous Class III water as well as the unremitting "numbers section" or the chunky waves at the

A major reason behind the popularity of rafting is that anyone, including those who have never tried watersports before, can participate.

base of the Royal Gorge, both Class IV–V. In Idaho, the Middle Fork of the Salmon, flowing through the heart of the Frank Church-River of No Return Wilderness Area offers a real backcountry experience, while the Gallatin River near Big Sky in Montana features the heart-pounding "Mad Mile"

Rafting on the Arkansas River in Colorado.

of Class III–IV rapids. In Wyoming, the Snake River at Jackson Hole delivers Class III–IV rapids, plus the state's most scenic float trips, right past the majestic Teton Range.

KAYAKING AND CANOEING

Many of the rivers used by rafters are also popular with kayakers, although on all but the gentlest of rivers kayaking requires a certain amount of experience and the ability to roll the craft. Since kayakers are more likely to ride the river independently, a good knowledge of the river and/or the ability to read river maps is vital. If you're in any doubt about your ability, go for a rafting trip instead. Canoeing is a relaxing way to discover calmer waterways and lakes, and most major lakes in the Rockies will have outfitters who can rent canoes by the hour, half-day, or longer. This quiet and traditional Native American method of water transport allows you to get close to waterfowl, pull up and enjoy picnics on secluded lakeside or riverside beaches, or just get in a low-key workout.

OTHER WATER SPORTS

Other water sports are available in the Rocky Mountain states, but to a very different degree compared to coastal regions or states with vast

water skiing are Bonny Reservoir, Grand Lake, Shadow Mountain and Green Mountain. Dillon Reservoir in Summit County allows motorboating and sailing, but swimming, windsurfing, and water-skiing are not permitted. Lakes and reservoirs near metropolitan areas are abundant and full watersport activities are usually permitted. Chatfield and Cherry Creek Recreation areas near Denver are particularly popular and easily accessible. Last but not least, a trip to Rifle Gap in the western part of Colorado, where artists Christo and Jeanne-Claude Javacheff

Kayaking the Colorado River.

Hot-air ballooning at the annual Erie Town Festival.

waterways. Because of the rugged mountain terrain, lakes tend to be smaller and winds changeable and unpredictable. While the cold and often shallow water does not lend itself to swimming, sailboarding or water skiing in many locations, sailing can be exciting and a test of ability – the small size of the lakes and the unpredictable winds require quick manoeuvring. Sailboarding and windsurfing with wetsuits is becoming increasingly popular at many lakes that allow body contact, largely because of the strong and active resident and visitor population and the relative ease of obtaining and carrying the required equipment.

A number of mountain lakes allow motorboats and water skiing. Some mountain lakes allowing

hung the 400ft (120 meter) high, 1,250-feet (380 meter) long orange "Valley Curtain" in 1970, may be worth the time and effort, not only for the sailing but also for the scenery.

CAVING

An alternative to hiking or biking high above the mountains is to explore the caves deep within them; caving (also called spelunking or potholing) attracts a small but dedicated number of visitors to the area. The largest concentration of limestone bedrock, creating caverns perfect for exploration by experienced cavers, is in Wyoming; indeed, a key publication for spelunkers is **Caves of Wyoming** by Hill, Sutherland and Tierney (University of Wyoming). In Montana, one of the few options is Azure Cave in the Little Rocky Mountains between Zortman and Landusky. Those that want to see a cave in the presence of a guide should head to the Cave of the Winds near Manitou Springs or the Glenwood Fairy Caverns (both in Colorado), or the Lewis and Clark Caverns State Park, near Bozeman in Montana.

While caving can be exciting, it can also be very dangerous, and cavers should be properly outfitted and guided to their destination. The lure of the unknown is probably the basis

Though some stables will rent horses to experienced riders, more common is a guided trail ride that can last anywhere between an hour to multi-day overnight forays.

you to a camp where the cook has steaming coffee and a hearty breakfast ready to appease the appetites of dudes and wranglers alike. For those less inclined to rise with the early birds,

Hiking in Grand Teton National Park.

Learning to ride horseback in Colorado.

for most of the spectacular stories about what lies underground, but those who venture into the deep should be well prepared. Climbers and cavers should always check in with the regional Forest Service office both upon entering and leaving the caves.

HORSEBACK RIDING

The pursuit with the longest history in the region is, of course, horseback riding.

Such guided backcountry trips usually require at a party of at least two. For full immersion into western life, you might like to spend time at a dude ranch; plan ahead for a breakfast ride at the crack of dawn in the crisp mountain air. The guide will have the horses ready and will take

there is always the evening steak ride or wagon ride. Guests are led to a hidden spot where the fire crackles and the steaks sizzle. The evening almost always includes tales of the Old West or the wranglers' experiences when they "was just young-uns" pushing cattle or riding their horses to school in blizzards long ago.

HOT-AIR BALLOONING

Of all the high-adrenaline sports offered in the mountains, the most thrilling, memorable, and expensive is perhaps hot-air ballooning. Short half-hour flights are the cheapest way to go, though most companies aim for a more leisurely experience, with at least an hour of airtime. Flights are offered by companies based

SKIING IN THE ROCKIES

To many, the Rocky Mountains are synonymous with winter sports and with around 60 ski areas in the region, it's easy to see why.

Even more so than the terrain – rugged ridges, steep drops, dense glades, and lonely bowls – the quality and amount of local snowfalls – dubbed "champagne powder" – keep skiiers coming back for more. Those used to icy slopes elsewhere will be surprised by how forgiving the snow is and are sure to be blown away after experiencing a legendary powder day.

WHERE TO GO

Resorts typically run their lifts from late-November through mid-April. Utah is particularly popular, with its resorts extraordinarily accessible from Salt Lake City. If après-ski is important to you, then you should head to Colorado, where ski towns party much harder than they do farther north – the best rule of thumb being that the older the associated town, the better the nightlife. This means that former mining towns like Aspen, Breckenridge, Telluride, and Crested Butte are good bets for raucous partying and are leagues ahead of newer rivals – particularly the all-inclusive resorts which tend to attract families.

Skiing fresh powder snow in the Utah mountains.

The most popular place to ski in Colorado is in Summit County, where Breckenridge, Keystone, Copper Mountain, and Arapaho Basin are all within close proximity. Within a short drive of Summit County are several other major ski areas, including the varied and challenging Winter Park, the idyllic backcountry paradise of Berthoud Pass and the massive slopes of Vail. The other major resorts in Colorado are harder to get to and include the four ski areas at Aspen, the state's après-ski capital, laid back Steamboat Springs in Northern Colorado, and the enjoyable Crested Butte and Telluride in Southern Colorado – each large enough to warrant their own airports.

Idaho is best known for the Sun Valley Resort, loaded with steep mogul runs and fine long intermediate level cruising opportunities. Other top resorts include Schweitzer Mountain Resort near Sandpoint and Silver Mountain Resort near Kellogg.

Montana's Big Sky, a half-hour drive north of Yellowstone National Park, has the biggest vertical drop of any resort in the US (over 4,000ft/1,219 meters), and is known for its good mix of intermediate-level terrain as well as a clutch of scary-looking expert trails. Big Mountain, near Whitefish, is another large and very worthwhile resort, known for varied routes and great glade skiing in between snow-covered trees – so-called "snow ghosts". The ski area of Red Lodge Mountain, Montana, is beside a happening party town and close to an outstanding network of cross-country trails.

Nearly all of Utah's major resorts are clustered within an hour's drive of Salt Lake City, and huge quantities of light, legendary snow fall consistently. Alta (for skiers only) and Snowbird, both in Little Cottonwood Canyon a half hour from Salt Lake City, are renowned for their laid-back nature and incredible terrain. In nearby Big Cottonwood Canyon are Brighton and Solitude, while the state's other most famous resorts – Park City, Deer Valley and the Canyons – are lined up in a row a few miles to the east.

Judged by many to be the best in the country, the ski scene in Wyoming is dominated by the world-class monster of Jackson Hole Mountain Resort – a challenge for even the most extreme of skiers. Not far away are a couple of other good resorts: Snow King Resort in Jackson and Grand Targhee Resort in Alta, reachable via Idaho.

in many Colorado towns including Boulder, Steamboat Springs, Vail, Aspen, and Colorado Springs. You can also get airborne in Jackson, Wyoming, and near Glacier National Park and Whitefish in Montana. The greatest annual hot-air balloon spectacles are held in Riverton and Rock Springs (both in Wyoming) around the same time in July. In Colorado both Grand Junction and Crested Butte also hold hot-air balloon festivals.

FISHING

The Rocky Mountains are a natural draw for anglers, with some of the finest stocks of fish in the Lower 48. The high mountain streams and lakes are a fisherman's dream, yielding brook trout, browns and firm-fleshed lake trout.

It's impossible to list the best fishing rivers in the Rockies simply because there are so many. Suffice to say there are enough "Blue Ribbon" or "Gold Medal" rivers throughout the region to make such terms nearly meaningless. In many places it's possible to fly-fish virtually from the roadside or even within some city centers, and if you're looking for solitude the lakes and rivers of the backcountry will provide infinite variety. Good access sites are often signposted, but you shouldn't assume you can fish anywhere you choose as some rivers run through private land and permission must be given by the landowner before you cast a line. It's often best to discuss spots and possible guided tours with a local outfitter. Depending on the area, bait or fly-fishing is recommended.

The main fishing season is June through October, although it's quite possible to fish year-round in many areas; ice fishing is a popular lake option in winter. Most lakes and reservoirs are open year-round, but there are often seasonal restrictions on rivers and streams. It's important to obtain the correct non-resident State Fishing Licenses before you set out.

Most mountain communities boast a fishing guide operation that not only has checked out the finest and most productive fishing spots but also constantly monitors the most effective bait choices for each season. Some guides all but guarantee that fishermen will leave with breakfast in their creels, but even if the fishing is unproductive, the Rocky Mountain scenery always makes the trip worthwhile. Guides can be hired to supply equipment as well as

expertise in most areas and, depending on the season and the location, will take their charges to their destination by boat or Jeep.

GOLF

Golf has also taken off as a popular summertime pursuit in the Rockies. More and more 18-hole courses designed by luminaries such as Jack Nicklaus and Robert Trent Jones II are springing up in the region. In Vail Valley alone, there are eight courses, and just an hour's drive away in Summit County is the beautiful but demanding

Playing golf on a beautiful desert golf course.

Keystone course.

The challenge to golfers extends beyond the usual as courses are frequently narrow and filled with many natural hazards. Designers have taken advantage of the natural lay of the land and complemented their courses with large stands of pine, mountain streams, rolls and hills, and turns that follow the valleys. Accurate ball placement is required on most mountain courses. In addition, because of the thin air, the ball travels farther than usual, so major adjustments in club use are required. The local pro shop will be able to advise, or a lesson with one of the local pros giving tips on how the course plays will work wonders in keeping scores low and spirits high.

The Colorado Renaissance Festival in Larkspur transforms this modern day town into a 16th-century Tudor village.

MOUNTAIN CELEBRATIONS

For the lover of sports or art, nature or culture, summer in the Rockies is a parade of festivals, concerts, and special events.

If you want to do as the locals do, plan your journey through the Rockies to coincide with some of these events. The Rockies have become the most well-known summer festival territory of the United States, with celebrations taking place across the region, though there are also plenty of events in the winter. Lists of happenings in most areas, from environmental and cultural events to athletic activities, are available from chambers of commerce and visitor center websites.

DENVER

Denver, Colorado's capital city, is teeming with events and festivals. The Denver Center for the Performing Arts has a wonderful theater company that stages both local and hit Broadway plays year-round. The Boettcher Concert Hall is the home to the well-known Colorado Symphony Orchestra, and one of the best musical auditoriums in the world. Great performers are frequently known to stop here on national tours.

Other events include the Denver Arts Festival in May, which showcases over 150 Colorado and national artists, and the Great American Beer Festival in October, which especially highlights the state's burgeoning craft beer industry.

In December, Denver hosts the Parade of Lights, culminating in what is said to be the world's largest display of Christmas lights. In January, the mile-high city kicks off the bronc-bustin' season with two weeks of parades, performers, and lots of high-stakes rodeo action at the National Western Stock Show and Rodeo.

TELLURIDE

Telluride stands apart from most Rockies ski resorts in that it has a full seasonal program

Telluride Mushroom Festival.

⊘ OPERA FESTIVALS

The Central City Opera Festival is one of Colorado's oldest summer festivals, held in July. This nationally famous festival takes place at the 1878 Opera House in the old gold mining town of Central City, 35 miles (56km) west of Denver. In Colorado Springs in the same month, the Opera Theatre of the Rockies also hosts the Vocal Arts Festival. Another nationally important event is the Colorado Music Festival held at the 1896 Chautauqua Auditorium in Boulder. For six weeks in summer, a series of chamber music concerts takes place; also of interest are the many lectures, symposia, concerts, films, and exhibits that take place throughout the year.

of worthwhile festivals that draw crowds from both near and far. Highlights include the Mushroom Festival (Aug), with guided forages into the woods, the Wine Festival (June), the Balloon Festival (June), and the Blues and Brews Festival (Sept), which combines live music with tastings from more than 150 craft breweries. The Jazz Festival, held since 1977 in the first week of August, has historically included performances by Herbie Hancock and Etta James.

Film buffs who also like the mountains will enjoy the popular Telluride Mountain Film Fes-

Hot-air balloons fill the sky in Colorado.

tival held in September, which brings together film-makers, film stars, climbers, mountain men, and outdoor enthusiasts, while Mountainfilm is an independent documentary film festival held in May.

The Telluride Bluegrass Festival is a spectacular four-day festival held in late June that attracts around 10,000 visitors for big name acts. It was started in 1973 by a small, local bluegrass band called Fall Creek, and the picturesque setting is a large field backed by the snow-peaked San Juans. It's also a carnival with food stands, craft booths, and musicians playing on stage while people relax, dance, chat, and hurl Frisbees. The atmosphere is extremely laid-back, with little groups of musicians jamming in the street or parking lots. Over the years, this festival has hosted the some of the finest folk and country musicians in the world, including Leon Russell, Willie Nelson, Roseanne Cash, The Band, New Grass Revival, and many others.

ASPEN

Like Telluride, Aspen features a full roster of festivals and events throughout the year. The Aspen X Games kicks things off in January, when top snowboarders and Big Air skiers compete at Buttermilk (it's free to watch). One of Aspen's biggest summertime attractions is the nine-week Aspen Music Festival, which includes chamber music and modern jazz and attracts internationally recognized musicians. The spectacular Snowmass Balloon Festival is held in September. Also usually in September is the five-day Aspen Filmfest, while Aspen Shortsfest in April is one of the premier short film festivals in North America. Year-round programs of concerts, plays, and dance performances are held by the Wheeler Opera House, DanceAspen, and Theatre Aspen.

WINTER FESTIVALS

Winter brings a host of events from the zany activities of Snowdown in Durango, Colorado, to dog sled races at Helena, Montana. Idaho's Sandpoint Film Festival (celebrating short films from around the globe) kicks things off in November, while horned helmets are de rigeur at the Ullr Fest (pronounced "oo-ler"). This Breckenridge, Colorado festival honors the Norse god of snow and is usually held in December with an "Ullr Parade" down Main Street. The four-day Vail Snow Days festival features live music, usually in mid-December. Also in Colorado, the Ouray Ice Festival and competition, held on the third weekend of January, celebrates the sport of ice climbing.

In February, boisterous winter carnivals are held in Whitefish, Montana, and Steamboat Springs, Colorado, while the renowned Lionel Hampton Jazz Festival is held in Moscow, Idaho.

SPRING AND SUMMER

In spring the mountains come alive with a variety of sporting events. More than 2,000 cyclists come to Durango, Colorado in May for three days of road and mountain biking events at the annual Iron Horse Bicycle Classic. In June, the town of

Salida in central Colorado hosts one of America's most prestigious kayak races, part of the FIBArk Whitewater Festival on the Arkansas River. Also in June, the annual Race to the Clouds pits 60 drivers against the clock in a white-knuckle auto race to the summit of Pike's Peak, Colorado. Finally, regatta week is held at Grand Lake Yacht Club, the world's highest registered yacht anchorage, in north central Colorado in mid-August.

Crested Butte's assortment of blossoms – including purple and white columbine, orange scarlet gilia, yellow mule's ear sunflowers, blue lupine, pink wild rose, and violet flax – are celebrated during June and July's Wildflower Festival, when a program of photography, painting, and herbal medicine workshops are offered. In Boulder, the Colorado Shakespeare Festival stages plays through the summer months, while the Colorado State Fair is usually held in Pueblo at the end of August. Also in August, the Rocky Mountain Folks Festival is held in Lyons, Colorado.

Colorado is also big on summer balloon festivals. Steamboat Springs hosts the Hot Air Balloon Rodeo in July, while in early September, the Colorado Springs Labor Day Lift Off sees hundreds of balloons float into the mountains. There's also the Creede Colorado Balloon Festival at the end of August and Snowmass Balloon Festival in September. Colorfest, held in Pagosa Springs at the end of September, features over 40 balloons filling the sky each morning.

In Utah, Park City's roster of summer events includes the International Music Festival, aka Beethoven Festival Park City (mid-July to mid-Aug), a month-long run of classical recitals, while the Salt Lake City Jazz Festival usually takes place in July (though it sometimes skips years on hiatus), and the Utah Jazz & Roots Festival is held in September. In August, the Raspberry Days Festival celebrates the harvest of Bear Lake's celebrated raspberry crop.

In Wyoming one of the biggest festivals is the Cody Stampede (July), which features parades, street performances, fireworks, and of course, a huge rodeo. The Wyoming Brewers Festival in Cheyenne brings together the region's best craft brewers every June, and Cheyenne Frontier Days is a massive celebration of Western culture held at the end of July (see page 107). The Wyoming State Fair is held in Douglas every August, 130 miles (209km) north of Cheyenne.

> *The famous Sundance Film Festival comes to Park City, Utah, in January, where the year's best independent and foreign films are screened to members of the Sundance Institute; screenings are usually not open to the public.*

In Idaho, the Festival at Sandpoint (July–Aug) features eight days of concerts on Lake Pend Oreille, while the Idaho Shakespeare Festival in

A movie theatre during the Sundance Film Festival.

Boise stages open-air performances through the summer. The state holds three state fairs: the North Idaho State Fair in Coeur d'Alene and the Western Idaho Fair in Boise, both in August, and the Eastern Idaho State Fair in Blackfoot in September.

In Montana, the Montana Folk Festival is a free outdoor music festival held in Butte in July, while the annual Montana State Fair is held in Great Falls (July–Aug).

POWWOWS

Some of the biggest Native American powwows in the nation are held in the Rocky Mountain region. Powwows are exclusively Native American festivals, where there is dancing, singing, eating and craft and cultural demonstrations – participants often dance into the night to the rhythm of drums. Outsiders are usually welcome, but it's always a good idea to check in advance and be careful to respectful of Native American culture. Instead of the glamour that some of the other Rocky Mountain festivals demonstrate, a sincerity and simple, earthy feeling unite all the participants here.

Powwows are held throughout the summer. Among the most popular in Montana are the Crow Fair, a huge celebration of Native American life and culture on the Crow Indian Reservation, the Arlee Fourth of July Powwow on the

The Denver March Powwow is another major event, featuring more than 1,500 Native American dancers from nearly 100 tribes, while the Southern Ute Fair Powwow is a three-day celebration held annually in September at the Sky Ute Fairgrounds in Ignacio, Colorado.

CELEBRATIONS OF THE OLD WEST

The traditions of the Old West are kept alive throughout the Rockies region with rodeos, reenactments and rendezvous. Little Bighorn Days in Hardin, Montana, is a four-day festival in June

World Champion bareback rider, Kelly Timberman.

Participant at the Fort Bridger Rendezvous.

Flathead Indian Reservation, and North American Indian Days on the Blackfeet Indian Reservation. Among the powwows in Wyoming are the Ethete Celebration, the Eastern Shoshone Indian Days Powwow at Fort Washakie, Big Wind Powwow on the Wind River Reservation, and the Plains Indian Museum Powwow at the Buffalo Bill Historical Center in Cody.

In Idaho the Shoshone-Bannock Indian Festival features a variety of arts and crafts stalls selling exquisite Native American jewelry, leather goods, beadwork and other Native American items. If you attend this event, you can either stay at Pocatello and commute daily or camp out on the reservation in areas specifically prepared for campers.

that celebrates the sights and sounds of the Old West, including an 1876 Grand Ball and Custer's Last Stand Reenactment.

Rodeos, held throughout Wyoming and other states during the summer, often provide the focus for all sorts of festival events, from live country music to communal cookouts. A list of dates and locations can be obtained from state visitor bureaus and local chambers of commerce websites. As far as rodeos go, the "Big Daddy of 'em all" is Cheyenne Frontier Days, which began in 1897 when 15,000 people cheered cow-pony races, pitching and bucking broncos, a pony express demonstration and a mock battle between Sioux warriors and US cavalrymen. It was so successful, it lasted two days.

In Montana, too, you can join the locals in foot-stompin' rodeos that go on almost every weekend during the summer, from the College National Finals Rodeo in Bozeman to the Wild Horse Stampede in Wolf Point. Another special event is the State Fiddling Championship every July in Polson, where visitors enjoy the music of the Montana Old Time Fiddlers Organization on the south shore of Flathead Lake.

For travelers with a taste for old-fashioned fun, a variety of mountain men rendezvous re-create 19th-century fur-trappers' gatherings

Today, Frontier Days lasts 10 days. The world's best rodeo is combined with a fabulous mile-long parade, superstar entertainers, free breakfasts, square dancing, Native American dancing, and an excellent Old West Museum.

Renaissance Festival, held for eight weekends between late June and early August. Situated at the base of the Rocky Mountains in Larkspur,

Entertainment at the Colorado Renaissance Festival.

Native American dancer at the Julyamsh Powwow.

with historic re-enactments, traditional games, cookouts, crafts, and entertainment. The Green River Rendezvous at the Museum of the Mountain Man in Pinedale, Wyoming, is held on the second full weekend in July, while Fur Trade Encampments are often re-created at Bent's Old Fort National Historic Site in Colorado. The Fort Bridger Rendezvous is held at Fort Bridger State Historic Site in Wyoming each September, commemorating the celebration of the fur trade rendezvous that occurred in the Rocky Mountains between 1825 and 1840.

COLORADO RENAISSANCE FESTIVAL

For a taste of something a bit more unusual considering the surroundings, visit the Colorado

between Colorado Springs and Denver off I-25, this is an event at which the whole family can experience the atmosphere of a medieval European marketplace, with nearly 200 craftspeople demonstrating and selling their wares to curious onlookers. A colorful cast of village characters welcomes the public to the magic merriment of a fantasy kingdom. Entertainers include combat jousters, sword swallowers, belly dancers, and wandering players. Shakespearean actors roam the fairgrounds while witty young lasses and lads joke and flirt with visitors. Nibble on turkey drumsticks, tempura steak on a spit, and spicy sausages. It's all fun, continuous entertainment on 20 acres (eight hectares) of the 16th-century-themed Renaissance Amusement Park.

WILDLIFE

One of the real thrills of traveling the Rocky Mountains region is the chance to see some of North America's most distinctive wildlife in its natural habitat.

Adult grizzly bear in Yellowstone National Park.

A curious baby coyote in Rocky Mountain National Park.

The determining factors for the kinds of animals and birds you might encounter while exploring here are altitude, terrain and vegetation. All three are inextricably linked, with altitude and terrain also determining what kinds of vegetation can grow in a given area; the mountains are thus made up of a number of distinct ecosystems, each one supporting particular types of animals and birds.

BUFFALO

By far the two most spectacular animals to be seen here are the grizzly bear and the buffalo (also known as the American bison). They are the largest, and some of the most dangerous animals found in the Rockies today. Although a few buffalo

herds are privately owned, travelers will find the largest herds at refuges such as Yellowstone National Park in Wyoming, Wind Cave National Park and Custer State Park in South Dakota, as well as a National Wildlife Refuge located in far-flung Moiese, Montana.

Visitors to Yellowstone in winter and summer are sure to see herds of buffalo grazing stolidly. The adult male is huge, standing up to 7ft (2 meters) tall and weighing up to a whopping 2,000 pounds (900kg). These massive animals can easily outrun humans in a stampede, and when threatened, they will defend themselves by goring with their short, curved horns. They are not to be approached on foot or surrounded by a group under any circumstances.

BEARS

Grizzly bears do their best to avoid humans, but backpackers in wilderness areas may encounter these huge omnivores. Grizzlies have poor sight and hearing and may move toward the unknown in order to understand it. They will try to flee from humans unless in pain, feeling trapped, or someone comes between a sow and her cubs. The best advice, of course, is to keep your distance.

Adult females weigh between 350 to 450 pounds (150 to 200kg) and males from 800 to

even adapted quite happily to foraging in garbage dumps at national parks and "begging" for food at campsites or by roadsides. Modern management policies have helped to alleviate this harmful behavior, but human encounters with black bears are a constant concern for park rangers. As well as black, this bear may be brown or reddish ("cinnamon") in color, but almost all of them will have a brown face and a white blaze on its chest. Adults are 5 to 6ft tall (about 2 meters) and weigh between 200 to 500 pounds (90 to 230 kg).

Yellow-bellied marmots along Beartooth Highway.

A cougar, also known as a mountain lion.

1,000 pounds (360 to 450kg). Their coloring ranges from dark brown to straw-colored blond with silvery tipped hairs, giving them the grizzled look for which they are named. A noticeable hump at the shoulders and an indented face above the snout distinguish them from their bear cousins. Fewer than 1,500 grizzlies are thought to exist in the United States outside the state of Alaska, and the majority of that number are to be found in Wyoming and Montana, particularly in Glacier and Yellowstone National Parks and their adjacent wilderness areas.

Black bears may present more danger to people simply because there are more of them, and because over time they have become less and less afraid of human presence. Some have

⊘ BIGHORN SHEEP

The title of Rocky Mountain mascot goes to the extraordinary Rocky Mountain bighorn sheep – there is no more indelible image than a lone bighorn majestically perched on a rocky ledge, lord of all he surveys. Both rams and ewes grow horns, although the two are easily distinguished as the ram has the classic "C"-shaped horns, while the ewe's grow as almost vertical spikes, up to 8 inches (20cm) long. Rams put on an extraordinary display during the rutting season, roughly mid-November through December, when they square off and crack horns with sickening impact to assert their authority and establish mating rights.

MOOSE, ELK, AND DEER

Four members of the deer family are common to the Rockies, including the moose. With the largest bulls reaching 7ft (2.1 meters) at the shoulder and weighing from 1,000 to 1,400 pounds (450 to 630kg), their antlers are the largest of any mammal, with five to seven prongs spreading out from solid "shovels" nearer the head. Record antler widths from prong to prong begin at 5ft (1.5 meters). Moose are fond of marshy areas and the grasses that grow along riverbanks. They are strong swimmers and will even take to open waters.

in the Rockies, as is the pronghorn, which local residents call an "antelope." Herds of pronghorn can be seen in open grasslands and even sometimes along busy roads.

WOLVES AND MOUNTAIN LIONS

The gray wolf (*canis lupus*) is native to the Glacier Country region in northern Montana and is making a steady comeback to Greater Yellowstone, with packs now established around the park's borders in forested areas of Montana, Wyoming and Idaho, as well as within Yellowstone itself;

A small pack of eastern timber wolves gather on a rocky slope.

The slightly smaller elk also carries large antlers, in this case open prongs sweeping upward and back from the head, nearly as large as the moose's. The larger bulls weigh up to 900 pounds (408kg), and sport huge "racks" or sets of antlers, which alone can weigh as much as 50 pounds (23kg). The most dramatic time to observe elk is during the fall rut, which generally begins in September and may go on into early November. The bulls strut and display their necks and antlers to the cows, but the most extraordinary part of their display is an unearthly call to a potential mate called "bugling" – a bizarre ear-piercing squeal.

Mule deer and white-tailed deer, smaller relatives of the moose and elk, are also common

it's unlikely that there are any wolf packs in Utah, though a small group was reported in Colorado in 2019. A gray (or "timber") wolf is roughly the size of an Alsatian dog, but with longer, leaner legs. Despite the name, a gray wolf's coat may be any color from snow white to jet black, with most falling somewhere in between as a blend of browns and creams or blueish-grays. Wolves keep very much to themselves, so any sighting is well worth bragging about.

Even more secretive – as well potentially dangerous – is the mountain lion; also referred to as a puma or cougar, this sleek, handsome animal has perhaps the most accurate Latin name of all – *felis concolor*, the "one-colored cat." Mountain lion sightings have increased throughout the Rockies in recent years, and while some would suggest that this is evidence of expanding populations, it's more likely that their habitat is shrinking under pressure from suburban development, bringing them into closer proximity with humans.

COYOTES AND RODENTS

Affectionately known to some Native American peoples as the "singing trickster," the coyote is a highly adaptable predator common in the Rockies. Sometimes confused with wolves from afar, coyotes are much smaller, and unlike wolves, it pops out from its rocky hideaway, and the yellow-bellied marmot, which closely resembles a groundhog. Marmots are inveterate sunbathers, and may be seen on exposed, sunny rock outcrops at lower mountain elevations and almost anywhere on the alpine tundra.

BIRDS AND FISH

Nearly every manner of bird can be found in the Rockies, from bald eagles – relatively rare in the Lower 48 – to colorful songbirds and trumpeter swans, the world's largest waterfowl. As for fish,

It's not difficult to see how the bighorn sheep got its name.

they'll often appear by roadsides and in populated areas where a free meal might present itself.

The largest rodent in North America, the beaver designs and builds wetland habitat for countless plants and animals. Its dam-building creates ponds and marshy meadows which in turn support wetland grasses and trees such as willow and cottonwood, as well as waterfowl and grazing animals like moose, elk, and deer.

Among the other interesting animals that you'll need a fair bit of luck to catch a glimpse of are the bobcat, badger, river otter, raccoon, muskrat, weasel, and pine marten. More common are the pika, a small but rotund rodent that announces its presence by squeaking loudly as

there's no shortage of them in the numerous mountain lakes and rivers, and even if you've no interest in casting for them yourself, you can't fail to notice the many people throwing a line in any available stream. Various species of trout are most prevalent, notably rainbow, lake, and cutthroat; there are also some remaining pockets of salmon, though the future of this once plentiful fish looks uncertain.

The beaver is battling to make a comeback in the Rockies, and the overall balance of many mountain ecosystems depend upon its success.

Blue skies and beargrass in bloom at the Rocky Mountain Range of Glacier National Park.

A herd of bison at Rocky Mountain Arsenal National Wildlife Refuge against the Denver skyline.

An abandoned Farmhouse in Idaho.

Skiing in Sun Valley, Idaho.

INTRODUCTION

A detailed guide to the whole of the region, with principal sites clearly cross-referenced by number to the maps.

Tabor Opera House.

Sprawling across five states and encompassing several booming cities, the Rockies offer miles of trackless wilderness, a bounty of outdoor recreation and a surprisingly cosmopolitan urban scene. From the charming Victorian mountain towns of central Colorado to the windswept grasslands of Montana's Big Sky Country, from downtown Denver to the ghost towns of the Idaho Panhandle, the Rocky Mountains bring together the many charms of the American West.

Among the region's natural wonders are some of the most celebrated wilderness preserves in the world. Yellowstone, the world's first national park, is perhaps the best-known, although several others, including Rocky Mountain and Mesa Verde in Colorado, Grand Teton in Wyoming, Glacier in Montana, and a number of smaller parks and monuments are equally worthy of attention.

The Million Dollar Cowboy Bar.

In the winter, the mountains are groomed for skiing. The Rockies boast some of the best snow and most challenging slopes in the world. Ski resorts like Aspen and Vail in Colorado, Park City in Utah and Jackson in Wyoming are well-known for attracting a high-powered mix of Hollywood stars, corporate bigwigs, and government officials, but are just as popular with skiers and snowboarders from all walks of life.

For travelers in search of urban pleasures, Salt Lake City, Denver and the Front Range cities offer lively stores, restaurants, museums, theaters, and special events; relatively small towns and resorts like Telluride, Jackson, Sun Valley, and Boulder offer a surprising variety of shopping and dining, too.

History buffs can visit legendary places like the Little Bighorn Battlefield, where George Armstrong Custer and the Seventh Cavalry made their famous "last stand" against the Sioux and Cheyenne, Fort Bridger in Wyoming, where thousands of westering pioneers bought supplies for their journey on the Oregon Trail, or Leadville in Colorado, where local miners saw Oscar Wilde perform at Tabor Opera House and sipped drinks at the Silver Dollar Saloon.

The Rockies are truly a national treasure; come share in the adventure.

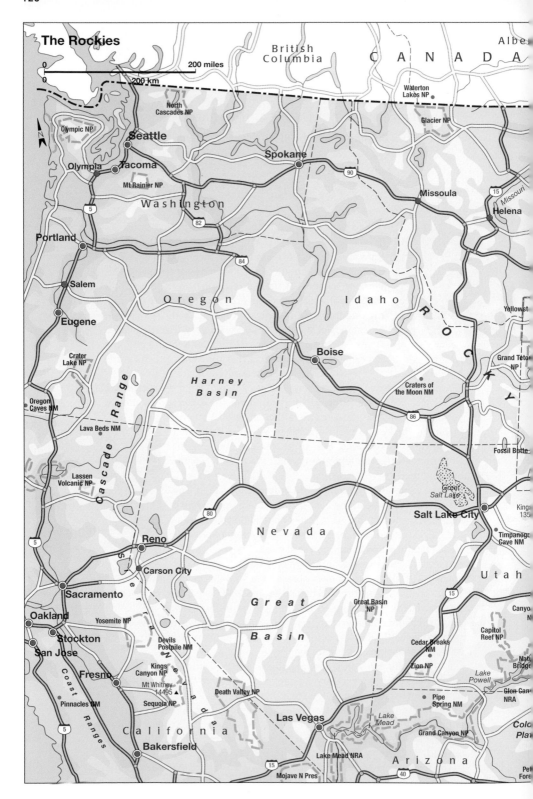

The Rockies

0 ____ 200 miles
0 ____ 200 km

British Columbia

C A N A D A

Albe

Waterton Lakes NP

Glacier NP

North Cascades NP

Olympic NP

Seattle

Olympia

Tacoma

Mt Rainier NP

W a s h i n g t o n

Spokane

90

Missoula

Missouri

15

Helena

82

Portland

Salem

Eugene

O r e g o n

I d a h o

R O C K Y

84

Crater Lake NP

Boise

Yellowst

Grand Této NP

Oregon Caves NM

H a r n e y   B a s i n

Craters of the Moon NM

Lava Beds NM

86

Fossil Butte

Lassen Volcanic NP

C a s c a d e   R a n g e

Great Salt Lake

80

Salt Lake City

Kings 135

N e v a d a

Timpanogos Cave NM

5

Reno

U t a h

Carson City

Sacramento

G r e a t

Great Basin NP

15

Canyo N

Oakland

Yosemite NP

Stockton

B a s i n

Capitol Reef NP

San Jose

Devils Postpile NM

Cedar Breaks NM

Natu Bridge

Fresno

Kings Canyon NP

Zion NP

Lake Powell

Pinnacles NM

Mt Whitney 14495 ▲

Death Valley NP

Glen Can NRA

Sequoia NP

Pipe Spring NM

Colo Pla

C a l i f o r n i a

S i e r r a   N e v a d a

Las Vegas

Lake Mead

Grand Canyon NP

Bakersfield

C o a s t   R a n g e s

Lake Mead NRA

A r i z o n a

Pe Fore

5

15

Mojave N Pres

40

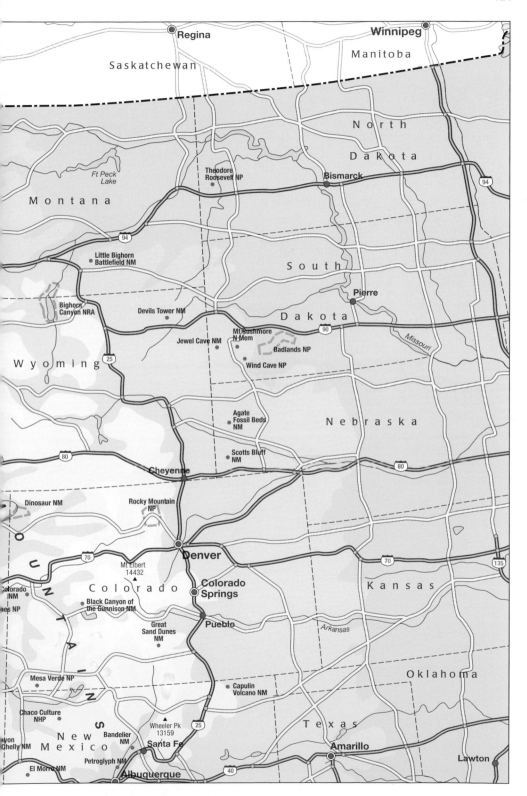

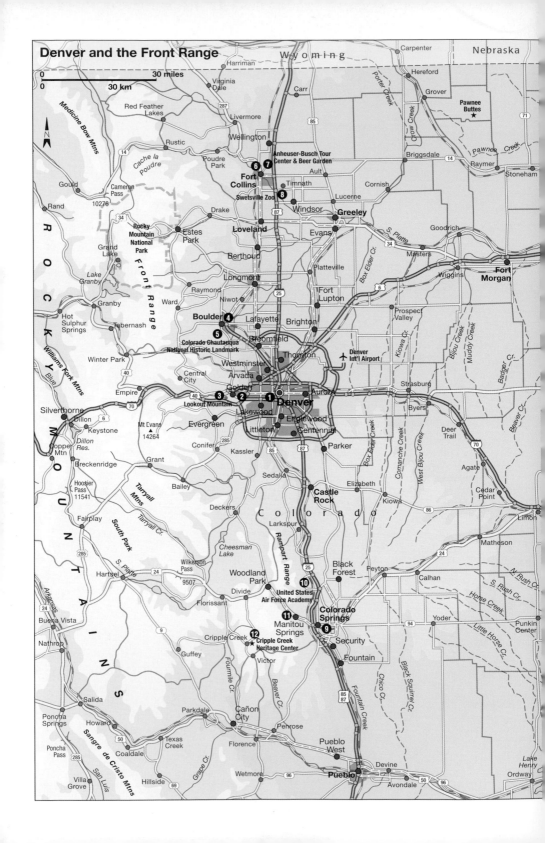

DENVER AND THE FRONT RANGE

The jagged mountain peaks of Colorado's Front Range – the foothills of the Rockies that rise from the Great Plains along a north-south axis – are lined by a booming urban strip that encompasses Denver, the vibrant state capital.

A good 600 miles (965km) from another city of even vaguely similar size, Denver and its surrounding area is unique in the Rockies for its great mix of urban diversions and outdoor adventure. To the west are 200 miles (322km) of towering snow-topped peaks rising to 14,000ft (4,270 meters) and creased by narrow river canyons. This is among the most awe-inspiring alpine scenery to be found in the world, where amber plains and mountain majesty meet. Denver itself bustles with life all year round, as does its northern neighbor, the progressive college town of Boulder. The sleepy brewery town of Golden is well-placed for outdoor adventures and close to the start of the stunning Peak-to-Peak Highway, while Colorado Springs offers a host of attractions and proximity to Pike's Peak, one of America's most celebrated mountains.

DENVER: THE MILE HIGH CITY

The Front Range's chief city is, of course, Colorado's capital, **Denver ❶**

The city that grew up along the Platte was both solid and wild. Newspaper editor Horace Greeley wrote that Denver had "more brawls, more pistol shots with criminal intent than in any other community with equal numbers on earth." Throughout the 1860s the entire region was subject to raids by Arapaho displaced from their lands by

an influx of American miners – they had supposedly been guaranteed ownership of the area by the Fort Laramie Treaty of 1851. Still, Denver quickly became an imposing city – in part because, in 1863, after a series of disastrous fires, the city fathers ordered all new buildings to built of brick. Soon miners who had found fortune high in the mountains were spending their wealth building mansions in Denver. When cattle boomed in Colorado during the 1870s, Denver became known as the Queen City of the Plains, a

Main attractions
16th Street Mall, Denver
Denver Art Museum
Clyfford Still Museum
Denver Botanic Gardens
Coors Brewery
Lookout Mountain
Boulder
US Olympic & Paralympic Museum
Manitou Springs
Pikes Peak

Maps on pages 122, 124

Colorado State Capitol Building.

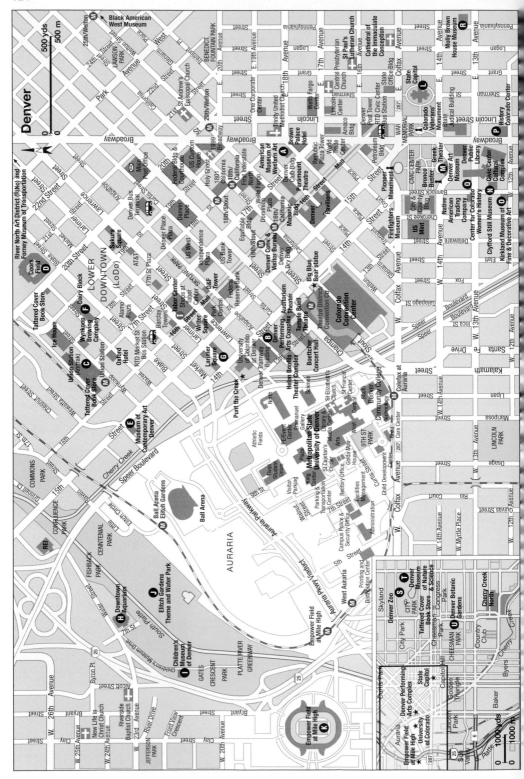

Denver

124

Black American West Museum

500 yds
500 m

0

N

River North Art District (RiNo) and Forney Museum of Transportation →

BENEDICT FOUNTAIN PARK

LAWSON PARK

St Andrew's Episcopal Church

Main Post Office

Federal Bldg & Courthouse

US Custom House

Holy Ghost

Trinity United Methodist Church

Lincoln Center

Wells Fargo Center

One Corporate Center

Denver Bus Terminal

Denver Place Plaza

California First Interstate North

1801 California

California First Interstate

Wells Fargo

Denver Club Bldg

American Museum of Western Art

Brown Palace Hotel

Amoco Bldg

Denver Post Tower

RTD Civic Center Bus Station

State Office Bldg

Central Presbyterian Church

St Paul's Lutheran Church

Cathedral of the Immaculate Conception

Molly Brown House Museum **R**

Coors Field **D**

Tattered Cover Book Store

Ice House

Wynkoop Brewing Company **F**

Dairy Block

Union Station **A**

Union Station

Oxford Hotel

RTD Market St Bus Station

Sakura Square

Independence Plaza

AT&T

17th St Plaza

US West

US Bank Tower

Federal Reserve Bank

Equitable Bldg

Dominion Plaza

Masonic Bldg

Paramount Theatre

World Trade Center

Republic Plaza Tower

Petroleum Bldg

Pioneer Monument

Greek Theater **V**

Denver Art Museum

Denver Public Library

LOWER DOWNTOWN (LoDo)

Tattered Cover Book Store

Tabor Center

Shops at Tabor Center

Barclay Towers

Park Central

D&F Tower

16th Street Mall

Writer Square

Larimer Square **G**

University of Denver Building

Denver Tramway Building

Helen Bonfils Theater Complex

Denver Performing Arts Complex

Auditorium Theater

Temple Buell Theatre

Denver Comm & Visitor Bureau

Denver Dry Bldg

Big Blue Bear statue ★

Theatre District/ Convention Ctr

Colorado Convention Center

Denver Pavilions

Civic Center Cultural Complex **U**

City & County Bldg

Bannock Street

Native American Trading Company

Center for Colorado Women's History

Clyfford Still Museum **Q**

Kirkland Museum of Fine & Decorative Art **O**

Bronco Buster

US Mint

Firefighters' Museum

Museum of Contemporary Art Denver **E**

Boettcher Concert Hall

St Elizabeth's Church

St Francis Center

Colfax at Auraria **M**

Community College of Denver

Colorado Veterans' Monument **L**

State Judicial Building

State Capitol

WAR MEMORIAL PARK

History Colorado Center

Colorado Center **P**

COMMONS PARK

CONFLUENCE PARK

FISHBACK PARK

CENTENNIAL PARK

REI **J**

Ball Arena Elitch Gardens **M**

Ball Arena

Elitch Gardens Theme and Water Park

Museum of Contemporary Art Denver **E**

AURARIA

Punt the Creek ★

Metropolitan State University of Denver

Auraria Parkway

Tivoli Student Union

Visitor Parking

Parking & Transportation Services Center

Campus Police & Security Office

Printing and Distribution Center

West Auraria **M**

Empower Field at Mile High

Emmanuel Gallery

PE/Event Center

St Cajetan's Center

Golda Meir House

Arts

9TH ST PARK

Rectory Office

Facilities Management

Administration

Child Development Center

Care Center

LINCOLN PARK

Downtown Aquarium **H**

Children's Museum of Denver **I**

Elitch Gardens Theme and Water Park

Empower Field at Mile High **K**

New Life in Christ Church

Riverside Baptist Church

JEFFERSON PARK

PLATTE RIVER GREENWAY

CRESCENT PARK

GATES CRESCENT PARK

PLATTE RIVER GREENWAY

(inset map)

Skyland

CITY PARK

Denver Zoo **S**

Denver Museum of Nature & Science **T**

City Park

Cheesman Park

Tattered Cover Book Store

Denver Botanic Gardens **N**

CHEESMAN PARK

Country Club

Cherry Creek North

Cherry Creek

Empower Field at Mile High ★

Denver Performing Arts Complex ★

State Capitol ★

University of Colorado

Auraria

Golden Triangle

Capitol Hill

Baker

Byers

0   1000 yds
0   1000 m

nickname accurately denoting its location in sight of, but not actually in the Rocky Mountains.

Today, Denver is indisputably the metropolis of the Rocky Mountain states. The energy boom of the 1980s (*Dynasty* fans will remember that the Carrington oil empire was headquartered here) gave it a skyline that at many angles dwarfs the Rockies. The city's current artsy, liberal population coexists happily with a dynamic business community driven by the energy and tech sectors.

Denver's attractions can be seen in three or four full days, depending on how much you want to explore the outlying areas. Most of the major sights are located Downtown and just to the south in the Capitol Hill and Golden Triangle district. The River North Art District (RiNo) is a relatively modern creation, an old warehouse district best known today for its bars and restaurants. Farther east, City Park is home to Denver Zoo and the Museum of Nature & Science. The city also has a passion for beer – Denver is said to be the brewpub capital of the world – and for sports, be it skiing, jogging, or cheering on the Colorado Rockies (baseball) and the fanatically supported Denver Broncos (football).

Chances are good that the weather will be sunny; the city averages 300 days of sunshine a year. July highs average about 88°F (31°C) but low humidity makes the heat tolerable, while February lows can sink to 16°F (-9°C) but the sunshine keeps things cheerful. As for the elevation, Denver boasts that it is the mile-high city, so you may huff and puff a bit in the high altitude – though not nearly to the extent that you will when visiting, for example, towering 10,000ft (3,048-meter) Leadville.

DOWNTOWN DENVER

Downtown Denver is anchored by the **16th Street Mall** (www.the16thstreetmall. com), a mile-long pedestrian promenade lined with shops and restaurants and served by a free shuttle bus. The skyscraper-heavy central business district at the southern end of Downtown is home to the **American Museum of Western Art** Ⓐ (1727 Tremont Place; tel: +1 303-293 2000; www.anschutzcollection.org; Mon, Wed, and Fri 10am–4.30pm), housed in the Navarre Building, which in the 1890s was allegedly Denver's finest brothel. Bierstadt, Remington, and Georgia O'Keeffe are some of the artists represented here. A few blocks west sprawls the **Colorado Convention Center**, with its famous **Big Blue Bear** statue on 14th Street, and the buildings of the **Denver Performing Arts Complex** Ⓑ (www.artscomplex.com); its 10 theaters make it second only to New York's Lincoln Center in capacity.

The 16th Street Mall links the central business district to "LoDo" (Lower Downtown) at the northern end of Downtown, a former warehouse district now home to bars, restaurants, the renovated **Union Station** Ⓒ

⊙ Drink

Denver has a well-earned reputation as craft-brewing hub, with microbreweries and taprooms scattered throughout the city. The state's oldest brewpub is Wynkoop Brewing Co (https://wynkoop.com) in Downtown Denver, but other local favorites include Black Shirt Brewing (www.blackshirtbrewingco.com) in RiNo, Great Divide Brewing (https://greatdivide.com) in Five Points, and Denver Beer Co (https://denverbeerco.com) across the river at 1695 Platte Street.

Renovated Union Station in Downtown Denver.

⊙ Shop

Denver is home to one of the best independent bookstores in the US: the Tattered Cover (www.tatteredcover.com), established in 1971 and now with three branches in the city. The most central is at 1701 Wynkoop Street (Union Station, open daily 10am–8pm), with another at 1991 Wazee Street, and one just south of City Park at 2526 East Colfax Avenue.

Dinosaur skeletons at the Denver Museum of Nature and Science.

development, and **Coors Field D**, the Colorado Rockies' ballpark (www.mlb.com/rockies). The **Museum of Contemporary Art Denver E** (1485 Delgany Street; tel: +1 303-298 7554; http://mcadenver.org; Tue–Thu noon–7pm, Fri noon–9pm, Sat and Sun 10am–5pm), was designed by star architect David Adjaye and features changing exhibitions, while the **Dairy Block F** (www.dairyblock.com) is another dining and shopping complex. Larimer Square **G** (www.larimersquare.com), the stretch of Larimer Street between 14th and 15th streets, features artfully restored brick buildings from the 1880s, now housing boutiques and outdoor cafés.

Along the Platte River on the west side of Downtown are a number of Denver's family-friendly attractions. The most high profile attraction here is the **Downtown Aquarium H** (700 Water Street; tel: +1 303-561 4450; www.aquariumrestaurants.com; Mon–Thu 10am–9pm, Fri 10am–10pm, Sat 9am–10pm, Sun 9am–8pm), dedicated to underwater ecosystems around the world, while the superb **Children's**

Museum of Denver I (2121 Children's Museum Drive; tel: +1 303-433 7444; www.mychildsmuseum.org; Mon, Tue, Thu, Fri 9am–4pm, Wed 9am–7pm, Sat and Sun 10am–5pm) relies on a range of intriguing interactive playscapes to get kids to learn. Kids will also love the **Elitch Gardens Theme & Water Park J** (2000 Elitch Circle; tel: +1 303-595 4386; www.elitchgardens.com; late Apr–Oct daily 10.30am–4pm, with some exceptions) for its white-knuckle rides – including the Mind Eraser, which catapults you at 60mph through terrifying corkscrew loops – and fun waterslides and pools. Home of the NFL's beloved Denver Broncos (www.denverbroncos.com), **Empower Field at Mile High K** football stadium also contains the Colorado Sports Hall of Fame and Museum.

CAPITOL HILL & GOLDEN TRIANGLE

Just to the south of Downtown, clustered around Civic Center Park, lies the historic Capitol Hill and Golden Triangle neighborhood. Presiding with gilded dignity over the city is the **Colorado State Capitol L** (200 East Colfax Avenue; tel: +1 303-866 2604; Mon–Fri 7.30am–5pm; free) – with its "Mile High" marker on the 13th step. Completed in 1908 after 18 years of construction, the capitol building is topped by a gold-plated dome, and a city ordinance forbids high rises from interfering with its view. On the south side of Civic Center Park lies the Daniel Libeskind-designed **Denver Art Museum M** (100 W 14th Avenue Parkway; tel: +1 720-865 5000; www.denverartmuseum.org; daily 10am–5pm). Holdings include particularly good contemporary and Native American art collections. When abstract painting pioneer Clyfford Still died in Maryland in 1980, his will stipulated that his estate be given to any American city willing to establish a museum dedicated solely to his work. It wasn't until 2004 that Denver

stepped up, and seven years later the **Clyfford Still Museum**  (1250 Bannock Street; tel: +1 720-354 4880; www.clyffordstillmuseum.org; Tue–Sun 10am–5pm) opened next to the art museum, a wonderful space for a rotating collection of 825 Still paintings and 1575 works on paper. Opened in 2018 with a striking façade of yellow terracotta bars, the **Kirkland Museum of Fine & Decorative Art** ⓞ (1201 Bannock Street; tel: +1 303-832 8576; www.kirklandmuseum.org; Tue–Sat 11am–5pm, Sun noon–5pm) features three core collections: international and decorative art; Colorado and regional art; and the work of local painter Vance Kirkland (1904–1981), whose 1910–1911 studio and art school building was transported here.

History buffs should check out the enlightening **History Colorado Center** ⓟ (1200 North Broadway; tel: +1 303-447 8679; www.historycolorado.org; daily 10am–5pm); there are exhibits of pioneer and Native American artifacts, and historic photographs by William Henry Jackson and others. The history of women in Colorado, and especially the struggle for equality, is commemorated at the **Center for Colorado Women's History at the Byers-Evans House** ⓠ (1310 Bannock Street; tel: +1 303-620 4933; Mon–Sat 10am–4pm, Sun 1–4pm). Built in 1883, the house has been restored to how it looked during the period between 1912 and 1924. One unforgettable Colorado woman was Margaret Tobin, who moved to Leadville and married a prospector who conveniently struck it rich. Known as "Unsinkable" Molly Brown, she tried to buy her way into Denver society, survived the sinking of the *Titanic* in 1912, and became one of the city's best loved figures, cemented by the eponymous musical and the Debbie Reynolds movie of 1964. Today a tour of the sandstone and lava stone **Molly Brown House Museum** ⓡ (1340 Pennsylvania Street; tel: +1 303-832 4092; https://

mollybrown.org; Tue–Sun 10am–4.30pm) brings her whole, exciting saga to life.

FIVE POINTS AND RINO

Northeast of Downtown, Five Points was once known as the "Harlem of the West" thanks to its many jazz joints. Created to house Black railroad workers in the 1870s, today it's still the heart of Denver's African American community and an up-and-coming district of coffeehouses, craft breweries, and museums. The enlightening **Black American West Museum** (3091 California Street; tel: +1 720-242 7428; www.bawmhc.org; Fri and Sat 10am–2pm) has intriguing details on Black pioneers and outlaws, and debunks Western myths: one third of all 19th-century cowboys were Black, and many were former slaves who left the South after the Civil War. The museum is housed in the former home and clinic of Colorado's first female Black doctor, Justina Ford (1871–1952), who purchased this property in 1911.

The renovated warehouses of adjacent **River North Art District** (RiNo)

A relaxed wander around the Botanic Gardens.

⊘ Shop

Around two miles south of Downtown Denver, the Art District on Santa Fe contains more than 30 art galleries and studios. It's historically a Latino area, represented by colorful street murals and the exhibitions at Museo de las Americas (www.museo.org), as well as at restaurants such as El Taco de México, Santiago's Mexican, and El Noa Noa.

Fermentation tanks inside the Coors Miller Brewery.

have been converted into art galleries, studios, and restaurants, including Denver Central Market (www.denvercentralmarket.com). Fans of old cars, bikes and trains will love the **Forney Museum of Transportation** (4303 Brighton Boulevard; tel: +1 303-297 1113; www.forneymuseum.org; Mon–Sat 10am–5pm), which has a truly massive collection of more than 600 interesting artifacts.

CITY PARK

Along Colorado Boulevard east of downtown lies **City Park**, which contains the **Denver Zoo** ❺ (2300 Steele Street; tel: +1 720-337 1400; www.denverzoo.org; daily Mar–Oct 9am–5pm, Nov–Feb 10am–4pm) and the **Denver Museum of Nature and Science** ❼ (2001 Colorado Boulevard; tel: +1 303-370 6000; www.dmns.org; daily 9am–5pm) – the latter known for its mineral collections and dinosaur and mammal fossils, from T. Rex to the world's largest woolly mammoth. Not far away, the **Denver Botanical Gardens** ⓤ (1007 York Street; tel: +1 720-865 3500;

www.botanicgardens.org; daily May–Sept 9am–8pm; Oct–Apr 9am–5pm) have a lovely Japanese garden and one of the world's largest collections of alpine plants. Various exhibitions are held in the iconic Science Pyramid and the stylish Freyer-Newman Center, which opened in 2020.

GOLDEN

Wedged between the Rockies and Denver's western suburbs, the sleepy town of **Golden** ❷ was established as a mining camp during Pike's Peak Gold Rush in 1859. It became capital of Colorado Territory in 1862, but was soon eclipsed by Denver (which replaced it as capital just five years later). Today it's best known as the site of the gargantuan **Coors Brewery** (1221 Ford Street; tel: 303-277 2337; www.coorsbrewerytour.com; Mon and Thu–Sat 10am–4pm (June–Aug also Tue and Wed), Sun noon–4pm). Downtown, marked by its "Golden Arch" over Washington Street, has been revitalized since the 1990s, and its stores and restaurants make for a pleasant stroll.

⊘ RED ROCKS PARK

Tucked away in the hills west of Golden, the remarkable sandstone outcrops of Red Rocks Park are best known for the Red Rocks Amphitheatre (18300 W Alameda Parkway, Morrison; www.redrocksonline.com). This spectacular 9000-capacity venue, squeezed between two glowing 400-foot (122-meter) red-sandstone monoliths, has been the setting for thousands of rock and classical concerts since completion in 1941 (though the location itself has hosted concerts since 1906); U2 recorded *Under a Blood Red Sky* here in 1983. The surrounding park features several trails and viewpoints, while the Visitor Center contains displays on the history of the site and the Performers' Hall of Fame. Just down the road, the Trading Post (the original park store completed in 1931) contains the Colorado Music Hall of Fame (https://cmhof.org).

Based here since 1874, the Colorado School of Mines runs an illuminating **Mines Museum** (1310 Maple Street; tel: +1 303-273 3815, www.mines.edu/museumofearthscience; Mon–Sat 9am–4pm, Sun 1–4pm), with a diverting selection of pre-electricity mining lamps, as well as a huge collection of rocks, minerals, and fossils.

Among the peaks that rise sharply behind downtown Golden is **Lookout Mountain** ❸, the final (and highly photogenic) resting place of Buffalo Bill Cody, the famed frontiersman and showman who died in Denver in 1917. The views of Denver, framed by the two flat-topped mountains, are spectacular, and the modest gravesite itself is free – you'll have to pay to see the gruesome artifacts in the adjacent **Buffalo Bill Museum** (tel: +1 720-865 2160; www.buffalobill.org; May–Oct daily 9am–5pm; Nov–Apr Tue–Sun 10am–5pm) which include a pistol with a handle fashioned from human bone. The mountain lies on the **Lariat Loop**, a 40-mile (64km) National Scenic Byway that takes in the grandest mountain scenery in a half-day's drive from Denver.

BOULDER

Some 27 miles (43km) northwest of Downtown Denver, **Boulder** ❹ is one of the country's liveliest college towns, filled with a youthful population that divides its time between phenomenally healthy daytime activities and almost equally unhealthy evening ones. Founded in 1858 by a prospecting party who erroneously felt that the nearby Flatiron Mountains – enormous sandstone monoliths that lean against the first swell of the Rockies – "looked right for gold." Boulder bloomed with the addition of a railroad and university in the 1870s and hasn't stopped growing since. Thanks largely to the presence of the University of Colorado-Boulder and its 35,000 students, the small town has fostered an offbeat, liberal vibe. Additionally, Boulder's mountainous location – ideal for cycling, hiking, and climbing – has attracted scores of outdoors enthusiasts, who continue to flock here.

Downtown Denver.

Your first Boulder stop should be **Pearl Street Mall**, one of the most successful downtown pedestrian malls in the nation, where two- and three-story Victorian buildings have been restored to house clothing boutiques, music shops, bookstores, and cafés.

Nearby, state-of-the-art **Museum of Boulder** (2205 Broadway; tel: +1 303-449 3464; https://museumofboulder. org; Mon and Thu–Sun 9am–5pm, Wed 9am–8pm) chronicles the history of the city in a 1950s Masonic Lodge building. The **Boulder Museum of Contemporary Art** (1750 13th Street; tel: +1 303-443 2122; https://bmoca.org; Tue–Sun 11am–5pm), across the creek from the exceptional **Dushanbe Teahouse** (www. boulderteahouse.com), holds high-quality temporary art exhibits from a global roster of artists.

The manicured campus of **University of Colorado Boulder** (CU; www. colorado.edu), founded in 1876, lies two miles (3.2km) southeast of Pearl Street mall, home of the beloved Colorado Buffaloes sports teams and marked by distinctive sandstone red-tiled buildings and a handful of museums. The well-respected Colorado Shakespeare Festival (https://cupresents.org/ series/shakespeare-festival) is held here each summer. The **CU Art Museum** (tel: +1 303-492 8300; www.colorado.edu/ cuartmuseum; Tue–Fri 10am–4pm, Sat 11am–4pm; free) boasts a collection of around 9500 art works, though exhibits tend to rotate. Highlights are paintings by Elizabeth Murray and Marsden Hartley, and minimalist sculptures by Sol LeWitt and Jackie Winsor. The University of Colorado **Museum of Natural History** (tel: +1 303-492 6892; www.colorado.edu/cumuseum; Mon–Sat 9am–5pm, Sun 10am–4pm; free) will appeal to aficionados, with five exhibition galleries of engaging and interactive displays exploring global natural and human history.

BOULDER OPEN SPACE AND MOUNTAIN PARKS

On the southwest fringe of Boulder, the landmark Flatiron peaks are the centerpiece of the **Boulder Open Space and Mountain Parks**. This network of mountains and valleys is laced with trails and copious amounts of rough climbing taking in Bear Peak, Green Mountain, Flagstaff Mountain, and Mount Sanitas. Almost at the foot of the Flatirons lies the **Colorado Chautauqua National Historic Landmark** ❺, a community of wooden cabins and houses first opened as a retreat for Texans in 1898 as part of a movement in the US to foster adult education and cultural entertainment. On the Chautauqua's western edge, the **Ranger Cottage** (May–Sept Mon–Fri 9am–4pm, Sat and Sun 9am–5pm, Oct–Apr daily 9am–4pm; free) is home to a small but informative nature center and friendly, knowledgeable staff. Pop in to get free maps, brochures, hiking suggestions, and the latest information about weather and trail conditions. Various trails lead south from Ranger

Dushanbe Teahouse, Boulder.

Cottage following the contours of the mountain below the Flatirons to the intriguing **NCAR Visitor Center** (https://scied.ucar.edu/visit; Mon–Fri 8am–5pm; Sat and Sun 9am–4pm; free), designed by I.M. Pei. This pink-sandstone facility sheds light on the National Center for Atmospheric Research (NCAR), which monitors global climate. Beyond the Chautauqua complex, Baseline Road becomes Flagstaff Road as it ascends **Flagstaff Mountain** (6,850ft/2,088 meters).

FORT COLLINS

The site of an 1860s fur-trapping fort built on the banks of the Cache la Poudre River, the modern city of **Fort Collins ⑥** anchors the north end of the Front Range. Like Boulder, it's a college town, with **Colorado State University** (www.colostate.edu) dominating the social scene – and surely responsible in part for the town's growing number of brew pubs. In the last few years, Fort Collins' downtown has been renovated and rechristened Old Town; it's a pleasant place to shop and quaff

a microbrew or two. Not far away, the **Fort Collins Museum of Discovery** (408 Mason Court; tel: +1 970-221 6738; https://fcmod.org ; Tue–Sun 10am–5pm) explores music, science, and history via state-of-the-art displays on everything from locally-found fossils to a "wind wall" and the history of cycling and Fort Collins' musical heritage. **The Avery House** (328 West Mountain Avenue; tel: +1 970-221 0533; http://poudrelandmarks.org/avery-house; Sat and Sun 1–4pm), a Victorian-era mansion, brings to life turn-of-the-century Fort Collins.

Fort Collins is major a beer-making hub, with the Anheuser-Busch brewery opening in 1988 – today the **Anheuser-Busch Tour Center & Beer Garden ⑦** (2351 Busch Drive, just north of I-25 Exit 271; tel: +1 970-490 4691; www.budweisertours.com; tours June–Sept daily 10am–4pm, Oct–May Wed–Mon 11am–4pm) offers a fun introduction to the brewers of Budweiser, the chance to see the famous Budweiser Clydesdale horses, and have a few drinks in the outdoor Biergarten.

Pro Rodeo Hall of Fame in Colorado.

⊙ CRAFT BEER CAPITAL

Stunningly, Fort Collins produces 70 percent of all the craft beer made in Colorado. Most of the 20-plus breweries here offer taprooms or tours of their facilities. You can also join guided tours with the Magic Bus (https://themagicbustours.com) or Beer and Bike Tours (www.beerandbiketours.com). The annual Colorado Brewers' Festival, held in late June, provides further grist (or yeast) for connoisseurs of the amber liquid in the form of tastings and beer-themed celebrations. Coopersmith's Pub & Brewing (5 Old Town Square; https://coopersmithspub.com) was Fort Collins' first brewpub in 1989, known for its Not Brown Ale, Scrumpy Cider, and Irish Stout. Other highlights include the beer garden at Equinox Brewing Co (https://equinoxbrewing.com), and Funkwerks (https://funkwerks.com).

Fort Collins also has a prime example of folk art. A little south of town, farmer Bill Sweat has created a metal menagerie of dinosaurs and other creatures from old car, truck, and tractor parts. The **Swetsville Zoo** 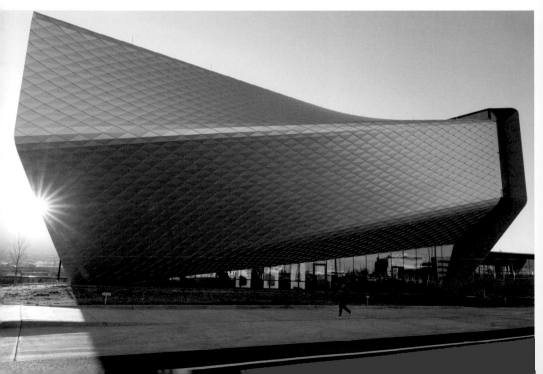 (4801 E Harmony Road; tel: +1 970-484 9509; by donation) will enchant any lover of American ingenuity.

COLORADO SPRINGS

South of Denver, new suburbs stretch along I-25 much of the way to **Colorado Springs** ❾, the second largest city in the state. Sprawling for 10 miles (16km) alongside the interstate, it was founded as a health resort in 1871 by railroad tycoon William Jackson Palmer. Today the city of more than half a million remains a tourist magnet, and for good reason: it is peppered with family-friendly attractions under the shadow of Pikes Peak, and happily coexisting with some major defense industry contractors and a high military presence – most notably Fort Carson, Peterson Air Force Base, and the US Air Force Academy.

With its wide, tree-lined streets, Downtown Colorado Springs is crammed with restaurants, shops, and a handful of attractions that will primarily appeal to history, art, and sports aficionados. Housed in the Italianate-style 1903 El Paso County Courthouse, the enlightening **Colorado Springs Pioneer Museum** (215 South Tejon Street; tel: +1 719-385 5990; www.cspm.org; Tue–Sat 10am–5pm) charts local history from prehistoric times to its military present-day basis, with rare Arapaho, Cheyenne, and Ute artifacts. The **Colorado Springs Fine Arts Center** (30 West Dale Street; tel: +1 719-634 5581; https://fac.coloradocollege.edu; Tue–Sat 10am–7.30pm, Sun 10am–5pm) at Colorado College boasts an excellent permanent art collection alongside intriguing traveling exhibitions. Colorado Springs is also home to one of the most important **US Olympic & Paralympic Training Centers**, with guided tours (1hr; www.teamusa.org/csotc) offering a unique insight into what makes the world's most successful Olympic medal winners. The

The US Olympic and Paralympic Museum (USOPM) opened in 2020 in Colorado. Springs.

stunning **US Olympic & Paralympic Museum** (200 South Sierra Madre Street; tel: +1 719-497 1234; https://usopm.org; Sun–Fri 10am–5pm, Sat 9am–6pm) opened in 2020, with the exterior made up of diamond-shaped reflective aluminum panels.

The most popular man-made attraction in Colorado is the **United States Air Force Academy** ⑩, located 15 miles (24km) north of downtown on I-25. The huge **Barry Goldwater Visitors Center** (2346 Academy Drive; tel: +1 719-333 2025, www.usafa.edu/visitors; Mon–Fri 9am–5pm; free) chronicles the history of the academy through films and exhibits. Nearby the iconic aluminum, glass, and steel **Cadet Chapel** is also free to visitors (though renovations will keep the interior closed until 2023). Designed by Walter Netsch of Skidmore, Owings & Merrill and completed in 1962, the interfaith chapel features 17 spires that soar 150ft (46 meters) into the sky.

Other area highlights include the **Pro Rodeo Hall of Fame** (101 Pro Rodeo Drive; tel: +1 719-528 4764; www.prorodeohalloffame.com; Tue–Sun 9am–5pm) where videos and displays explain the sport's various disciplines and how it developed out of the needs of early ranch work. The **Garden of the Gods** (1805 North 30th Street; tel: +1 719-634 6666; www.gardenofgods.com; daily May–Oct 5am–10pm, Nov–Apr 5am–9pm; free) is a city park as spectacular as many national parks; red sandstone towers and spires testify to the erosive power of wind and water.

MANITOU SPRINGS

The "springs" for which the city is named actually flow from nearby **Manitou Springs** ⑪. Five miles (8km) west of Downtown Colorado Springs on Hwy-24, it's an attractive if touristy town of stately Victorian buildings, shops, restaurants, and the still pumping natural springs. The main sight in town is **Miramont Castle** (9 Capitol Hill Avenue; tel: +1 719-685 1011; www.miramontcastle.org; June–Aug daily 9am–5pm, Sept–May Tue–Sun 10–4pm) built in 1895. The extravagant former residence of (wealthy) French priest

South Gateway Rock formation at the Garden of the Gods Park.

Jean Baptiste Francolon, who came looking for a cure for his tuberculosis, is a medley of architectural styles. If you don't have time to visit any of the ancient pueblos further south, the **Manitou Cliff Dwellings** (10 Cliff Road; tel: +1 719-685 5242; www.cliffdwellings-museum.com; daily: May–Aug 9am–6pm, Mar, Apr, Sept, and Oct 9am–5pm, Nov 9am–4pm, Dec–Feb 10am–4pm) will provide a decent introduction to the great Anasazi culture of the southwest. The small on-site museum contains artifacts, pottery, and descriptions of Anasazi life, but the centerpiece is the strip of impressive dwellings themselves. Set enigmatically into the red sandstone cliff side, it's hard to drag your eyes away from them.

CRIPPLE CREEK

Due west of Colorado Springs, **Cripple Creek** ⑫ was among the last and richest of Colorado's mining boom towns. Gold discovered in 1891 lured thousands of miners here: by the turn of the century Cripple Creek was the fourth largest city in the state.

Manitou Cliff Dwellings.

The boom lasted only 20 years, and for much of the 20th century Cripple Creek was a rather quiet tourist town, best known for the melodramas at the historic Imperial Hotel. But since 1991, when gambling was legalized here, the new versions of the town's gold mines have been its casinos. False-fronted Western buildings have been filled with clanging slots and beeping video poker machines, and crowds stream from one gambling hall to the next. The merits of the transformation are hotly debated – but if you want to test your luck in a suitably frontier atmosphere, this is the place to do it, though you don't have to lose your weight in quarters to enjoy Cripple Creek and the nearby town of **Victor**, whose run-down condition preserves a more acute sense of history.

Get an introduction to the area at the **Cripple Creek Heritage Center** (tel: +1 719-689 3315; www.visitcripplecreek.com; daily 9am–5pm; free) set high on a bluff at the eastern entrance to town, while the **Cripple Creek District Museum** (510 Bennett Drive; tel: +1 719-689 9540, https://cripplecreek-museum.com; daily late May to mid-Oct 10am–5pm), is the best place to gain an appreciation of the frontier town's raucous history. One of the last mines to close in the area was the **Mollie Kathleen Gold Mine** (tel: +1 719-689 2466; www.goldminetours.com; May–Oct daily 9am–5pm) just down the road from the Heritage Center on Hwy-67, which now gives tours led by ex-miners to gold veins 1,000 feet (305 meters) underground. Finally, the **Cripple Creek and Victor Narrow Gauge Railroad** (520 E Carr Avenue; tel: +1 719-689 2640; https://cripplecreekrailroad.com; late May to early Oct daily 10am–5pm) is a narrow-gauge steam train ride that runs from the old depot beside the District Museum. It's a scenic four-mile (6.5km) tour past several abandoned mines, including the site of the original gold strikes.

PIKES PEAK

Physically and spiritually, Colorado Springs is dominated by Pikes Peak, the 14,110-ft (4,301-meter) mountain that has inspired generations of Native Americans, pioneers, and visitors.

The first white American to spot the mountain was Zebulon Pike in 1806 (though Spanish explorers are thought to have seen it in the 1700s). After a failed attempt to climb it, he wrote "no human being could have ascended to its summit." Fourteen years later, botanist Edwin James proved him wrong by bagging the peak, and by the end of the century trails had been built to carry rich tourists to the top. Since then it has inspired gold-seekers, settlers, and even songwriters; perhaps most famously, Katherine Lee Bates' "America The Beautiful" was inspired by the "purple mountain majesty" of Pikes Peak – set to music, it quickly became the United State's unofficial second anthem. From the bleak and windswept top today, it's possible to see Denver 70 miles (113km) north, and the endless prairie to the east, while to the west mile upon mile of giant snowcapped peaks rise into the distance. The new Pikes Peak Summit Visitor Center opened in 2022, with tourist information, exhibits, and a café with phenomenal views; the complex also includes a Utilities facility and a High-Altitude Research Laboratory.

You can make a trip to the summit of Pikes Peak in a number of ways. The most obvious is to drive on the fully paved Pikes Peak Highway (www.pikespeak.us.com), which climbs 7,000ft (2,134 meters) in 19 miles (31km) from Cascade, three miles (5km) west of Manitou Springs.

You can also hop aboard the Pikes Peak Cog Railway (www.cograilway.com), which has been hauling tourists since 1891. Red carriages of the thrilling railway grind their way up an average of 847ft (258 meters) per mile (1.6km) on a 90-minute journey to the summit; from 11,500ft (3,505 meters) onward they cross a barren expanse of tundra. The train leaves from 515 Ruxton Avenue in Manitou Springs, and round-trips take 3 hours 15 minutes.

If you're hardy, hike the 11.8-mile (19km) Barr Trail up the mountain from Manitou Springs. The steepest part of the trail comes first, leveling out as it ascends to the Barr Camp Cabins, seven miles (11km) from the trailhead and a mile-and-a-half (2.4km) below the tree-line. Beyond here, the alpine tundra takes over, harboring numerous delicate plants, flowers, and bighorn sheep. As the air gets thinner, the last few miles of switchbacks make the rocky slopes a hard climb. Average hikers manage the trail in 12 hours: 8 hours up and 4 hours down.

Pike's Peak is open year-round, weather permitting; call tel: 719-385 7325 and select option 1 for current road conditions. The peak complex tends to open 7.30am–7pm daily in the summer, and 9.30am–4pm October to Memorial Day.

Pikes Peak soaring over the Garden of the Gods.

Gorgeous fall colors over Longs Peak and Bear Lake.

ROCKY MOUNTAIN NATIONAL PARK

In north-central Colorado, the snow-mantled peaks of Rocky Mountain National Park rise high above fresh green alpine valleys and glistening lakes – the park is often referred to as the "top of the continent."

With 71 peaks reaching over 12,000ft (3,650 meters), and with large sections inhabited by elk herds, moose, black bears, and bighorn sheep, any visitor to Rocky Mountain National Park is immediately humbled by the magnitude and grandeur of the surrounding landscape. The showpiece of the park is Trail Ridge Road, the 45-mile (72km) stretch of US-34 that connects the small gateway towns of Estes Park (38 miles/61km northwest from Boulder), and Grand Lake (on the east and west sides of the park respectively), but to really appreciate the region's beauty it's best to leave the car and get hiking.

A unique feature of the park is the marked differences found with the changing elevations. In an exhilarating trip over the Trail Ridge Road, you will travel through a series of diverse ecological zones that range from montane forest to those similar to the Alaskan Arctic. At lower levels, open stands of ponderosa pine and juniper grow on the slopes facing the sun; on cooler northern slopes, Douglas firs reach skyward. Groves of aspen appear here and there, and meadows and glades are speckled with wildflowers. Looming above this are forests of subalpine fir trees. Grotesque, twisted trees hug the ground at the upper edges of this zone. One-third of the park is actually above the tree line, where trees

disappear and the harsh, fragile world of alpine tundra predominates. More than one-quarter of the plants here can also be found in the Arctic.

HISTORY

The modern Ute and Arapaho were the most recent Native American inhabitants of the Rocky Mountain National Park region. In 1820 US military man Stephen H. Long, on an expedition ordered by Congress to investigate the region and explore possibilities of trading with the Native Americans, was the first to

Map on page 138

A Steller's jay at Emerald Lake.

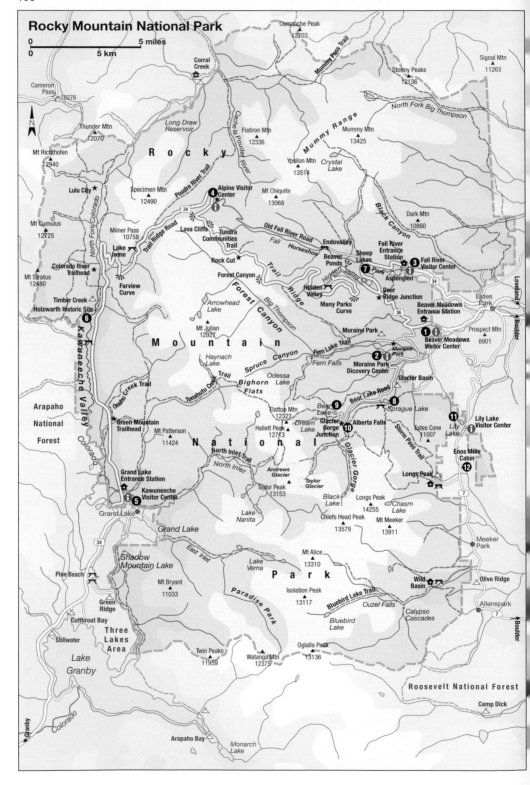

Rocky Mountain National Park

0 — 5 miles
0 — 5 km

N

Comanche Peak
12703

Signal Mtn
11263

Corral Creek

Mummy Pass Trail

Stormy Peaks
12136

North Fork Big Thompson

Cameron Pass
10276

Thunder Mtn
12070

Long Draw Reservoir

Flatiron Mtn
12336

R o c k y

Mummy Mtn
13425

Mt Richthofen
12940

Specimen Mtn
12490

Poudre River Trail

Alpine Visitor Center 4

Mt Chiquita
13068

Mummy Range

Ypsilon Mtn
13514

Crystal Lake

Black Canyon

Dark Mtn
10860

Lulu City ★

Mt Cumulus
12725

Milner Pass
10758

Lake Irene

Lava Cliffs

Tundra Communities Trail

Old Fall River Road

Fall

Horseshoe

Endovalley

Sheep Lakes

Fall River Entrance Station

Park 7

Fall River Visitor Center 3

Loveland

Colorado River Trailhead

Mt Stratus
12480

Farview Curve

Rock Cut

Forest Canyon

Trail

Ridge

Hidden Valley

Hidden Valley Cr.

Aspenglen

Deer Ridge Junction ★

Beaver Meadows Entrance Station

Estes Park

Timber Creek

Holzwarth Historic Site 6

Arrowhead Lake

Mt Julian
12927

Forest Canyon

Big Thompson

Many Parks Curve

Moraine Park

Beaver Meadows Visitor Center 1

Prospect Mtn
8901

M o u n t a i n

Haynach Lake

Spruce Canyon

Fern Lake Trail

Fern Falls

Moraine Park

Moraine Park Discovery Center 2

Glacier Basin

Arapaho

National

Forest

Kawuneeche Valley

Colorado

Green Mountain Trailhead

Onahu Creek Trail

Tonahutu Creek Trail

Bighorn Flats

Odessa Lake

Bear Lake Road

Bear Lake 9

Sprague Lake 8

N a t i o n a l

Mt Patterson
11424

Flattop Mtn
12323

Hallett Peak
12713

Dream Lake

Glacier Gorge Junction 10

Alberta Falls

Estes Cone
11007

Lily Lake

Lily Lake Visitor Center 11

North Inlet Trail

Andrews Glacier

Taylor Glacier

Glacier Gorge

Storm Pass Trail

Enos Mills Cabin 12

Grand Lake Entrance Station

Kawuneeche Visitor Center 5

North Inlet

Taylor Peak
13153

Black Lake

Longs Peak
14255

Chasm Lake

Longs Peak

7

Grand Lake

Lake Nanita

Lake Verna

Mt Alice
13310

Chiefs Head Peak
13579

Mt Meeker
13911

Meeker Park

Shadow Mountain Lake

East Inlet

Mt Bryant
11033

P a r k

Isolation Peak
13117

Bluebird Lake Trail

Wild Basin

Olive Ridge

Pine Beach

Paradise Park

Ouzel Falls

Calypso Cascades

Allenspark

Green Ridge

Cutthroat Bay

Stillwater

Three Lakes Area

Bluebird Lake

Boulder

Lake Granby

Twin Peaks
11959

Watanga Mtn
12375

Oglalla Peak
13136

Roosevelt National Forest

Camp Dick

Granby

Colorado

Arapaho Bay

Monarch Lake

see and record Longs Peak, the highest mountain in the park, which now bears his name. The first white man known to have lived in the region was Joel Estes; in 1860, he settled his entire family in the grassy meadows of the forest-rimmed valley that now bears his name – most Native Americans had been displaced or forcibly removed by this time. The establishment of the national park is historically linked with the name of one man – Enos A. Mills, the "father" of the park and a famous naturalist. His enthusiastic reports and lectures laid the groundwork that eventually led to legislation that set aside the area as a national park in 1915. The Fall River Road first opened to traffic in September 1920, with the epic Trail Ridge Road completed in stages between 1929 and 1938.

VISITOR CENTERS

Stop at one of the four Rocky Mountain visitor centers to become acquainted with the park. The park headquarters and **Beaver Meadows Visitor Center ❶** (daily 9am–4.30pm, with some exceptions) is three miles (4.8km) west of Estes Park on US-36. The **Moraine Park Discovery Center ❷** (late May to mid-Oct daily 9am–5pm) lies on Bear Lake Road (off US-36), some 1.5 miles (2.4km) from the Beaver Meadows Entrance. Taking the alternative route west, US-34 (Fall River Road), the **Fall River Visitor Center ❸** (daily 9am–5pm) is five miles (8km) west of Estes Park.

The central **Alpine Visitor Center ❹** (see below) is on Trail Ridge Road, while on the western side of the park, the **Kawuneeche Visitor Center ❺** (daily 9am–4.30pm; with some exceptions) lies one mile (1.6km) north of Grand Lake on US-34. Guided walks, campfire talks, and many other park services begin in early June and extend into September.

TRAIL RIDGE ROAD

Trail Ridge Road (usually open late May to mid-Oct) is the highest-elevation paved road in any US national park (cresting at 12,183ft/3,713 meters), affording a succession of mesmerizing views – several short hiking trails also start from convenient parking lots along the way. Majestic peaks and

> ⊙ **Fact**
>
> Rocky Mountain National Park (tel: 1+ 970 586 1206, www.nps.gov/romo) is officially open daily (24hr), though most of the through roads are closed due to snow October to May. One-day passes are $25/vehicle. In addition, from late May to early Oct you must apply for a timed-entry permit (see website).

A mountain meadow on Rocky Mountains Trail Ridge Road.

⊙ Tip

Free shuttle buses (usually late May to early Oct, daily 7am–7pm; check the park website) run through the park: from Estes Park to Glacier Basin Park & Ride, between Fern Lake/ Moraine Park Discovery Center and Sprague Lake (every 20min), and between Glacier Basin/ Sprague Lake and Bear Lake (every 15min).

The high peaks of Continental Divide rise over Sprague Lake.

alpine tundra are at their most breathtaking to either side of the Alpine Visitor Center (late May to early Oct daily 9.30am–4.30pm), halfway along at Fall River Pass (11,796ft/3,595 meters). If you're generally happy to admire the scenery from your car, the visitor center is really the only requisite stop along the way, for its exhibits explaining the flora and fauna of the tundra and also its simple, good-value cafeteria. Good areas for wildlife viewing (especially elk) lie a little further east around Timber Creek. Nevertheless, the four-mile (6.4km) Ute Trail down to Milner Pass is a bracing way to take in this harsh but stunning environment.

Built in 1917 by German immigrants John and Sophia Holzwarth on the west side of the park (13 miles/21km on from the Alpine Visitor Center), the **Holzwarth Historic Site ⑥** (exterior and grounds open 24hr) and dude ranch offer a glimpse into the life of Colorado homesteaders. The "Mama Cabin" retains many of its original furnishings, linens, and even its Admiral Blue stove. The interior is usually open

in the summer; check the park website for details.

OLD FALL RIVER ROAD

An alternative scenic drive through the park follows the Old Fall River Road (aka US-34, usually open May–Sept), completed in 1920. Running east–west (one-way) along the bed of a U-shaped glacial valley, it doesn't have open mountain vistas, but it's much quieter than the Trail Ridge Road, and there's far more chance of spotting wildlife: roaming the area are moose, coyote, mountain lions, and black bears. Just six miles (10km) west of Estes Park, stop at the **Sheep Lakes ⑦**, where bighorn sheep are commonly seen from May through mid-August and there's a small information station. The road rejoins Trail Ridge Road a few miles on at Deer Ridge Junction.

BEAR LAKE ROAD

Bear Lake Road branches south off Trail Ridge Road just beyond Beaver Meadows Visitor Center, with the Moraine Park Discovery Center another 1.5 miles

(2.4km) south, displaying exhibits on the park's flora and fauna. Some five miles (8km) on, **Sprague Lake** ❽ is another popular picnic and hiking spot. Breathtaking views of the Continental Divide can be enjoyed from a half-mile-long (800-meter) lake loop trail. Another four miles (6km) southwest from Sprague Lake, gorgeous **Bear Lake** ❾ is tucked into the spruce and fir forest at the base of Hallett Peak and Flattop Mountain. The short but hilly Bear Lake Trail loop trail is enhanced with interpretive panels. Just to the south, thundering **Alberta Falls** ❿ are accessible from the Glacier Gorge Trailhead.

LILY LAKE

Around six miles (10km) south of Estes Park on Hwy-7, **Lily Lake** ⓫ is an idyllic spot, with an easy mile-long (1.6km) loop trail smothered in wildflowers in the spring and early summer. Enos Mills, the "father of Rocky Mountain National Park", enjoyed walking to here from his home, two miles (3.2km) further south along Hwy-7. His fascinating **Enos Mills Cabin** ⓬ dates back

to 1885 and is open year-round by appointment (tel: +1 970 586 4706).

SEASONS AND WEATHER

Primarily because of differences in altitude, slope, and exposure, the high country of Rocky Mountain National Park produces a variable weather pattern. Another consideration is the drastic difference between day and night temperatures; summer days reach well into the 80s Fahrenheit (up to 26°C) and drop into the 40s (4°C) at night.

Millions of people come to Rocky Mountain National Park each year, and they can testify as to how difficult it is to secure a spot at a campsite during the peak summer season. A beautiful time of year to consider a trip to Rocky Mountain National Park is in September or October when the weather is pleasant, the aspens have turned golden, and the crowds have thinned. Winter means snow in the Rockies, and snow means skiing – cross-country skiing in the lower valleys, winter mountaineering in the high country, and down-hill skiing at Hidden Valley.

A sunny late summer evening at Alberta Falls.

CENTRAL COLORADO

Colorado's image and unrivalled reputation as a formidable winter (and now summer) resort destination derives from the cluster of snowcapped peaks and incredible ski areas in Central Colorado. This is North America's rooftop.

Geologists tell us that the Rockies began rising some 65 million years ago; over the last 100,000 years they were repeatedly sculpted by glaciers. In terms of human settlement, the Ute people have probably been here longest; but of course the discovery of gold here in the 1850s brought the crowds in waves. The mining boom ended abruptly with the 1893 silver crash, but not before major towns like Leadville, Central City, and Breckenridge were decorated with grand Victorian mansions and opera houses. The economy then limped along until its focus began to switch in the early 20th century from the rich seams of precious ore buried deep within the mountainsides to the precious winter snows above them. Today almost all the local ski resorts also promote themselves as summer destinations, when the region's seemingly boundless alpine tundra, thick dark forests, and immense peaks are a haven for excellent hiking, biking, fishing, and kayaking.

The region is sewn together by I-70, an incredible feat of engineering completed in 1992 that runs west from Denver to Utah, across the Continental Divide. While anyone can be seduced by the plush comforts of Central Colorado – the smart shops of Aspen, the fine dining at Vail – you will find it rewarding to experience the region's history

A mountain goat standing alone on a rock.

as well. Walk the streets of Leadville, for example, and you can almost hear the ghosts of miners, pioneers, and outlaws.

CENTRAL CITY AND BLACK HAWK

Once crumbling Victorian mining towns, **Central City** ❶ and the adjoining smaller town of **Black Hawk** ❷ have transformed themselves into shiny, pseudo-Victorian casino resorts, a short drive west of Denver. Central City originally began as an

◎ Main attractions

Aspen
Crested Butte
Georgetown Loop Railroad
Leadville
Peak-to-Peak Highway
Steamboat Springs
Top of the Rockies
  National Scenic Byway
Vail
Winter Park

Map on page 145

Argo Gold Mine & Mill in Idaho Springs offers daily tours.

amalgamation of mining camps along steep-sided Gregory Gulch in 1859. Soon dubbed "the richest square mile on earth," it grew quickly, partly thanks to publicity of *New York Tribune* writer Horace Greely, who was inspired to write the famous lines, "Go West young man and grow with the country." The end of mining had virtually wiped out both towns by the 1950s, but casinos were introduced in the 1990s – though, it has to be said, much more successfully in Black Hawk; its Main Street is now dominated by them.

Though gambling dominates, the rich history of the region is preserved at the **Central City Opera House** (124 Eureka Street; tel: 303-292 6700; https://centralcityopera.org), built in 1878 and which still hosts a fabulous opera season every summer. A good impression of what the frontier town must have been like in the mining days can be gained at the **Gilpin History Museum** (228 East High Street; tel: 303-582 5283; www.gilpinhistory.org; late May to early Oct daily 10am–4pm). The museum also manages other historic

properties in town: Thomas House, Coeur d'Alene Mine Shaft House, and Washington Hall are all open in the summer.

Established in 1918, the scenic **Peak-to-Peak Highway** runs 55 miles (88.5km) along the Front Range from Central City north to Estes Park and the adjacent Rocky Mountain National Park (see p. 137). Views on much of the route are sensational, with the high peaks of the Continental Divide to the west and thousands of square miles of plains to the east. A worthy detour off the Peak-to-Peak highway, the **Golden Gate Canyon State Park** ❸ (92 Crawford Gulch Road; tel 303-582 3707; daily 5am–10pm) features 35 miles (56km) of trails, crossing through aspen forests and lush meadows, and giving fantastic views over the Indian Peaks Wilderness and the Continental Divide.

IDAHO SPRINGS

Some 33 miles (53km) west of downtown Denver on I-70, the scruffy little town of **Idaho Springs** ❹ was the scene of one of the first important gold finds in the Rocky Mountains in 1859. It was silver, however, that became Idaho Spring's most lucrative ore, with the town growing to be a hub for a silver district that included Black Hawk and Central City. You can get a closer glimpse into the town's mining past at the **Argo Mill & Tunnel** (2350 Riverside Drive; tel: 503-567 2421; https://argomilltour.com; daily 10am–5pm, with exceptions), the biggest structure on the north side of the valley. Guided tours (1hr 15min) run deep into the Double Eagle mine, and the five-story Argo Mill and museum, with gold panning also offered. Even more enjoyable is the **Phoenix Gold Mine** (800 Trail Creek Road; tel 303-567 0422; www.phoenixgoldmine.com; daily 10am–5pm, with exceptions). Mining still takes place here, but is now secondary to entertaining tours given by ex-miners,

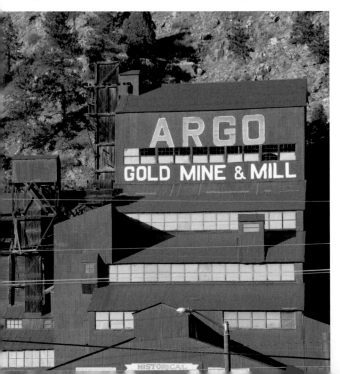

during which visitors head down 600ft (183 meters) to view a three-foot-long (0.9-meter) vein of gold ore, wield 19th-century excavating tools and try their luck at panning for gold. **Mount Evans** ⑤ (14,265ft/4,348 meters) is Colorado's easiest 14,000ft peak to bag, since there's a narrow road, the Mount Evans Scenic Byway (typically open June–Aug), almost all the way to the summit from Idaho Springs, 28 miles (45km) away.

NORTH CENTRAL COLORADO

Winter Park, 67 miles (108km) northwest of Denver, was established in 1938 and its wide, ever-expanding variety of ski and bike terrain, friendly atmosphere, family attractions, and good-value lodgings draw more than a million visitors a year. The ski resort (www.winterparkresort.com) also has exceptional facilities for kids and skiers with disabilities, and comprises three interconnected mountain peaks – Winter Park itself, Mary Jane, and the Vasquez Ridge. Summer visitors enjoy 600 miles (965km) of excellent mountain-biking trails.

Another 30 miles (48km) to the northwest, in the Colorado River Valley, **Hot Sulphur Springs** ⑥ exudes an altogether more genteel air than its neighbors. The eponymous town springs – allegedly loaded with such health-giving goodies as sodium, chloride, magnesium, potassium, calcium, and fluoride – are now enclosed in a

◉ Eat

Idaho Springs is the home of the original **Beau Jo's** (1517 Miner Street; tel: 303-567 4376, www.beaujos.com), famed locally for its "Colorado-style mountain pie" pizzas and now a small chain. The extra thick-crust style pizza debuted here in 1973, a chewy delight topped with a thick blanket of cheese, numerous sauces, and a bewildering choice of toppings.

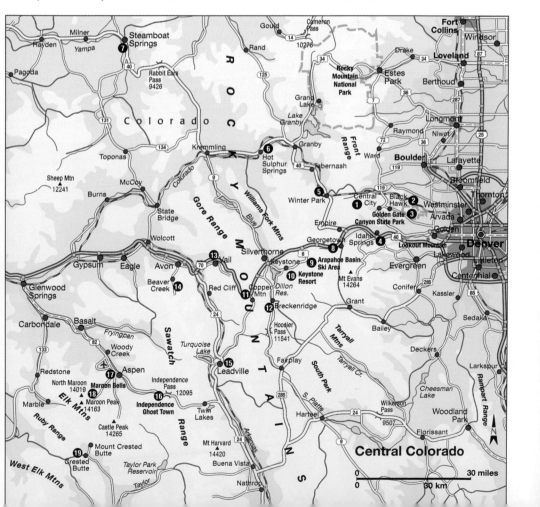

Central Colorado

peaceful spa resort (www.hotsulphursprings.com), which, together with the enlightening **Pioneer Village Museum** (110 East Byers Avenue; tel: 970-725 3939; https://grandcountyhistory.org; Wed–Mon 10am–4pm), comprise fair reasons for a day visit or even an overnight stay. The museum features a meticulous collection of buildings salvaged from elsewhere in the region, including a 1924 schoolhouse that now contains ancient Native American artifacts.

Surrounded by wide, snowy valleys, **Steamboat Springs** ❼, 70 miles (113km) northwest of Hot Sulphur Springs, is where Colorado's skiing industry was born in 1913; it was promoted by Carl Howelsen, a Norwegian ski-jumper. Famous for its prodigious light dry snow – "champagne powder" as it's called hereabouts – **Steamboat Ski Resort** (tel: 970-879 6111; www.steamboat.com) boasts the second-highest lift-served mountain in Colorado and is generally considered to be one of the country's best all-round wintersports venues. In summer the Silver Bullet gondola will get you straight onto the Steamboat Bike Park network of winding trails.

GEORGETOWN

Nestling deep at the head of the Clear Creek Valley beside a lake and surrounded by soaring mountains, **Georgetown** ❽ has a marvelous setting – but for the I-70 running so close past the town. Like Central City, Georgetown dates from Colorado's first gold boom (which happened in the late 1850s and 1860s), although silver proved to be in larger supply than gold. Today it's an unusually pretty little place at the foot of Guanella Pass. Victorian homes and businesses have been lovingly restored, notably the **Hotel de Paris** (409 6th Street; tel: 303-569 2311, https://hoteldeparismuseum.org; late May to Sept Mon–Sat 10am–5pm, Sun noon–5pm), built in 1875 by Louis Dupuy, a Frenchman of mysterious repute who announced that he was going to build the finest hostelry in the Rockies. See if he succeeded, by taking one of the regular guided tours (1hr). Similarly lavish, the Gothic Revival

Georgetown Loop Railroad runs between Georgetown and Silver Plume.

Hamil House Museum (305 Argentine Street; tel: 303-569 2840, https://historicgeorgetown.org; late May–late Sept Thu–Sun noon–3pm; call ahead), was once considered one of the most elegant Victorian homes in the Rockies, with a luxuriously furnished, polished hardwood interior containing some odd touches such as camel-hair wallpaper. Originally constructed in 1867, it was given a lavish makeover in the 1870s by silver baron William Arthur Hamill (whose great-great-grandson is Mark Hamill, aka Luke Skywalker).

Georgetown is also home to the **Georgetown Loop Railroad** (646 Loop Drive; tel: 303-569 2030, www.georgetownlooprr.com; late Apr–early Oct daily 10am–3.50pm). Back in 1884 this was one of the engineering feats of the world, defeating a 6 percent grade by means of pretzel-twisting tracks and bridges over Upper Clear Creek Canyon. Today, instead of ore steam trains carry tourists 4.5 miles (7.2 km) to the village of Silver Plume and give visitors the only access to the historic **Lebanon Silver Mine** at the halfway point (optional walking tours of the mine are extra). The narrow-gauge railroad was disbanded and finally sold for scrap in 1939, before being revived and entirely rebuilt by enthusiasts in 1984.

You can also get a feel for what it was like to be a hard rock miner by venturing over 1000ft (305 meters) into the town's **Capital Prize Gold Mine** (1016 Biddle Street; tel: 303-569 2468; www.capitalprizegoldmine.com; June–Oct daily 11am–3pm, by appointment rest of year), home to several rich veins of silver and gold since the 1860s, and still working today. Enthusiastic tour guides provide background and 45min–1hr tours along the main tunnel.

SUMMIT COUNTY

The purpose-built ski resorts, old mining towns, snow-covered peaks, alpine meadows, and crystal lakes that make up **Summit County** lie alongside I-70,

roughly 70 miles (113km) west of Denver. This section of the interstate was one of the last in the national system to be completed, and is justly regarded as an engineering marvel: it crosses the Continental Divide via the Eisenhower Tunnel, at 11,158ft (3,400 meters), before snaking high above Vail Pass.

The county contains four major ski areas, and there are ticket packages that allow you to ski all of them in one vacation. The highest in altitude of the Summit County ski resorts and the smallest, **Arapahoe Basin ❾** ("A-Basin"; tel: 970-468 0718; www.arapahoebasin.com) is a favorite of intermediate and advanced skiers, while **Keystone ❿** (tel: 970-496 4500; www.keystoneresort.com) is known for good intermediate and beginner terrain, as well as the biggest night-ski operation in the US. **Copper Mountain ⓫** (tel: 970-968 2318; www.coppercolorado.com) has a vertical drop of 2,700ft (823 meters) and does a good job of separating its advanced, intermediate, and beginner runs. Each resort runs a chairlift or gondola to the top of the

Mid-season skiing at Araphoe Basin ski resort.

○ Eat

It's unlikely that lettuce farmer Frank Bienkowski ever expected his secluded cabin to become the poshest place to eat in the Vail valley, but in winter diners travel 20 minutes to **Beano's Cabin** at Beaver Creek Mountain (www.beavercreek.com) via a snowcat-drawn open-sleigh to enjoy a five-course gourmet meal. The food is superb and there are plenty of entrées to choose from. Reservations required. Open mid-Dec to Sept 5–9pm.

A bike shop on Main Street, Leadville.

mountains for access to great hiking and cycling trails in the summer – Keystone is particularly outstanding for its mountain-bike trails with world-class downhill and cross-country trails.

Breckenridge ⑫ (tel: 970-453 5000; www.breckenridge.com) is the oldest and largest of the Summit County ski areas (spanning five peaks), and the most interesting for non-skiers. Founded in 1859 as a Gold Rush camp, it boasts a large historic district (with multi-colored gingerbread-style homes from the 1890s and early 1900s), touristy but tasteful stores, art galleries, and excellent restaurants. The town's local history museum, the **Edwin Carter Discovery Center** (111 South Ridge Street; tel: 970-453 9767; www.breckheritage.com; Tue–Sun 10am–3pm; free), provides an insight into the local characters who shaped the town's beginnings. One of them was Edwin Carter, a naturalist from New York, who in the late 19th century campaigned for the protection of the local environment as it was progressively attacked by opencast mining. You can also learn

about the fascinating history of the formerly enslaved African American activist and prospector Barney Ford at the museum which bears his name, **Barney Ford House Museum** (111 East Washington Avenue; tel: 970-453 9767; www.breckheritage.com; Tue–Sun 10am–3pm; free), a restored 1882 Victorian home. To complete the picture of what the early days of Breckenridge were like, head two miles (3.2km) northeast of town to the **Country Boy Mine** (542 French Gulch Road; tel: 970-453 4405; www.countryboymine.com; daily: Apr–Aug 9am–5pm; Sept–Mar 10.30am–4pm), where the tours take you 1000ft (305 meters) into a gold and silver mine founded in 1887.

VAIL

Compared to most other Colorado ski towns, **Vail ⑬**, 15 miles (24km) west of Summit County on I-70, is a new creation: just a handful of farmers lived here before the resort opened in 1962. Vail's real forte is its bowl skiing and boarding. The ski-area extends from one vast treeless bowl to another,

○ BABY DOE

Horace Tabor was a Leadville storekeeper and one-time mayor who grubstaked prospectors in exchange for potential profits; this meant that he would provide his clients with material, provisions, or money that allowed them to work, in return for a share in any profits that came as a result of the work he had enabled. In 1878 he hit the jackpot when two of his clients developed a silver mine that produced $20 million within a year. Tabor purchased the profitable Matchless Mine with his one-third share, and later in the 1880s became a US senator. He left his wife Augusta to marry local waitress "Baby Doe" McCourt, a major scandal at the time (her first husband was one Harvey Doe). However, by the time of his death in 1899, Tabor was financially ruined, wiped out in the Silver Panic of 1893. He told Baby Doe, "Hang on to the Matchless," and legend has it she did – at least for a while (actual ownership is murky). Initially with one of her daughters and then alone, she lived in a former tool shed beside the mine for 36 more years until she froze to death there, penniless, in 1935. Today you can learn about Baby Doe's bizarre saga and take a surface tour of her cabin and the Matchless Mine (East 7th Street; tel: 719-486 1229; www.mininghalloffame.org; late May to late Sept daily 11am–4.45pm), 1.25 miles (2km) east of Leadville.

providing an experience unlike anywhere else in Colorado.

Today the town sprawls 8 miles (13km) or so along the narrow Gore Creek valley floor, comprising a series of village districts beginning with Vail Village itself – the area's main social center – and running west to Lionshead, Cascade Village, and West Vail. Vail Resorts (www.vail.com), which operates the ski areas at Vail, owns an even more exclusive gated resort, **Beaver Creek** ⓮ (www.beavercreek.com), 11 miles (18km) farther west on I-70 (the small towns of Avon, Eagle-Vail and Edwards extend the resort area still farther along the valley). Each area is pedestrianized and linked by free shuttle buses to the ski lifts. The villages themselves are mostly uninspiring collections of Tyrolean-style chalets and concrete-block condos, pockmarked by pricey fashion boutiques and often painfully pretentious restaurants; the real highlights are the stunning mountain scenery and activities on offer. Indeed, given the exceptional quality of the snow, and the sheer size and variety of terrain, Vail is a formidable winter sport destination. Note, however, that unlike Aspen, Vail is essentially just a big resort, and is often deserted out of season.

In summer you can use the lifts to go mountain biking, best at Vail, and hiking, best at the quieter Beaver Creek. A good six-mile (9.6km) round-trip heads out-and-back to Beaver Lake, taking around three or four hours. You can also check out the **Colorado Snowsports Museum** (231 South Frontage Road; tel: 970-476 1876, www.snowsportsmuseum.org; daily 11am–6pm; free), which charts centuries of man's efforts to slide down mountains, while former president Gerald Ford and his wife Betty – longtime Vail residents – established the **Betty Ford Alpine Gardens** (522 S Frontage Road; tel: 970-476 0103; https://bettyfordalpinegardens.org; daily 10am–4pm) here in the 1980s as a lovely place to gaze upon the gorgeous flowers.

LEADVILLE

From Vail you can take Hwy-24 south over 10,242-ft (3,122-meter) Tennessee Pass to **Leadville** ⓯. Ringed by snow-capped mountains at an elevation of more than 10,000ft (3,048 meters), the atmospheric old mining town enjoys a magnificent vista of mounts Elbert and Massive, Colorado's two highest peaks. Leadville is rich in character and history, its old red-brick streets abounding with tales of gunfights (Doc Holliday fought his last here), miners dying of exposure, and graveyards being excavated to get at the seams. Gold was discovered in 1860, but silver took over in the 1870s and later copper and zinc; by 1880 Leadville was the second largest town in Colorado. After a 17-year shutdown, the Climax molybdenum mine reopened in 2012, resuming Leadville's longest tradition.

Leadville wealth helped create major American fortunes, like that of Marshall Field and the Guggenheims,

Legendary saloon bar in Leadville.

but its most fabled millionaire was probably Horace Tabor.

In summer you can still enjoy melodrama in the sumptuous **Tabor Opera House** (308 Harrison Avenue; tel: 719-486 8409; www.taboroperahouse.net; tours late May to mid-Oct Tue–Sun noon–5pm), which Horace built in 1879 to bring some culture to his adopted town. In 1882, garbed in black velvet knee britches and diamonds, Oscar Wilde addressed a host of dozing miners here. Also established in 1879, the **Silver Dollar Saloon** (315 Harrison Avenue; tel: 719-486 9914; https://legendarysilverdollarsaloon.com; daily noon–1am) remains a grand place for a drink, while the restored **Delaware Hotel** (700 Harrison Avenue; tel: 719-212 1781; www.delawarehotel.com) lets guests sleep in baronial comfort.

The **National Mining Hall of Fame & Museum** (120 West 9th Street; tel: 719-486 1229, www.mininghalloffame.org; Tue–Sun 9am–4.45pm) charts mining techniques from historic times to the present, and you can take a walk through a replica of an underground hard-rock mine. The building was originally the Leadville High School, built in 1900.

For a more illuminating romp through the town's grim early history, head for the **Heritage Museum** (102 East 9th Street; tel: 719-486 1878; www.leadvilleheritagemuseum.com; late-May to Sept daily 10am–5pm), where glass cases hold snippets on local fraternal organizations, quack doctors, music-hall stars, and the like, while a host of smoky photographs portray the lawless boomtown that in two years grew from a mining camp of 200 people into Colorado's second-largest city. The museum occupies the old red-brick Carnegie Library, completed in 1904.

For a good view of the surrounding terrain, hop aboard the **Leadville, Colorado & Southern Railroad** (326 East 7th Street; tel: 719-486 3936; www.leadvillerailroad.com; late May to mid-Oct, 1–3 times daily, mid- to late Oct, Sat and Sun twice daily; Holiday Express runs from mid-Nov), a 2hr 30min train ride (round-trip) deep into the mountains, on carriages re-configured as open observation cars.

The Eagle Bahn Gondola in Vail.

TOP OF THE ROCKIES NATIONAL SCENIC BYWAY

By far the most spectacular way to reach Aspen from Leadville is to drive over **Independence Pass** via the **Top of the Rockies National Scenic Byway** (aka Hwy-82), a scintillating route that passes the pretty village of Twin Lakes and crosses the Continental Divide at 12,095ft/3,687 meters. On the western side the road winds along the Roaring Fork River, past **Independence Ghost Town ⑯** (late June to early Oct daily 10am–6pm; free, suggested donation $5), into Aspen. The pass is generally closed between November and late May; the alternate route via I-70 and Glenwood Springs adds an extra 70 miles (113km) to the trip from Denver.

ASPEN

While there's more than a grain of truth to the image of **Aspen ⑰** as a celebrity hangout, it's a perfectly accessible and appealing place for ordinary folks to visit, and in summer at least the room rates are affordable for all but those on shoestring budgets. Indeed, unlike in resorts like Vail, which are often deserted out of season, affordable housing and local development have made this a real working town where ski bums really do mingle with millionaires. While spending too much time in Aspen itself is something of a waste given the virtually limitless recreation opportunities in the neighboring mountains, hanging out around the town's leafy pedestrianized streets or browsing in the chichi stores and galleries makes for a pleasant way to spend a couple of hours.

For Aspen, it all began in 1879 when Walter Clark arrived from Leadville, hoping to find silver. He did; lots of it, and Aspen boomed. By 1893 Aspen was the third largest city in Colorado, with a population of 12,000 people – more than live here today. But the crash of 1893 devastated the town, and it wasn't until the 1940s that a new generation discovered it. The US Army's famed 10th Mountain Division ski troops were stationed nearby, which helped showcase the ski potential offered by the Aspen slopes. After the

Independence Ghost Town.

A view over Aspen.

war, Austrian-born Friedl Pfeiffer and businessman Walter Paepcke joined forces to form what became the Aspen Skiing Corporation (Paepcke also created what is now the Aspen Institute, a respected think-tank, and also helped found the annual Aspen Music Festival).

Cycling is the main summer pursuit around Aspen, though the Roaring Fork River, surging out of the Sawatch Range, is excellent for kayaking and rafting during a short season that's typically over by early to mid-July. Come summer, Aspen is also a hiker's delight. An easy way to get your bearings and enjoy great valley views is to take the **Silver Queen Gondola** from 601 Dean Street to the summit of Aspen Mountain (mid-June to early Sept daily). **Elk Camp Gondola** (same times) runs up Snowmass.

Among the most beautiful day trips in the region is the one to **Maroon Bells Recreation Area** ⑱, centered on the twin purple-grey peaks of the Maroon Bells peaks themselves (14,014ft/4,271 meters and 14,156ft/4,315 meters

respectively). Still regarded as sacred ground by Ute, the lake- and-mountains vista is said to be the most photographed scene in America. Hiking trails lead from the car park around dark blue Maroon Lake, where mesmerizing views of the Bells blend with the equally jaw-dropping Pyramid Peak (14,018ft/4,273 meters) and the reddish crags of the Sievers Mountains. Longer trails lead up to Crater Lake (10,076ft/3,071 meters), nearer the base of the mountains, where moose sometimes graze. It's very popular – so much so that in summer you can only get there by hiking, mountain biking, or public transit – but it is extraordinarily lovely.

The town of Aspen itself shows what can happen when superb scenery meets lots of money. Hyman Avenue and Galena Street are high-altitude Rodeo Drives, with the most famous names in American fashion displaying their wares in store windows. For a taster of Aspen's history visit the **Wheeler/Stallard Museum** (620 West Bleeker Street; tel: 970-925 3721; https://aspenhistory.org; Tue–Sat

11am–5pm), a Queen-Anne style home built around 1888 for Jerome Wheeler, considered the town's founding father. Before Wheeler went bankrupt he built its two most magnificent Victorian buildings, both completed in 1889; the Hotel Jerome, now one of the most luxurious (and expensive) hotels in Aspen, and the magnificently restored **Wheeler Opera House** (320 East Hyman Avenue; tel: 970-920 5770; https://wheeleroperahouse.com), which remains a stirring place to enjoy music, theater, or dance. Focused on contemporary work, the stylish **Aspen Art Museum** (637 East Hyman Avenue; tel: 970-925 8050; www.aspenartmuseum.org; Tue–Sun 10am–6pm; free) shows traveling exhibitions by top artists from around the globe.

CRESTED BUTTE

Not far south from Aspen as the crow flies – but a considerably longer trip as the car drives – the ski resort and beautiful Victorian mining town of **Crested Butte** ⑲ sits about 30 miles (48km) north of Gunnison at the upper end of the Gunnison Valley. Crested Butte's relative remoteness has in many ways been a blessing. It has managed to hang on to much of its small-town appeal while still being known for some of the best skiing – and, increasingly, best mountain biking – in the state (there's also fishing, hiking, and kayaking in summer). The old town is resplendent with gaily painted clapboard homes and businesses, with all the action taking place among the low-rise, historic buildings, bars, and restaurants on Elk Avenue. For a quick introduction to the town's history, head over to the **Crested Butte Mountain Heritage Museum** (331 Elk Avenue; tel: 970-349 1880; https://crestedbuttemuseum.com; call for opening times), with exhibits that cover the development of skiing and mountain biking in the region. In skiing and snowboarding circles, **Crested Butte Mountain Resort** (www.skicb.com) is best known for its extreme terrain, with lifts serving out-of-the-way bowls and faces that would only be accessible by helicopter at other resorts. In summer the action switches to zip-line tours, rafting, horseback riding and the trails of Crested Butte Mountain Bike Park.

Aspen Valley in fall.

⦿ SKI ASPEN

Today, Aspen boasts four ski mountains, all operated by Aspen Skiing Company (tel: 970-925 1220, www.aspensnowmass.com), with **Aspen Highlands** and **Snowmass** featuring their own "villages". **Highlands** balances intermediate and beginner runs with expert runs, and has the greatest vertical drop of any ski area in Colorado. **Aspen Mountain** itself is for skilled intermediate and expert skiers, while **Buttermilk** caters to beginners and intermediates. Twelve miles (19 km) northwest of Aspen, **Snowmass** offers some 2,000 acres (810 hectares) of varied ski terrain. But downhill skiing is by no means all Aspen has to offer; skilled cross-country skiers may want to ski from hut to hut on the **10th Mountain Trail** (www.huts.org), founded by veterans of the Army's 10th Mountain Division.

Colorado National Monument.

WESTERN COLORADO

Coloradans who live on the Western Slope – the western third of the state, where the Rockies drop toward the Utah border – will tell you that only here will you see the true Colorado.

They have a point. Venture along the Colorado, the Yampa, and the Gunnison rivers, then up into the San Juan Mountains, and you'll see the cattle, cowboys, and wide open spaces that sum up the American West. Tourism helps fuel western Colorado's economy, as it does in the rest of the state —Telluride couldn't live without its skiers or Durango without its mountain bikers. But you won't encounter the chic crowds and high prices here that you would at Aspen or Vail; western Colorado makes its visitors amply welcome, but it doesn't bend itself out of shape for them. Maybe that's what makes this region such an exhilarating place to explore.

GRAND JUNCTION

Western Colorado's chief metropolis is **Grand Junction ❶**, founded in 1882 among red sandstone bluffs at the confluence of the Gunnison and Colorado rivers. At 4,586ft (1,397 meters), Grand Junction has notably warmer weather than many higher-elevation Colorado cities, and a longer growing season. The city flourished in the 1950s as prospectors scoured the nearby mountains for uranium and boomed again in the 1970s when oil shale was the sought-after bonanza. Both those booms went quickly bust, but today Grand Junction thrives as tourists and new residents come to enjoy sunny skies, relatively

balmy temperatures, and a location that makes it a natural base for exploring the rest of western Colorado.

Although initial impressions may be unfavorable – a sprawl of factory units and sales yards lines the I-70 Business Loop – the tiny downtown is much nicer, with leafy boulevards hemming in a small, tree-lined historic district dotted with sculptures and stores. The **Museum of the West** (462 Ute Avenue; tel: 970-242 0971; https://museumofwest-ernco.com; Tue–Sat 10am–4pm) takes you through 10,000 years of Colorado

Main attractions
Black Canyon of the Gunnison
Colorado National Monument
Dinosaur National Monument
Durango and Silverton Narrow Gauge Railroad
Flat Tops Trail Scenic Byway
Grand Mesa
Mesa Verde National Park

Map on page 157

Grand Junction and the Colorado River.

> **◎ Tip**
>
> The Grand Junction area is prime mountain biking territory, with a network of trails just outside the city; visit Ruby Canyon Cycles at 301 Main Street (tel: 970-241 0141, https://rubycanyoncycles.com; Mon–Fri 9am–6pm, Sat 9am–5pm) for trail information and rentals, or Over the Edge Sports in Fruita (202 East Aspen Avenue; tel: 970-858 7220, https://otesports.com; daily 9am–6pm).

settlement, from Ice Age man to 19th-century pioneers to today. A museum offshoot some 12 miles (19km) west of town, **Dinosaur Journey** (550 Jurassic Court, Fruita; tel: 970-858 7282; https://museumofwesternco.com; daily 10am–5pm) testifies to Grand Junction's paleontological importance. The interactive museum features robotic displays of several kinds of dinosaurs, in addition to a collection of giant, locally excavated bones – all helping to create a vivid picture of these prehistoric beasts.

COLORADO NATIONAL MONUMENT

Southwest of Grand Junction, the mesmerizing **Colorado National Monument** ❷ (1750 Rim Rock Drive, Fruita; tel: 970-858 3617, www.nps.gov/colm; daily 24hr) encompasses 20,000 acres (8,094 hectares) of maze-like sandstone canyons where more than 200 million years of wind and water erosion have gouged out rock spires, domes, arches, pedestals, and balanced rocks along a line of cliffs a few miles south of the city. The park has two entrances at either end

A Grand Mesa sunset.

of twisting, 23-mile (37km) Rim Rock Drive, which links a string of spectacular overlooks with the visitor center at the north end of the park (exit 19, I-70). Short hikes along the way afford views of several monoliths, while longer treks get right down to the canyon floor.

GRAND MESA

East of Grand Junction rises **Grand Mesa** ❸, the world's largest flattop mountain, a lava-capped plateau with an average elevation of 10,000ft (3,048 meters). The mesa's 200-plus lakes lure fishermen; other visitors come to savor the high mountain scenery, fall colors, and the half-dozen small mountain lodges that are scattered about the area. The 78-mile (125-km) long Grand Mesa Scenic and Historic Byway (aka Hwy-65) runs across the mesa, ending in **Cedaredge's** ❹ **Pioneer Town** (388 South Grand Mesa Drive; tel: 970-856 7554; www.pioneer-town.org; late May–early Oct Tue–Sat 10am–4pm, Sun 10am–1pm), where a collection of historic buildings – saloon, jail, and general store among them – has been gathered together to form a handsome composite of a typical 19th-century frontier town.

GLENWOOD SPRINGS

About 90 miles (144km) northeast of Grand Junction on I-70 is the resort town of **Glenwood Springs** ❺. At the confluence of the Roaring Fork and Colorado rivers, the town was long used by the Ute people as a place of relaxation thanks to its hot springs, but it was silver magnate Walter Devereux who brought the springs to the outside world's attention. First came the world's largest outdoor mineral pool in 1888, then elegant hostelries like the ornate Hotel Colorado, opened in 1893.

Today Glenwood Springs wears its heritage gracefully. The restored **Hotel Colorado** has been tastefully decorated with teddy bears and other Teddy Roosevelt memorabilia – the former

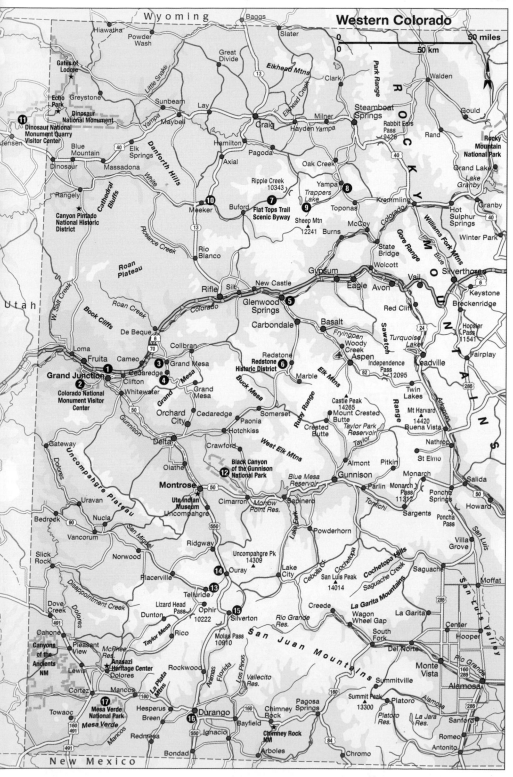

Western Colorado

president was an early guest. You can soak weary muscles in the **Glenwood Hot Springs Pool** (410 North River Street; tel: 970-947 2955; www.hot-springspool.com; daily: summer 7.30am–10pm; rest of year 9am–10pm), soothe your sinuses in the nearby **Yampah Hot Springs Spa Vapor Cave** (709 East 6th Street; tel: 970-945 0667; https://yampah-spa.com; daily 9am–9pm), and brush up on local outlaw history at the **Frontier Museum** (1001 Colorado Avenue; tel: 970-945 4448, www.glenwoodhistory.com; June–Sept Mon–Sat 10am–4pm; Oct–May Mon–Sat 1–4pm), which also focuses on the indigenous Ute as well as the area's pioneering history. Check out the museum's satellite **Doc Holliday Collection** (732 Grand Avenue; tel: 970-945 9175; daily 10am–4pm) in the former Hotel Glenwood where the famous gunfighter died in 1887. Doc Holliday is buried in **Linwood Cemetery** overlooking the town.

REDSTONE

Take highways 82 and 133 south from Glenwood Springs and you come to another highly unusual resort town, built on the banks of the Crystal River. In the 1880s, coal baron John Osgood founded **Redstone** N to house workers for his coal mines and coke ovens. Osgood's men had to obey rigorous rules. They were required to shower before appearing on the street, and to discourage drunkenness in other workers. In return Osgood provided a company town with unusually pleasant living conditions. Miners with families lived in a line of cozy cottages; bachelors were quartered in the Tudor-style **Redstone Inn** (www.redstoneinn.com). Eventually Osgood became so enamored of this beautiful valley that he built his own grand mansion, **Cleveholm Manor**, in 1902. More than a century later, Osgood's town has found a new lease of life: the cabins now serve as art galleries, fashionable stores, and second homes. The Redstone Inn is now a very attractive hotel and Cleveholm Manor is the **Redstone Castle** (https://theredstonecastle.com), a baronial bed-and-breakfast inn. Come summer, Redstone is lively with artists, craft artisans, and their customers.

Glenwood Springs in summer.

FLAT TOPS TRAIL SCENIC BYWAY

The area north of Glenwood Springs is Colorado's loneliest quadrant, a beautifully empty land of rolling mountains and spacious cattle ranches. For 82 scenic miles (132km), the partially paved **Flat Tops Trail Scenic Byway** ❼ (aka County Rd 8) winds its way through the Flat Tops Wilderness, beginning in the town of **Yampa** ❽, 30 miles (48km) south of Steamboat Springs. Soak up the dazzling views across the White River Valley from 10,343-ft (3,153-meter) Ripple Creek Pass, then make a detour (via Forest Road 205) to pristine **Trappers Lake** ❾. Sparked by the preservation efforts of Arthur Carhart in 1919, the lake is often considered the birthplace of the wilderness movement. Trappers Lake Lodge (www.trapperslake.com) rents cabins and boats, and there are five barebones campgrounds nearby. The byway ends at the small ranching town of **Meeker** ❿ on the White River, home of the Meeker Classic Sheep Dog Championship Trials (usually held the first Wednesday through Sunday after Labor Day in September).

DINOSAUR NATIONAL MONUMENT

To the northwest of Meeker, **Dinosaur National Monument's** ⓫ 300 sq. miles (777 sq. km) lie partly in Colorado and partly in northeastern Utah. But Dinosaur's true locale is the Jurassic period, 140 million years ago, when this arid portion of the Colorado Plateau was home to the largest animals ever to roam the earth. The monument has played an unrivaled role in the history of American paleontology. Among the most important finds here were the first known brontosaurus (now called apatosaurus) fossils.

Dinosaur is more than bones, though. Its dramatic landscape begs to be explored by car, by foot, or by raft. The Colorado half of the monument lies just northeast of the isolated town of Dinosaur, the site of the main **Canyon Visitor Center** (just off Hwy-40), which has video presentations and exhibits on the fossilized finds (note that there are

A fossil at Dinosaur National Monument.

⊙ Fact

Dinosaur National Monument is officially open daily, 24hr, but check the website (www. nps.gov/dino) for the latest conditions. Entrance is $25 per vehicle. The Quarry Visitor Center (in Utah; tel: 435-781 7700) is usually open June–Aug daily 8am–4.30pm, Sept– May Mon–Fri 8am– 4.30pm. The Canyon Visitor Center (tel: 970-374 3000) in Colorado is usually open late May to Sept daily 9am–5pm.

Black Canyon of the Gunnison.

no fossils in situ on the Colorado side). Take the 31-mile (50-km) drive from here on unpaved Harper's Corner Road and then the 2-mile (3km) hike to Echo Park overlook and you'll see the meeting of the Green and Yampa rivers thousands of feet below. If you want to see this view from river level, you have lots of options to choose from. Commercial river runners operate many one- to five-day trips on both rivers.

Heading west into Utah on Hwy-40 you reach **Jensen**, where you can access the second part of the monument. Hwy-149 leads north to the enclosed dinosaur **Quarry Exhibit Hall** (next to the Quarry Visitor Center; opening times vary), where a tilted layer of sandstone has been painstakingly exposed to display an incredible three-dimensional jigsaw of fossilized dinosaur bones, left in situ for imaginative visitors to piece together. In summer a shuttle bus runs from the Quarry Visitor Center to the Exhibit Hall (daily 8am–5pm, every 15 minutes); the rest of the year park rangers lead car caravans to the site.

Overnight visitors will find two developed campgrounds (and five more basic ones) inside the monument. For motels, your widest range of choices can be found in Vernal, Utah, 35 miles (56km) west of the Colorado border.

BLACK CANYON OF THE GUNNISON NATIONAL MONUMENT

To explore the region south of I-70, return to Grand Junction and follow Hwy-50 along the Gunnison River to the mind-boggling **Black Canyon of the Gunnison National Monument** ⑫ (tel: 970-249 1914, www.nps.gov/blca; daily 24hr; South Rim Visitor Center daily: late May–early Sept 8am–6pm; late Apr–late May & early Sept–Oct 8am–5pm; Nov–late Apr 9am–4pm). Fifty-three miles (85km) long (12 miles/19km of which lie within the monument), up to one mile (1.6km) deep, its sheer walls composed of dark gray schist and gneiss, Black Canyon wasn't really plumbed until 1901, when William Torrence and Abraham Lincoln Fellows floated the length of the Gunnison River

on a rubber raft. Today most visitors see the canyon from South Rim Drive, lined with viewpoints: Gunnison Point behind the visitor center, the Pulpit Rock overlook, and Painted View Wall, where the vast scale and height of the streaky cliffs really hits home, are the best. South Rim Road ends at High Point (8,289ft/2,526 meters), and the start of the Warner Point Trail (1.5 miles/2.4km return). The more remote North Rim Road (closed in winter) is 11 miles (18km) from the little town of Crawford (near Delta) off Hwy-92 (the last 7 miles/11km are unpaved). The monument has three campgrounds, or you can find numerous motels in nearby Delta and Montrose.

TELLURIDE

Scenic US-550 runs south from Montrose and the Black Canyon of the Gunnison all the way to Durango, part of the spectacular **San Juan Skyway loop**. Turn off in Ridgway to make the side-trip to **Telluride** ⑬, set in a picturesque valley at the flat base of a bowl of vast steep-sided mountains. In the gold and silver booms of the 1880s and 1890s, Telluride boasted a dozen bordellos and twice that number of saloons, and it was briefly home to the young Butch Cassidy, who robbed his first bank here in 1889. By 1930, though, all the mines had closed and the town's population was down to 512. The town seemed destined for oblivion until 1968, when a Californian investor started developing the surrounding slopes and the town's reputation as a great ski area was launched.

Telluride today capitalizes on its sumptuous setting in the San Juan Mountains and the Victorian architecture left over from its boom days. With long, steep, and demanding runs, **Telluride Ski Resort** (https://tellurideskiresort.com) is known as an expert's mountain, but novices and intermediates will find suitable slopes, too. And at any time of year the town itself (much of it a National Historic District) is charming, with Victorian buildings converted to galleries, restaurants, and bed-and-breakfast inns. The fascinating **Telluride Historical Museum** (201 West Gregory Avenue; tel: 970-728

An areal view of Telluride.

3344, www.telluridemuseum.org; June–Oct Mon–Sat 11am–5pm, Thu until 7pm, limited winter hours) recalls days when the town had 26 saloons and 12 brothels, and miners sledded down from mines on their shovels in winter. Summer hiking opportunities are excellent; one three-mile (4.8km) round-trip walk leads from the head of the valley, where the highway ends at Pioneer Mill, up to the 431ft (131 meter) Bridal Veil Falls, the tallest in Colorado.

OURAY

Back on US-550 heading south, the attractive mining community of **Ouray** ⑭ is named after the Ute chief who promoted cooperation with the invading Anglo settlers, a tactic he later regretted when the US government eventually forced the Utes to leave Colorado and live on reservations in Utah. Ouray began in the 1870s as a booming silver town, but was saved after the silver-market crash by the discovery of gold in 1896, allowing the local economy to hum on. Today, Ouray's small downtown area is lined with grand Victorian structures,

built with the spoils of silver and gold mining – industries detailed in the **Ouray County Museum** (420 6th Avenue; tel: 970-325 4576, www.ouraycountyhistorical-society.org; late-May–Oct Mon–Sat 10am–4.30pm, Sun noon–4.30pm), housed in the old miner's hospital of 1887.

What helps set Ouray apart from nearby mining towns are its famed hot springs, the largest of which is **Ouray Hot Springs** (1220 Main Street; tel: 970-325 7073; https://ourayhotsprings.com; Mon–Fri noon–7pm, Sat and Sun 1–8pm, with exceptions), beside the Uncompahgre River at the north end of town. The complex contains a large heated mineral swimming pool and five smaller soaking pools. The original source of the springs is a mile up the river in Box Canyon. Just south of town, a one-way-loop dirt road leads to **Box Cañon Falls Park**, where a straightforward trail, partly along a swaying wooden parapet, leads into narrow Box Canyon and the namesake falls, where Canyon Creek thunders through a tiny cleft in the mountain at the far end. The Box Cañon Visitor Center (tel: 970-325 7080; early May to

A steam engine train travels from Durango to Silverton through the San Juan Mountains.

⊘ FESTIVE TELLURIDE

Telluride stands apart from most ski resorts in having an off-season program of worthwhile summer festivals that actually draw crowds and top performers from both near and far. The Telluride Bluegrass Festival (tel: 970-449-6007, https://bluegrass.com) runs over four days in late June and celebrates all kinds of music (though primarily, of course, bluegrass), while the Telluride Jazz Festival (tel: 970-728 7009, www.telluridejazz.org) is held in the first week of August. The Chamber Music Festival (tel: 970-369 5669, www.telluridechambermusic.org) is another longstanding August event, beginning with an incredible outdoor sunset concert. The Telluride Film Festival (tel: 510-665 9494, www.telluride-filmfestival.org) is held on the first weekend in September.

Oct daily 8am–8pm) contains interpretive exhibits that describe the geology, wildlife and history of the area. Many birders come to canyon to observe the rare colony of black swifts that nest here.

SILVERTON

The twisting 23-mile (37km) stretch of Hwy-550 between Ouray and **Silverton** ⓖ is known as the Million Dollar Highway, a gorgeous section of the Skyway that snakes over the 11,018ft (3,358 meter) Red Mountain Pass. At its peak in around 1890, Silverton had 2,000 residents. It has maybe one quarter of that today, but it thrives as the northern terminus of the Durango & Silverton Narrow Gauge Railroad.

First stop in Silverton should be the captivating exhibits at the **San Juan County Historical Society** (1559 Greene St; tel: 970-387 5838, www.sanjuancountyhistoricalsociety.org; late May to early Oct daily 10am–4.30pm), comprising the 1902 County Jail and connected Mining Heritage Center, housed in the old Caledonia Boardinghouse.

For a better impression of a miner's daily toil, head to the **One Hundred Gold Mine Tour** (721 County Road 4A; tel: 970-387 5444, www.minetour.com; tours late May to mid-Oct), three miles (4.8km) northeast of town. Mine tours (1hr) head a third of a mile (530 meters) into Galena Mountain, where old mining tools aren't just exhibited but operated as well. Tours begin with a three-minute underground train ride to a large cavern, where there are noisy air-powered stoppers and a mucker scooping rock into a cart.

DURANGO

Thanks to a splendid setting amid the San Juan Mountains, **Durango** ⓰, founded in 1880 as a refining town and rail junction to serve Silverton, 45 miles (72km) north, is southwest Colorado's largest city. The city continues to bustle with students and tourists, and the place has an unexpectedly youthful, energetic buzz. The north–south Main Avenue is the hub of Durango's urban action, lined with restaurants, souvenir shops, and Southwestern art galleries – almost all housed

⊘ Tip

Whitewater rafting on the Animas River is a must-do activity in Durango. The most popular trips are the fairly tame family-friendly excursions on the Lower Animas; class II and III waters south of town. But the real gem for those with the courage, money, and time are the rafting trips farther upstream. The 28 miles (45km) of the Upper Animas provides continuous class III water with several Class IV and V sections (see https://durangorafting.com or https://mild2wildrafting.com).

Ouray Box Canyon Waterfall.

⊘ BIKING DURANGO

Durango is a world-class center for off-road biking, and the venue for one of the largest bike races in the entire US – the annual Iron Horse Bicycle Classic (http://ironhorsebicycleclassic.com) – a nail-biting event in which riders race the narrow-gauge railway train 47 miles (76km) and over an elevation gain of 5,700ft (1,737m) to Silverton. The event began in 1972 as a friendly wager between two brothers and has since mushroomed into a major three-day carnival over Memorial Day (late May). For rentals, equipment and advice contact Mountain Bike Specialists (949 Main Avenue; tel: 970-247 4066; www.mountainbikespecialists.com), or Pedal the Peaks (598 Main Avenue; tel: 970-259 6880, www.ptpdurango.com). Classic local rides include Telegraph Hill, Haflin Creek Trail and Hermosa Creek Trail.

⊘ Fact

Mesa Verde lies 35 miles (56km) west of Durango. Entry is $30 per vehicle May to Oct, and $20 the rest of the year, all tickets valid for a week. The park visitor center (tel: 970-529 4465; www. nps.gov/meve) lies on US-160 at the entrance to the park, around 40min drive below the mesa-top sites (daily 9am–3pm, with exceptions).

in Victorian red-brick buildings. The gaudiest landmark may be the **Strater Hotel** (https://strater.com), built in 1887 for the then extravagant cost of $70,000 and still a charming place to stay. The Strater also houses the Diamond Belle Saloon, featuring "Belle Girls" in period costume.

For another trip into the Western past, board the **Durango and Silverton Narrow Gauge Railroad** (479 Main Avenue; tel: 877872 4607; www.durangotrain.com; May–Oct, 1–3 times daily), which makes a 45-mile (72km) trip north to Silverton on a river-hopping, mountain-hugging route laid out in 1881. Total trip time is eight hours, including two hours for sightseeing in Silverton.

MESA VERDE NATIONAL PARK

To the west of Durango, Hwy-160 leads about 36 miles (58km) to **Mesa Verde National Park** ⑰. The site preserves dramatic masonry cliff dwellings built by Ancestral Puebloan farmers more than 800 years ago. You can easily spend a few days exploring the park, which ranges from the early Basketmaker period of about 1,400 years ago

to the much later Pueblo period. The site was abandoned about AD 1300, though it's not entirely clear why.

All the park's ruins are located 20 tortuous miles (32km) up from the **visitor center**; you must purchase tickets here to visit Balcony House, Cliff Palace, and Long House (tickets are not required for Spruce Tree House or Step House on Wetherill Mesa). Some 15 miles (24km) beyond the visitor center, the road forks to reach two constellations of remains: Chapin Mesa to the south, and Wetherill Mesa to the west. The **Chapin Mesa Archeological Museum** (daily: Apr–Aug 8am–6.30pm; Sept and Oct 8am–5pm; Nov–Mar 9am–4.30pm) holds the best displays on the Ancestral Puebloans and also sells tour tickets after the visitor center closes in late fall. From here the eastern Cliff Palace Loop takes in the highlight, **Cliff Palace**, tucked 100ft (30.5 meters) below an overhanging ledge of pale rock, and the largest Ancestral Puebloan cliff dwelling to survive anywhere. It holds 217 rooms and 23 kivas (ritual spaces), each thought to have belonged to a separate family or clan.

Cliff Palace at Mesa Verde.

BUTCH CASSIDY & THE SUNDANCE KID

The two most engaging characters to roam the Rocky Mountains, Butch Cassidy and the Sundance Kid remain legends not only of the Old West but of a romantic outlaw existence.

Thanks in large part to being mythologized in the classic 1969 Hollywood movie, *Butch Cassidy and the Sundance Kid* (which starred Paul Newman and Robert Redford), these two former thieves and cattle-rustlers continue to cast a long shadow across the Rockies.

Butch Cassidy was born Robert LeRoy Parker in the Mormon town of Beaver, Utah in 1866. Taught the fine art of cattle rustling by local ranch-hand Mike Cassidy, Robert borrowed his mentor's last name, then picked up the handle "Butch" while working as a butcher in Rock Springs, Wyoming. He pulled his first bank job in Telluride, Colorado in 1889, and soon found himself in the company of a like-minded group of villains known collectively as the Wild Bunch. There were several female members of the gang, including Laura Bullion, who was likely born in Texas. Among their male members was one Harry Longabaugh – the Sundance Kid – who picked up his nickname following a jail stint in Sundance, Wyoming in 1887. Longabaugh was born in Mont Clare, Pennsylvania, in 1867, and came West at the age of 15, settling near Cortez, Colorado. He worked primarily as an itinerant ranch-hand throughout the Rockies, only turning to crime full-time in the 1890s.

The Wild Bunch used Hole-in-the-Wall, near Kaycee in Wyoming's Big Horn Mountains, as a base, and often laid low through the winter months in Brown's Hole (now a wildlife refuge), a broad river valley in remote northwest Colorado and Utah. They were also known to visit (and get quite raucous in) the southern Wyoming towns of Baggs, Rock Springs, and Green River. The gang, however, was eventually undone by their own vanity and love of a good time. During a visit to Fort Worth, Texas, five of them posed for a photograph in smart suits and derby hats, looking so dapper that the photographer proudly placed the photo in his shop window, where it was seen by a detective from the famous Pinkerton's agency. Despite their reputation, it's thought that Butch and Sundance didn't kill anyone during their spree of robberies and heists – though other gang members such as Kid Curry certainly did, and gunfights with lawmen were common.

Having masterminded some major railroad robberies in the late 1890s, and wearying of life on the run, Butch and Sundance sailed for South America in 1901. They traveled to Argentina and finally Bolivia, where they supposedly died in a hail of bullets at the hands of Bolivian soldiers in 1908 (as depicted in the film) – the rest of the gang had been arrested or killed back in the US in the years before. Yet rumors of the outlaw's survival began almost immediately; residents of Baggs claimed Cassidy had visited for several days in 1924, while Josie Bassett, an old girlfriend from Butch's Brown's Hole days, insisted that he died an old man in Johnnie, Nevada, some time during the late 1930s. The last of the Wild Bunch is thought to have died in Memphis, Tennessee, in 1961.

Robert Leroy Parker, known as Butch Cassidy, was the leader of tvhe Wild Bunch Gang in the American Old West.

$4,000 Reward

WILL BE PAID FOR THE CAPTURE OF ROBERT LEROY PARKER

DEAD OR ALIVE

Age, 36 years (1901)
Weight, 165 lbs.
Complexion, Light.
Eyes, Blue.
Nationality, American.
Marks, two cut scars back of head, small scar under left eye, small brown mole calf of leg.

Height, 5 ft. 9 in.
Build, Medium.
Color of hair, Flaxen.
Mustache, sandy if any.
Occupation, Cowboy, Rustler.
Criminal occupation, bank robber & Highwayme cattle and horse thief.

ROBERT LEROY PARKER
ALIAS
"BUTCH" CASSIDY

Caves at Logan Canyon.

NORTHERN UTAH

As the Rockies rumble north through Colorado, the spectacular Wasatch Mountains poke an elbow into Northern Utah, harboring top-notch ski resorts, pristine alpine peaks, and 19th-century Mormon farming towns.

At one time, Ute, Shoshone, and Bannock people roamed over these mountains in search of game and wild foods. Later, mountain men trapped fur-bearing animals along its cold streams and rivers. Attracted by its remoteness, Mormons established Salt Lake City in 1847 and began settling the northern valleys shortly after. Their isolation came to an end 23 years later, however, when America's first trans-continental railroad was completed. The final spike was driven into place in 1869 at Promontory Summit just northwest of Salt Lake City.

The heart of the remaining farm economy, Cache Valley, is a good place to begin a visit to the region around Great Salt Lake's northern shore. Well-watered by Bear River and its tributaries, the beautiful green valley is almost completely surrounded by steep mountain ridges. It's here that you pick up US-89, which winds its way north via Logan up to Yellowstone National Park, eight hours away, making by far and away the most scenic driving route between Salt Lake City and northern Wyoming. Not to be missed along this stretch are the wonderful hiking, fishing, and lazing about to be had in Logan Canyon, as well as some fine swimming in the impossibly blue waters of Bear Lake, which straddles the Utah/Idaho border.

A small wooden house near Bear Lake.

OGDEN

The Ogden River drains west out of Pineview Reservoir down Ogden Canyon to the city of **Ogden** , all named after Peter Skene Ogden, the British fur trapper who passed this way in the 1820s. This is where Miles Goodyear, commonly considered Utah's first non-Native American settler, built his home in 1846. He raised a garden and traded horses he bought in California to overland migrants. He eventually sold everything to early Mormon settlers, and is now commemorated

⊙ Main attractions

Aggie Ice Cream
American West Heritage Center
Bear Lake
Golden Spike National Historical Park
LeBeau's
Logan Canyon Scenic Byway
Maddox Ranch House
Powder Mountain
Shooting Star Saloon

⦿ **Map on page 169**

The Ogden River.

at **Fort Buenaventura Park**, a reconstruction of his log stockade off 24th Street in West Ogden. The actual **Miles Goodyear Cabin** is located next to the **Daughters of Utah Pioneers Museum** (2104 Lincoln Avenue, at 21st Street), which honors those who founded Utah. Both are one block west of the local Mormon Temple, dedicated in 1972, and the older Ogden Tabernacle.

Ogden grew with the railroad, becoming Utah's first non-Mormon city after the tracks arrived in 1869. It was then Utah's commercial connection to the outside. **Union Depot** at 25th Street and Wall Avenue wasn't built until 1924, but it is a classic reminder of the railroad's importance to the city (though passenger services no longer call here). It houses the **Museums at Union Station** (https://ogdencity.com; Wed–Sat noon–4pm), with various collections of prints, photographs, decorative arts, costumes, paintings, sculpture, toys, and railroad ephemera, including the John M. Browning Firearms Museum and the Utah State Railroad Museum/Eccles Rail Center.

The most unusual building in town is **Peerys Egyptian Theater** (2439 Washington Boulevard; tel: 801-689 8700; www.ogdenpet.com), completed in 1924 and decorated in an ornate faux-Egyptian style – it remains a movie theater and performance center. Stroll Historic 25th Street to see more examples of the city's grand architecture, now converted into restaurants, art galleries, and bars.

Families will appreciate the **Treehouse Museum** (347 22nd Street; tel: 801-394 9663; www.treehousemuseum.org; Tue–Sat 10am–4.30pm), an interactive wonderland in which kids can make music, dress up in costumes, and romp through the dozens of mini exhibits that range from fish tanks to a rodeo arena. Younger kids will also love the **Odgen's George S Eccles Dinosaur Park and Museum** (1544 Park Boulevard; tel: 801-393 3466; www.dinosaurpark.org; Mon–Sat 10am–5pm, with exceptions) where life-size (and life-like) dinosaur statues prowl the gardens and kids can run around and climb on many of them.

OGDEN VALLEY

The mountains east of Ogden are best known for the trails and uncrowded powder at three ski resorts: **Snowbasin** ❷ (www.snowbasin.com), huge **Powder Mountain** ❸ (www.powdermountain.com); and **Nordic Valley** ❹ (www.nordicvalley. ski), considered the best learning hill in the West with some of the best night skiing. All three morph into hiking and mountain-biking hubs in the summer.

The valley is anchored by ragged-edged **Pineview Reservoir** and the town of **Huntsville** ❺, the home of the late David O. McKay, one of the Mormon church's most revered prophets (tours of the David O McKay Home on request; tel: 801-633 7368). Tours are also available of the **historic Robert F.**

Aldous Cabin, built in 1861 (East 200 South and South 7400 East; June–Aug Sat 11am–1pm).

BRIGHAM CITY

A few miles north of Odgen lies **Brigham City** ❻, most successful of Brigham Young's 19th-century experiments in cooperative Mormon living. The town was founded in 1851 and later played an important role in Brigham Young's United Order, an organization dedicated to the notion of communal property. Today, the town is best known for the **Box Elder Tabernacle** (251 South Main Street; free guided tours in summer), a dramatic Mormon church structure with gleaming white spires completed in the 1890s.

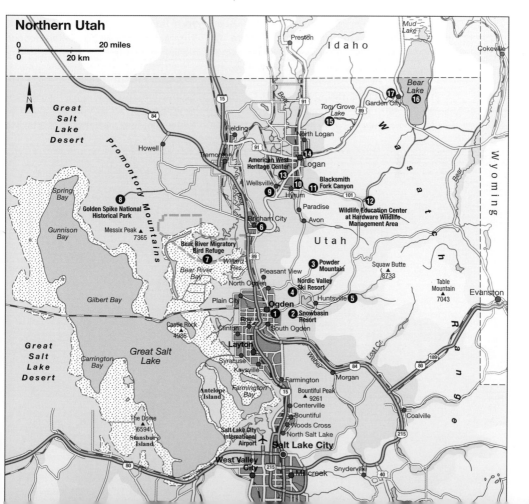

On the southern outskirts of Brigham City, the **Maddox Ranch House** (1900 South Hwy-89; tel: 435-723 8545; https://maddoxfinefood.com; Tue–Sat 11am–9.30pm) has become a destination in its own right, a drive-in diner that's a genuine Utah institution. Open since 1949, it's best known for buffalo steaks and burgers, as well as its "famous" fried chicken and freshly made rolls with raspberry honey butter. Reserve ahead to avoid a long wait for a table. In late summer, northern Utah's peaches ripen – the peach harvest is celebrated every year in September during "Peach Days"– and are sold in the many fruit stands along this stretch of Hwy-89, known as the "Fruit Way."

Just west of Brigham City are the extensive marshlands of the **Bear River Migratory Bird Refuge** (www.fws.gov/refuge/bear_river_migratory_bird_refuge), best visited in the fall or spring when hundreds of species of migrating birds pass the Great Salt Lake's shores. You can drive the one-way 12-mile (19km) Auto Tour, or

Golden Spike National Historic Park.

stroll 1.5 miles (2.4km) of trails near the Wildlife Education Center (I-15, exit 363).

GOLDEN SPIKE NATIONAL HISTORICAL PARK

High in the Promontory Mountains 30 miles (48km) northwest of Brigham City, the **Golden Spike National Historical Park** ❽ (tel: 435-471 2209; www.nps.gov/gosp; daily 9am–5pm, with exceptions) commemorates the completion of America's first transcontinental railroad in 1869. Work on this historic project began more than six years earlier, with the Central Pacific building east from Sacramento, California, and the Union Pacific building west from Omaha, Nebraska. The site where the last spike was driven stands near the modern Visitor Center, and is commemorated by a polished wooden tie with a plaque.

WELLSVILLE

Some 16 miles (26km) northeast from Brigham City on Hwy-89 is the Cache Valley's oldest settlement, **Wellsville**

9. The town sits at the foot of the Wellsville Mountains, which climb 5,000ft (1,500 meters) from the valley floor, a rise made more impressive by their narrow base. They have one of the steepest mountain faces in the United States. A few miles east of Wellsville is another colorful early Mormon settlement, **Hyrum 10**. Outside it is Hyrum State Park with boating and camping facilities, and to the east, the **Blacksmith Fork Canyon 11**, a high walled gorge with good fishing and plenty of picnic sites. Farther along Hwy-101 is the state-run **Wildlife Education Center at Hardware Wildlife Management Area 12** (https://wildlife.utah. gov/hardware-visit.html; free); the main attraction here is the annual winter feeding of hundreds of elk.

Heading north Hwy-89 between Wellsville and Logan, stop off at the **American West Heritage Center 13** (tel: 435-245 6050, www.awhc.org), a living museum that explores the diverse cultures that shaped the Cache Valley from 1820 to 1920; steam powered tractors, harvesters, wagons, and other antique farm equipment is kept in operation.

LOGAN

Just north of the Wellsville Mountains in the middle of the cool and green Cache Valley, **Logan 14** is a small Mormon town and home of Utah State University, with decent restaurants and hotels making it a good place to stop. Upon approaching the city, you'll see the castle-like **Logan Temple** (175 North 300 East), the local Mormon church, an unornamented, gray limestone Gothic building with twin cupola-topped towers. Volunteer laborers constructed it between 1877 and 1884. Only Mormons in good standing may enter the temple, and a similar gray, cupola-crowned building is only two blocks west on Main Street. This is the **Mormon Tabernacle** (50 Main Street), begun in 1865 and completed in 1890.

The **Caine Lyric Theatre** (28 West Center Street; tel: 435-797 3040), built in 1913, is home to the modern Lyric Repertory Company (www.usu.edu/lyricrep), while the nearby Ellen Eccles

A Mormon temple in Logan.

⊘ BEAR RIVER MASSACRE

The Cache Valley extends several miles across the state border into Idaho, where there is a tragic historic site, sacred to Native Americans. Five miles (8 km) north of Preston, Idaho, on US-91 by the Bear River, is the **Bear River Massacre Site**, where a large band of Shoshone-Bannocks, accused of harassing overland migrants and settlers, camped in January 1863. It was there that federal troops from Fort Douglas in Salt Lake City attacked them. Led by Colonel Patrick E. Connor, the soldiers trapped the Native Americans in a ravine and, showing no mercy, killed at least 224 people. Their own casualties came to a total of 14 killed and 49 wounded. Miraculously, Shoshone leader Chief Sagwitch survived the massacre and later joined the Mormon Church.

⊘ Eat
Thanks to the plump, juicy raspberries grown in Bear Lake Valley, Garden City has become celebrated for raspberry shakes, a mouthwatering treat – essentially fresh raspberries blended with soft-serve ice cream. Traditionally, **LeBeau's** (69 North Bear Lake Boulevard; www.labeaus.com) has become the champion purveyor of raspberry shakes since 1981, but there are several other joints in town that do pretty good versions including **Zipz** (75 North Bear Lake Boulevard; www.zipzbearlake.com) and **Hometown** (105 North Bear Lake Boulevard; www.htbearlake.com). These kind of places tend to open May through September.

Walking along the shore at Bear Lake.

Theatre (43 South Main Street; tel: 435-752 0026, www.cachearts.org) dates from 1923 and also remains in use.

LOGAN CANYON

The **Logan Canyon Scenic Byway** (aka US-89) begins just outside Logan at an altitude of 4,700ft (1,433 meters) and runs along the Logan River for 37 miles (60km) through the Wasatch-Cache National Forest before topping out at 7,800ft (2,377 meters), a couple of miles (3.2km) above the western shore of Bear Lake. Steep limestone walls, fields of wildflowers, and astonishing fall foliage in reds, yellows, and greens line the road, which can be driven in under an hour. But it's worth spending at least half a day walking a trail or two, or simply driving up to **Tony Grove Lake** ⑮ (halfway along), and unpacking a picnic basket.

BEAR LAKE

It's quite something when you crest the final hill at the eastern end of Logan Canyon and get a full view of **Bear Lake** ⑯. At around 20 miles (32km) long and 8 miles (13km) wide, its waters are colored a stunning turquoise – the product of billions of limestone particles suspended in the water – making it very hard to resist a stop for a spot of fine freshwater swimming. Split pretty evenly between Utah and Idaho, the lake gets plenty of attention from residents of both states coming to swim, water-ski, sail, fish, and lounge on its beaches.

Garden City ⑰ is the nearest thing to a town on the western shore, though it's basically a string of holiday cottages that straggle for several miles to the north and south. The two main recreation areas nearby, State Park Marina and Rendezvous Beach, are both state parks and require a fee for day-use. The former, located on the north side of Garden City, is the place for boating activities like water-skiing and sailing; craft including catamarans and jet-skis can be rented here. Rendezvous Beach, on the southwestern shore about 8 miles (13km) south of Garden City, is a popular sandy spot perfect for swimming, sailing, and basking in the sun.

On the eastern side of the lake, Cisco Beach eventually gives way to Bear Lake State Park in Idaho, with North Beach an especially beautiful spot for a swim; note that in summer the parking lot usually fills by noon.

Indeed, while waterside settlements like Laketown and St Charles still retain much of their character, Bear Lake is showing signs of overdevelopment. Its beaches and nearby hillsides are crowded with resorts and summer homes, and the quality of its once crystal clean water is deteriorating. It once drained one way, into Bear River; now Bear River's water is pumped back into the lake during the high runoff, a process that is gradually altering the temperature and ecology of the lake. To see truly rural Utah, travel south from Bear Lake on State highways 30 and 16 to rustic, isolated Randolph and Woodruff.

A western meadowlark singing at the Bear River Migratory Bird Refuge in Utah.

Salt Lake City as night begins to fall.

SALT LAKE CITY

Salt Lake City, the capital of Utah, is by far the state's largest and most cosmopolitan urban center, with a superb setting in the shadow of the snow-capped Wasatch Front.

The city (and much of Utah) is of course primarily associated with the Church of Jesus Christ of Latter-Day Saints (or Mormons). The city was founded in 1847 by hardy Mormon settlers led by Brigham Young; at that point it lay outside the official boundaries of the USA. Today, over 60 percent of Utah's 3-million-strong population are Mormons (see page 77). Mormon history provides much of what makes the city so interesting, but the area around the city offers great hiking and cycling in summer and autumn and, in winter, superb skiing. Outsiders tend to imagine Salt Lake City as decidedly short on fun, but so long as you're willing to switch gears and slow down, its unhurried pace and the positive energy of its people can make for an enjoyable experience.

TEMPLE SQUARE

The geographical – and spiritual – heart of **Salt Lake City ❶**, **Temple Square** (50 East North Temple Street; daily 9am–9pm; free) is the world headquarters of the Mormon Church. Its focus, the iconic **Temple Ⓐ** itself, was completed in 1893 after 40 years of intensive labor – the multi-spired edifice rises 210ft (64 meters) above the city. Only confirmed Mormons may enter the Temple, and only for the most sacred Latter-Day Saints (LDS) rituals

Temple Square in Salt Lake City.

– marriage, baptisms, and "sealing," the joining of a family unit for eternity. While the Temple itself is likely to be closed until 2024 for a major rebuilding program, the Conference Center, Tabernacle, and **Assembly Hall Ⓑ** (50 South Temple Street; daily 10am–6pm; free) will remain open to the public during construction. The latter was completed in a Neo-Gothic style in 1882 and is still used as a place of worship. Within the spotless, landscaped Temple Square itself are also statues of Joseph and Hyrum Smith and the

❂ Main attractions
Alpine Loop
Antelope Island State Park
Big Cottonwood Canyon
Temple Square
Ruth's Diner
Spiral Jetty
Snowbird
Timpanogos Cave National Monument
Utah Olympic Park
Utah State Capitol

Maps on pages 176, 178

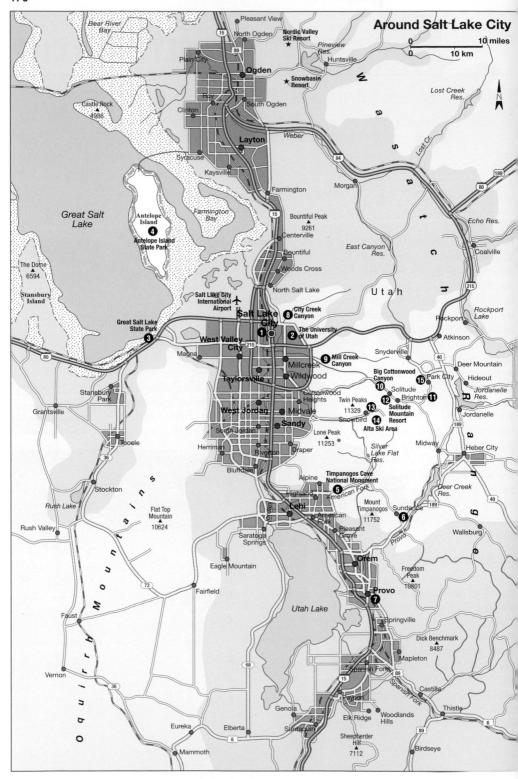

Around Salt Lake City

0 ⎯⎯⎯⎯⎯⎯⎯ 10 miles
0 ⎯⎯⎯⎯⎯⎯⎯ 10 km

Pleasant View

Nordic Valley
Ski Resort ★

*Pineview
Res.*

North Ogden

Ogden

Huntsville

★ Snowbasin
Resort

W a s a t c h

*Lost Creek
Res.*

Plain City

Roy

South Ogden

Layton

Weber

Lost Cr.

Clinton

Syracuse

Kaysville

Morgan

Echo Res.

Farmington

**Great Salt
Lake**

*Castle Rock
▲ 4986*

Antelope
Island

④ Antelope Island
State Park

*Farmington
Bay*

Bountiful Peak
▲ 9261
Centerville

*East Canyon
Res.*

Coalville

*The Dome
6594*

*Farmington
Bay*

Bountiful

Woods Cross

U t a h

Rockport
Lake

**Stansbury
Island**

North Salt Lake

Rockport

Atkinson

*Great Salt
Lake*

Salt Lake City
International
Airport ✈

Great Salt Lake
State Park

③

**Salt Lake
City**

⑧ City Creek
Canyon

①

② The University
of Utah

Snyderville

Deer Mountain

Magna

**West Valley
City**

⑨ Mill Creek
Canyon

Hideout

Stansbury
Park

Taylorsville

Millcreek
Wildwood

Big Cottonwood
Canyon

⑩ Solitude

⑮ Park City

*Jordanelle
Res.*

Grantsville

Cottonwood
Heights
Twin Peaks
▲ 11329

⑫ Brighton ⑪
⑬ Solitude
Mountain
Resort

Jordanelle

Tooele

West Jordan

Midvale
Sandy
South Jordan

Snowbird
⑭ Alta Ski Area

Midway

Heber City

Stockton

Herriman
Riverton Draper

Lone Peak
▲ 11253

*Silver
Lake Flat
Res.*

Rush Lake

Bluffdale

Alpine
Highland

Timpanogos Cave
National Monument
⑤

*Deer Creek
Res.*

Wallsburg

Flat Top
Mountain
▲ 10624

American Fork

Mount
Timpanogos
▲ 11752

Sundance ⑥

Rush Valley

Saratoga
Springs

Lehi

American
Fork
Pleasant
Grove

Provo

Faust

Eagle Mountain

Orem

Freedom
Peak
▲ 10801

Fairfield

Provo ⑦

Oquirrh Mountains

Utah Lake

Springville

Vernon

Dick Benchmark
▲ 8487

Mapleton

Genola

Spanish Fork

Payson

Spanish Fork

Castilla

Eureka

Elberta

Santaquin

Elk Ridge

Woodlands
Hills

Thistle

Mammoth

Sheepherder
Hill
7112

Birdseye

Seagull Monument, commemorating the 1848 "Miracle of the Gulls" (when a flock of seagulls saved the Mormon harvest by eating scavenging crickets). Visits usually begin at the **Conference Center**  (60 North Temple Street; tel: 801-240 8945; www.churchofjesuschrist. org; daily 10am–6pm; free), where there are exhibits, a 17-minute orientation film, a replica of Christus, and a 19th-century statue of Christ by Danish sculptor Bertel Thorvaldsen.

You can also explore the odd oblong shell of the **Mormon Tabernacle**  (50 North West Temple Street; tel: 801-240 2534; daily 10am–6pm; free), completed in 1867 as a place for church members to gather and hear their leaders. No images of any kind adorn its interior, where a guide laconically displays its remarkable acoustic properties by tearing up a newspaper and dropping a nail. There's free admission to the Mormon Tabernacle Choir's 9.30am Sunday broadcast and its rehearsals on Thursday evenings at 7.30–9.30pm. Organ recitals take place from Monday to Saturday at noon and on Sunday at 2pm.

Other sights include the marbled and chandeliered lobby of the **Joseph Smith Memorial Building**  (15 E South Temple Street; tel: 801-531 1000; Mon–Sat 11am–9pm; free), once the entrance to the luxurious Hotel Utah, completed in 1911. Today it's home to the Nauvoo Café and Legacy Theater, which shows films throughout the day that explore the Mormon church and its history.

In the southeast corner of Temple Square, the **Beehive House**  (67 East South Temple Street; tel: 801-240 2681; Mon–Sat 10am–6pm; free), is a plain white New England-style home, with wraparound verandas and green shutters. Erected in 1854 for Mormon leader Brigham Young (it also served as offices for the church for many years), it's now restored as a small museum of Young's life. Completed

in 2009, the **Church History Library**  (45 North West Temple Street; tel: 801-240 3310; Mon–Fri 10am–5pm, Sat 10am–3pm; free) houses Mormon Church records, with materials that chronicle the history of the church from 1830 to the present day. Visitors can view a short video and then peruse exhibits that contain foundational documents of the Mormon Church, everything from Joseph Smith's journal (1835), to various original Book of Mormon scriptures. There's also the **Family History Library**  (35 North West Temple Street; tel: 801-240 6996, www.familysearch.org; Mon–Sat 9am–5pm; free), the world's most exhaustive genealogical library, and the **Church History Museum**  (45 North West Temple Street; tel: 801-240 3310; Mon–Sat 10am–6pm; free), which charts the rise of the Mormon faith in art and artifacts.

DOWNTOWN

Commercial Salt Lake City lies immediately south of Temple Street, with a spate of shopping malls like City Creek

⊙ Tip

Salt Lake's bike share program is GREENbike (www.greenbikeutah.org), with stations all over downtown; 24/hr passes are $7 (unlimited 30min rides; $5 for next 30min then $5/hr thereafter).

Assembly Hall and the Seagull Monument.

Center (https://shopcitycreekcenter.com), skyscrapers and secular attractions. The stylish **Utah Museum of Contemporary Art** ❶ (20 South West Temple Street; tel: 801-328 4201; https://utahmoca.org; Tue–Thu and Sat 11am–6pm, Fri 11am–8pm; free, suggested donation $8) offers a break from all things Mormon, with carefully curated changing exhibits of contemporary art in all mediums. Family-friendly attractions include the **Discovery Gateway Children's Museum** ❿ (444 West 100 South Street; tel: 801-456 5437; www.discoverygateway.org; Mon and Wed–Sat 10am–6pm, Sun noon–6pm), and the **Clark Planetarium** ❶ (110 South 400 West Street; tel: 385-468 7827; https://slco.org/clark-planetarium; Sun–Thu 10am–7pm, Fri and Sat 10am–10.45pm), which features IMAX movies and exhibits on space exploration.

CAPITOL HILL

Just north of Temple Square lies the secular Capitol Hill area. Completed in 1916, the neoclassical **Utah State Capitol** ❿ (350 North State Street;

tel: 801-538 1800, https://utahstatecapitol.utah.gov; Mon–Thu 7am–8pm, Fri–Sat 7am–6pm; free) contains the two state legislative chambers, a ceremonial supreme court chamber, and the working offices of top state officials. Inside rises a 165-foot (50-meter) rotunda, arching over the building's core attractions: the 23-karat gold-leaf state reception room, an exhibition hall dedicated to Utah's history, and marble staircases leading to the galleried chambers of state government. Operated by the Daughters of Utah Pioneers, the nearby **Pioneer Memorial Museum** ❿ (300 North Main Street; tel: 801-532 6479; http://www.dupinternational.org; Mon–Sat 9am–5pm; free) features a quirky mixture of displays and memorabilia from the early days of Mormon settlement in the Great Salt Lake region; portraits, antique guns, quilts, old clothing, a Conestoga wagon, a 1902 fire engine, Victorian hair art, articles associated with the Mormon Battalion, and the original carved eagle from the city's Eagle Gate.

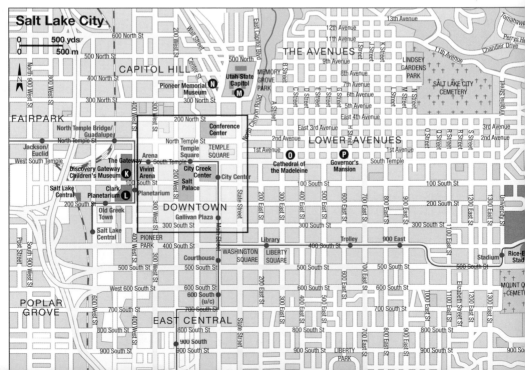

East of City Creek Canyon is the **Avenues Historic District**, featuring a wide variety of architectural styles, including many restored Victorian houses. Highlights here include the Roman Catholic **Cathedral of the Madeleine** ⓞ (331 East South Temple Street; tel: 801-328 8941, www.utcotm.org; daily 8am–6pm; free) a gray sandstone Romanesque-style church with stained-glass sanctuary windows, and the mansions of two prominent Utah silver magnates who owned the Silver King Mine in Park City: the **Keith Brown Mansion** (529 East Temple Street), and the **Thomas Kearns Mansion** (603 East Temple Street), completed in 1902 and now the official **Governor's Mansion** ⓟ (tel: 801-245 7330 for tours).

UNIVERSITY OF UTAH

Some three miles (4.8km) east of Downtown, a handful of attractions lie around the landscaped campus of the **University of Utah** ❷. The **Natural History Museum of Utah** ⓠ (301 Wakara Way; tel: 801-581 6927; https://nhmu.utah.edu; daily 10am–5pm) highlights the state's eight federally recognized Native American tribes, and its extraordinarily rich fossil heritage, while the Utah **Museum of Fine Arts** ⓡ (410 Campus Center Drive; tel: 801-581 7332, www.umfa.utah.edu; Tue–Sun 10am–5pm, Wed till 8pm) features over 20,000 original works of art from all over the world.

Utah's pioneer past comes to life at **This Is the Place Heritage State Park** ⓢ (2601 Sunnyside Avenue South; tel: 801-582 1847; www.thisistheplace.org; daily 9am–5pm), comprising various historic properties salvaged from around the state.

GREAT SALT LAKE

Northwest of the city, the **Great Salt Lake** itself is pretty much as its name suggests, huge and extremely salty. Its shoreline doesn't warrant much of a visit, although the lake's **Antelope Island** does afford the opportunity to view a glorious sunset and the state's only bison herd.

In the late 19th century, the lake's shores were lined with extravagant

Dinosaur skeletons at the Natural History Museum of Utah.

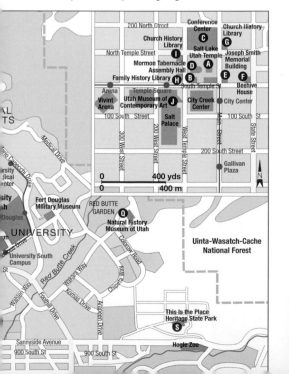

resorts, and steamboats and pleasure cruisers plied its waters. After years of mysterious decline, when enough of its contents evaporated to make it the world's second-saltiest body of water (after Israel's Dead Sea), it began equally mysteriously to refill in the 1980s; it reached its largest size in 1988, and began to recede again in 2002. Now roughly 75 miles (121km) long by 28 miles (45km) wide (though its size fluctuates), the lake has no outlet, so water flowing in from the Bear, Weber, and Jordan rivers steadily evaporates, leaving behind 2 million tons of salt each year – which contributes to a salt extraction industry.

Tiny **Great Salt Lake State Park** ❸ (tel: 801-828 0787, www.stateparks.utah.gov; daily 8am–sunset), 19 miles (30km) west of Downtown Salt Lake City via I-80, is the most convenient spot to take in the lake's bizarre charms, though **Antelope Island State Park** ❹ (tel: 801-725 9263; daily 6am–10pm), 40 miles (64km) north of Salt Lake City, is more attractive. The island terrain is dramatically different to that of the Salt Lake Valley, with clusters of red sand dunes, rocky ridges, and even small depressions of stinky marshland. Besides the experience of floating in water so dense with minerals you can barely sink, the island affords views of glorious lake sunsets and is also home to the state's only wild bison; from the 12 animals introduced in 1893, the herd has grown to between 500–700.

ALPINE LOOP

The 20-mile (32km) **Alpine Loop Scenic Drive** (open late May to late Oct), snakes through the rugged alpine canyons of the Wasatch Range, just to the south of Salt Lake City, following Hwy-92. The highway climbs up American Fork Canyon around Mount Timpanogos, continues through Uinta National Forest then drops into Provo Canyon and joins US-189. From the northern end at Lehi, the first major attraction is the stunning subterranean passageways of **Timpanogos Cave National Monument** ❺ (tel: 801-756 5239, www.nps.gov/tica; daily May–Sept). Farther along lies **Sundance Mountain**

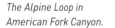
The Alpine Loop in American Fork Canyon.

☉ SPIRAL JETTY

One of the most unusual (and remote) sights on the Great Salt Lake is Robert Smithson's "Spiral Jetty," considered to be the sculptor's most important work. Created in 1970 on the northwest arm of the lake, near Rozel Point, this giant, swirling earthwork has been permanently visible since 2002, though it has at times been completely submerged. Smithson used some 6,000 tons of black basalt rock and earth from the adjacent shore to form a coil 1,500ft (457 meters) long and approximately 15ft (4.5 meters) wide. The site can be accessed via 16 miles (26km) of gravel roads from the Golden Spike National Historic Site Visitor Center, and has been maintained by the Dia Art Foundation since 1999 (www.diaart.org). Visitors must "leave no trace" at the site.

Resort **❻** (www.sundanceresort.com), best known for its annual film festival and its former owner Robert Redford (the Hollywood legend sold the resort in 2020). From here the route drops into the **Provo Canyon**, where the Provo River Parkway provides opportunities for hiking. **Provo ❼** itself is home to Utah Valley University and Brigham Young University, with the latter campus sprinkled with several free (and very interesting) museums; the **Museum of Paleontology** (tel: 801-422 3680; https://geology.byu.edu/museum; Mon–Fri 9am–5pm; free); the **BYU Museum of Art** (tel: 801-422 8287; https://moa.byu.edu; Mon, Thu, and Fri 10am–9pm, Tue and Wed 10am–6pm, Sat 10am–4pm; free); and the **Monte L. Bean Life Science Museum** (tel: 801-422 5050; https://mlbean.byu.edu; Mon–Fri 10am–9pm, Sat 10am–5pm; free).

WASATCH CANYONS

Salt Lake City is nestled at the base of the **Wasatch Mountains** – in winter, these are blanketed in the dry, light snow that draws skiers from all over the world to the low-key resorts of Alta, Snowbird, Brighton, and Solitude, as well as the more famous ones around Park City. The trails that serve skiers and snowboarders in winter give hikers access to alpine lakes and sweet-smelling stands of pines in the summer; mountain-bikers too can navigate the trails of the **Wasatch Canyons**.

The first water source used by Mormon pioneers settling the Salt Lake Valley in 1847, **City Creek Canyon ❽** is heavily used by local bikers, walkers, and joggers today, as the eight miles (13km) of paved Canyon Road begin just northeast of downtown beside Capitol Hill. Better hiking trails, featuring unbeatable views over the Salt Lake Valley, can be found in **Mill Creek Canyon ❾** to the southeast. It's also a good choice for mountain bikers, but if you're going to visit just one of the

Wasatch Canyons – even for a short hike – it should be **Big Cottonwood Canyon ❿**. Less developed than Little Cottonwood and also unscarred by mining activities, it's just a thirty-five minutes drive from downtown Salt Lake City (via Hwy-190). Of the two ski resorts in Big Cottonwood, **Brighton ⓫** (https://brightonresort.com) has taken advantage of its proximity to Salt Lake by becoming the local boarders' hill, tapping into the large population of school-age riders by providing cheap lift tickets. **Solitude ⓬** (www.solitude-mountain.com) meanwhile, could be fairly described as the most low-key place to ski in the Wasatch Canyons. From June to October, **Guardsman Pass Road**, which connects Big Cottonwood to Park City is open. There's a pull-out just below the top of the pass on the Park City side where you can park your car and take a short, steep hike to fantastic views of the ski-lifts, canyon hiking trails, and some tiny but beautiful alpine lakes.

About forty minutes' southeast of downtown Salt Lake, **Little Cottonwood**

Downtown city skyline of Salt Lake City with the Wasatch mountains in the background.

○ Eat

It's worth driving up scenic Emigration Canyon, on the east side of Salt Lake City, to eat at **Ruth's Diner** (4160 Emigration Canyon Road; tel: 801-582 5807; www.ruthsdiner.com; Mon, Thu and Sun 8am–9pm, Fri and Sat 8am–10pm), a quintessential Salt Lake breakfast spot since 1930. With a lovely outdoor patio, set in and around old railroad carriages, Ruth's serves up a wide selection of home-style roasts and chops, great salads and some of Utah's best breakfast plates. All breakfasts come with their celebrated fluffy delights, "Mile High biscuits."

The winding road to the Deer Valley Ski Resort.

Canyon boasts Utah's two finest ski areas. **Snowbird** (tel: 800-640 2002, www.snowbird.com) was created in 1971 by millionaire mountaineer-adventurer Dick Bass, the first man to summit the highest peak on each of the seven continents. In contrast, the first lift carried skiers up the slopes of **Alta** ⑭ (tel: 801-359 1078, www.alta.com) in 1937, and the resort has done its best to remain enveloped in a time-warp ever since. The lodging is defiantly old-world, with not so much as an elevator to be seen, and the slopes are completely snowboard free.

PARK CITY

Park City ⑮ is the largest ski area in Utah. The first mining camp here, just 30 miles (48km) east of downtown Salt Lake City, was established in the late 1860s. In 1872, George Hearst laid the foundations of the Hearst media empire by paying $27,000 for a claim here that became the Ontario Silver Mine, worth $50 million. Today Park City's restored Main Street now makes only token gestures towards mimicking the mountain mining community it used to be, with stores and restaurants instead striving to emulate the upscale ski resorts found elsewhere in the Rockies. Obviously, though, the ritzy stores and restaurants wouldn't exist if not for the town's glorious mountain environment. In summer there's decent hiking and truly phenomenal lift-served mountain biking. The three local ski areas – **Park City Mountain** (www.parkcitymountain.com), **The Canyons** (now part of the former), and **Deer Valley** (www.deervalley.com) – each has its own charms and quirks of character. There's no clear consensus over which is the best of the three, but fortunately all are close enough to try even if you are only staying a short while. Nearby **Utah Olympic Park** hosted the 2002 Winter Olympics and though it serves today as a training facility it contains the free Alf Engen Ski Museum, and the Eccles Salt Lake 2002 Olympic Winter Games Museum (both daily 9am–6pm), plus offers guided tours (https://utaholympiclegacy.org/activity/summer-guided-tours).

○ SUMMER IN PARK CITY

Just like winter, summer in Park City, also revolves to a large extent around the ski resorts' chairlifts. Both the PayDay Express and Crescent Express at Park City Mountain Resort, and the Silver Lake Express and Sterling Express at Deer Valley give hikers and bikers access to some amazing trails among the ski runs and old closed-down mines high above town. Bikers after a real leg workout can take on steep trails like the Sweeney Switchbacks. Two places with large selections of good rental bikes are Jans Mountain Outfitters, 1600 Park Avenue (www.jans.com) and Cole Sport, 1615 Park Avenue (www.colesport.com). Other staple activities in and around Park City include whitewater rafting and fly-fishing on the nearby Provo and Weber rivers.

Medicine Bow Mountains.

SOUTHERN WYOMING

Pronghorn antelope all but outnumber people in wide-open Wyoming, the ninth largest but least populous state in the union, with just over 581,000 residents.

This is classic cowboy country, replete with dude ranches, rodeos, and country-music dance halls, and the inspiration behind the TV series *Shane and The Virginian*, as well as countless Western novels. The state emblem, seen everywhere, is a hat-waving cowboy astride a bucking bronco, and a favorite bumper sticker reads, "Wyoming is what America used to be."

Unlikely as it may seem, this conservative state was the first to grant women the right to vote in 1869 – a full half-century before the federal government. This was done on the grounds that the enfranchisement of women would attract settlers and increase the population, thereby hastening statehood (which came in 1890). The "Equality State" also elected the first female US governor, Nellie Tayloe Ross, in 1924. Today the home state of former vice president Dick Cheney is solidly Republican.

Geologically, Wyoming is effectively a giant plateau broken by a series of precipitous mountain ranges, with its eastern third being high-elevation prairie – a sea of rolling grassland and scrub. All roads tend to lead to Yellowstone (see page 203) and Grand Teton (see page 198) national parks, but southern Wyoming is rich in history; the state capital, Cheyenne, is here, along with numerous forts and towns associated

with the Oregon Trail, the 19th-century route to the West Coast.

CHEYENNE

Established in 1867 as little more than a hardscrabble camp for workers on the Union Pacific railroad, **Cheyenne ❶** as the current capital of Wyoming has grown to a population of around 65,000, though its sleepy center rarely feels busy. Much activity revolves around the F E Warren Air Force Base, one of the nation's largest intercontinental missile bases. Cowboy culture is big

⚙ **Main attractions**

Cheyenne Frontier Days Old West Museum
Flaming Gorge National Recreation Area
Fort Laramie National Historic Site
Fossil Butte National Monument
Independence Rock
National Historic Trails Interpretive Center
Snowy Range Scenic Byway

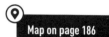

Map on page 186

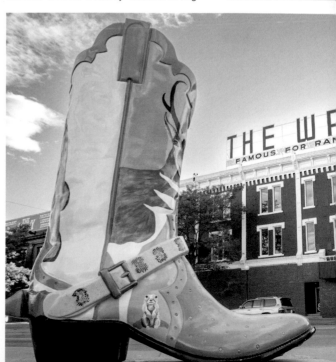

Shoe sculpture outside the Wrangler Building.

◎ Eat

For a slice for classic Americana in Cheyenne, belly up to the **Luxury Diner** (1401 West Lincolnway; tel: 307-638 8971, www.luxurydiner.com), housed in a converted railroad dining car from 1926. It serves all the home-made classics; huge breakfasts, excellent corned beef, BLTs with amazing sweet potato fries and the hefty "Luxury Burger." Great cheesecake, too. For something a little more contemporary, sample the excellent craft beers at **Freedom's Edge Brewing** (1509 Pioneer Avenue; tel: 307-635 9245; www. freedomsedgebrewing.com).

here, too, as the ranchwear stores and honky-tonks attest; furthermore, the 10-day Cheyenne Frontier Days festival celebrates cowboy culture in grand style, unchallenged as Wyoming's premier annual event.

Lincolnway, also known as 16th Street, is the retail and entertainment heart of town. Today only freight trains trundle through the handsome 1886 Union Pacific depot, now the **Cheyenne Depot Museum** (121 West 15th Street; tel: 307-632 3905; www.cheyennedepotmuseum.org; May–Aug Mon–Fri 9am–6.30pm, Sat 9am–5pm, Sun 11am–3pm; Sept–Apr Mon–Fri 9am–5pm, Sat 9am–3pm, Sun 11am–3pm), though it still anchors Cheyenne's compact downtown. If you're short of time, book a trip on the **Cheyenne Street Railway Trolley**, a 90-minute "Wild West Trolley Tour loop," beginning and ending outside the museum (see www.cheyenne.org/things-to-do/cheyennetrolley for the latest schedule).

A few blocks north of the station, the elegant but restrained Renaissance Revival-style **Wyoming State Capitol**, with its distinctive gold-leaf smothered dome, was completed in 1890 (200 West 24th Street; tel: 307-777 5861; www.wyomingcapitolsquare.com; open for self-guided tours Mon–Fri 8am–5pm;). Nearby **Wyoming State Museum** (2301 Central Avenue; tel: 307-777 7022; https://wyomuseum.wyo.gov; Mon–Sat 9am–4.30pm; free), chronicles the history of the state with hands-on displays, and special emphasis on its mineral resources and its Native American cultures – don't miss the Great Turtle Petroglyph. Two blocks away, the stately Georgian-style **Historic Governors' Mansion** (300 East 21st Street; tel: 307-777 7878; June–Sept Mon–Sat 9am–5pm, Sun 1–5pm; Dec and Jan–May Wed–Sat 9am–5pm; free) was completed in 1904, its period rooms reflecting the modest tastes of its tenants. The governors moved out in 1976.

Frontier Days transforms the town every July, but at other times you can visit **Cheyenne Frontier Days Old West Museum**, in Frontier Park (4610 Carey Avenue; tel: 307-778 7290; www.cfdrodeo.com/cfd-old-west-museum; daily 9am–5pm), which chronicles the history of the

◎ FRONTIER DAYS

Founded back in 1897 as a way to boost the local economy, **Cheyenne Frontier Days** (www.cfdrodeo.com) in late July is now one of the nation's premier Western festivals (hence its slogan, "the daddy of 'em all"), attracting thousands to its huge outdoor rodeo, big-name country and western concerts, parades, chuckwagon races, air shows and cook-outs. The action takes place at the specially built grounds in Frontier Park on Carey Avenue, a couple of miles north of downtown Cheyenne. Things only calm down at breakfast time – when thousands of free pancakes are served up to replenish sugar reserves – and during the four stately parades of antique horse-drawn carriages, traps and buggies, which start out at 9.30am on Tuesday, Thursday and on both Saturdays.

festival and displays a wonderful collection of vintage stagecoaches and horse-drawn carriages from the 1860s on. Look out also for a rare elk hide painting by Shoshone leader Chief Washakie.

WEST TO LARAMIE

The 50-mile (80km) drive west from Cheyenne to Laramie is quickest via I-80, but Hwy-210 (Happy Jack Road), which runs parallel and just to the north, is worth taking for the better scenery. The highway undulates across familiar Wyoming grasslands and plains studded with bizarrely shaped boulders and outcrops. Twenty-two miles (35km) before Laramie, the twin reservoirs at **Curt Gowdy State Park ②** (1264 Granite Springs Road; tel: 307-632 7946) are set in the foothills of the Laramie Mountains. Named for a television sportscaster and Wyoming native, the park is primarily known for rainbow trout and kokanee salmon fishing, boating, and water-skiing (no swimming allowed), while hikers ply the surrounding hills.

The Arapaho word *vedauwoo* (pronounced vee-duh-voo) means "land of the earthborn spirits," and neatly describes the unique granite formations that mark the **Vedauwoo Recreation Area ③** (I-80 exit 329; tel: 307-745 2300; www.vedauwoo.org), 15 miles (24km) east of Laramie in the Medicine Bow-Routt National Forest. Once a sacred site for young indigenous men seeking visions and enlightenment, Vedauwoo now draws rock climbers who want to tackle the piled up mushroomed rock formations, hike around them, picnic beside them, or just ride mountain bikes on the area trails. Beginning just inside the pay-entrance to Vedauwoo is a trailhead which leads to the much-visited Turtle Rock loop trail (2.8 miles/4.5km), allowing a circumnavigation of the area's landmark rock feature. To reach Vedauwoo from Happy Jack Road, turn south onto unsealed County Road 700.

LARAMIE

Founded in 1868 as another "Hell on Wheels" camp for the Union Pacific railroad, **Laramie ④** is far more genteel today thanks to the **University of Wyoming** (UW), whose campus

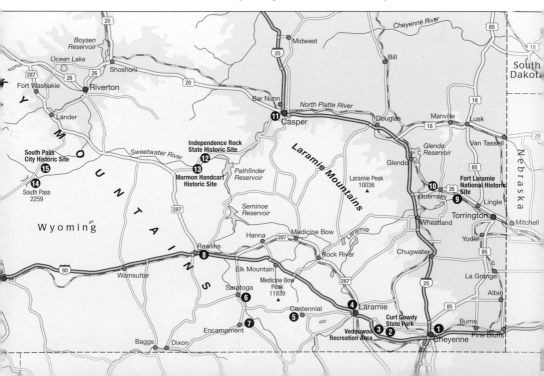

○ Drink

Laramie's oldest tavern, the **Buckhorn Bar & Parlor** (114 Ivinson Street; tel: 307-742 3554; www.buckhornbarlaramie. com) is a classic, open since 1900 and sprinkled with historic relics. It's open daily 8am to 2am. A short drive south on I-80, the **Cavalryman Steakhouse** (4425 South 3rd Street, US-287; tel: 307-745 0141, www. wyomingsteakhouse.com) is an atmospheric spot for a tasty Western steak, an old, wood-paneled clubhouse on the former site of Fort Sanders.

Red Canyon.

spreads east from the town center. At first Laramie seems typical of rural Wyoming, but behind downtown's Victorian facades lurk vegetarian cafés, day spas, and secondhand bookstores. The pleasant campus is home to a handful of free museums, the best of which is the **Geological Museum** (1000 East University Avenue; tel: 307-766 2646; www.uwyo.edu/geomuseum; Mon–Sat 10am–4pm; free), home to some marvelous fossilized dinos, including a rare 75-foot (23-meter) apatosaurus (brontosaurus) skeleton, the most complete specimen ever found (aka "Big Al"), and a collection of 50-million-year-old freshwater fossil fish. The **Art Museum** (2111 East Willett Drive; tel: 307-766 6622; www.uwyo.edu/artmuseum; Tue–Sat 10am–5pm; free) is housed in the futuristic Centennial Complex, which also contains the American Heritage Center, and features nine galleries housing a series of changing exhibits throughout the year.

The impressive Victorian stone structure which houses the **Laramie Plains Museum** (603 East Ivinson Avenue; tel: +1 307 742 4448; http://laramiemuseum.org; Mon–Sat 9am–6pm, Sun 1–4pm), was built in 1892 by Laramie's most revered business, banking, and civic magnate, Edward Ivinson. The house has been decked out with superb period furnishings, crockery, century-old kitchen appliances – even the Ivinsons' 50th anniversary formal dress – and today provides a fascinating glimpse into Laramie's past.

The centerpiece of the ambitious **Wyoming Territorial Prison Historic Site** (975 Snowy Range Road; tel: 307-745 6161; May–Sept daily 9am–4pm, Oct–Apr Wed–Sat 10am–3pm), just west of town, is the old prison itself, in business from 1872 to 1903. Its minuscule cells and rooms contain informative displays on the history of the site and some of its colorful ex-convicts – there's a whole room dedicated to Butch Cassidy, incarcerated here for 18 months in 1896 for cattle-rustling. Other buildings include the broom factory where prisoners were set to work, historic log structures, and the 1910 horse barn.

MEDICINE BOW MOUNTAINS

Just outside Laramie, Hwy-130 (aka the **Snowy Range Scenic Byway**) dips into the huge wind-gouged bowl of Big Hollow and starts the steep climb up the **Medicine Bow Mountains**, one of Wyoming's most picturesque drives. The byway cuts through the former mining town of **Centennial** ❺, where there's a handy **Visitor's Center** (tel: 307-742 9730; late May to early Oct Thu–Mon 9am–5pm; free), though the stark and often chilly beauty of the Snowy Range does not really become apparent until you reach Sugarloaf Recreation Area, roughly 20 miles (32km) farther on. The byway reaches its summit at 10,847-ft (3,306-meter) Snowy Range Pass nearby (closed in winter). Stop at the Libby Flats Observation Area, where the sweeping valley-forest panorama stretches clear to Colorado. Twelve miles beyond the western edge of the Medicine Bow Range, sleepy **Saratoga** ❻ is a spa resort known for its healing hot springs, while a short detour south of the byway leads to **Encampment** ❼, a virtual ghost town remembered mostly for its 1890s copper boom. Modern visitors can see such curiosities as a two-story outhouse and a folding oak bathtub at the **Grand Encampment Museum** (807 Barnett Avenue; tel: 307-327 5308; https://gemuseum.com; late May to Sept Tue–Sat 9am–5pm).

RAWLINS

There would be little reason to stop at the tiny prairie town of **Rawlins** ❽, 100 miles (161km) west of Laramie on I-80, but for the unmissable **Wyoming Frontier Prison** (500 West Walnut Street; tel: 307-324 4422; www.wyomingfrontierprison.org; Mon–Thu 9am–noon and 1–4pm, with exceptions). In service from 1901 till 1981, this huge jail with dingy cells, peeling walls and echoing corridors can make for a creepy experience – not least due to the fascinating anecdotes told by the exceptional guides. The darkest moment comes as the gas chamber (in use from 1937 until 1965) is revealed.

FORT LARAMIE

North of Cheyenne, Wyoming's largely untouched high prairies have preserved

A concord coach in a Cheyenne Frontier Days parade.

◎ **Eat**

Some 42 miles north of Rock Springs on US-191, the claim to fame of the tiny town of Farson is its giant ice cream cones, served at local landmark **Farson Mercantile** (4048 US-191; tel: 307-273 9511; https://farsonmerc.com; daily 10am–7pm, with exceptions). It also sells sandwiches, pizza, and a range of local gifts and souvenirs. The red-brick building dates back to the 1930s.

Independence Rock.

numerous sites associated with the great wagon trails that cut across the nation to California and Oregon in the mid-19th century. **Fort Laramie National Historic Site** (tel: 307-837 2221, www.nps.gov/fola; visitor center daily late May to early Sept 9am–7pm, rest of year 8am–4pm; free), established as a private fur-trading fort in 1834, later became the largest military post on the Northern Plains and an important stop on the trails. Nearby, the town of **Guernsey** ⑩ has two notable pioneer trail sites. **Register Cliff** (open sunrise–sunset; free), overlooking the North Platte River is covered with the signatures of emigrants who camped in the vicinity. After they left here, the pioneers were forced onto a narrow ridge of sandstone, their wagon wheels wearing ruts up to 5ft (1.5 meters) deep in some places. Visitors can still stand in the grooves at **Oregon Trail Ruts State Historic Site**.

CASPER

At **Casper** ⑪, Wyoming's second largest city, travelers on the Oregon Trail

left behind the Platte River, which they had followed for more than 400 miles (645km). **Fort Caspar** (4001 Fort Caspar Road; tel: 307-235 8462; http://www.fortcasparwyoming.com; May–Sept daily 8.30am–5pm, Oct–Apr Thu–Sat 8.30am–5pm) was established to protect the emigrants as they crossed the Platte for the long, dry trek across central Wyoming. The fort and city were originally spelled Caspar in honor of Caspar Collings, an Army officer who died in a battle with Native Americans near here. Get an overview of trail history at the **National Historic Trails Interpretive Center** (1501 North Poplar Street; tel: 307-261 7700; https://nhtcf.org; summer Tue–Sun 8am–5pm; rest of year Tue–Sat 9am–4.30pm; free). Other attractions include the **Nicolaysen Art Museum** (400 East Collins Drive; tel: 307-235 5247; https://thenic.org; Tue–Sat 10am–5pm) and the **Tate Geological Museum** (2332 Lisco Drive; tel: 307-268 2447; www.caspercollege.edu/tate-geological-museum; Mon–Sat 10am–4pm; free). Casper's biggest annual event is the **Central Wyoming Fair and Rodeo** (http://centralwyomingfair.com), held the last week of July.

TRACING THE OREGON-CALIFORNIA TRAILS

Some 58 miles (93km) southwest of Casper, imposing **Independence Rock** ⑫ (tel: 307-577 5150; open 24hr; free) was a major landmark on the Oregon-California trails and is also inscribed with pioneer graffiti. A few miles southwest, **Devil's Gate**, a gorge on the Sweetwater River, was another dramatic trail landmark, now accessible from the **Mormon Handcart Historic Site** ⑬ (47600 Hwy-220, Alcova; tel: 307-328 2953; daily summer 9am–9pm, rest of year 9am–4pm; free). This major Mormon pilgrimage site commemorates the Mormon "handcart pioneers" (who actually pulled their own carts all the way to Salt Lake City, horses being too expensive), and especially the tragic circumstances of those stranded near

here at Martin's Cove in 1856 – students re-enact portions of the trek each year.

Finally, **Historic South Pass** 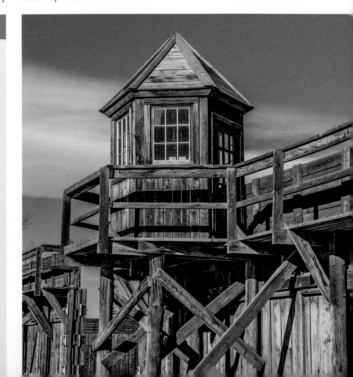 (elevation 7,412ft/2,259 meters), some 180 miles (290km) west of Casper, was the easiest Rockies crossing point used by trail emigrants (it's the lowest point on the Continental Divide), today traversed by Hwy-28, with wagon ruts still visible in several places. Nearby **South Pass City** (tel: 307-332 3684; www.southpasscity. com; May–Sept daily 10am–6pm) was built in 1867 during a gold rush but is now a ghost town, preserved as a state historic site with about two dozen of its original 300 structures still standing.

SOUTHWEST WYOMING

Southwest Wyoming is anchored by the small city of **Rock Springs**, though the real draws lie in the surrounding countryside. Hwy-191 south of Rock Springs (aka **Flaming Gorge-Green River Scenic Byway**), and Hwy-530 south of Green River, are the main gateways to the **Flaming Gorge National Recreation Area** (https://utah.com/flaming-gorge), named by explorer John Wesley Powell for its bright red canyons. Inspiring views can be found at Firehole Canyon (off Hwy-191), and various fishing and boating rentals are available at several marinas. The river hasn't been free running since the dam at Red Canyon in Utah was completed in 1964. The resulting Flaming Gorge Reservoir forms the centerpiece of the recreation area, with the **Red Canyon Visitor Center** (Red Canyon Road, off Hwy-44; tel: 435-789 1181; Mon–Fri 10am–5pm, Sat and Sun 9am–6pm, with exceptions; free) on the Utah side boasting a dramatic overlook and attractive nearby campground.

Some 100 miles (161km) west of Rock Springs, **Fossil Butte National Monument** (tel: 307 877 4455; www. nps.gov/fobu; visitor center Mon–Sat 8am–4.30pm, with exceptions; free) a 1,000-foot (306-meter) high cliff, 10 miles (16km) west of Kemmerer, used to be covered by a vast freshwater lake. When the prehistoric lake dried up, it left behind an array of fossilized creatures. This is the home of the famous Green River Formation – the steep fossil beds that cap Fossil Butte itself.

A wooden lookout tower at Wyoming Territorial Prison.

Ø FORT BRIDGER

Some 76 miles (122km) southwest from Rock Springs on swift I-80, **Fort Bridger State Historic Site** (tel: 307-782 3842; grounds open year-round, buildings May–Sept daily 9am–5pm) is one of Wyoming's most fascinating relics of the Old West. Jim Bridger, the famous mountain man, teamed with his buddy Louis Vasquez to establish a trading post here for the growing emigrant traffic in the early 1840s. The post was favored not just by those bound for Oregon but by the growing ranks of Mormons headed west. Mormons wound up buying the fort in 1855 and torching it two years later in the face of federal pressures. The federal government took over, rebuilt the post, and ran it until it was abandoned in 1890. The restored site does an excellent job of interpreting the many chapters of Fort Bridger's past.

OREGON TRAIL

Like wagon ruts on the prairies, the Oregon Trail, extending 2,000 miles (3,220 km) from Missouri to the Pacific Northwest, left an indelible mark on the American West.

As early as the 1830s, fur trappers and missionaries spread word of the Oregon Country – a vast region of rich river valleys and snowy mountains, reaching from Russian Alaska to Spanish California. Never mind that the US and Britain disputed who owned it: by Manifest Destiny, Americans felt, Oregon was theirs. Hurt by the economic panic of 1837, midwestern farmers listened receptively to stories of the fertile Willamette Valley. Emigration societies lobbied Congress to encourage western settlement. Missouri Senator Thomas Hart Benton sent his son-in-law, the dashing explorer John Fremont, to survey the land between the Missouri River and the Rocky Mountains and publicize its potential as a western travel route.

THE GREAT EMIGRATION

In May 1843 the first pioneer party gathered near Independence, Missouri: an estimated 1,000 men, women, and children in 120 wagons accompanied by 2,000 horses and cattle. Guided at points by Protestant missionary Marcus Whitman and then by Whitman's Cayuse guide, Stickus, the party arrived in Oregon six months later, effectively doubling the territory's American population. The die was cast, and by the spring of 1845 some 3,000 pioneers were pointing their covered wagons toward Oregon. The next year, the Oregon Treaty officially awarded the land south of the 49th parallel to the United States.

Oregon trail parkway in Scotts Bluff National Monument, Nebraska.

Chimney Rock in the North Platte River Valley.

Entrance to Independence Rock State Historic Site.

A cascading waterfall on the Oregon Trail.

The Route

The trail the pioneers followed began at Independence, forded the Kansas River and then cut west via Fort Kearney along the Platte River for over 600 miles (966km), across Nebraska and into Wyoming; Independence Rock marked the halfway point. Fort Laramie, Wyoming, was the first place where wagon trains could obtain supplies, albeit at inflated prices. Fort Laramie was also where some pioneers reconsidered and turned their wagons back toward home. Pioneers crossed the Rockies at low, relatively gentle South Pass, but then had to brave the rugged terrain and river crossings of Idaho's Snake River country and the Blue Mountains before following the Columbia River west toward the Willamette Valley. The most formidable terrain lay near the trail's end. As the trail disappeared into the Columbia River gorge, pioneers were forced to float wagons, livestock, and themselves downstream on homemade rafts. Not all survived. Within a few years, the Oregon Trail journey grew easier. By the 1860s, 330,000 people had made the journey, and the time required to travel the trail had been cut from six months to three.

…unlight streaming through the water mist at Silver Falls
…the Willamette Valley in Oregon.

…sign pointing to Oregon Trail Road at Scotts Bluff
…ational Monument.

The ruins of a hospital at Fort Laramie National Historic Site.

A bison in front of Grand Teton Mountain range.

JACKSON HOLE AND GRAND TETON

The jagged tooth-like peaks of the Tetons, which stretch 40 miles (64km) north of the town of Jackson, make a magnificent spectacle, rising abruptly to soar 14,000ft (4,267 meters) above the valley.

Protected by the Grand Teton National Park, a string of gem-like lakes is set tight at the foot of the mountains. The region also encompasses the broad, sagebrush-covered Jackson Hole river basin (a "hole" was a pioneer term for a flat, mountain-ringed valley), broken by the gently winding Snake River, rich in elk, bison, and moose – it's a lot more common to see the latter here than in Yellowstone. The town of Jackson itself is the busiest base for summer tourism in the vicinity of the Tetons, and is also home to one of the Rockies' most challenging ski mountains, Jackson Hole Mountain Resort.

HISTORY

For thousands of years prior to the early 1800s, Native Americans held undisputed dominion over Teton country. They frequently crossed the passes into the basins on warring expeditions or to hunt and fish, but they didn't stay long. The winters were too severe in Jackson Hole for permanent settlement and the land was left virtually untouched.

The first European-American to see the 50-mile (80km) long valley was explorer John Colter, who visited its wonders in 1807. In subsequent years the region was traversed by Native American tribes such as the Bannock, Blackfeet, Crow, Gros Ventre and

Shoshone, and a handful of fur trappers – "Jackson's Hole" was named after "Davey" Jackson, who caught beavers here in the 1820s. By 1840, the fur trade's best days were over and most of the big companies, such as the one owned by Jedediah Smith, William Sublette, and Jackson, were dissolved. Teton country was then deserted for about 20 years except for bands of Native Americans who rode in to hunt and fish.

Unbelievable stories told by mountain men of the wonders of Jackson Hole country were confirmed by the

Main attractions
Grand Targhee Resort
Grand Teton National Park
Jackson Hole Mountain Resort
Jackson Lake Lodge
Jenny Lake
National Elk Refuge
Million Dollar Cowboy Bar
Mormon Row
Snake River float trip

Map on page 196

A stagecoach in downtown Jackson.

Hayden Expedition of 1871 and 1872, which filed the first official reports on Teton fossils, geology, and mammals. Homesteaders arrived in the valley in the 1880s, and the town of Jackson was named in 1893.

Creating a national park in Jackson Hole was discussed as early as 1890, but many of those interested in preservation owned ranches in the area that they felt should be protected. This distinguished the Tetons from Yellowstone, where no one had ever lived. The greatest single park benefactor was millionaire philanthropist John D. Rockefeller Jr, who in the 1920s began purchasing privately-owned lands within the area to preserve them (much to the disapproval of locals). Unaware of the operation at hand, Congress voted to create Grand Teton National Park in 1929. The park was about one-third the size of today's preserve, protecting only the immediate mountain range and very little of the valley floor. Rockefeller's land was initially used to create the separate 221,000-acre (89,000 hectare) Jackson Hole National Monument in 1943, but this was finally folded into the park in 1950.

JACKSON

Crammed with touristy boutiques, art galleries, Old West bars, and excellent restaurants, **Jackson ❶** makes for an enjoyable base, 5 miles (8km) from Grand Teton National Park's southern boundary. Centered around shady Town Square, which is marked by an arch of tangled elk antlers at each corner, the Old West-style boardwalks of downtown burst with visitors in summer. The free **Town Square Shoot Out** recreates a Western gunfight (Mon–Sat 6pm), and the family-friendly **Jackson Hole Rodeo** (447 Snow King Avenue; tel: 307-733 7927, http://jhrodeo.com; late May to early Sept Wed and Sat 8pm) adds to the Western kitsch. The **Jackson Hole Historical Society and Museum** (225 North Cache Street; tel: 307-733 2414; https://jacksonholehistory.org; Wed–Sat 10am–5pm, with exceptions) offers a look at life in the valley as it really was, from prehistoric times to the frontier era.

A bull elk in the snow.

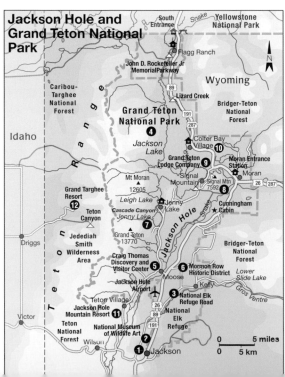

Just south of the town center, **Snow King Resort** (tel: 307-201 5464, https:// snowkingmountain.com) is an affordable, family-friendly ski resort that's also lit for night skiing; in summer you can take the chairlift up to the summit of Snow King Mountain (7,808ft/2,380 meters) for fine views of Jackson.

Around 2.5 miles (4km) north of the Town Square on US-191/US-89, in a building that looks like a castle, the **National Museum of Wildlife Art** ❷ (2820 Rungius Road; tel: 307-733 5771, www.wildlifeart.org; May–Oct daily 10am–5pm, Nov–Apr Tue–Sat 10am–5pm) houses an impressive art collection featuring wild animals from all over the world.

NATIONAL ELK REFUGE

North of Jackson town center, the **National Elk Refuge** ❸ (tel: 307-733 9212; www.fws.gov/refuge/national_ elk_refuge; sunrise to sunset; free), was established in 1912 at a time when nearly 20,000 elk in the Jackson Hole region were starving during a severe winter. Residents of the valley raised $1,000 to buy hay for them, and the Wyoming State Legislature appropriated $5,000 for additional feed. Congress then set aside 1,000 acres (405 hectares) as a winter refuge for elk. Since that time, the area has expanded to 24,700 acres (10,000 hectares). Around 11,000 elk now migrate to the refuge in late October and November, leaving for higher pastures in early May; a herd of bison of just over 1,000 also winter in the refuge, and bighorn sheep can also usually be seen on or near the Refuge Road during the winter months. Visitors may take sleigh rides among the elk from mid-December to early April (45min–1hr; daily 10am–4pm; $30). The **Historic Miller Ranch** (late May to mid-Sept daily 10am–4pm; free), a two-story log home built by pioneer Robert Miller and his wife in 1895, is also part of the refuge. Note that only the first 3.5 miles (5.6km) of the scenic Refuge Road that cuts through the preserve is open from December through April each year in order to protect the wintering wildlife.

⊙ Drink

Built in the early 1930s, Jackson's Million Dollar Cowboy Bar (25 North Cache Street; tel: 307-733 2207; www. milliondollarcowboybar. com), is a touristy but essential pit stop, with saddles for bar stools and live country and western; the nearby Silver Dollar Bar & Grill (50 North Glenwood Street; tel: 307-733 2190) really has silver dollar coins inlaid into its bar.

Grand Teton National Park in fall.

GRAND TETON NATIONAL PARK

The blue-gray, pyramid-like Tetons incorporated within **Grand Teton National Park ④** (www.nps.gov/grte; open year-round 24hr; $35 per vehicle, valid for seven days) are among the most memorable features of the American West. Soaring more than a mile (1.6 km) above the Sagebrush Flats and moraine lakes of Jackson Hole, the imposing peaks are a striking example of the fault-block type of mountain formation (in contrast to the results of volcanic action in Yellowstone). The Teton Range actually comprises 12 main peaks, though there are five clearly dominant summits; in order from south to north, these are Nez Perce (11,901ft/3,627 meters), Middle Teton (12,804ft/3,903 meters), Grand Teton (13,770ft/4,197 meters, naturally the tallest of the bunch), Mount Owen (12,928ft/3,940 meters), and Teewinot Mountain (12,325ft/3,757 meters).

There are only two entrance stations to the national park, where you pay to enter; one is at the southern end just beyond Moose on Teton Park Road, and the other is at Moran Junction, just after Hwy-26/289 branches off to the east, on the park's eastern edge. The third point of entry is at the north end of the park (US-191/US-89), from Yellowstone; there is no entrance station for Grand Teton here (if you're going to Yellowstone first, it's cheaper to buy a joint ticket for Grand Teton when there), but you can collect a park map and information nearby at Flagg Ranch Information Station (check website for current hours). The 26-mile stretch of US-26/89/191 that connects Moose and Moran Junction technically runs through the park, but you can use this section of road without going through an entrance station or paying for a permit.

MOOSE

Some 12 miles (19km) north of Jackson, Teton Park Road splits off US-191/US-89 and crosses the Snake River at **Moose**, the small national park headquarters. It's home to the beautifully designed **Craig Thomas Discovery**

A scenic trip along Snake River.

& Visitor Center ❺ (100 Discovery Way; tel: 307-739 3399; May–Oct daily 8am–5pm, with exceptions), where the park's geology, ecology, and human history (including some artifacts from the Vernon Indian Art Collection) are explained through illuminating exhibits, artwork, and movies. It also has free wi-fi.

Nearby, **Menors Ferry Historic District** on the Snake River preserves Bill Menor's 1894 homestead cabin and store, and the 1916 Maud Noble Cabin, with exhibits on the portentous meeting that took place here in 1923 to discuss the formation of the park. A little farther north on main US-191/US-89, you can detour to **Mormon Row Historic District ❻**, a short drive off the highway via Antelope Flats Road. This is where Mormon homesteaders settled in the early 1900s, and several timber barns and homes remain standing; look for the Moulton Barn, positioned photogenically with the snow-capped Tetons in the background.

JENNY LAKE

From Moose, Teton Park Road continues 8 miles (13km) north to crystal-clear **Jenny Lake ❼**, a hub for boating, kayaking, and wonderfully scenic hiking trails that is subsequently heavily overcrowded in the summer peak season. Drivers can enjoy the 5-mile (8km) Jenny Lake Scenic Loop (one-way southbound), which provides a few overlooks of the mountains soaring above the lake's southwest shore.

Head to the **Jenny Lake Visitor Center** (403 South Jenny Lake Drive; tel: 307-739 3392; mid-May to late Sept daily 9am–5pm, with exceptions) for information about ferries across the lake (https://jennylakeboating.com). Take the ferry for a face-to-face encounter with towering, partly hunch-backed Grand Teton, Wyoming's second highest mountain, and, at Inspiration Point, a 1-mile/1.6km uphill hike from the dock via cascading Hidden Falls

(also reachable by a 2-mile/3.2km hike along the south shore of the lake). Note that at peak periods in July you might have to wait more than an hour to take the ferry. You can also take a one-hour scenic cruise of the lake here.

JACKSON LAKE

From Jenny Lake, Teton Park Road continues north (via a series of overlooks) to **Jackson Lake**, the largest body of water in the region. En route, a narrow side road up **Signal Mountain ❽** (7,727ft/2,355 meters) offers a breathtaking panorama of the Tetons and especially the wide valley of Jackson Hole. Once you've crossed Jackson Lake Dam and rejoined US-191/US-89 north, the **Jackson Lake Lodge ❾** (100 Jackson Lake Lodge Road; tel: 307-543 3100; www.gtlc.com) is an essential stop even if you're not staying here. A gorgeous park hotel, built in 1955, it offers fabulous views of the mountains from its bar and back terrace. Nearby Oxbow Bend Turnout on the Snake River is a good place to spot wildlife in the early morning.

Paddleboarding on Jackson Lake.

Another 5 miles (8km) north is **Colter Bay Village** , containing stores, a gas station, cabins, and a marina where you can rent boats. The **Colter Bay Visitor Center** (640 Cottonwood Way; tel: 307-739 3594; mid-May to early Oct daily 8am–5pm) displays 35 artifacts from the David T. Vernon Indian Arts Collection, an ensemble of rare Native American artwork donated to the park by billionaire Laurance Rockefeller in 1976. From here it's just 18 miles (29km) north to Yellowstone South Entrance.

SKI RESORTS

Other than Snow King within Jackson itself, the region offers two excellent ski resorts, increasingly also operating as bases for summer activities. Jackson Hole Mountain Resort is a massive mountain with a huge vertical drop and terrain best suited to upper intermediate to extreme downhillers; Grand Targhee on the west side of the Teton range has less development and mind-boggling snow statistics.

Teton Village lies at the base of **Jackson Hole Mountain Resort** (tel: 307-733 2292; www.jacksonhole.com). In the summer you can ride the Aerial Tram straight up to Rendezvous Mountain for hiking and mind-bending views, or the Bridger Gondola to Gondola Summit for fine dining (you can also hike between the two points). There's also a popular downhill bike park on the slopes, while back in Teton Village kids will enjoy the pop jet fountains, climbing wall, and bungee trampolines.

Grand Targhee Resort (3300 Ski Hill Road, Alta; tel: 307-353 2300; www.grandtarghee.com) can be visited from Jackson too, as it's about an hour's drive away – it's in Wyoming but can only be accessed from the Idaho town of Driggs. Storms strafe the west side of the Tetons all winter long, giving rise to the local expression "a three-inch day" – a day spent skiing in snow three inches above your belly button. So while accommodation is limited and there's no real nightlife to speak of, this is the perfect resort for those who look forward to a full day of intense skiing or boarding, just to do it all over again the next day.

The hiking trails in Grand Teton National Park offer some stunning views.

⊘ GRAND TETON HIKES

Hiking trails in Grand Teton National Park waste no time in getting to the highlights. To climb one of the craggy Tetons themselves you need to be an experienced mountaineer: guides can usually take fit newbies up Grand Teton in two days after two days of training – contact Exum Mountain Guides (South Jenny Lake; tel: 307-733 2297; http://exumguides.com). Easier hikes include Leigh Lake Trail (1.8 miles/2.9km round-trip), a popular walk following the sandy beaches of String Lake up to Leigh Lake, where the imposing Mount Moran bursts out dramatically from the shore. The Taggart Lake-Bradley Lake Loop Trail is a moderate hike of just over 5 miles (8km) up an aspen-covered moraine and around these two lakes at the base of the Tetons; expect lots of wildlife and wildflowers en route. The Phelps Lake Overlook Trail is a pleasant stroll of just under 2 miles (3.2km) round-trip from the Death Canyon Trailhead, with views of the lake, the canyon and Jackson Hole. The Death Canyon Trail (7.9 miles/12.7km round-trip) is a more adventurous, but suitably rewarding amble up the macabrely named Death Canyon itself, reaching a verdant plateau on a well-graded trail adjacent to crashing creek waters and spectacular views of Phelps Lake and the surrounding peaks (2,100ft/640 meters elevation gain).

SNAKE RIVER

Grand Teton National Park and Jackson Hole have no monopoly on the Snake River, one of the cleanest rivers in the country. Only 40 of its 1,000 miles (1,609km) pass through Jackson Hole on its journey from the Continental Divide near Yellowstone National Park to its confluence with the Columbia River near Pasco, Washington.

The Snake harbors a wealth of aquatic life, owing to the enriching quality of the abundant shoreline. The fish, in turn, become a tasty meal, and not only for skillful anglers. Herons, mergansers, eagles, ospreys, otters, and other terrestrial predators also rely on the park's aquatic food pyramid. Of the several varieties of game fish luring thousands of fishermen to the waters of the Tetons, the Snake River cutthroat trout – found only in the Snake's watershed – is unique. Fishing regulations within the park conform to Wyoming law.

A highlight of the region is to take a float trip on the Snake River. As the Teton range glides by, you may see bald eagles, ospreys, moose, Canada geese, beaver, otters, and a variety of ducks in the same primitive setting appreciated by the territory's first inhabitants. For a truly exciting experience, go on a whitewater excursion between Hoback Junction and Alpine, where the Snake River Canyon constricts the river into producing mostly Class-III rapids.

Among the long-time reliable operators for both float and rafting trips are Barker-Ewing (945 West Broadway, Jackson; tel: 307-733 1000; www.barker-ewing.com), Dave Hansen Whitewater (225 West Broadway, Jackson; tel: 307-733 6295; www.davehansenwhitewater.com), and Sands Whitewater & Scenic River Trips (1050 South Hwy-89, Jackson; tel: 307-733 441; www.sandswhitewater.com).

Another alternative to getting onto the river is in a kayak or canoe; Rendezvous River Sports and Jackson Hole Kayak School (945 West Broadway, Jackson; tel: 307-733 2471; www.jacksonholekayak.com), offers instruction and river trips.

Skiiers contemplate the Tetons.

Yellowstone National Park's Grand Canyon.

YELLOWSTONE NATIONAL PARK

America's oldest and easily its most famous national park, Yellowstone National Park attracts millions of visitors every year for good reason; the sheer diversity of what's on offer is mind-bending.

Not only does Yellowstone deliver jaw-dropping mountain scenery, from the scintillating colors of the Grand Canyon of the Yellowstone to the deep-azure Yellowstone Lake and wildflower-filled meadows, but it's jam-packed with so much wildlife you might think you've arrived at a safari park. Shambling grizzly bears, vast herds of heavy-bearded bison (buffalo) and horned elk mingle with marmots, prairie dogs, eagles, coyotes, and more than a dozen elusive wolf packs on the prowl. What really sets Yellowstone apart, however, is that this is one of the world's largest volcanic zones, with thermal activity providing half the world's geysers, thousands of fumaroles jetting plumes of steam, mud pots gurgling with acid-dissolved muds and clays, and, of course, hot springs. The park might not look like a volcano, but that's because the caldera is so big – 34 by 45 miles (54 by 72 km) – and because, thankfully, it hasn't exploded for 640,000 years.

MAMMOTH HOT SPRINGS

The small village-like center of **Mammoth Hot Springs ❶** (with lodgings, general stores, and gas station), at the northern tip of the Yellowstone Loop Road, was once Fort Yellowstone, with most of the stolid buildings constructed here between 1891 and 1913 now used

Canary Spring.

for park administration. Elk are often seen grazing on the grass in winter. Today, the old bachelor officers' quarters of 1909 house the **Albright Visitor Center** (tel: 307 344 2263; daily 9am–5pm), the park's sole year-round information center, with movies and exhibits on the human history of the park and a small art gallery of Yellowstone-related paintings (some by Thomas Moran). The main attraction here, though – the **hot springs** – are clearly visible south of the center; terraces of barnacle-like deposits cascade down a vapor-shrouded

Map on page 204

mountainside. Tinted a marvelous array of greys, greens, yellows, browns, and oranges by algae, they are composed of travertine, a form of limestone which, having been dissolved and carried to the surface by boiling water, is deposited as tier upon tier of steaming stone.

TOWER-ROOSEVELT AND THE LAMAR VALLEY

The main landmark of Yellowstone's Tower and Roosevelt area, 20 miles (32km) east of Mammoth Hot Springs, is the high peak of **Mount Washburn** ❷; its lookout tower can be reached by an enjoyable hike (5–6 miles/8–9.6km return, depending on which trailhead you use). For an easier hike, take the trail that leads down to the spray-drenched base of 132ft (40 meter) **Tower Fall**, 2.5 miles (4km) south of Tower Junction.

From Tower Junction, the Northeast Entrance Highway wanders through the meadows of serene **Lamar Valley** ❸ – often called "North America's Serengeti" for its abundant wildlife, where life-and-death struggles between predators (grizzlies, wolves, mountain lions) and prey (elk, pronghorn, mule deer and especially bison) play out daily. This is the most spectacular route to Montana, via the Beartooth Highway.

THE GRAND CANYON OF THE YELLOWSTONE

The Yellowstone River roars and tumbles for 20 miles (32km) between the

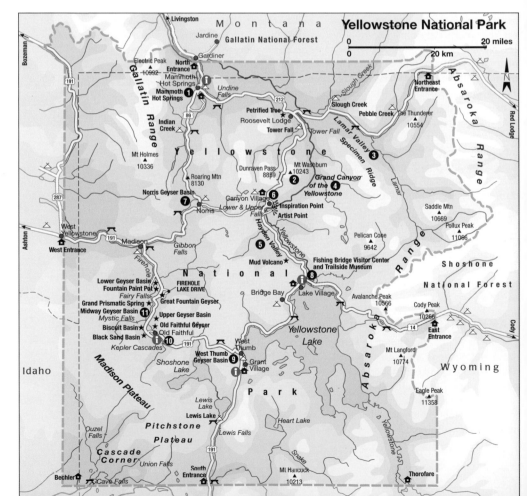

sheer red, pink and golden-hued cliffs of the **Grand Canyon of the Yellowstone ❹** (some 800–1200ft/244–366 meters high), its course punctuated by two powerful waterfalls: 109ft (33 meter) **Upper Falls** and its downstream counterpart, thunderous 308ft (94 meter) **Lower Falls**. On the south rim, Artist Point looks down hundreds of feet to the river canyon, where frothing water swirls between mineral-stained walls. Nearby, Uncle Tom's Trail descends steeply to a spray-covered platform in the canyon, gently vibrating in the face of the pounding Lower Falls. A few miles south, the river widens to meander through tranquil **Hayden Valley ❺**, one of the finest spots in Yellowstone to view wildlife from the road.

To get oriented, visit the **Canyon Visitor Education Center** (tel: 307-344 2550; late Apr to Oct daily 9am–5pm, with exceptions) in **Canyon Village ❻**, the most visitor-friendly center in the park; all the services, shops, and restaurants are close together on a horseshoe-shaped cul-de-sac. The education center highlights the natural wonders of the park and its "supervolcano" status through multimedia exhibits and films – it's the best overall introduction to Yellowstone.

NORRIS GEYSER BASIN

Some 12 miles (19km) west of Canyon Village is the less crowded **Norris Geyser Basin ❼**, where two separate trails explore a pallid landscape of whistling vents and fumaroles. **Steamboat** is the world's tallest geyser, capable of forcing near-boiling water over 300ft (91 meters) into the air; full eruptions are entirely unpredictable. The **Echinus Geyser** is the largest acid-water geyser known; every 35 to 75 minutes it spews crowd-pleasing, vinegary eruptions of 40 to 60ft (12–18 meters). Get oriented at the **Norris Geyser Basin Museum** (tel: 307-344 2812; late May to mid-Oct daily 9am–5pm), which chronicles the history of Yellowstone's geothermal activity. Nearby, the modest **Museum of the National Park Ranger** (tel: 307-344 7353; late May to late Sept daily 9am–4pm) charts the development of

Grand Prismatic Spring.

Eat

Each of Yellowstone's lodges and villages boasts official dining rooms, typically open May–Sept 7–10am, 11.30am–2.30pm and 5–10pm, offering similar menus of pricey but usually high-quality food: breakfast buffets, lunches and more elaborate dinners. Each location also usually features a workaday cafeteria open similar hours with cheaper options such as bison burgers and sandwiches, as well as a general store.

the park ranger since 1916, with exhibits and films in an old army log cabin.

YELLOWSTONE LAKE

North America's largest alpine stretch of water, deep and deceptively calm **Yellowstone Lake** fills a sizeable chunk of the eastern half of the Yellowstone caldera. At 7,733ft (2,357 meters) above sea level, it's high enough to be frozen half the year, and its waters remain perilously cold through summer. You'll see the lake 16 miles (27km) south of Canyon Village (passing the Mud Volcano and Sulphur Caldron), where the small **Fishing Bridge Visitor Center and Trailside Museum** ❽ (tel: 307-344 2450; late May to mid-Oct daily 9am–5pm, with exceptions) has displays on lake biology and stuffed waterbirds found around here, including Trumpeter swans. Nearby **Lake Village** has hotels and places to eat, while rowboats, along with larger motorboats and powerboats, can be rented from the Bridge Bay Marina, also the place to catch scenic cruises (mid-June to early Sept).

At **West Thumb Geyser Basin** ❾, 21 miles (34km) south from Lake Village, where hot pools empty into the lake's tranquil waters and fizz away into nothing, it's easy to see why early tourists would have made use of the so-called Fishing Cone by cooking freshly caught fish in its boiling waters. A couple of miles south, the **Grant Visitor Center** (tel: 307-344 2650; daily: late May to mid-Oct 9am–5pm, with exceptions) has a small exhibit examining the role of forest fires in Yellowstone, using the major fires of 1988 as examples. These destructive wildfires brought Yellowstone's environmental policies into sharp focus; park authorities insisted the burn was a natural part of the forest's ecocycle, clearing out 200-year-old trees to make way for new growth, but the sight of the country's flagship national park in flames was seen by some as a public relations disaster. The aftermath did indeed see a burst of new growth, and the scarred mountainsides have now largely recovered. The park has averaged 26 fires, and 5,851 acres (24 sq km) burned per year

Old Faithful geyser.

VISITING THE PARK

The key to appreciating Yellowstone is to take your time, plan carefully and exercise patience with the inevitable crowds. First-time visitors are often surprised – and disappointed – to find just how congested the park can get. Allow for a stay of at least three days to see the park fully. Most of Yellowstone's top sights are accessible from the 142-mile (228-km) Loop Road, a figure-of-eight circuit fed by roads from the park's five entrances, though the traditional North Entrance is the one marked by the iconic 1903 Roosevelt Arch. Although the speed limit is a radar-enforced 45mph, journey times are hard to predict. Wildlife traffic jams, usually caused by stubborn herds of bison parking themselves on the pavement, are not unusual and should be expected; it's advisable to avoid night driving in Yellowstone for the same reason.

since then, with only 2016 (when 70,285 acres/284 sq km burned) coming close to the 1988 disaster.

OLD FAITHFUL AND AROUND

For well over a century, the dependable **Old Faithful** ⑩ (17 miles/27km west from West Thumb) has erupted more frequently than any of its higher or larger rivals, making it the most popular geyser in the park – for many, this is what Yellowstone is all about. As a result, a half-moon of concentric benches, backed by a host of visitor facilities, now surround it at a respectful distance on the side away from the Firehole River. On average, it "performs" for expectant crowds every 65 to 92 minutes; approximate schedules are displayed nearby. The first sign of activity is a soft hissing as water splashes repeatedly over the rim; after several minutes, a column of water shoots to a height of 100 to 180ft (30–55 meters) as the geyser spurts out a total of 11,000 gallons (41,640 liters). As soon as it stops, everyone leaves, and you'll suddenly have the place to

yourself. **The Old Faithful Visitor Education Center** (tel: 307-344 2751; daily 9am–5pm, with exceptions; closed mid-Mar to mid-Apr and early Nov to mid-Dec) features interactive exhibits explaining Yellowstone's thermal features. Check out also the **Old Faithful Inn**, a Yellowstone landmark built in 1904, featuring the oldest log-and-wood-frame structures in the world and a seven-story lobby.

Two miles of boardwalks lead from Old Faithful to dozens of other geysers in the Upper Basin. If possible, try to arrive when **Grand Geyser** is due to explode. This colossus blows its top on average just twice daily, for 12 to 20 minutes, in a series of four powerful bursts that can reach 200ft (61 meters). Other highlights along the banks of the Firehole River, usually lined with browsing bison, include the fluorescent intensity of the **Grand Prismatic Spring at Midway Geyser Basin** ⑪, particularly breathtaking in early evening when human figures and bison herds are silhouetted against plumes of mineral spray.

Herd of bison at sunset in Hayden Valley.

THE HISTORY OF YELLOWSTONE

Yellowstone was America's first national preserve, setting the standard for what became the US National Park Service, but it has a complex history that goes back much further.

Native Americans have been hunting and fishing in the Yellowstone region for thousands of years – likely the ancestors of today's Nez Perce, Kiowa, Crow, Lakota Sioux and Shoshone tribes. In 1805, based on information received from Native Americans, explorers Lewis and Clark sent a progress report to President Jefferson that included a map on which "Yellow-Stone" appeared in English, thereby permanently naming the watercourse as the Missouri River's principal tributary. Seven years before, a full rendering of the river's name into English (from French) was made by explorer-geographer David

Theodore Roosevelt's Yellowstone camp in 1903.

Thompson, who had visited the Mandan villages near present-day Bismarck, North Dakota – the yellowish sandstone bluffs conspicuous along the lower course of the river supposedly inspired the name that was later also applied to the park.

In 1807, mountain man John Colter was the first European-American to actually visit Yellowstone, but no one believed his descriptions of the bubbling pools of "Colter's Hell." Though trapper Osborne Russell encountered the Tukudika band of Shoshone (meaning "Sheep Eaters") in the Lamar Valley in the 1830s, it wasn't until the Cook–Folsom–Peterson Expedition of 1869 and the Hayden Geological Survey of 1871 that the region was first surveyed in detail, and features like Old Faithful Geyser were named. Remarkably, President Grant created Yellowstone National Park a year later in 1872 to preserve it from development, the first in America. Native American tribes were effectively excluded from the national park (most had been decimated by disease by this point), and tourism gradually increased.

At first, management of the park was beset by problems, with Congress devoting enthusiasm but little funding toward its protection. Irresponsible tourists stuck soap down the geysers, ruining the intricate plumbing, and bandits preyed on stagecoaches carrying rich excursionists. Congress took the park out of civilian hands in 1886, and put the army in charge. By the time they handed over to the newly created National Park Service in 1917, the ascendancy of the automobile in Yellowstone had begun, and visitor numbers began to boom.

The conflict between tourism and wilderness preservation has raged ever since. The elimination of predators such as mountain lions and wolves in the 1920s allowed the elk herd to grow insupportably large; the former policy of permitting bears to feed from tourist scraps resulted in maulings. These issues have since been addressed (wolves were reintroduced in 1995, for example), but ecologists now warn that the park cannot stand alone as some pristine paradise, and must be seen as part of a much larger "Greater Yellowstone Ecosystem;" this notional ecosystem encompasses Yellowstone, the Tetons, the Snake River Valley south of Jackson to just over the Idaho border, and the northern Wind River Mountains.

GOLDEN GATE

A curious pronghorn.

NORTHERN WYOMING

Northern Wyoming is a thinly populated region of vast sagebrush plains, wild, untouched mountain ranges and small towns that retain the atmosphere and architecture of the Old West.

With millions of visitors pouring into Yellowstone and Grand Teton national parks every year, all roads tend to lead to the northwestern corner of the state, but there is plenty to see en route. Much of the state's history is associated with the great wagon trails that led across this vast, generally empty landscape, littered with old army forts, dinosaur fossils, and likeable Old West towns such as Cody and Buffalo. Without doubt the highlight of the region is the stunning Wind River Mountain Range, widely considered to be Wyoming's most scenic and challenging backcountry area for hiking, climbing, and angling. Flanked by a trio of friendly towns in Lander, Dubois, and Pinedale, the Wind Rivers are also home to large populations of Shoshone and Arapaho people, who have lived in central Wyoming for thousands of years. From the greenly forested Bighorn Mountains to the grassy flatlands and dry, windy buttes of the Wind River Indian Reservation, the terrain does not stay the same for long.

THE WAPITI VALLEY

The drive east from Yellowstone National Park to Cody is extremely beautiful, running alongside the Shoshone River through the open **Wapiti Valley**, which President Theodore Roosevelt once called "the most scenic

50 miles in the world." This stretch of US-14/16/20, known as the **Buffalo Bill Cody Scenic Byway**, is rich in wonderous wildlife such as bighorn sheep, pronghorn antelope and mule deer. Six miles (9.7km) west of Cody, the main features of **Buffalo Bill State Park** (tel: +1 307 587 9227; open 24hr) are the **Buffalo Bill Reservoir**, and the **Buffalo Bill Dam and Visitor Center** (4808 North Fork Hwy; tel: +1 307 527 6076; https://bbdvc.com; May–Sept daily Mon–Fri 9am–6pm, Sat and Sun 9am–5pm).

Main attractions
Bighorn Canyon National Recreation Area
Bighorn Mountains
Cody Nite Rodeo
Devil's Tower National Monument
Irma Hotel
Thermopolis
Wapiti Valley
Wind River Range
Wind River Wild Horse Sanctuary

Map on page 212

Buffalo Bill Dam in Cody.

○ **Drink**

Cody's most celebrated inn is the Irma Hotel (1192 Sheridan Avenue; tel: +1 307 587 4221; www.irmahotel.com), founded by Buffalo Bill himself in 1902. The Irma's most famous feature is its gorgeous imported European cherrywood bar in the Silver Saddle Saloon – a gift to Cody from Queen Victoria.

CODY

The "rodeo capital of the world" and located on the North Fork of the Shoshone River, the city of **Cody ❷** was the brainchild of a group of investors. In 1896, these investors persuaded "Buffalo Bill" Cody to become involved in their development company, knowing his approval would attract homesteaders and visitors alike; the city is named after him for the part he played in founding it. In summer, tourism is huge business here, but underneath all the Buffalo Bill-connected attractions and paraphernalia, Cody manages to retain the feel of a rural Western settlement. The wide main thoroughfare, Sheridan Avenue, holds souvenir and ranchwear shops and hosts parades during early

July's annual **Cody Stampede Rodeo** (tel: +1 307 587 5155; www.codystampederodeo.com). In summer the **Cody Nite Rodeo** takes place nightly at the open-air arena at 519 West Yellowstone Avenue on the western edge of town (June–Aug daily 8pm; same contact info).

Just east of the rodeo grounds off US-14, the 26 buildings gathered at **Old Trail Town** (1831 Demaris Drive; tel: +1 307 587 5302; www.oldtrailtown. org; mid-May–Sept daily 8am–6pm), include cabins and saloons frequented by Butch Cassidy and the Sundance Kid. The buildings date between 1879 and 1901, and include a re-created general store, trapper's cabin, and blacksmith's shop.

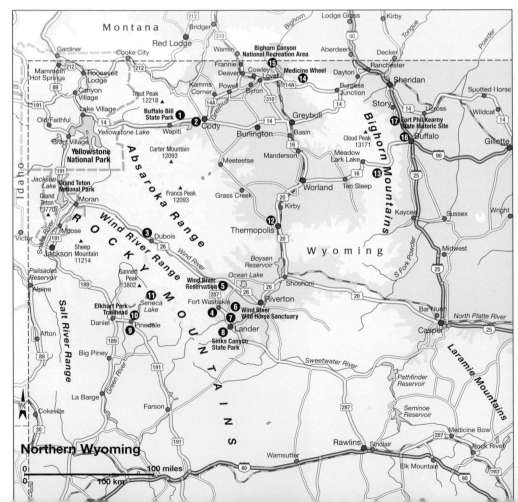

Northern Wyoming

BUFFALO BILL CENTER OF THE WEST

By far the biggest year-round attraction in Cody is the massive **Buffalo Bill Center of the West** (720 Sheridan Avenue; tel: +1 307 587 4771; www.centerofthewest.org; May to mid-Sept daily 8am–6pm; mid-Sept to Oct daily 8am–5pm; Mar, Apr, and Nov daily 10am–5pm; Dec–Feb Thu–Sun 10am–5pm), a complex of five interconnected museums. The most intriguing is the **Buffalo Bill Museum**, charting the extraordinary life of William Cody himself, from frontier legend to one of the first global celebrities thanks to his Wild West show. The **Plains Indian Museum** tackles aspects of Native American culture by theme not tribe (with just one tiny section on the wars of the 19th century). Its huge collection of rare artifacts ranges from headdresses and shields to clubs and painted buffalo hides. The **Whitney Western Art Museum** contains a high-quality collection of Western-themed paintings from Albert Bierstadt and Charles Russell, a whole room dedicated to Frederic Remington, John James Audubon engravings, George Catlin lithographs, and the iconic Medicine Robe by Maynard Dixon. The **Draper Natural History Museum** focuses on the fauna and flora of the Yellowstone region, while the **Cody Firearms Museum** is one of the largest collections of guns in the world.

WIND RIVER RANGE

If the throngs in Cody and the national parks have you yearning for isolation, consider a trip south to the **Wind River Range**. The "Winds" runs for around 100 miles (160km) and are home to over 40 mountains topping 13,000ft (3,962 meters) – including Wyoming's highest mountain, **Gannett Peak** (at 13,804ft/4,207 meters). Much of the range is encompassed by the Shoshone National Forest on the east side, and Bridger-Teton National Forest on the west. No roads cross the mountains, but there are some great bases from which to explore them, including Pinedale from the west, and Lander or Dubois from the east.

Young cowboys discussing a rodeo competition.

DUBOIS

The former logging town of **Dubois** ❸ ("dew-BOYS"), squeezed into the tip of the Wind River valley, is an oasis among the badlands. The town turned to tourism after its final sawmill closed in 1987; it doesn't hurt that it's located 60 miles (96km) southeast of Grand Teton National Park via dramatic Togwotee Pass (9,544ft/2,909 meters). Home to the biggest herd of bighorn sheep in the lower 48 states, Dubois celebrates that fact with the impressive **National Bighorn Sheep Center**, (10 Bighorn Lane; tel: +1 307 455 3429; https://bighorn.org; June–Aug daily 9am–5pm; Sept–May Tue–Sat 10am–4pm). Along with running 3–4-hour 4WD sheep-spotting tours (Nov–Mar only), the center has detailed exhibits on the majestic mascot of the Rockies.

WIND RIVER RESERVATION

Southeast from Dubois, the **Wind River Indian Reservation** ❹ is shared by the Eastern Shoshone and Northern Arapaho. The reservation is centered on the small town of **Fort Washakie** ❺, where the **Rupert Weeks Traditional Center** (90 Ethete Road; tel: +1 307 332 9106; Mon–Fri 8am–4.45pm; free) displays exhibits related to the Shoshone tribe. Ask here, or at the **Wind River Trading Co** (tel: +1 307 332 3267; Mon–Sat 9am–6pm, Sun 9am–5pm) on the main road, for directions to the Washakie Cemetery for the memorial to **Chief Washakie**, leader of the Shoshone in the 19th century, and the **Sacajawea Cemetery** (resting place of the Shoshone heroine). Some historians agree that the grave, with a headstone dated 1884, is Sacajawea's true resting place. Others insist that she died in 1812 near what is now Mobridge, South Dakota. Each June the reservation hosts Wyoming's largest Powwow, **Eastern Shoshone Indian Days**, a festival of dancing, games, and music (check https://windriver.org for details).

To the south lies the **Wind River Wild Horse Sanctuary** ❻ (Hwy-287; tel: +1 307 438 3838; www.windriverwildhorses.com; Mon–Fri 9am–5pm, Sat 9am–4pm, with exceptions) where guided tours take in herds of wild mustangs and a visitor center (free) explores Native American horse culture and history.

LANDER

Occupying a prime location for forays into both the Wind River Mountains and the Wind River Indian Reservation, the prosperous and friendly town of **Lander** ❼ is also a world-renowned rock-climbing hub. Lander's history is preserved on the edge of town at the **Museum of the American West** (1445 West Main Street; tel: +1 307 335 8778; www.museumoftheamericanwest.com; May–Oct Mon–Sat 9am–4pm), where 10 historic buildings portray pioneer life from 1880 to 1930. Next door, the **Fremont County Pioneer Museum** (1443 West Main Street; tel: +1 307 332 4137; https://fremontcountymuseums.com; Mon–Sat 9am–5pm) is crammed

A misty sunrise in the Wind River Range.

with local artifacts going back to pre-historic times.

Sinks Canyon State Park ❽ (tel: +1 307 332 6333; daily 6am–10pm; visitor center mid-May to mid-Sept daily 9am–5pm) offers easy to moderate hiking, biking, and even climbing – it's just 6 miles (9.7km) south of Lander via Hwy-131. Here the Middle Fork of the Popo Agie River (pronounced roughly "puh-PO-juh") flows down the canyon and disappears into a subterranean limestone cavern (the "Sinks"), reappearing another quarter-mile below in a calm pool (the "Rise") filled with huge rainbow trout; fishing is forbidden. The main wall and sandstone buttresses in Sinks Canyon are popular with rock climbers, though the most celebrated climbing area is at **Wild Iris**, around 25 miles (40km) south of Lander on Hwy-28.

PINEDALE

On the west side of the Wind River Range, a scenic 77-mile (124km) drive from Jackson on US-189/191, tiny **Pinedale ❾** offers excellent access to outdoor pursuits, while the **Museum of the Mountain Man** (700 East Hennick Road; tel: +1 307 367 4101; https://museumofthemountainman.com; May–Oct daily 9am–5pm), commemorates its role as a rendezvous for fur trappers in the 1830s. Hats and other products made from beaver fur are displayed, alongside several of the firearms favored by the fur-trappers. The prize piece, however, is a c.1853 rifle owned by legendary explorer and mountain man Jim Bridger. A 16-mile (26km) road winds east from Pinedale past **Fremont Lake** to **Elkhart Park Trailhead ❿**, from where horse-worn paths lead past beautiful **Seneca Lake ⓫** and up rugged Indian Pass to glaciers and snowy peaks.

THERMOPOLIS

The Wind River follows US-26 then US-20 north of the Wind River Reservation, carving an impressive and deep canyon through the Owl Creek Mountains. The river was dammed to form Boysen Reservoir in 1952, and north of here it eventually flows through the spa town of **Thermopolis ⓬** where it becomes known as the Bighorn River. The dominant feature of **Hot Springs State Park** (220 Park Street; tel: +1 307 864 2176; Mon–Fri 7.30am–4pm; free) is the sculpted mineral terraces of Big Spring; this gusher pours out 8,000 gallons (36 kiloliters) of water each day at temperatures of about 128°F (53°C). You can soak in the waters – renowned for their healing properties – at the **State Bath House** (Tepee Street; Mon–Sat 8am–5.30pm, Sun noon–5.30pm; 20min time limit; free), or try the waterslides and hot pools at two commercial complexes nearby: **Star Plunge** (https://star-plunge.com) and **Hellie's Tepee Pools** (https://tepeepools.com). There's also a bison herd in the park.

The **Hot Springs County Museum** (700 Broadway Street; tel: +1 307 864 5183; https://thermopolismuseum.

☉ Drink

Tiny Pinedale is remarkably well-served by bars and restaurants. Wind River Brewery (402 Pine Street; tel: +1 307 367 2337; www.windriverbrewingco.com) serves interesting craft beers, while local cowboys and tourists mingle at the "World Famous" Corral Bar (30 West Pine Street; tel: +1 307 367 2469) and Stockman's Saloon & Steakhouse (117 West Pine Street; tel: +1 307 367 3695; www.stockmans.biz).

Hot Springs State Park in Thermopolis.

com; Mon–Sat May–Sept 9am–5pm, Oct–Apr 9am–4pm) is also worth a look, with its Native American artifacts and displays of frontier life, including an elk hide painted by Chief Washakie and the original Hole-in-the-Wall bar of Butch Cassidy fame.

The **Wyoming Dinosaur Center** (110 Carter Ranch Road; tel: +1 307 864 2997; https://wyomingdinosaurcenter. org; daily mid-May to mid-Sept 8am–6pm, mid-Sept to mid-May 10am–5pm), displays 20 full-size dinosaur skeletons and is crammed with interpretive exhibits. Wyoming has become a dinosaur hotspot since the first major fossils were excavated in the 1870s – it even has a "state dinosaur," the triceratops.

BIGHORN MOUNTAINS

The massive and heavily wooded **Bighorn Mountains ⑬** – a spur of the main Rockies chain – soar abruptly from the plains to over 9,000ft (2,743 meters), marking the eastern side of the wide Bighorn Basin. Two scenic byways cut across the northern Bighorns:

Bighorn Canyon National Recreation Area.

US-14 (58-mile/93-km **Bighorn Scenic Byway**) and US Alt-14 (the 27-mile/43-km **Medicine Wheel Passage Scenic Byway**) are both accessed from I-90 some 13 miles/21km north of the unremarkable town of Sheridan. US Alt-14 is the most spectacular. The road (typically closed Nov–May due to snow), edges its way up Medicine Mountain, on whose windswept western peak the mysterious **Medicine Wheel ⑭** (1.5 miles/2.4km on gravel road, then a 3-mile/4.8km return hike; 24hr; free, rangers summer only 8.30am–6pm) – the largest such monument still intact – stands protected behind a wire fence. Local Native American legends offer no clues as to the original purpose of these flat stones, arranged in a circular "wheel" shape with 28 spokes and a circumference of 245ft (75 meters) – though the pattern suggests sun worship or early astronomy. Constructed between 1200 and 1700, accounts of its design published in 1885 mention a series of small huts, each one positioned at the end of a spoke, which may have functioned as sanctuaries for prayer and meditation.

Before US Alt-14 gets to Lovell, Hwy-37 turns north to the **Bighorn Canyon National Recreation Area ⑮** (tel: +1 307 548 5406; www.nps.gov/bica; open 24hr), an unexpected red-rock wilderness straddling the border between Wyoming and Montana. No road runs the full length of the canyon, which since being flooded by the 525ft (160 meter) Yellowtail Dam (only accessible from Montana) has become primarily the preserve of water-sports enthusiasts. The Devil's Canyon overlook, just off Hwy-37, three miles over the border into Montana, affords landlubbers an opportunity to gauge the knee-knocking 1000ft-plus (305-meter) drop into the abyss. The **Cal S. Taggart Bighorn Canyon Visitor Center** (tel: +1 307 548-2251; daily 8.30–4.30pm, with exceptions) is just east of Lovell on US Alt-14.

The southern Bighorns are traversed by a third route, US-16 between Worland and Buffalo. The 47-mile (76-km) **Cloud Peak Skyway Scenic Byway** winds through Ten Sleep Canyon and climbs high into the mountains with a summit of 9,666ft (2,946-meters) near Powder River Pass.

BUFFALO

Snuggled among the southeastern foothills of the Bighorn Mountains, easy-going **Buffalo** ⑯ remains largely unaffected by the bustle of the nearby I-90/I-25 junction; winters here are mild compared to other areas of Wyoming, thus prompting locals to refer to the town as the state's "banana belt." Although Main Street, now lined with frontier-style stores, used to be an old buffalo trail, the place was actually named after Buffalo, New York. The **Jim Gatchell Memorial Museum** (100 Fort Street; tel: +1 307 684 9331; https://jimgatchell.com; summer Mon–Sat 9am–5pm, Sun noon–5pm; rest of year Mon–Fri 9am–4pm), houses a fine collection of Old West curiosities pertaining to soldiers, ranchers, and Native Americans.

FORT PHIL KEARNEY

The remains of **Fort Phil Kearney** ⑰ (528 Wagon Box Road, Banner; tel: +1 307 684 7629; May–Sept daily 8am–6pm; Oct Wed–Sun noon–4pm), one of the bloodiest of the western army forts, stand 17 miles (27km) north of Buffalo, off I-90, on Hwy-193. Only operative from 1866 to 1868, it was repeatedly stormed by the Sioux, Apache, and Cheyenne, and finally destroyed by jubilant Sioux when it was abandoned in 1868. A museum beside the site of the partially rebuilt fort tells the story of the 1866 Fetterman Massacre, when Captain William Fetterman (who bragged that with 80 men he could defeat any amount of Native Americans in battle without trouble) ignored strict orders and was lured into the path of over 1,000 Sioux warriors. Fetterman and all of his 80 soldiers were killed, the first US Army defeat ever to leave not even a single survivor.

Devils Tower National Monument.

ⓞ DEVILS TOWER

Although not even remotely associated with the Rocky Mountains, **Devils Tower National Monument** (tel: +1 307 467 5283; www.nps.gov/deto; open 24hr) – tucked into the northeast corner of Wyoming – is one of the region's most intriguing natural attractions. The country's first national monument in 1906, it took Steven Spielberg's use of it in *Close Encounters of the Third Kind* to make this eerie 867ft (265-meter) volcanic outcrop a true national icon. Plonked on top of a thickly forested hill, itself a full 400ft (122 meters) above the peaceful Belle Fourche River, the tower resembles a giant wizened tree stump; but, painted ever-changing hues by the sun and moon, it can be hauntingly beautiful. Plains tribes such as the Arapaho and Crow still consider it sacred.

BUFFALO BILL

He was born William Frederick Cody in Iowa Territory in 1846, but the world came to know him as Buffalo Bill. To the millions who saw his Wild West show, he was the very embodiment of the Western frontier.

Though a great deal of his reputation was based on fancy – much of it of his own making – he was a true son of the West. Cody took his first step into legend at age 15 when he signed on with the Pony Express. For two years, he rode across the plains, evading Native Americans and road agents and once riding 320 miles (515km) in 22 hours when he found that his relief had been killed in a drunken fight. He later won acclaim as a Native American fighter, Army scout, and buffalo hunter and befriended such celebrated figures as Wild Bill Hickok and Kit Carson.

BIRTH OF A LEGEND

In 1869, while working as a scout in Nebraska, Cody was introduced to Ned Buntline, a writer who came West looking for material; Cody was just the type he was looking for. Upon returning East, Buntline penned dozens of novels featuring the young plainsman. The protagonist from the books was virtually unrecognizable as the real Buffalo Bill, but the character made him famous nonetheless. For a decade beginning in 1872, Cody spent part of each year acting in his own theatrical productions.

William "Buffalo Bill" Cody on horseback, leading a column of mounted soldiers.

The statue of Buffalo Bill in front of the historical center Cody that bears his name.

Buffalo Bill's Rough Riders Review, 1901.

oosed portrait of Buffalo Bill in 1907.

uffalo Bill sculpture at The Buffalo Bill Center of The
est in Cody.

The Buffalo Bill Center of the West includes five museums
and is the oldest in the West.

The Wild West Show

Cody soon came up with something more suited to his talents as a
showman. It was a rollicking, circus-like exhibition of riding, roping,
and shooting with real-life cowboys and Native Americans. He called it
Buffalo Bill's Wild West, and it ran for more than 20 years. In 1885 a
dead-shot named Annie Oakley joined the company. Even old Sitting
Bull joined for a time, although not before negotiating the right to sell
photographs of himself.

In 1887, the troupe made a triumphant tour of England. Queen
Victoria, breaking with tradition, attended the entire performance, and
was so enthralled that she invited Cody to perform at Windsor Castle.

The tour was Cody's crowning achievement, but his theatrical
success was marred by personal failure. Money passed through his
hands as quickly as it poured in, and he was forced to work off his
debts right up until to the end. He drank too much and became
estranged from his wife before dying in 1917 at the age of 71, at his
sister's home in Denver. He was buried on Lookout Mountain just
outside the city.

Chief Sitting
Bull signed on
with Buffalo
Bill's Wild
West Show,
negotiating
exclusive
rights over the
sale of
photographs of
himself.

Sunset over Mount Rushmore Memorial.

THE BLACK HILLS

An offshoot of the Rockies on the South Dakota-Wyoming border, the Black Hills rise like an island of granite in a sea of grass.

To the Sioux their value was and still is immeasurable, a kind of spiritual safe place where warriors went to speak with Wakan Tanka (the Great Spirit) and await visions. Assuming the Black Hills to be worthless, the US government signed the Treaty of Fort Laramie in 1868 with the Lakota, Yanktonai Dakota and Arapaho, ceding them to the Great Sioux Reservation. However, once the Custer Expedition of 1874 confirmed rumors of gold in the hills, it wasn't long before fortune-hunters came pouring in, and mining camps sprang up like weeds. Finally, in the controversial "Agreement of 1877," the US government unilaterally modified the 1868 treaty, clawing back the Blacks Hills – what the Sioux dubbed the "sell or starve" rider, and something they have protested ever since. In 1979 the Sioux famously rejected a government offer to recompense them $106 million for the loss of the Black Hills, believing that the land would one day be returned to them. The interest on the deal has by now compounded to well over $1 billion, and the land has yet to be returned.

Today, much of the region is encompassed within Black Hills National Forest. Even though they're mountains in the classic sense – the highest of the lot, Harney Peak, rises 7,242ft (2,207 meters) – they were dubbed Paha

The Needles Eye Tunnel.

Sapa, or Black Hills, as the blue spruce and Norway pine trees blanketing them appear black from a distance.

South Dakota's second largest settlement, Rapid City, is the region's commercial center, but apart from visiting family-oriented attractions such as nearby Reptile Gardens (www.reptile-gardens.com) and Bear Country USA (www.bearcountryusa.com), there's little reason to base yourself here. Indeed, though there's plenty of kitsch fun in the form of theme parks, crazy golf and the like throughout the Black Hills

⊘ Main attractions
Crazy Horse Memorial
Custer State Park
Deadwood
Jewel Cave National Monument
Lead
Mammoth Site
Mount Rushmore National Memorial
Spearfish Canyon
Wind Cave National Park

Map on page 222

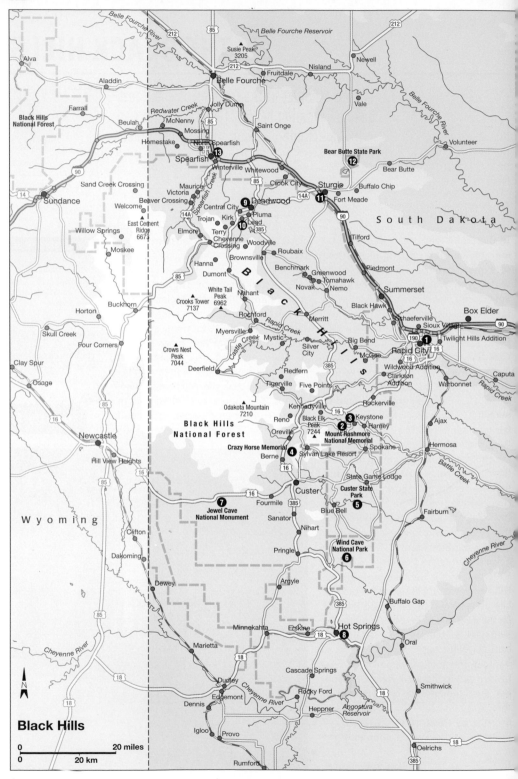

Black Hills

Alva
Aladdin
Beulah
Farrall
Black Hills National Forest
Redwater Creek
Jolly Dump
McNenny
Mossing
Homestake
North Spearfish
Spearfish
Winterville
Whitewood
Crook City
Belle Fourche
Susie Peak 3205
Fruitdale
Nisland
Newell
Belle Fourche Reservoir
Vale
Volunteer
Saint Onge
Bear Butte State Park
Bear Butte
Buffalo Chip
Sturgis
Fort Meade
South Dakota
Sand Creek Crossing
Sundance
Maurice
Victoria
Beaver Crossing
Welcome
East Cement Ridge 6673
Willow Springs
Moskee
Central City
Deadwood
Trojan
Kirk
Pluma
Lead
Elmore
Terry
Cheyenne Crossing
Woodville
Hanna
Brownsville
Roubaix
Dumont
Benchmark
Greenwood
Tomahawk
Nahant
Novak
Nemo
Tilford
White Tail Peak 6962
Crooks Tower 7137
Rochford
Merritt
Black Hawk
Summerset
Schaeferville
Sioux Village
Box Elder
Myersville
Mystic
Big Bend
McGee
Rapid City
Twilight Hills Addition
Horton
Buckhorn
Skull Creek
Four Corners
Crows Nest Peak 7044
Silver City
Wildwood Addition
Caputa
Clay Spur
Osage
Deerfield
Redfern
Tigerville
Five Points
Clarkson Addition
Warbonnet
Odakota Mountain 7210
Kennedyville
Reno
Black Elk Peak 7244
Keystone
Rockerville
Harney
Ajax
Newcastle
Black Hills National Forest
Oreville
Mount Rushmore National Memorial
Spokane
Hermosa
Hill View Heights
Crazy Horse Memorial
Berne
Sylvan Lake Resort
State Game Lodge
Fourmile
Custer
Custer State Park
Blue Bell
Fairburn
Jewel Cave National Monument
Sanator
Nihart
Clifton
Pringle
Wind Cave National Park
Dakoming
Dewey
Argyle
Buffalo Gap
Minnekahta
Erskine
Hot Springs
Oral
Marietta
Cascade Springs
Smithwick
Dudley
Edgemont
Rocky Ford
Dennis
Heppner
Angostura Reservoir
Igloo
Provo
Rumford
Oelrichs

Wyoming

Belle Fourche River
Cheyenne River
Rapid Creek
Castle Creek
Spearfish Creek
Battle Creek

0   20 miles
0   20 km

there's also plenty of history, and no place is much farther than a 90-minute drive from the show-stoppers of Mount Rushmore and its ambitious work-in-progress counterpart, the Crazy Horse Memorial. Yet it's the outdoor activities, rich wildlife, and extraordinary scenery that make the Black Hills special, from the bison herds of Custer State Park to the magical caverns of Wind Cave National Park.

RAPID CITY

Nestled on the eastern front of the Black Hills is **Rapid City ❶**, the largest settlement in the area and primary transport hub. Its historic Main Street still has an Old West feeling, and the **Journey Museum and Learning Center** (222 New York Street; tel: +1 605 394 6923; www.journeymuseum.org; Thu–Sat 10am–5pm, Sun 1–5pm), has fine collections on Black Hills history and Native American culture. The **Museum of Geology** (Technology Court, O'Harra Bldg, 3/F; tel: +1 605 394 2467; www.sdsmt.edu/Academics/Museum-of-Geology; Mon–Sat 9am–6pm, late May to early Sept, 9am–4.30pm early Sept to late May; free) on the South Dakota School of Mines and Technology campus offers an instructive overview of the geologic forces that shaped the hills and the prehistoric creatures that once roamed the area.

MOUNT RUSHMORE NATIONAL MEMORIAL

It's about 24 miles (39km) from downtown Rapid City to **Mount Rushmore National Memorial ❷** (13000 Hwy-244, Keystone; tel: +1 605 574 2523; www.nps.gov/moru; grounds open daily 5am–9pm, visitor center daily late May to mid-Aug 8am–10pm, mid-Aug to Sept 8am–9pm; Oct to late May 8am–5pm; free, parking charge), along Hwy-16 and scenic Iron Mountain Road (Hwy-16A).

One of America's best-known monuments, Mount Rushmore is unarguably the linchpin of the Black Hills' tourist circuit. The memorial was created by sculptor Gutzon Borglum, who chose the faces and heads of four certifiably great American presidents: George Washington, Thomas Jefferson, Abraham Lincoln, and his idol, Theodore Roosevelt. Sixty years old when the project began in 1927, Borglum died shortly prior to the dedication of the last head – Roosevelt's – in 1941. An incredible engineering feat, each head is about 60ft (18 meters) from chin to crown – by way of comparison, the Statue of Liberty's head is just 17ft (5 meters). Exhibits at the Lincoln Borglum Visitor Center explain the creation of the monument; scale models, tools, and other paraphernalia are on display at Borglum's Sculptor's Studio. The best times to view Mount Rushmore are at dawn or dusk, when there are fewer people and better natural lighting.

Just outside the monument is the tiny town of **Keystone ❸**, where visitors can pan for gold at the **Big Thunder Gold Mine** (604 Blair Street; tel: +1 605 666 4847; www.bigthundermine.com; daily Apr and Oct 9am–5pm, May

A herd of buffalo grazing in Custer State Park.

and Sept 9am–6pm, June–Aug 8am–8pm), or catch a 20-mile (32km) round trip on the vintage **1880 Train** (103 Winter Street; tel: +1 605 574 2222; www.1880train.com; early May to Dec, check website for current schedule) between Keystone and Hill City.

CRAZY HORSE MEMORIAL

An even larger sculpture is being made of Sioux warrior Crazy Horse at the **Crazy Horse Memorial** ❹ (12151 Avenue of the Chiefs; tel: +1 605 673 4681; https://crazyhorsememorial.org; daily mid-Mar to mid-May 8am–7pm, mid-May–Sept 8am–8pm, Oct to mid-Mar 9am–5pm, with exceptions), on Highway 385/16 about 15 miles (24km) from Mount Rushmore.

In 1939, prompted by the sight of the Rushmore monument, Sioux leader Henry Standing Bear wrote to Korczak Ziolkowski, who had just won first prize for sculpture at the New York World's Fair, telling him that Native Americans "would like the white man to know that the red man has great heroes, too". Less than a decade later, Ziolkowski moved permanently to the Black Hills to undertake a vastly ambitious project, depicting the revered warrior Crazy Horse on horseback. The work Ziolkowski began on Thunderhead Mountain in 1948 didn't stop with his death in 1982; his widow, and now his children and grandchildren continue to realize his vision. Ziolkowski refused to accept federal or state funds, instead relying entirely on admissions and contributions: the 90-foot (27-meter) high face was completed in 1998, and by 2022, the hand of Crazy Horse was gradually taking shape; the arm, shoulder, hairline, and the top of the horse's head should be complete by 2035. When it is completed, the sculpture will be 563ft (172 meters) high and 641ft (195 meters) long, dwarfing Mount Rushmore.

The main viewing terrace at the Welcome Center is nearly a mile from the carving itself (shuttle buses trundle to the base for an extra charge). Admission also includes the Indian Museum of North America, Mountain Carving Gallery, and the Ziolkowski log home and studio.

The Crazy Horse Memorial in progress.

CUSTER STATE PARK

The buffalo, pronghorn, and prairie-dog rich plains of **Custer State Park** ❺ (tel: +1 605 255 4515; https://gfp.sd.gov/parks/detail/custer-state-park; daily 24hr) are some of the most enticing sections of the Black Hills. The **Needles Highway** (Hwy-87; closed mid-Oct to mid-Apr) winds for 14 miles (22.5km) through pine forests and past the eponymous jagged granite spires in the park's northwestern corner, between Sylvan and Legion lakes. In the southeastern reaches of the park, the 18-mile (29-km) Wildlife Loop undulates through rolling meadows rich with antelope, deer, and "begging burros" (tame four-legged panhandlers who'll stick their snouts through the windows of slow-moving vehicles in search of snack handouts), as well as the herd of 1,300 bison for which the park is known; elk and bighorn sheep are harder to spot.

For a fuller appreciation of the beauty of Custer State Park, set out on one of its myriad hiking and biking trails. A good, short introductory hike is the three-mile (4.8km) Lovers Leap Trail, which begins near the park's main visitor center, on Hwy-16A in the park's eastern section. One of the park's most prominent hikes is the six-mile (9.7-km) trek from Sylvan Lake up Harney Peak, where you are rewarded by expansive views from the stone lookout tower perched atop the summit.

The dramatic **Iron Mountain Road** (Highway 16A) leads through tunnels and over picturesque bridges back to Mount Rushmore. This gorgeous route runs 17 miles (27km) up via three curly twists in the road called "pigtail bridges," each an engineering and design triumph.

WIND CAVE NATIONAL PARK

Beneath wide-open rangelands, **Wind Cave National Park** ❻ (tel: +1 605 745 4600; www.nps.gov/wica; park 24hr, visitor center daily 8am–4.30pm, with exceptions; park entry free; cave tours charge), directly south of Custer State Park, comprises over 100 miles (161km) of underground passages etched out of limestone. Rangers lead a variety of cave tours from the visitor center, pointing out delicate features such as frostwork and boxwork along the way. If you come in summer, forget the standard walking tours and opt for the ones that allow you to crawl around in the smaller passages, or explore the caves by candlelight – call ahead for reservations.

If you lack the inclination to delve into the Dakotas' dank bowels, driving through the park is another quintessential Black Hills experience. Like Custer, its native grass prairies are home to deer, antelope, elk, coyote, prairie dogs, and a sizeable herd of bison.

JEWEL CAVE NATIONAL MONUMENT

The third longest cave system in the world at 209 miles/337km (and counting), **Jewel Cave National Monument** ❼ (tel: + 1 605 673 8300; www.nps.gov/jeca; visitor center mid-May to

There are some great places to eat in Hot Springs, beginning with Red Shed Smokehouse (corner of River Street and Hwy-385; tel: +1 218 277 0582), which knocks out incredible pulled pork sandwiches from a large food cart. For dessert try Two Cows Creamery (237 North River Street; tel: +1 605 745 3838; www.twocowscreamery.com).

Wind Cave National Park.

mid-Sept daily 8am–5.30pm, mid-Sept to mid-May Wed–Sat 8.30am–4.30pm) – about 35 miles (56km) west of Wind Cave – is another maze of passages, caverns, and astounding calcite crystal formations. The tours only cover half a mile, but there are 723 steps up and down (reservations crucial in July). Discovered in 1900, this cave system contrasts radically from the Wind Cave, with its frostwork formations like a subterranean coral reef without water, all bubbles and a thick crust of mostly grey crystals. Look out for the famous "bacon formation," an amazing ribbon of striped crystal.

HOT SPRINGS

The Black Hills' southern anchor, the pretty town of **Hot Springs** ❽ became the region's first tourist destination in the 1890s thanks to its balmy, mineral-rich spring waters (a legacy maintained at Evans Plunge water park; www.evansplunge.com). Though it's surrounded by numerous motels, its downtown is (as yet) largely uncommercialized, with several utilitarian yet handsome sandstone structures passed by the sprightly Fall River – this never freezes thanks to the hot spring water, with a small waterfall and trail along the steaming river in the center of town.

The unique **Mammoth Site** (1800 Hwy-18 bypass; tel: +1 605 745 6017; www.mammothsite.org; mid-May to mid-Aug daily 8am–8pm; mid-Aug to mid-May check website for hours) on the edge of town is the only in situ display of mammoth fossils in the USA, with some 60 unearthed so far, from around 26,000 years ago. Inside its dome, fascinating guided tours explain how these 10-ton mammoths (along with camels, bears, and rodents) were trapped in a steep-sided sinkhole and gradually became covered by sediment; complete skeletons are easy to pick out in the excavation site.

DEADWOOD

Few places encapsulate the mystique of the American West like **Deadwood** ❾ (around 40 miles/64km from Rapid City), a Gold Rush town with a spectacular setting and a pantheon of

Historic saloons, bars, and shops bring visitors to Main Street in Deadwood.

iconic former residents such as Wild Bill Hickok and Calamity Jane. Yet the truth is that Deadwood was only briefly the wild town of legend (settled by miners in the early 1870s, the Gold Rush was over by 1877), and by the 1880s it was a prosperous trade and supply center. In the 1920s it was consciously developed into a parody of the "Wild West," but by the 1980s Deadwood was virtually bankrupt; it was only the legalization of gaming and casinos in 1989 that saved it. Though its handsome buildings are now wonderfully preserved (most of the Wild West tack is long gone and the whole town is a National Historic Landmark), and elegant houses line the slopes, casinos now dominate business here, making it something of a year-round resort – adjust your expectations accordingly and Deadwood can still be lots of fun.

Deadwood's Main Street is the best place to soak up the town's historic roots, though its otherwise stately Victorian buildings are liberally sprinkled with casinos and gift stores. Wild West ground zero is **Saloon #10** (657 Main Street; tel: +1 605 578 3346; www.saloon10.com; daily 8am–2am), a working bar which commemorates the shooting in 1876 of Hickok by Jack McCall while holding two aces, a pair of eights and the nine of diamonds – forever after christened the "Dead Man's Hand". In the summer actors restage the shooting several times daily, and Hickok's chair is preserved above the door.

Confusingly, the spot where this shooting actually happened is down the street at the **Wild Bill Bar** (624 Main Street; tel: +1 605 717 0600), a replica of the original Nuttall and Mann's Saloon No. 10. You can also attend the recreated family-friendly **Trial of Jack McCall** at the Wild Bill Theatre (624 Main Street; tel: +1 800 344 8826; www.deadwoodalive.com; late May to late Sept Mon–Sat 8pm). Kids will also enjoy the staged "gunfights" on Main Street (late May to late Sept Mon–Sat 2pm, 4pm and 6pm; free).

In 1876, a year after the discovery of gold in Deadwood, 6,000 diggers swarmed in to stake their claims; the

Where

The historic Bullock Hotel (633 Main Street; tel: +1 605 578 1745, www.historicbullock.com) was built in Deadwood around 1895, and still offers a range of period-themed rooms, from lavish suites to more affordable "full rooms." This being Deadwood, there's also a small casino downstairs, open 24hr, and a ghost; Deadwood's first Sheriff, Seth Bullock.

Early morning waterfall at Spearfish Canyon.

Days of '76 Western Museum (18 Seventy Six Drive; tel: +1 605 578 1657; www.deadwoodhistory.com; May–Sept daily 9am–5pm, Oct–Apr Tue–Sun 10am–4pm) commemorates this portentous event and the annual rodeo that began in Deadwood in 1923 (held every August), with exhibits of Western and Native American artifacts, photos and artwork.

The **Mount Moriah Cemetery** (10 Mt Moriah Drive; tel: +1 605 578 2600; late May to mid-Oct daily 8am–6pm, limited access rest of year) above the town is a major attraction thanks to the resting place of James Butler Hickock, aka Wild Bill Hickok (1837–76), spy, scout, bullwhacker, stagecoach driver, sheriff, and gambler who spent just a few weeks in Deadwood prior to his murder here in 1876. Martha "Calamity Jane" Canary (1852–1903), an illiterate alcoholic whose checkered career included stints as scout, sex worker, nurse, and even stage performer, arrived around the same time as Hickok; despite barely knowing him, she was buried 27 years later beside Hickok's bronze monument and bust.

A long-horned rider at Sturgis Motorcycle Rally.

LEAD

In utter contrast to Deadwood just three miles (4.8km) north, **Lead** ⑩ (pronounced "Leed") is a quiet working town, operated and virtually controlled by Homestake Mining until 2002 and dripping with history. The Homestake gold claim was founded in 1876; George Hearst was the geological genius who bought it one year later. His son Randolph was the newspaper magnate and inspiration for *Citizen Kane*. By the time of its closure in 2002, a maze of shafts dropped 8,000ft (2,438 meters) below the town, today partly reborn as the futuristic Sanford Underground Research Facility, which operates a lab to detect dark matter.

Start your visit to Lead at the **Sanford Lab Homestake Visitor Center** (160 West Main Street; tel: +1 605 584 3110; www.sanfordlabhomestake.com; daily 9am–5pm; free), which offers a short video on the history of the town and the Sanford Lab, plus views over the mind-blowing 1,250ft/381 meter-deep, one mile-/1.6-km wide Open Cut. Guided tours (1hr) leave from here, with a narrated bus tour through the town and a visit to the old hoist room for the mine (now serving the Sanford Lab) – there's no actual tour of the mine itself.

The grand 1914 **Historic Homestake Opera House** (313 West Main Street; tel: +1 605 584 2067; www.homestake-operahouse.org; Mon–Sat 10.30am–4.30pm; is being gradually restored after a fire, with shows taking place despite ongoing work. Tours take in the ornate main theatre and the interpretive exhibit upstairs. The nearby **Black Hills Mining Museum** (323 West Main Street; tel: +1 605 584 1605; https://blackhillsminingmuseum.com; Apr to late Oct Mon–Sat 9am–5pm) is an absorbing introduction to the region's gold-digging history.

STURGIS

About 16 miles (26km) to the northeast from Deadwood is **Sturgis** ⑪, founded in 1878 as a military camp. Among the colorful figures who settled in town was gambler "Poker" Alice Tubbs (1851–1930), a cigar-chomping Englishwoman who opened a brothel and casino in 1910 in what is now the clapboard **Poker Alice House** (aka "Poker's Palace") – today it's part of **Sturgis Motel** and available for overnight stays (1802 Junction Avenue; tel: +1 605 347 2506; www.thesturgismotel.com).

Sturgis was also the last home of Annie Tallent (1827–1901), the first white female settler in the Black Hills in 1874. The little stone house she rented towards the end of her life is dubbed **Annie Tallent House** (1603 Main Street; closed to the public), built in 1898.

Sturgis livens up each August when the **Sturgis Motorcycle Rally** (tel: + 1 605 720 0800; www.sturgismotorcyclerally.com) packs the otherwise sleepy town. An abundance of Harley-Davidson souvenirs stock the downtown stores year-round, and even if you've rolled into Sturgis on four wheels, the **Sturgis Motorcycle Museum & Hall of Fame** (999 Main Street; tel: +1 605 347 2001; www.sturgismuseum.com; daily 10am–4pm, with exceptions) is worth a visit.

To the east of town, the **Fort Meade Museum** (50 Sheridan Street; tel: +1 605 347 9822; www.fortmeademuseum.org; May–Sept Tue–Sat 10am–5pm) – home of the Seventh Cavalry after the Battle of Little Bighorn – recounts life at a frontier outpost. A few miles north, the volcanic mass of **Bear Butte State Park ⑫** (trail open 30min before sunrise to 30min after sunset) is considered sacred by the Sioux and other Native Americans; stay on the 1.85-mile (3km) trail while hiking to the summit, and don't disturb medicine bags and prayer ribbons that have been left as offerings.

SPEARFISH

The last stop in the Black Hills is **Spearfish ⑬**, about 20 miles (32km) northwest of Sturgis via I-90. The town stands at the terminus of **Spearfish Canyon Highway**, a tortuous 26-mile (42-km) drive through a stunning granite gorge.

An abandoned open pit mine close to Lead.

⊘ THE MICKELSON TRAIL

One of the most rewarding ways to enjoy the beauty of the Black Hills is to traverse the 109-mile 175km) "rail-to-trail" George S. Mickelson trail on foot or by mountain bike; the crushed limestone and gravel trail follows the old Deadwood to Edgemont rail line, abandoned in 1983 and restored as a multi-use trail in 1998. The route cuts through spruce and ponderosa pine forests and includes 100 converted railroad bridges and four rock tunnels.

Hardcore cyclists cover the trail in a day (heading south is a bit easier), but there are plenty of places to break the journey; careful planning is required if you have no car to pick you up, though. You must purchase trail passes online before setting out; see https://gfp.sd.gov/parks/detail/george-s--mickelson-trail.

The foothills of the Bear Tooth Mountains.

EASTERN MONTANA

Eastern Montana really is Big Sky country, a region of turbulent rivers, heavily wooded forests and sparkling blue lakes beneath a vast, deep blue sky that seems to stretch for a million miles.

The Blackfeet and Shoshone once hunted bison here and today the state remains a bastion of Western culture: a land of cowboys, ranches, and 19th-century ghost towns, because of course, when the gold ran out so did the people. Native Americans fought hard to hold onto their land; the crushing defeats they inflicted on the US Army include the legendary victory at Little Bighorn.

The eastern two-thirds of the state is dusty high prairie – sun-parched in summer and wracked by blizzards in winter – that attracts far fewer visitors. Yet the plains are intermittently broken by mountains, of which the most impressive are the icy Beartooth Range, crammed between the town of Red Lodge and Yellowstone National Park. Rafting down the Missouri River as it bends near Fort Benton, or following the history-haunted course of the Little Bighorn River are images of Eastern Montana the traveler will not be able to forget in a hurry. Come May, when the grass on the hills greens up, you'd be forgiven for thinking you were in a more spacious Ireland. Even winter has a softer side, for this is the land of the "chinook", the warm, dry winds that sweep down from the Rockies to give immediate aid to shivering eastern Montanans – a good chinook can raise temperatures by 30°F (16.6°C) in under

The Beartooth Highway mountain pass.

10 minutes. Most visitors traverse the state east to west on I-94/I-90 from Wyoming and the Dakotas, following the Yellowstone River, but an alternative is the Hi-Line, which charts a lonely course along the top of the state towards the Rockies.

MILES CITY

Wild West history is everywhere in **Miles City** , a small settlement on the plains and badlands along the Yellowstone River. At 501 Main Street stands the **Olive Hotel**, where Gus

Main attractions

Beartooth Scenic Highway
C.M. Russell Museum of
  Western Art
Fort Benton
Little Bighorn Battlefield
  National Monument
Medicine Rocks State Park
Upper Missouri National
  Wild and Scenic River
Yellowstone Art Museum
Wolf Point Wild Horse
  Stampede

Map on page 232

McRae died in Larry McMurtry's novel *Lonesome Dove*, and not far away, the **Montana Bar** (612 Main Street) is just what you'd want a Western bar to look like. The **Range Riders Museum** (435 West Main Street; tel: +1 406 232 6146; www.rangeridersmuseum.com; mid-Apr to mid-Oct Mon and Wed–Sun 8am–5pm) is one of the best small museums in Montana, with good collections of firearms and Native American artifacts and a scale-model replica of Fort Keogh, the 1878 army fort that got Miles City started.

Miles City still has weekly livestock auctions, and in May comes the festival-like **Miles City Bucking Horse Sale** (https://buckinghorsesale.com) for rodeo stock buyers and breeders. Miles City also has some literary connections; it features in Robert Pirsig's *Zen and the Art of Motorcycle Maintenance*, and is the setting for Emily M. Danforth's *The Miseducation of Cameron Post*, made into a movie in 2018 – though it wasn't filmed in Montana.

Another intriguing area attraction is **Medicine Rocks State Park ❷** (Hwy-7 to Ekalaka; tel: +1 406 377 6256; daily 7am–10pm), whose Swiss-cheese like formations inspired a young visitor from the East, Teddy Roosevelt, to call it "As fantastically beautiful a place as I have ever seen".

LITTLE BIGHORN BATTLEFIELD NATIONAL MONUMENT

With the exception of Gettysburg, no other US battle has gripped the American imagination like the Battle of the Little Bighorn in June 1876, the biggest defeat of US forces by Native Americans in the West and the scene of the much-mythologized "Custer's Last Stand." Once seen as a tragic hero, Custer is better known today for a series of blunders leading up to the battle, and the decisive Native American victory – of combined Arapaho, Lakota Sioux, and Cheyenne warriors – helped shape the legends of leaders Sitting Bull and Crazy Horse.

The **Little Bighorn Battlefield National Monument ❸** (756 Battlefield Tour Road, Crow Agency; tel: +1

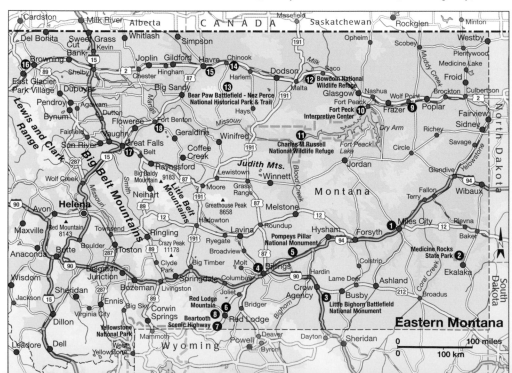

Eastern Montana

406 638 2621, www.nps.gov/libi; daily Apr to Oct 8am–6pm, Nov–Mar 8am–4.30pm) is located on the current Crow Indian Reservation in the Little Bighorn Valley. You can trace the course of the battle on a self-guided driving tour through the grasslands, between the visitor center and Last Stand Hill itself, and the Reno-Benteen Battlefield five miles (8km) away; there are also several hiking trails. What makes Little Bighorn so unique is that the landscape has remained virtually unchanged since 1876. Equally unusual, white headstone markers show where each cavalryman was killed (Custer himself was reburied in 1877 at the West Point Military Academy in New York State), while red granite markers do the same for Native American warriors, making for an extremely evocative experience. The visitor center only contains a small exhibit on the battle, so to get the most out of the site, listen to a ranger talk or take a free ranger tour; there are also fascinating hour-long bus tours with Crow-operated Apsaalooke Tours (tel: + 1 406 638 3897), and you can also use your phone to access audio tour commentary.

BILLINGS

With a population of around 190,000, **Billings** ❹ is Montana's big city, with a booming economy and even a couple of skyscrapers (though the state's tallest building, First Interstate Tower, is a modest 272ft/83 meters). Founded in 1882 on the Yellowstone River, Billings was originally a railroad town; today the nearby Bakken and Heath shale oil fields continue to fuel the city's explosive growth. Downtown, bounded on its north side by the 400ft/122-meter crumpled sandstone cliffs of the Rimrock (or just "the Rims"), centers on the tent-like Skypoint structure covering the intersection of Second Avenue and Broadway. While there are plenty of shops and restaurants here, this isn't likely to be the version of Montana you've come to experience – make time instead for the city's cultural attractions and the intriguing historic sites nearby.

The most prominent historical property downtown is the **Moss Mansion**

Little Bighorn Battlefield National Monument.

Pompey's Pillar National Monument.

(914 Division Street; tel: + 1 406 256 5100; www.mossmansion.com; June–Aug Mon and Wed–Sat 10am–4pm, Sun noon–3pm, rest of year Thu–Mon noon–3pm), a sturdy 1903 red-sandstone manse built for P.B. Moss (1863–1947), an entrepreneur who made a fortune running most of the businesses and utilities in Billings from the 1890s. His daughter lived in this house virtually unaltered until it became a museum in 1984, so the contents are in mint condition, lavishly furnished and decorated in various styles, from a Moorish-themed entrance hall and somber English oak dining room to a pretty pink French parlor.

The modest **Yellowstone Art Museum** (401 North 27th Street; tel: +1 406 256 6804; www.artmuseum.org; Tue–Sun 10am–5pm, Thu till 8pm), partly housed in the town's 1910 jail, is mostly filled with traveling art exhibits, but the excellent permanent collection galleries specialize in Montana art from the mid-20th century onward; highlights include the Western books, paintings and posters by cowboy illustrator Will James (1892–1942), who lived here in later life, and contemporary works from Theodore Waddell, who was born in Billings in 1941; ironically, both spent time in the jail's drunk tank. Make time also for the Visible Vault behind the museum (included), where all 7,000-plus items in the permanent collection are stored and you can view resident artists at work.

Billings's other cultural highlights include the **Western Heritage Center** (2822 Montana Avenue; tel: +1 406 256 6809; www.ywhc.org) and the **Yellowstone County Museum** (1950 Terminal Circle; www.ycmhistory.org; Tue–Sat 10.30am–5.30pm) both of which emphasize Montana and Yellowstone Valley history.

POMPEYS PILLAR NATIONAL MONUMENT

Just 28 miles (45km) northeast of Billings, overlooking the Yellowstone River, **Pompeys Pillar National Monument ❺** (3039 US-312; tel: +1 406 875 2400; www.pompeyspillar.org;

May–Sept daily 8.30am–4.30pm) would just be a 150ft/45-meter tall sandstone outcrop with modest appeal if not for its fascinating historical connections: the rock was named by explorer William Clark for Sacagawea's son when he passed here in 1806, but he also carved his signature into its stone flanks. It's now protected by glass (surrounded by graffiti going back to the 1880s and reached via a boardwalk), but history buffs will get chills being up close and personal with the only physical evidence of the Corps of Discovery's 1804–06 expedition. The excellent visitor center provides details of the expedition.

RED LODGE AND BEARTOOTH SCENIC HIGHWAY

The small but popular resort town of **Red Lodge ❻** lies along Bear Creek, 60 miles (97km) south of Billings at the foot of the awe-inspiring Beartooth Mountains – whose jagged peaks and outcrops contain some of the oldest rocks on earth – and in winter acts as a base for skiers using the popular

Red Lodge Mountain ❼, six miles (9.7km) west on US-212 (tel: +1 406 446 2610; www.redlodgemountain. com). Originally founded to mine coal for the trans-continental railroads, Red Lodge's future was secured by the construction of the 65-mile (105km) **Beartooth Scenic Highway ❽** (usually open late May to early Oct) connecting to Cooke City at the northeastern entrance to Yellowstone National Park, a jaw-dropping ride of tight switchbacks, steep grades, and vertiginous overlooks (allow 2–3 hours to drive to the park entrance). Even in summer the springy tundra turf of the 10,940ft (3,335-meter) Beartooth Pass is covered with snow that (due to algae) turns pink when crushed. All around are gem-like corries, deeply gouged granite walls, and huge blocks of roadside ice.

THE HI-LINE

Some 200 miles (322km) north of Billings, lonely US-2 – named the **Hi-Line** for the route followed by the Great Northern Railroad – is an isolated,

Fort Benton.

bleak but beautiful stretch of road that runs from North Dakota to Glacier National Park, passing small communities, Native American reservations, and awe-inspiring vistas.

Not far from the North Dakota border, US-2 enters the **Fort Peck Indian Reservation** (www.fortpecktribes.org), home to Assiniboine, Nakota, Lakota, and Dakota Sioux peoples. **Wolf Point** , the largest community on the reservation, hosts the **Wolf Point Wild Horse Stampede** (www.wolfpoint-chamber.com) each July; mixing Native American dances and feats of horsemanship, it's considered by many to be one of the best and most exciting rodeos in Montana.

Just outside the reservation's southwestern border lies the irregular expanse of 130-mile-long **Fort Peck Lake**, with 1500 miles (2414km) of shoreline, which the New Deal created in the 1930s by damming the Missouri River – the immense **Fort Peck Dam** stretches across the river here for more than three miles (5km). The **Fort Peck Interpretive Center** (tel:

+1 406 526 3493; May–Sept daily 9am–5pm, Oct–Apr Mon–Fri 10am–4pm) highlights the main attractions of the C. M. Russell National Wildlife Refuge, as well as dam history and local fossils, and also contains the two largest aquariums in Montana. In the adjacent **Charles M. Russell Wildlife Refuge** (tel: +1 406 438 8706; www.fws.gov/refuge/charles_m_russell) itself, you can spot pronghorn antelope, elk, deer, and bighorn sheep.

Back on US-2, **Malta** is the gateway to the **Bowdoin National Wildlife Refuge** (194 Bowdoin Auto Tour Road; tel: +1 406 654 2863; www.fws.gov/refuge/bowdoin), crowded with geese and ducks during the spring and fall migration, before the road cuts through the **Fort Belknap Indian Reservation**, home to the A'aninin (Gros Ventre) and the Nakoda (Assiniboine) tribes.

At **Chinook** you can branch south on Cleveland Road some 15 miles (24km) to **Bear Paw Battlefield** (tel: +1 406 357 3130; www.nps.gov/nepe; daily sunrise–sunset), part of the Nez Perce National Historical Park & Trail. In 1877, when Chief Joseph led his band of Nez Perce from Oregon to hoped-for exile in Canada, the US Army caught up with and defeated them here; it was here that Chief Joseph delivered his moving speech that ended, "From where the sun now stands, I will fight no more forever." The **Blaine County Museum** (501 Indiana Street; tel: +1 406 357 2590; https://blainecountymuseum.com; May–Sept Mon–Sat 9am–5pm, Sun noon–5pm, Oct–Apr Mon–Fri 1–5pm) back in Chinook, also tells Chief Joseph's story.

Havre is the chief town in the central portion of the Hi-Line, where the chief attraction is **Havre Beneath the Streets** (120 3rd Avenue; tel: +1 406 265 8888; https://havrebeneaththestreets.com; call for current times), a recreated frontier town located – you guessed it – underground.

The final section of US-2 before Glacier runs across the **Blackfeet**

Moss Mansion.

Indian Reservation. At **Browning** ⑯, headquarters of the Blackfeet tribe, the **Museum of the Plains Indian** (19 Museum Loop; tel: +1 406 338 2230; www.doi.gov/iacb/museum-plains-indian; June–Sept Tue–Sat 9am–5pm, Oct–May Tue–Thu 11am–3pm, with exceptions) has good exhibits and a gift shop with an excellent selection of jewelry and crafts. The museum also sponsors the **North American Indian Days** celebration in July.

GREAT FALLS

Great Falls ⑰ has always made an impact on visitors. When Lewis and Clark made their voyage up the Missouri River in 1805, they were struck by the series of waterfalls along the river: "a sublimely grand spectacle," Lewis wrote. Today, a large city has grown up along the Missouri here, and the falls themselves have been somewhat diminished by a series of hydroelectric dams. In addition to the Charlie Russell Museum (see box), other Great Falls attractions include the **Paris Gibson Square Museum of Art** (1400 1st Avenue North; tel: +1 406 727 8255; www.the-square.org; Tue 10am–9pm, Wed–Fri 10am–5pm, Sat 10am–3pm, with exceptions), and the **Lewis and Clark Interpretive Center** (4201 Giant Springs Road; tel: +1 406 727 8733; Tue–Sat 9am–5pm, Sun noon–5pm). The **River's Edge Trail** gives you the views of the falls that so impressed Lewis and Clark; just outside town is **Giant Springs Heritage State Park** (4803 Giant Springs Road; tel: +1 406 727 1212; daily sunrise–sunset) whose springs also earned the explorers' praise. You can see what's left of the "Great Falls of the Missouri" at the **Ryan Dam** (14 bumpy miles/23km from the city center by car).

FORT BENTON

Northeast of Great Falls, Hwy-87 takes you to **Fort Benton** ⑱. Tucked into a small valley along the Missouri River, Fort Benton is a delight. Established in 1846 as a fur trading post, it became Montana's "port" – the farthest upstream reach of the Missouri River to which steamboats could navigate.

Display at the Lewis and Clark Interpretive Center.

Antler Rake and Scapula Hoe
Women made handy tools by tying antlers and bones to sturdy sticks. As they worked in the fields of vegetables and corn, they worked for a successful harvest.

Pottery
Round-bottomed pots...

⊘ CHARLIE RUSSELL

Grand Falls can lay claim to one of the greatest artists of the American West, probably the main reason many visitors come to the city today. The rowdy son of a wealthy Missouri family, **Charles Marion Russell** (1864–1926) was sent to Montana at age 16 to knock some sense into him. Instead, he grew so enamored of the cowboy life that he stayed out West, working first as a wrangler and then gaining immortality as an artist who depicted cowboys and Blackfeet chiefs, cattle drives, campfires, and buffalo hunts. Russell spent much of his working career in Great Falls; during the latter portion he painted in a log-cabin studio he built to remind himself of his happy younger days on the range. Today that studio and Russell's house are incorporated into the **C.M. Russell Museum of Western Art** (400 13th Street North; tel: +1 406 727 8787; https://cmrussell.org; May–Oct Wed–Mon 10am–5pm, Nov–Apr Thu–Mon 10am–5pm), which contains an incomparable collection of Russell paintings, drawings, and sculptures. Other galleries are devoted to contemporary Western artists and to the Browning Firearms Collection. Every March the museum sponsors the C.M. Russell Auction of Original Western Art, which draws rich patrons from around the world to bid on the best of Western oils and sculpture.

🔍 CUSTER'S LAST STAND

Tragic military hero, self-aggrandizing blunderer or murderer of Native American civilians – the legacy of George Armstrong Custer remains complex and controversial to this day.

During an erratic career, Custer was one of the major American military icons of the mid- to late-19th century. Born in Ohio in 1839, he was never particularly studious and graduated last in his class at West Point in 1861. Nevertheless, the young man went on to become the army's youngest-ever brigadier general, seeing action at Gettysburg in 1863 during the US Civil War. He attracted national attention through his presence at the ultimate Union victory at Appomattox in 1865, with his own troops blocking the Confederate retreat; his coverage in the press began a life-long love affair with publicity. Though he thought about leaving the army after the war, in 1866 he was appointed lieutenant colonel of the newly created 7th Cavalry Regiment.

Battle of Little Bighorn monument.

However, Custer was also suspended for going AWOL in Kansas, and found notoriety in 1868 for allowing the murder of almost 100 Cheyenne women and children at the Battle of Washita River. His most (in)famous moment, though, came on June 25, 1876, at the Battle of the Little Bighorn, known to Native tribes as the Battle of the Greasy Grass. The action was part of the Great Sioux War, and provoked the US government's desire to obtain ownership of the Black Hills (land that was sacred to the Sioux). It was Custer's expedition into the Black Hills in 1874 that had discovered gold, precipitating the war.

Custer's was the first unit to arrive in the Little Bighorn Valley. Disdaining to await reinforcements, he set out to raze a village along the Little Bighorn River – which turned out to be the largest-ever gathering of Indigenous peoples of the Great Plains. As a party of his men pursued fleeing women and children, they were encircled by 2,000 Lakota and Cheyenne warriors emerging from either side of a ravine. The soldiers dismounted in order to attempt to shoot their way out, but were soon overwhelmed; simultaneously, Custer's command post on a nearby hill was wiped out, while a another group, under Major Marcus Reno and Captain Frederick Benteen remained in a defensive formation about four miles (6.4km) away and could offer no help. Total US casualties included 268 dead and 55 severely wounded.

Although American myth up to the 1960s established Custer as an unquestioned hero (largely encouraged by Custer's indomitable wife, Elizabeth Bacon Custer, who lived on until 1933), archeologists and historians have since discounted the idea of Custer's Last Stand as a heroic act of defiance in which Custer was the last cavalryman left standing; the battle lasted less than an hour, with the white soldiers being systematically and effortlessly picked off. This most decisive Native American victory in the West – led by Sitting Bull and warriors like Crazy Horse – was also their final great show of resistance. With so many US soldiers killed, an incensed President Grant piled maximum resources into a military campaign that brought about the effective defeat of Indigenous peoples of the Great Plains by the end of the decade, and the 7th Cavalry's "revenge" at Wounded Knee in 1890.

During Montana's gold rush, river trade boomed, with as many as 50 steamboats a season docking here. That trade and Fort Benton's position at the south end of the Whoop-Up Trail to Canada helped make it Montana's largest city for a while; it was also among the state's most lawless, with Front Street called "the bloodiest block in the West."

Today, Fort Benton is anything but busy or violent as it drowses alongside the river in the shade of cottonwood trees. It's a town that takes considerable pride in the past, with its old brick business district nicely restored. Among the highlights are Fort Benton's museums (+1 406 622 5316; http://fortbentonmuseums.com; all open June–Sept Mon–Sat 10.30–4.30pm, Sun noon–4pm, with exceptions): the **Museum of the Northern Great Plains** (1205 20th Street), focusing on 19th-century homesteaders; the **Museum of the Upper Missouri** (Old Fort Park), which details Fort Benton's glory days as a river port; the **Upper Missouri River Breaks Interpretive Center** (701 7th Street), highlighting the history of the river itself;

and **Historic Old Fort Benton** and the **Starr Gallery of Western Art** (Old Fort Park) – built in 1846, the fort blockhouse is Montana's oldest building.

Farther down the street is the stately **Grand Union Hotel** (www.grandunion-hotel.com), built in 1882, and the rather touching **Shep Memorial**, a statue of a dog named "Shep:" when his master died and was shipped back east for burial, this devoted pooch waited faithfully at the Fort Benton train station for years, hoping in vain for his master's return.

Fort Benton and nearby Virgelle also serve as gateways for trips down the **Upper Missouri National Wild and Scenic River** (tel: +1 406 622 4000), which protects a 149-mile (240km) stretch of the river downstream from here. Much of the Missouri in Montana has been considerably altered by dams: this is one place where you can see it much as it was in the 19th century, rolling through beautifully eroded country on its way east. Experienced travelers can make their own voyages in rented canoes; the less experienced can join guided trips.

The confluence of the Marias and Missouri Rivers.

SACAGAWEA

Of the many characters in the chronicles of American history, few are as idealized as Sacagawea (or Sacajawea), the young Shoshone girl who, at age 16, served as guide and interpreter for the Lewis and Clark expedition of 1804–6.

Sacagawea, or Bird Woman, was kidnapped by the Hidatsa tribe as a girl and later sold as a wife to French-Canadian trapper Toussaint Charbonneau. The couple encountered Lewis and Clark's Corps of Discovery at Fort Mandan in what is now North Dakota in the winter of 1804. Charbonneau was hired as a guide and interpreter, but it was his pregnant, 16-year-old wife who proved the most helpful. In February, Sacagawea gave birth to a son, Jean Baptiste, known to the other members of the party as "Little Pomp." She carried the child in a cradleboard on her back during the entire 3,000-mile (4,828km) adventure.

Statue of Sacagawea and her son Jean-Baptiste Charbonneau.

LEWIS AND CLARK EXPEDITION

Sacagawea's ability to find food in the wilderness and make peace with suspicious Native Americans was vital to the group's survival, and her courage and even-tempered nature made her one of the most reliable and well-liked people on the expedition. She was particularly helpful when the party reached her native tribe, the Shoshone, in Montana. After a reunion with her brother, Chief Cameahwait, she helped procure 21 horses and two guides for the arduous trek over the Bitterroot Mountains.

Lewis and Clark National and State Historical Parks.

Earth lodge replica at Knife River Village, the site where Sacagawea met Lewis and Clark for their expedition.

A postage stamp showing Lewis and Clark's Expedition.

Later life and legacy

The expedition reached the Pacific in November 1805, and Sacagawea and Charbonneau returned to Fort Mandan the following year. In 1809 she traveled to St Louis, where William Clark educated and raised Little Pomp. What happened next is unclear; some accounts have Sacagawea dying as a young woman in Dakota Territory in 1812, while other reports say that she lived with the Comanche tribe, before finally settling with the Shoshone in Wyoming. A woman later identified as Sacagawea died on the Wind River Reservation in 1884 at nearly 100 years of age. She is buried in Fort Washakie, where "she sleeps with her face toward the sunny side of the Rocky Mountains." Near her grave is a monument to Jean Baptiste who, after traveling in Europe, came back to the Rockies to work as a mountain man, dying in 1866.

Today, Sacagawea is considered one of the most important women in American history – a pivotal figure in the opening of the West and a paragon of courage and dignity. There are said to be more statues of her than any other woman in US history.

...atue of Lewis and Clark at the end of the Lewis and ...ark trail.

...lliam Clark's inscription on Pompey's Pillar.

Sign depicting Lewis, Clark, and Sacagawea with her baby indicating a point of interest on the Lewis and Clark Trail in Montana.

Mountain goats at Glacier
National Park.

GLACIER NATIONAL PARK

1,000 miles (1,600km) of flowing rivers, thick forests, breezy meadows and awe-inspiring peaks, not to mention two thousand lakes, make up one of America's finest attractions: Glacier National Park.

The park takes its name from the huge flows of ice that carved these immense valleys some 20,000 years ago, and although the park does hold 25 small (rapidly retreating) glaciers, some worrying estimates predict that they could disappear completely by 2030. The park is also a haven for bighorn sheep, mountain goats, black and grizzly bears, wolves, and mountain lions. In the summer months this is prime hiking and whitewater rafting territory, while huckleberries litter the slopes in the fall. Outside of summer, the crisp air, icy-cold waterfalls, and copious snowfall give the impression of being close to the Arctic Circle; in fact, the latitude here is lower than that of London. Its plunging waterfalls, radiant wildflower meadows, and swirling turquoise streams have left millions of visitors slack-jawed with admiration since the 1890s. The naturalist John Muir called it "the best care-killing country on the continent," and Ernie Pyle, the war correspondent who saw a quite bit of the world in his time, said he "wouldn't trade one square mile of Glacier for all the other parks put together."

HISTORY

The ancestors of the Kootenai, Salish, Pend d'Oreille, and Kalispel tribes have hunted here for more than 10,000 years. By the time European explorers and fur trappers arrived in the 18th century, the powerful Blackfeet confederation controlled the plains on the east side of Glacier, while the Salish, Pend d'Oreille, and Kootenai occupied the forested western side. By the end of the 19th century, though, these tribes had been laid low by smallpox epidemics and illicit land deals, byproducts of the westward expansion of the United States. They were ultimately confined to the Blackfeet Indian Reservation on Glacier's eastern border, and the Flathead Indian Reservation along

⊙ Main attractions
Glacier Park Lodge
Going-to-the-Sun Road
Grinnell Glacier
Hidden Lake
Iceberg Lake
Logan Pass
Many Glacier Hotel
St Mary Lake
Two Medicine Lake

Map on page 244

Hiking Grinnell Glacier Trail.

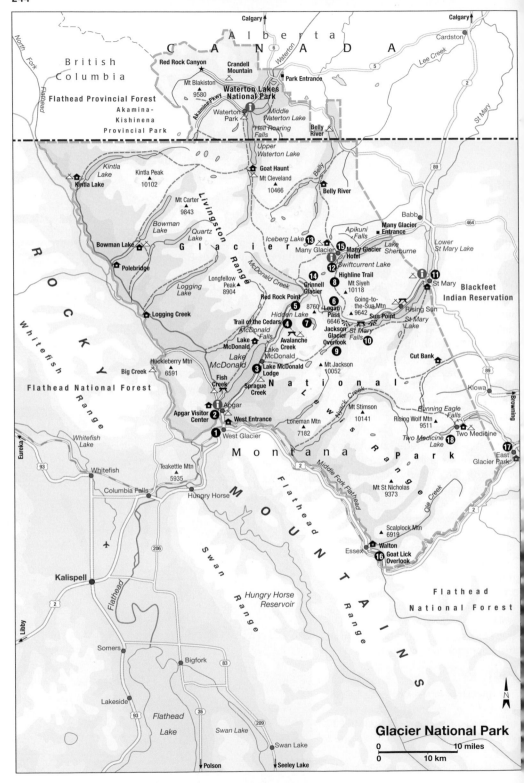

Glacier National Park

CANADA

Alberta

Calgary ↑   Calgary ↑

Cardston

Lee Creek

British Columbia

North Fork Flathead

Flathead Provincial Forest

Akamina-
Kishinena
Provincial Park

Red Rock Canyon ★

Crandell Mountain

Waterton

Park Entrance

Mt Blakiston ▲ 9580

Akamina Pkwy

Waterton Park ℹ

Waterton Lakes National Park

Middle Waterton Lake

Hell Roaring Falls

Belly River

Upper Waterton Lake

Kintla Lake

Kintla Peak 10102

Mt Carter 9843

Bowman Lake

Quartz Lake

Bowman Lake

Polebridge

Goat Haunt

Mt Cleveland 10466

Belly River

Babb

Many Glacier Entrance

Apikuni Falls

Iceberg Lake **13**

Many Glacier **15**

Many Glacier Hotel ℹ **12**

Lake Sherburne

Lower St Mary Lake

464

Logging Lake

Longfellow Peak ▲ 8904

McDonald Creek

Red Rock Point **5**

Grinnell Glacier **14**

Swiftcurrent Lake

Highline Trail **8**

Mt Siyeh 10118

St Mary ℹ **11**

Blackfeet Indian Reservation

Logging Creek

Hidden Lake **4** **7**

Trail of the Cedars

8760 **6**

Logan Pass 6646

Going-to-the-Sun Mtn 9642

Rising Sun

Sun Point

Huckleberry Mtn 6591

Big Creek

Lake McDonald

McDonald Falls

Lake McDonald

Avalanche Creek

Jackson Glacier Overlook

St Mary Falls **10**

St Mary Lake

Cut Bank

89

Flathead National Forest

Whitefish Range

Whitefish Lake

Lake McDonald Lodge **3**

Fish Creek

Sprague Creek

Mt Jackson 10052

9

National

Kiowa

Apgar Visitor Center **2**

Apgar

West Entrance

1

West Glacier

Nyack Creek

Mt Stimson 10141

Running Eagle Falls

Rising Wolf Mtn 9511

Browning

Teakettle Mtn 5935

Loneman Mtn 7182

Montana

Two Medicine Lake

Two Medicine **18**

Park

East Glacier Park **17**

Eureka

93

Whitefish

Columbia Falls

Hungry Horse

206

Middle Fork Flathead

Mt St Nicholas 9373

Ole Creek

2

Kalispell

2

Libby

Swan Range

Hungry Horse Reservoir

Scalplock Mtn 6919

Walton

Essex

Goat Lick Overlook **16**

Flathead National Forest

Somers

Bigfork

83

Lakeside

36

Flathead Lake

Swan Lake

209

Polson ↓   Seeley Lake ↓

N

the Flathead River, home to the Confederated Salish and Kootenai Tribes of the Flathead Nation.

With the expansion of the Great Northern Railway over Marias Pass in 1891, more homesteaders from the east arrived, and tourism was rapidly developed in the 1890s. Mining also briefly flourished on the east side of the park in the 1890s, but no large copper or gold deposits were ever located. This area first received protection from Congress as a forest preserve in 1900, and Glacier finally became a national park in 1910. Going-to-the-Sun Road was completed in 1932.

WEST GLACIER

The park's main, western entrance is at **West Glacier** ❶ on US-2, 25 miles (40km) east of Whitefish and just 35 miles (56km) south of the Canadian border. Here you'll find the Amtrak station, a cluster of accommodation (including Alpine-style Belton Chalets, dating back to 1910), and the park headquarters. The helpful **Apgar Visitor Center** ❷ (tel: +1 406 888 7800; www.nps.gov/glac; mid-May to mid-Oct daily 8am–5pm), lies 2 miles (3.2km) north of the West Entrance on Going-to-the-Sun Road.

GOING-TO-THE-SUN ROAD

The 53-mile (85-km) **Going-to-the-Sun Road** (usually passable between June and mid-Oct) across the heart of Glacier National Park is one of the most mesmerizing drives in the country; traversing it from west to east can take several hours, creating the illusion that you'll be climbing forever, with each successive hairpin bringing a new colossus into view. Beginning at West Glacier, the road runs east along 10-mile (16km) **Lake McDonald**. Lined with cedar trees and warm enough to swim in during late summer, the lake has many beaches that offer sweeping vistas of the mountains. Toward the lake's northern end, the road passes

Lake McDonald Lodge ❸ (open mid-May to mid-Sept). This grand hotel opened in 1914 with an ideal shoreline location and a picturesque Swiss chalet design, offering spacious lodge rooms or small rustic cabins outside the complex; there's also Russell's Fireside Dining Room, Jammer Joe's Grill & Pizzeria, and Lucke's Lounge, open to non-guests. Beyond the lake the road follows McDonald Creek, a lovely watercourse that curls through the ancient cedar and hemlock forest of the park's warmer, moister west side. The **Trail of the Cedars** ❹ loops through a cathedral stand of ancient cedar, hemlock and cottonwood trees, while a bit farther along at **Red Rock Point** ❺, the creek zigzags between tilting blocks of vermilion mudstone and whirls into a deep turquoise pool.

LOGAN PASS

Beyond Lake McDonald Creek the road starts to climb up the Garden Wall ridge, as snowmelt from waterfalls gushes across the road, and the winding route nudges over the Continental Divide at

A lodge at Glacier National Park.

⊙ Eat

The multicolored Two Sisters Café (3600 Hwy-89, Babb; tel: +1 406 732 5535) lies between Babb and St Mary on Hwy-89 (east side of Glacier), famous for its outlandish decor, home-made pies, rainbow trout, bison burgers, chilli, and desserts. In East Glacier Park, Whistle Stop (1024 Hwy-49; tel: +1 406 226 9292) serves up huge breakfasts and huckleberry pies.

Sunset over St Mary Lake and Wild Goose Island.

Logan Pass ❻ (6,646ft/2,025 meters) – a good spot to step out and enjoy the views. Valley walls plunge from sight, and row upon row of summits reach off in all directions. Jagged peaks loom directly overhead. Waterfalls spill over cliffs just a hundred yards from the visitor center parking lot, and broad meadows of wildflowers spread right at your feet. The **Logan Pass Visitor Center** (daily late June to early Sept 9am–7pm, rest of Sept 9am–4pm) houses exhibits on the flora and fauna found in the sub-alpine region of the park. Note that this area is usually mobbed by visitors in the summer; plan to arrive early or visit later in the afternoon.

The most popular trail in the park also begins at Logan Pass, following a boardwalk for 1.5 miles (2.4km) across wildflower-strewn alpine meadows framed by towering craggy peaks, en route to serene **Hidden Lake** ❼. Another hike follows the **Highline Trail** ❽ across cliffs and avalanche slopes to grassy meadows overlooking McDonald Valley. Chances of seeing mountain goats are excellent on either hike.

Back on Going-to-the-Sun Road, four miles (6.4km) on, there's an overlook at **Jackson Glacier** ❾, one of the few glaciers visible from the roadside. It's the seventh largest in the park, but has shrunk by over 30 percent since the 1960s.

ST MARY AND ST MARY LAKE

From the Jackson Glacier Overlook the road descends to **St Mary Lake**, a 10-mile (16km) body of crystal-clear water that occupies an enormous depression gouged out by one of the huge valley glaciers thousands of years ago. A short trail leads to scenic **St Mary Falls** ❿ at the western end, while Sun Point offers a tremendous view of the entire lower valley as well as the surrounding peaks. The tiny community of **St Mary** ⓫ lies at the eastern end of the lake, at the East Entrance to the park, right on the edge of the Great Plains. At **St Mary Visitor Center** (mid-May to mid-Oct daily 8am–5pm) a park film is shown throughout the day, and exhibits chronicle the Native American history of the region.

MANY GLACIER

If you have time, explore some of the more remote sections of the park by car, bike or on foot, beginning with **Many Glacier**, 20 miles (32km) northwest of St Mary via its own park entrance off Hwy-89. The road ends at **Swiftcurrent Lake** ⑫, where an easy two-mile (3.2km) loop trail runs along the lakeshore, and an exciting five-mile (8km), one-way trail heads to **Iceberg Lake** ⑬, so called for the blocks of ice that float on its surface even in midsummer. Another popular option is to make the journey to the foot of the **Grinnell Glacier** ⑭ via two boat trips and two hikes (https://glacier-parkboats.com). **Many Glacier Hotel** ⑮ (open June to mid-Sept) is a stately, alpine-style lodge built by the Great Northern Railway in 1915, right on Swift-current Lake (non-guests can visit the Swiss Lounge, Heidi's Snack Shop, and the lakeside Ptarmigan Dining Room).

SOUTHERN LOOP

US-2 runs around the southern border of the park for 85 miles (137km) between West Glacier and St Mary. It's not as dramatic as Going-to-the-Sun Road, but it's still very scenic and is open year-round; en route you'll pass **Goat Lick Overlook** ⑯, a good place to spot mountain goats. In the remote village of **East Glacier Park** ⑰ there's another Amtrak station and the **Glacier Park Lodge** (open June to late Sept), best known for the massive Douglas fir and cedar columns (with bark still attached) in its huge, phenomenal lobby, brought over from the Pacific Northwest in 1913 by the Great Northern Railway. Non-guests are welcome to come in for a look, or to stop by the Great Northern Dining Room, Empire Bar, and Country Corner convenience store.

Just north of East Glacier Park, the **Two Medicine** section of the park has a separate entrance off Hwy-49. This is a less crowded center for hiking and boating, focused on beautiful **Two Medicine Lake** ⑱ itself, where the road ends. The area got its name from a tradition of two Blackfeet tribes, the Bloods and the Piegans, who often held their annual sun dance in adjacent medicine lodges.

An inquisitive ground squirrel.

⊘ GLACIER TOURS AND ACTIVITIES

Travelers arriving by public transportation can travel around the park via the bright-red 1936 "jammer" buses (so called because of the need to jam the gears into place) that provide narrated sightseeing tours from the main lodges (tel: +1 406 892 2525; www.glaciernationalpark-lodges.com/red-bus-tours; east side early June to late Sept; west side late May to late Oct). Free Glacier Shuttles (July to early Sept only) also run along Going-to-the-Sun Road: one between Apgar Visitor Center and Logan Pass (with a transfer to smaller bus at Avalanche Creek), and one between Logan Pass and St Mary Visitor Center (with a transfer at Sun Point). Purchase tickets from www.recreation.gov.

Sun Tours (tel: +1 406 226 9220; www.glaciersuntours.com) offers daily half-day and full-day guided tours of the park in summer led by members of the Blackfeet tribe.

Tour boats also explore all the large lakes, and kayak rentals are available. Contact Glacier Park Boat Co (tel: +1 406 257 2426; https://glacierparkboats.com). Several companies offer excellent whitewater rafting trips in and around Glacier National Park, mostly based at West Glacier. The Glacier Raft Company is a reputable operator offering half-day and full-day excursions (106 Going-To-The-Sun Road, West Glacier; tel: +1 406 888 5454; https://glacierraftco.com).

PARK GEOLOGY

Scan the flanks of any mountain in the park and you will soon see that it is composed of layer upon layer of sedimentary rock. These layers are the pages of Glacier's early geologic history, and their story reaches back roughly 1.6 billion years to a time when this portion of Montana was flat. Mud, sand and silt washed out onto this plain for several hundred million years, accumulated to depths of three to five miles (5–8 km) and turned to stone – much of it very colorful; vivid red and blue-green mudstone are the most notable deposits. The rock layers preserved ripple marks, mud cracks, and even impressions made by raindrops that fell more than a billion years ago. You can pass your hand over some of these ripple marks beside St Mary Lake.

This thick sheet of strata remained buried until just 70 million years ago, then rose through the surface as the earth's crustal plates collided along the western edge of North America. Like a car crash in slow motion, the western portion of the continent crumpled, gradually elevating chains of mountains. Here, though, the strata did not simply rise in place; it broke away in pieces and slid more than 35 miles (56km) eastward before finally coming to rest in what are now Glacier and Waterton parks. The mountains that rise abruptly from the Great Plains on the east side of the parks represent the edge of that colossal slab.

For tens of millions of years, erosion carried away the upper layers until all that remained were the oldest tiers of rock. Then came the great Ice Ages. At least three times in the past 200,000 years, enormous glaciers formed in the upper ramparts of the mountains and plowed their way down to the plains and river valleys. These great masses of ice sometimes exceeded depths of 2,000ft (610 meters), and their effects can be seen at every turn.

The steep, semicircular walls and flat floors of the park's spacious valleys trace the outlines of the largest glaciers. Huge mounds of morainal debris confine the park's big lakes. There are knife-edged ridges, horn-shaped

Views over the meadows and lakes in Glacier National Park.

peaks, cirques, and hanging valleys. All were created in one way or another by glaciers, but not by the 25 or so relative dwarfs that nibble away at the peaks today. The last of the titanic glaciers that shaped the park melted away about 6,000 years ago.

GLACIER FLORA AND FAUNA

Throughout this incredible spread of primitive country roam some of North America's most impressive and beautiful animals. Mountain goats (shaggy white beasts with sharp black horns) scamper among the park's highest pinnacles and cliffs. Bighorn sheep graze in the meadows at the timber line, never far from the protection of steep boulder fields and scree slopes. Grizzly bears wander the high-country basins, digging up ground squirrels and munching on roots, sedges, grasses, and berries. Glacier also abounds with animals common throughout the Northern Rockies – elk, moose, deer, black bear, and the mountain lion.

You also find wetlands throughout the park, thick with marsh grasses, cattails, reeds, and a cornucopia of insects, fish, amphibians, waterfowl, and semiaquatic mammals such as beaver, muskrat, and mink. They also attract osprey and large mammals, including moose.

Arms of prairie grass stretch into many of the eastern valleys, and grasslands appear as isolated pockets in the forests of the west side. The meadows support elk and deer as well as many types of small rodents, which attract predators such as wolves, mountain lions, hawks, owls, coyotes, and badgers.

Groves of aspen, cottonwood, and other deciduous trees shade the edges of meadows and give way at higher elevations to evergreens, which are better adapted to the shorter growing season. The middle slopes of the park's mountains consist mainly of lodgepole, spruce, and fir. However, warm Pacific air masses stall out on Glacier's western slopes and drop enough moisture to support stands of cedar and hemlock. East or west, the deep forest provides a home for black bears, mountain lions, deer, woodpeckers, flying squirrels, and pygmy owls.

Among the small valleys and basins that dot Glacier's high country, forests of Englemann spruce, whitebark pine, and subalpine fir grow alongside sprawling meadows carpeted with wildflowers, sedges, and grasses. Thickets of berry bushes crowd the avalanche slopes. Known as the subalpine zone, this niche is home to grizzly bears, bighorn sheep, wolverines, marmots, weasels, ground squirrels, and, in the highest reaches, mountain goats.

Finally, along the crest of the mountains, the trees give out almost entirely. Those that survive here hug the ground and seek cover from the wind by twisting and bending around rocks. A thin layer of grasses, sedges, and wildflowers also manages to eke out a supremely fragile existence, but few animals besides mountain goats and pikas (tiny hares) spend much time here.

⊙ Fact

Just across the Canadian border, **Waterton Lakes National Park** (www. pc.gc.ca/waterton) is well worth a visit. The park embraces three beautiful and very different valleys and, like Glacier, its mountains rise abruptly from the Great Plains. Upper Waterton Lake occupies a very long, narrow trough at the head end of the park's main valley, which extends south across the border into Glacier.

A moose and her calf at Swiftcurrent Lake.

BEAR WITH US

The Rocky Mountains are one of the few refuges left for the grizzly bear – a vanishing symbol of America's rich natural heritage.

Their invulnerability and ferocity when threatened have long earned grizzlies the respect they deserve. Lewis and Clark provided early scientific reports on grizzly bears; Captain Lewis recorded: "...these bears being so hard to die rather intimidated us all; I must confess that I do not like the gentlemen and had rather fight two Indians than one bear."

A THREATENED SPECIES

Grizzly bears in the lower 48 states are currently protected as a threatened species (the population in Alaska is far bigger). Of the thousands of grizzlies who once roamed freely throughout western America, fewer than 1,500 have survived in the lower 48, limited to Montana, Wyoming and Idaho. Affectionately referred to by mountain men as Old Ephraim, the grizzly was firmly planted in North America long before the first European ventured to these shores. The factor most responsible for the grizzly bear's demise in the United States was the introduction of the domestic cattle industry into the mountain valleys and open ranges west of the Great Plains. The slow-moving cattle were easy prey for the bears, and the grizzly quickly became the cattleman's foremost predatory enemy. New high-powered repeating rifles and packs of trained hunting dogs made slaughtering every possible grizzly bear relatively safe and easy.

Grizzly bears can be beautiful and terrifying in equal measure.

Grizzly bear claws are made for hunting.

A grizzly bear on its hind legs.

A female grizzly bear with her four cubs in tow.

Bear safety

Fatal maulings receive so much media attention that a somewhat exaggerated impression has been created of grizzly bears (not to mention the notorious mauling scene in the 2015 movie Revenant). Realistically, your biggest irritations while hiking in the Rockies are likely to be mosquitoes, flies, and blackflies, and tramping in the American wilderness is far safer than wandering around most cities. But make no mistake; the largest and most formidable of carnivorous North American animals, grizzly bears are potentially very dangerous. Most people blow a whistle while walking in bear country to warn them off. If confronted, don't run, make loud noises or any sudden movements, all of which are likely to provoke an attack – be reassured that most bear encounters end without injury. It can also help to talk calmly so the bear knows you are human and not prey. Be sure to get some useful tips from local park rangers on how to pack and store your food for camping so as not to attract unwanted visitors, and above all, have respect for the animals themselves.

...aking the water off after a swim.

...gns warning about grizzlies can be found all over the ...cky Mountains.

A grizzly bear in the snow at Grand Teton National Park.

A copper mine in Butte.

WESTERN MONTANA

Scenery is at its most dramatic in Western Montana, especially the phenomenal Glacier National Park and the surrounding mountain chains, with jagged peaks that rise over 12,000 feet (3,658 meters).

With the Continental Divide zigzagging through this part of the state, mountains dominate: the Rockies, the Bitterroots, the Madisons, and Gallatins. These landscapes featured heavily in 1990s movies *A River Runs Through It* and *The Horse Whisperer*, both filmed in part on Dennis Quaid's Montana ranch.

Each of Western Montana's small cities has its own proud identity, and most of them are conveniently located off the east–west I-90 corridor. Enjoyable Missoula is a laidback college town, a glimmer of liberalism in this otherwise libertarian state; the historic copper-mining hub of Butte was once a union stronghold, the elegant state capital Helena harkens back to its prosperous gold-mining years, and Bozeman, just to the south, is one of the hippest mountain towns in the USA, buzzing with out-of-towners in the peak months.

BOZEMAN

Founded in 1864, **Bozeman** ❶ lies at the north end of the lush Gallatin Valley some 145 miles (233km) west of Billings, a small, affluent college town of around 40,000 with a pleasant, lively Main Street and a couple of worthwhile museums. The city is also home to Montana State University (MSU), whose Bobcats sports teams enjoy enthusiastic support. The biggest game of the

year is the football match with bitter rivals, the Missoula-based University of Montana known as the Grizzlies, dubbed the "Brawl of the Wild" (usually in November; see https://msubobcats.com).

The small **Gallatin History Museum** (317 West Main Street; tel: +1 406 522 8122; www.gallatinhistorymuseum. org; Tue–Sat 11am–4pm, with exceptions) in the heart of town is crammed with all sorts of historical bits and pieces relating to the history of Bozeman and Gallatin County, from exhibits

⊘ Main attractions

Butte
Flathead Lake
Garnet Ghost Town
Gates of the Mountains
Helena
Museum of the Rockies
National Bison Range
Whitefish

Map on page 254

Tyrannosaurus Rex skeleton in Bozeman.

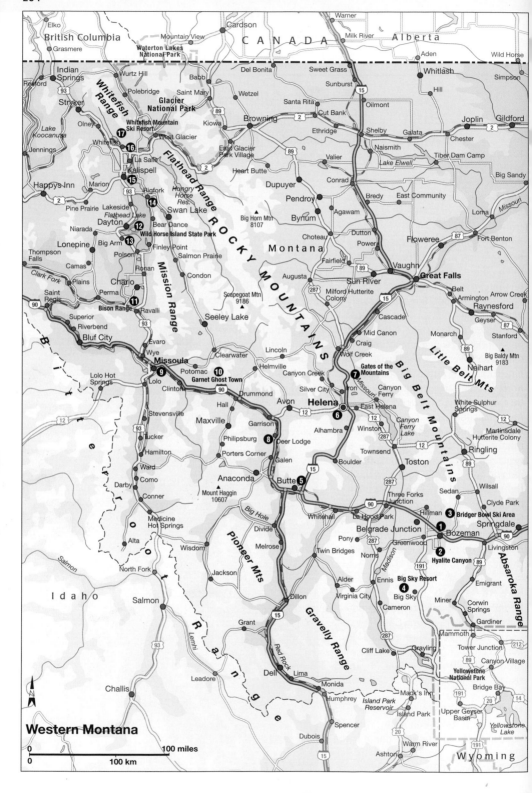

British Columbia

Elko
Grasmere

Mountain View

Cardson

C A N A D A

Warner

Milk River

Alberta

Aden

Wild Horse

Simpson

Rexford
Indian Springs

Grasmere

Wurtz Hill
Polebridge

Waterton Lakes
National Park

Del Bonita

Sweet Grass

Whitlash

Stryker

Babb

Saint Mary

Wetzel

Sunburst

Hill

15

Glacier
National Park

Kiowa

Browning

Santa Rita

Shelby

Oilmont

Galata

Joplin

Gildford

Whitefish Mountain
Ski Resort

West Glacier

East Glacier
Park Village

89

2

Cut Bank

Ethridge

Naismith

Chester

Olney
Whitefish
17
16
La Salle
Kalispell
15
Rigfork
14
Swan Lake

West Glacier

Heart Butte

89

Valier

Conrad

Lake Elwell

Tiber Dam Camp

Big Sandy

Happys Inn
2
Marion
Pine Prairie
Lakeside
Dayton
12
Niarada
Lonepine
Big Arm
13
Camas
Thompson
Falls
Plains

Hungry
Horse
Res.

Bear Dance

Finley Point

Salmon Prairie

Condon

Dupuyer

Pendroy

Bynum

Agawam

Choteau

Dutton

Power

Bredy

East Community

Loma

Fort Benton

Floweree

87

Missouri

Saint
Regis

90

Charlo
Perma
Ravalli

Rollins

Polson

Rohan

Fairfield

Augusta

Milford Hutterite
Colony

Sun River

Vaughn

Great Falls

Belt

Armington

Arrow Creek

Raynesford

Geyser

Stanford

87

Superior
Riverbend
Bluf City

Evaro
Wye

Missoula
9
Lolo

Potomac
10
Garnet Ghost Town

Clearwater

Lincoln

Wolf Creek

Cascade

Mid Canon

Craig

Monarch

Big Baldy Mtn
9183

Neihart

White Sulphur
Springs

Lolo Hot
Springs
12

Clinton

Drummond

Hall

Helmville

Canyon Creek

Silver City

Gates of the
Mountains
7

Canyon
Ferry

Canyon
Ferry
Lake

12

Martinsdale
Hutterite Colony

Ringling

Stevensville
Maxville
Garrison
93
Tucker
Hamilton
Philipsburg
Porters Corner
8
Deer Lodge

Avon

Helena
6

East Helena

Alhambra

Winston

Townsend

Toston

89

Ward
Como

Galen

Boulder

Sedan

Wilsall

Darby
Conner

Anaconda

Butte
5

15

Three Forks
Junction

Hillman

Clyde Park

Bridger Bowl Ski Area
3
1

Springdale

Mount Haggin
10607

Big Hole

Divide

Whitehall

La Hood Park

Belgrade Junction

Bozeman

Livingston

90

Medicine
Hot Springs
Alta

Melrose

Pony

287

Greenwood

Hyalite Canyon
2

89

Absaroka Range

Wisdom

Twin Bridges

Norris

191

Emigrant

North Fork

Jackson

Alder

Ennis

Big Sky Resort
4

Miner

Corwin
Springs

Salmon

Virginia City

Big Sky

Cameron

Gardiner

Grant

287

Mammoth

212

Idaho

Dillon

Cliff Lake

Grayling

Tower Junction

89

Canyon Village

Leadore

Red Rock

Dell

Lima

Monida

Mack's Inn

Yellowstone
National Park

Bridge Bay

20

14

Challis

Humphrey

Island Park
Reservoir

191

Upper Geyser
Basin

Spencer

Island Park

20

Yellowstone
Lake

Western Montana

Dubois

Warm River

Ashton

Wyoming

0   100 miles

0   100 km

15

on MSU and Gary Cooper (who went to high school here), to city founder, gambler and womanizer John Bozeman. The museum occupies the old jail of 1911, which was in operation until 1982.

South of downtown Bozeman, the huge **Museum of the Rockies** (600 West Kagy Boulevard; tel: +1 406 994 2251; https://museumoftherockies.org; daily 9.30am–4.30pm, with exceptions) is best known for its exceptional dinosaur collection, almost all of it obtained from digs in Montana. Among the many highlights is the world's largest-known skull of a Tyrannosaurus rex, a large ensemble of giant Triceratops skulls and skeletons, and landmark Deinonychus finds (the nasty little ancestor of the Velociraptor) that revolutionized the way scientists thought about dinosaurs; that modern-day birds are direct descendants of dinosaurs is a big theme of the museum. There are also sections on Native American culture and pioneer history, and in summer, the Living History Farm, an 1889 farmhouse and blossom-filled garden manned by costumed guides, is well worth a visit.

Other local attractions include the travelling art shows at the **Bozeman Art Museum** (2612 West Main Street; tel: +1 406 570 1419; https://bozemanartmuseum.org; Tue–Sat 11am–5pm), and the family-friendly exhibits at the adjacent **Montana Science Center** (2744 West Main Street; tel: +1 406 522 9087; https://montanasciencecenter.org; Mon–Sat 9am–6pm, Sun 11am–5pm).

Right on Bozeman's southern doorstep is **Hyalite Canyon** ②, an attractive region of waterfalls and hanging valleys laced with hiking and biking trails that includes the Hyalite Reservoir. A twenty-minute drive north of town is the Bridger Range, named after legendary mountain man Jim Bridger and home to **Bridger Bowl Ski Area** ③ (https://bridgerbowl.com).

GALLATIN VALLEY

South of Bozeman, US-191 emerges from flat plains into the twisting **Gallatin Valley** en route to Yellowstone National Park. Following the fast-moving, clear waters of the Gallatin River, the highway is framed on either side by steep crags and forested hillsides rising to the Gallatin Range to the east and the Madison Range to the west. Some of the Madisons' steep slopes are now occupied by **Big Sky Resort** ④ (https://bigskyresort.com), Montana's largest ski resort. Along with the skiing possibilities, Big Sky has added a number of dining and lodging options to the valley, as well as float trips on the Gallatin in the summer.

BUTTE

Eighty miles (129km) west of Bozeman, the former copper-mining colossus of **Butte** ⑤ (rhyme with "mute") burst into life after gold was discovered here in 1862. Set on the slopes of a steep hill, today it sports massive black steel headframes – "gallus frames" (gallows frames) to miners – grand architecture,

Ⓒ **Eat**

Granny's Gourmet Donuts (3 Tai Lane, at West Lincoln Street; tel: +1 406 922 0022), a tiny hole-in-the-wall near the MSU campus in Bozeman, has garnered something of a cult following for its freshly made donuts, just $1 each, from the addictive orange-cream flavor to the zingy strawberry. Cash only.

The Nurses Lakes and Gallatin National Forest.

Butte's Pork Chop John's (8 West Mercury Street; tel: +1 406 782 0812, www.porkchopjohns.com) has been knocking out fried breaded pork sandwiches since 1932, while Sparky's Garage (222 East Park Street; tel: +1 406 782 2301; www.sparkysrestaurant.com) is loaded with auto memorabilia. The American Chinese Pekin Noodle Parlor (117 South Main Street; tel: +1 406 782 2217) is a historic gem, open since 1911, with pink wooden booths.

Paddleboarding on the Hyalite Reservoir.

Cornish pasties and Irish and Serbian churches, all a legacy of its turbulent mining heyday. Though mining still takes place here, Butte's population has been on the decline for years, with around 34,500 current inhabitants. The historical section is known as Uptown, while below Front Street lies The Flats, where most people live today. At dusk it's all oddly attractive, when the golden light casts a glow on the mine-pocked hillsides, and the old neon signs illuminate historic brick buildings.

Grand remnants of Butte's past include **Copper King Mansion** (219 West Granite Street; tel: +1 406 782 7580; tours May–Sept daily 10am–4pm), completed for copper magnate William A. Clark in 1888. Along with frescoed ceilings, handcrafted mahogany and bird's-eye maple chandeliers and fireplaces, the "modern Elizabethan"-style mansion has been restocked with an incredible collection of period antiques, dolls, toys, clocks, paintings, and carpets; it also has the draw of being a working bed and breakfast. Nearby, Charles W. Clark,

the eldest son of William Clark, built the **Historic Clark Chateau** (321 West Broadway; tel: +1 406 491 5636; www.clarkchateau.org; May–Aug Thu–Sun noon–4pm, Sept–Apr Sat and Sun noon–4pm) in 1898, a mock-French castle with a splendid spiral staircase, exotic-wood-inlaid rooms, and wrought-iron decor. It now contains Victorian furniture and antiques, as well as a rotating selection of contemporary regional art.

Hard to imagine today, but Butte once had a thriving Chinese community, at its peak in the 1910s and commemorated at the **Mai Wah Museum** (17 West Mercury Street; tel: +1 406 723 3231; www.maiwah.org; June–Sept Tue–Sat 10am–4pm). The museum occupies two historic buildings; the Wah Chong Tai, erected in 1899 and a general store operated by the Chinn family until 1941, and the Mai Wah Noodle Parlour, built in 1909. The Wah Chong Tai section is crammed with all its original contents frozen in time, and a detailed exhibit on Butte's Chinatown, which emerged around here in

the 1870s. By the 1940s most Chinese had gone and many nearby buildings were demolished. The nearby **Dumas Brothel** (45 East Mercury Street; tel: +1 406 351 9922; https://dumas-brothel.com; call for hours) preserves the real brothel that operated here between 1890 and 1982.

BUTTE'S MINING HISTORY

In 1954 Anaconda Mining decided to open up the Berkeley Pit in Butte, an incredibly productive move that led to some 320 million tons of copper being extracted before the mine closed in 1982 thanks to the collapse in copper prices. Unfortunately, the company had to demolish half of Butte to create this giant hole, 1,800ft/549 meters deep, one mile (1.6km) wide and 1.25 miles (2km) long. When the whole thing flooded after closing, it became some of the most toxic water in the US. At the **Berkeley Pit Viewing Stand** (300 Continental Drive; tel: +1 406 723 3177; https://pitwatch.org; Mar–Nov daily 9am–5pm) you can take in the vast size of it all, and learn about the long-term efforts to clean it up.

The excellent **World Museum of Mining** (155 Museum Way; tel: +1 406 723 7211; https://miningmuseum.org; Apr–Oct daily 9.30am–5.30pm), on the far side of the Montana Technological University campus, is packed with fascinating memorabilia, and outside, the museum's 50-building Hell Roarin' Gulch re-creates a mining camp of the 1890s, complete with saloon, bordello, church, schoolhouse, and Chinese laundry. You can also take in an underground tour of the rickety old mine facilities, walking through tunnels below the surface (though the mine is completely flooded below 100ft/30 meters).

HELENA

Some 70 miles (112km) north of Butte on I-15, **Helena ⑥** is Montana's relaxed, tiny state capital, founded in 1864 when a party of gold prospectors hit the jackpot at Last Chance Gulch. During the boom years, more than $20 million in gold was extracted from the gulch, and 50 successful prospectors remained here as millionaires. Last Chance Gulch is now the town's attractive main street whose stately Victorian buildings are home to gift shops, restaurants, and bars; the gulch from the name still runs, but it is underground now and therefore not visible. Contrast this with the far more modest digs southwest of town in **Reeder's Alley** (www.reedersalley.com), a collection of miners' bunkhouses, wooden storehouses, and other humble stone and brick structures built between 1875 and 1884, now refurbished into smart stores and diners.

The Montana legislative branch has worked since 1902 out of the elegant **Montana State Capitol** (1301 East 6th Avenue; tel: +1 406 444 4789; https://mhs.mt.gov/education/Capitol; Mon–Fri 8am–5pm, Sat and Sun 9am–3pm; free), topped with a copper-clad dome and featuring an ornate, French

A French-inspired chateau in Butte.

◎ Eat

Big Dipper Ice Cream (www.bigdippericecream. com) has been a local Montana favorite since 1995, with unusual and delicious concoctions such as strawberry pink peppercorn sorbet. It has branches in Missoula, Helena, and Billings, with an ice cream truck called "Coneboy" also rolling around Missoula – It's also sold in Glacier National Park and at Yellowstone.

Renaissance interior adorned with stained-glass skylights and numerous murals. The most famous artwork lies in the House Chamber, where a huge mural completed by Montana artist Charles M. Russell in 1911 depicts a dramatic encounter between Native tribes and Lewis and Clark.

The illuminating **Montana's Museum** (225 North Roberts Street; tel: +1 406 444 2694; https://mhs.mt.gov; Mon–Sat 9am–5pm) opposite the Capitol, chronicles the history of the state in great detail with clear explanations and rare artifacts from each period. The new **Montana Heritage Center** should open in 2024 (https://montanamuseum. org). The Montana Historical Society runs the museum as well as tours of the **Original Governor's Mansion** (304 North Ewing Street; mid-May to mid-Sept Tue–Sat noon–3pm, mid-Sept to mid-May Sat noon–3pm).

Other local attractions include the **Holter Museum of Art** (12 East Lawrence Street; tel: +1 406 442 6400; https://holtermuseum.org; Tue–Sat 10am–5.30pm, Sun noon–4pm; free),

specializing in regional artists, and the science exhibits at the family-friendly **ExplorationWorks** (995 Carousel Way; tel: +1 406 457 1800; Tue–Sun 10am–5pm). One of the grandest Catholic cathedrals in the West is the **Cathedral of St Helena** (530 North Ewing Street; www.sthelenas.org), completed in 1924; it's modeled after the Cathedral of the Sacred Heart in Vienna.

GATES OF THE MOUNTAINS

One of the region's more worthwhile excursions is the two-hour guided boat tour through the stunning **Gates of the Mountains** ❼ (tel: +1 406 458 5241; https://gatesofthemountains. com; late May to late Sept), some 25 miles (40km) north of Helena off I-15. This dramatic stretch of the Missouri River, also known as Great White Rock Canyon, is a six-mile (9.7-km) gorge between sheer 1,200ft/366-meter limestone cliffs named by explorer Meriwether Lewis. While not as grand as Glacier National Park, the gentle cruise does offer plenty of scenic splendor, not to mention an eye-opening array of wildlife, including resident pelicans and bald eagles, bighorn sheep, and occasionally mountain lions and black bears (August is the best time for the latter).

DEER LODGE

Some 37 miles (60km) from Butte on I-90, **Deer Lodge** ❽ offers a trio of interesting attractions. The region's long-time importance as a ranching center is commemorated by the **Grant-Kohrs Ranch National Historic Site** (266 Warren Lane; tel: +1 406 846 2070; www.nps.gov/grko; daily late May to early Sept 9am–5.30pm, rest of year 9am–4.30pm), just north of town. This, the first ranch in Montana, was started by Johnny Grant in 1862 and expanded by German immigrant Conrad Kohrs, who built an empire stretching across four states and into Canada. The Kohrs'

Horse-drawn wagons at the World Museum Of Mining in Butte.

Victorian ranch house is a pinnacle of frontier luxury.

The castle-like building in town is in fact the **Old Montana Prison Museum** (1104 Main Street; tel: +1 406 846 3111; http://pcmaf.org; daily 10am–4pm, with exceptions), which is open for grimly fascinating tours; next door is the **Montana Auto Museum** (same details). From the Model T to the T-bird, it's a gleaming shrine to American chrome. The same organization runs the nearby **Frontier Montana Museum** (Thu–Sun noon–5pm) and Powell County Museum.

MISSOULA

Framed by the striking Bitterroot and Sapphire mountains on the banks of the Clark Fork River, vibrant and friendly **Missoula** ❾ is full of contrasts – bookstores, continental cafés, and gun shops – a place where students from the local University of Montana (UM) provide much of the town's energy. Founded in 1866, it's now the second biggest city in Montana. A little south of downtown, **Fort Missoula** was built in 1877 to protect the young

settlement against the Nez Perce; it's now a historical museum (tel: +1 406 728 3476; https://fortmissoulamuseum.org; Mon–Sat 10am–5pm, Sun noon–5pm late May to early Sept; Tue–Sun noon–5pm early Sept to late May).

One sign of Missoula's modern dynamism is the **Missoula Art Museum** (335 North Pattee Street; tel: +1 406 728 0447; https://missoulaartmuseum.org; Tue–Sat 10am–5pm; free), which displays challenging contemporary work in digital photography, painting, and sculpture (especially art related to the American West), and a range of eye-opening pieces by contemporary Native American artists.

On the UM campus, the **Montana Museum of Art & Culture** (tel: +1 406 243 2019; www.umt.edu/montanamuseum; Tue–Sat noon–6pm) boasts an incredibly rich collection of art highlighted by florid Renaissance-era Flemish tapestries, paintings and prints by Rembrandt, Delacroix, Joan Miró, Picasso, and Toulouse-Lautrec, and American art from Frederic Remington, Warhol, Rockwell, and many others.

Prairie church in the fog at Fort Missoula.

⊘ OUTDOOR MISSOULA

Missoula is a particularly good base for outdoor activities. Worthwhile hikes traverse the 60,000 acres (243 sq km) of the Rattlesnake National Recreation Area, which, despite the name, claims to be serpent-free; find more information at the local ranger station (Fort Missoula, Building 24; Mon–Fri 8am–4.30pm; tel: +1 406 329 3750; www.fs.usda.gov/lolo). Missoula is also excellent for cycling, and another good source of information and trail maps is the Adventure Cycling Association (150 East Pine Street; tel: +1 406 721 1776; www.adventurecycling.org). The Bicycle Hangar (1801 Brooks Street and 424 North Higgins Avenue, Tue–Sat 10am–6pm; tel: + 1 406 728 9537; www.bicycle-hangar.com) rents out good-quality mountain bikes.

The most developed of the city's small ski areas is Montana Snowbowl (tel: +1 406 549 9777; www.montanasnowbowl.com), 12 miles (19km) northwest. For state-park camping you'll need to backtrack east, either 25 miles (40km) on I-90 to small Beavertail Hill State Park (May–Oct; tel: +1 406 542 5500), which has 24 campsites with electricity and also two Sioux-style tipis to stay in, or 40 miles (64km) on Hwy-200 and a brief jog on Hwy-83 north to Salmon Lake State Park (same phone number), which is great for its fishing and swimming in the Clearwater River.

Operated by the pro-conservation/ pro-hunting Rocky Mountain Elk Foundation just outside town, the **Elk Country Visitor Center** (5705 Grant Creek Road; tel: +1 866 266 7750; https://rmef. org; check website for times; free) provides exhibits about the region's prodigious horned creatures, with a short walking trail supplying on-site examples of a few of the animals you can expect to see on more rugged hikes.

Fires are common in this part of the country during the dry season, and the associated dangers are highlighted at the Forest Service **Smokejumper Center** (5765 West Broadway St; tel: +1 406 329 4934; May–Oct daily 8.30am– 5pm; free), 10 miles (16km) out of town on US-93. A small visitor center explains methods used to train smokejumpers here – highly skilled firefighters who parachute into forested areas to stop the spread of wildfires.

GARNET GHOST TOWN

To get an in-depth look at the rugged days of the Old West, travel east from Missoula some 40 miles (64km) on I-90, then another 11 bumpy miles (18km) by single-lane Bear Gulch Road, to **Garnet Ghost Town**  (Garnet Range Road; tel: +1 406 329 3914; http://garnetghosttown.org; daily 9.30am–4.30pm, road open May–Dec 15 only). In the late 1890s this site was home to thousands of hard-rock gold miners doing a tough, perilous job – by 1905 many of the mines were abandoned and the town's population had shrunk to about 150. By the 1940s Garnet was a ghost town, and since the buildings have been kept in their semi-decayed state, the atmosphere is quite arresting: the quiet and lonely specter of vacant, wood-framed saloons, cabins, stores, and a jail, set amid acres of rolling hills that invite a leisurely stroll.

NATIONAL BISON RANGE

Conveniently located just off the route between Missoula and Glacier National Park, the **National Bison Range**  (58355 Bison Range Road, Hwy-212; tel: +1 406 644 2211; https://bisonrange. org; Visitor Center daily 8am–5pm, Red Sleep Drive mid-May to early Oct daily 6.30am–6pm) lies near the town of Moiese. Beyond the small Visitor Center, the 19 mile (30km) Red Sleep Mountain Drive loop road rises into the hills for stellar views of the surrounding mountains, before dropping down to plains that harbor small herds of 350– 500 bison – you might also see black bears, and plenty of pronghorn and deer. Note that it's strictly forbidden to leave your car, except on two marked hiking trails. The preserve was carved out of the Flathead Indian Reservation in 1908; after a long legal battle, the Confederated Salish and Kootenai Tribes became the stewards of the bison herd and range in 2020.

FLATHEAD LAKE

The alpine charms of 28-mile (45-km) long **Flathead Lake** provide a welcome diversion on the long route

A bison grazing at the Bison Range.

north toward Glacier National Park, reached by following US-93 north from I-90. Between Polson in the south and Somers in the north, US-93 follows the lake's curving western shore, while the narrower Hwy-36 runs up the east below the Mission Mountains, and is the summer home to countless roadside cherry and berry vendors. Surrounded by low-lying mountains, both routes offer handsome views of the deep blue waters, and the lake is a great place for hiking, boating, or just lazing on the shore for a few hours, though there are plenty of amusements in the nearby towns. About eight miles (13 km) above the lake's north shore, **Kalispell** ⑫ is the Flathead Valley's largest town, but the small resort of **Bigfork** ⑬ in the northeast is the more pleasant place to stay. Kalispell's major landmark is the **Conrad Mansion** (330 Woodland Avenue; tel: +1 406 755 2166; www.conradmansion.com; May to mid-Oct Tue–Sun 11am–5pm, mid-Oct to Apr Tue–Fri 10am–4pm), built in 1895 by a 19th-century railroad tycoon. The sprawling house is now open for tours, run by guides in full period dress.

WILD HORSE ISLAND STATE PARK

Wild Horse Island ⑭ (tel: +1 406 837 3041; daily sunset–sunrise), Flathead Lake's largest island, is a state park and can be reached by boat. Hiking on its terrific range of moderate to steep trails, which lead past knolls, ponderosa forest, and buttes up to fine lookouts over the lake, you're apt to see mule deer and the odd group of bighorn sheep – though unfortunately the eponymous wild horses are few (there are in fact just five of them) and therefore very rarely seen; those who do catch a glimpse are extremely lucky. To visit the island, rent a motorboat or kayak or contact Pointer Scenic Cruises (452 Grand Drive, tel: +1 406 837 5617; www.wildhorseislandboattrips.com;

May–Nov Mon–Sat only) in Bigfork, or Big Arm Boat Rentals and Rides (44227 A Street; tel: +1 406 260 5090; www.boatrentalsandrides.com; May to mid-Sept daily) which runs round-trip shuttles to the island from the village of **Big Arm** ⑮.

WHITEFISH

The old logging town of **Whitefish** ⑯, just 25 miles (40km) west of Glacier National Park, is now one of the most popular resorts in Montana, perched on the south shore of beautiful Whitefish Lake in the shade of the **Whitefish Mountain Ski Resort** ⑰ (tel: +1 406 862 2900; https://skiwhitefish.com). As one of the area's big-name winter sports draws, the resort is also excellent for hiking in summer, when you can trudge four hard miles (6.4km) up to a restaurant on top of the mountain; you can also take a chairlift ride, or cycle the roads around the lake and foothills – bikes can be rented from Glacier Cyclery (326 East 2nd Street; tel: +1 406 862 6446; www.glaciercyclery.com).

⊙ Shop

Eva Gates (456 Electric Avenue, Bigfork; tel. +1 406 837 4356; www.evagates.com) began making her wild berry preserves back in 1949, and her original store is still a great place to pick up souvenirs and picnic items like fudges, jams, teas, syrups, and sweets made with local huckleberries, strawberries, raspberries, cherries, and apples.

Whitefish Lake as the sun goes down.

Shoshone Falls and Snake River, Idaho.

IDAHO

Declared a state in 1890 after much political wrangling, Idaho was the last of the Western regions to be penetrated by white settlers and it remains perhaps the least known and visited.

In 1805, Lewis and Clark described central Idaho's bewildering labyrinth of razor-edged peaks and wild waterways as the most difficult leg of their epic trek. Often assumed to be all potato country today, Idaho has most of the world fooled; much of its mind-blowing scenery deserves national park status, but it has always lacked the major showstoppers (and therefore the crowds) of its neighboring states, a situation its famously conservative citizens have long been happy to maintain.

The state capital, Boise, is surprisingly urbane and friendly, but above all, this is a destination for the outdoors enthusiast. The state is laced with incredibly scenic highways, especially through the jaw-dropping Sawtooth Mountains, with Red Fish Lake offering some of the most mesmerizing scenery in the Rockies. Other natural wonders include Hells Canyon, America's deepest river gorge, and the black, barren Craters of the Moon. Hikers and backpackers have the choice of some eighty mountain ranges, interspersed with virgin forest and lava plateaus, while the mighty Snake and Salmon rivers offer endless fishing and especially whitewater rafting. You'll eat well here, too: the fresh trout is superb, and the state is also known for hops (and therefore microbrews), lamb, and, of course, fine potatoes.

The State Capitol Building of Idaho in Boise.

BOISE

The verdant, likeable capital of Idaho, **Boise** ❶ (pronounced "BOY-see"; never "zee") straddles I-84, just 50 miles (80km) east of the Oregon border, and was established in 1862 for the benefit of pioneers using the Oregon Trail. After adapting (or perhaps misspelling) the name originally given to the area by French trappers – *les bois*, meaning "the woods" – the earliest residents boosted the town's appearance by getting to work planting hundreds more trees.

⊙ Main attractions

Boise
Craters of the Moon
Custer
Hell's Canyon
Nez Perce National
  Historical Park
Red Fish Lake
Salmon River Scenic
  Byway
Sawtooth Scenic Byway
Shoshone Falls
Wallace

Map on page 264

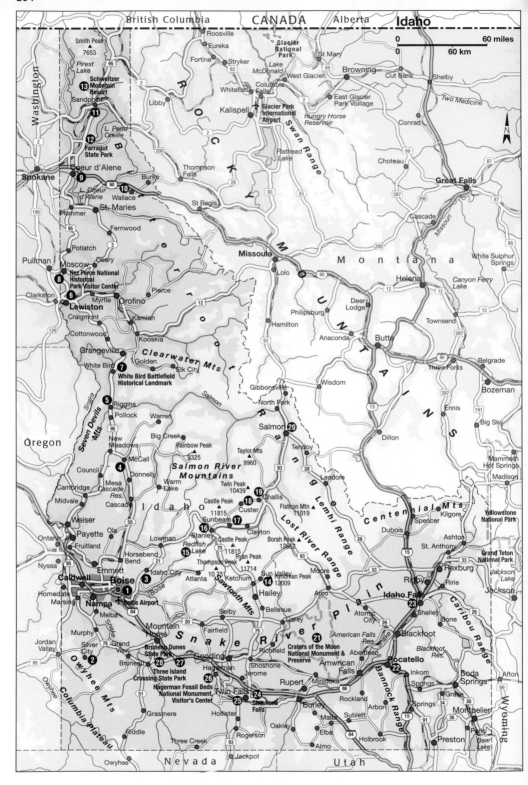

Today Boise is a friendly, cosmopolitan, and outdoorsy city, with great skiing, biking, and floating along the Boise River (the favorite way for locals to cool off in the summer), all within paddling distance of a host of excellent independent stores, restaurants, and bars.

Downtown is centered on the fountains at Grove Plaza, where the annual "Alive after Five" concert series sees different food and drink vendors take over the square (June–Sept every Wed 5–8pm).

Boise is also unique in having the largest Basque population in the world outside of the Basque heartland (in Spain and France), and is the home of **Boise State University** (BSU), whose football team the Broncos (with its famed all-blue field, lined with blue-painted turf) receives fanatical support from locals – their rivalry with University of Idaho in Moscow goes back a long way, though the two teams rarely meet these days. But perhaps Boise's best feature is the **Greenbelt**, a 25-mile (40km) bike path and hiking trail that crisscrosses the tranquil Boise River, linking various parks right in the heart of the city.

The centerpiece of downtown Boise is the **Idaho State Capitol** (700 West Jefferson Street; tel: +1 208 332 1012; https://capitolcommission.idaho.gov; Mon–Fri 6.30am–7pm, Sat and Sun 9am–5pm), with a fairly typical grand neoclassical domed exterior completed in 1912, but an unusual, striking interior clad in white marble with green veining. Get maps for a self-guided tour in the basement, where exhibits on the potentially dry subject of the history and structure of Idaho state government are surprisingly entertaining. Nearby, the **Old Boise Historic District** (https://old-boise.com) is an elegant area of stone-trimmed brick restaurants and shops (built mostly 1903–10).

The **Basque Museum and Cultural Center** (611 Grove Street; tel: +1 208 343 2671; https://basquemuseum.eus; Tue–Fri 10am–4pm, Sat 11am–3pm),

on the "Basque Block" of Grove Street, traces the heritage of the Basque shepherds of mountainous central Idaho through illuminating antiques, relics, photographs, and key manuscripts. The site includes the charming Cyrus Jacobs-Uberuaga boarding house, built in 1864.

The interactive **Idaho State Museum** (610 North Julia Davis Drive; tel: +1 208 334 2120; https://history.idaho.gov; Mon–Sat 10am–5pm, Sun noon–5pm) displays artifacts from Native American and Basque peoples, details the difficult experience of the Chinese miners of the 1870s and 1880s, and describes the lives of Idahoans from furriers to gold miners and ranchers.

Other attractions nearby include the **Boise Art Museum** (670 Julia Davis Drive; tel: +1 208 345 8330; http://www.boiseartmuseum.org; Tue–Sat 10am–5pm, Sun noon–5pm), **Zoo Boise** (355 Julia Davis Drive; tel: +1 208 608 7760; https://zooboise.org; daily 10am–5pm), and the family-friendly scenic exhibits at the **Discovery Center of Idaho** (131 West Myrtle Street; tel: +1 208

Old Idaho State Penitentiary Site.

343 9895; www.dcidaho.org; Mon–Sat 10am–4.30pm, Sun noon–4.30pm).

On the edge of town, the grim **Old Idaho Penitentiary** (2445 Old Penitentiary Road, off Warm Springs Avenue; https://history.idaho.gov; tel: +1 208 334 2844; daily summer 10am–5pm; rest of year noon–5pm) is an imposing sandstone citadel that remained open from 1870 until a major riot in 1973 finally persuaded the authorities to build modern facilities – some shared cells still had slop buckets instead of toilets. Exhibits include confiscated weapons and mugshots of former inmates, including one Harry Orchard, who murdered the state governor in 1905.

SILVER CITY AND IDAHO CITY

The Wild West is also still in evidence at **Silver City ❷**, a once-rowdy mining town reached over a 23-mile (37km) rough road off Hwy-78 (look for the sign east of Murphy), and **Idaho City ❸**, northeast of Boise via Hwy-21. Silver City is the sleepier – and thereby the more genuine – of the two ghost towns, but Idaho City is an easier drive.

PAYETTE RIVER SCENIC BYWAY

Hwy-55 north of Boise is known as the **Payette River Scenic Byway** (http://payetteriverscenicbyway.org) for its 110-mile (177km) run to McCall. It's a pretty drive, with views ranging from tight river canyons narrowly shared with the highway to broad swaths of farmland north of Cascade. Nearly all the land to the east (and much to the west) of Hwy-55 is part of Boise National Forest. Intriguing side roads lead to such little-known spots as Warm Lake, a recreation area, and Yellow Pine, home of a harmonica festival the first weekend of August.

Summer or winter, **McCall ❹** is a major Idaho sports capital. During the warmer months, Payette Lake is the center of attention, with many visitors choosing to set up camp at Ponderosa State Park just two miles (3km) from town. The McCall Winter Carnival, held in late January, features a major ice-sculpting competition, snowmobile races, parades, and fireworks; visitors arriving in other winter months will find

Road Bridge over the Payette River.

downhill skiing at Brundage Mountain (https://brundage.com) and cross-country skiing and snowmobile trails throughout the McCall-Cascade area.

HELLS CANYON NATIONAL RECREATION AREA

From McCall, Hwy-55 climbs steadily to merge with US-95 and follow the turbulent Little Salmon River. Just south of the outdoorsy town of **Riggins** ❺, 30 miles (48km) on, comes a good opportunity to see **Hells Canyon** from Idaho. With an average depth of 5,500ft (1,676 meters) this is the deepest river gorge in the US, though you wouldn't guess so due to its broad expanse and lack of sheer walls. Nevertheless, it is impressive, with Oregon's Wallowa and Eagle Cap ranges rising behind it and the river glimmering far down below. Heaven's Gate Overlook is the best viewpoint into the canyon from Idaho; from the south end of Riggins, allow a half-day to reach the overlook on a very steep and winding gravel road (Forest Road 517), best tackled in a 4WD. The canyon is also accessible by road from Oregon but the most exhilarating way to experience Hells Canyon is via a jet-boat ride – you won't easily forget the soaring cliffs, whitewater rapids, bald eagles, glimpses of black bears, and gorgeous scenery. On the Idaho side, Killgore Adventures is a reputable outfit, based in the small town of White Bird, 30 miles (48km) north of Riggins (tel: +1 208-839 2255; www.killgoreadventures.com).

NEZ PERCE NATIONAL HISTORICAL PARK

North-central Idaho is the homeland of the Nez Perce (or Nez Percé), whose leader – Chief Joseph – led the tribe on one of history's greatest marches in 1877 before finally surrendering with his famous "I will fight no more forever" speech. Unlike most sites of its kind, **Nez Perce National Historical Park** isn't a single spot but a collection of 38 separate places that are important to the tribe (known today as the Niimíipu). At the **Visitor Center** ❻ in Spalding, 10 miles (16km) east of Lewiston (39063 US-95, Lapwai; tel:

⊙ THE NIIMÍIPU

The first whites to encounter the Niimíipu were the weak, hungry, and disease-ridden Lewis and Clark expedition in 1805. The Niimíipu gave them food and shelter, and cared for their animals until the party was ready to carry on westward. Relations between the Niimíipu (called the "Nez Percé" by French-Canadian trappers because of their shell-pierced noses) and whites remained agreeable for more than 50 years, until the discovery of gold, and pressure for property ownership led the US government to persuade some renegade Niimíipu to sign a treaty in 1863 that took away three-quarters of tribal land. As settlers started to move into the hunting grounds of the Wallowa Valley in the early 1870s, the majority of the Niimíipu, under Chief Joseph, refused to recognize the agreement. In 1877, after much vacillation, the government decided to enact its terms and gave the tribe 30 days to leave.

Ensuing skirmishes resulted in the deaths of a handful of settlers, and a large army force began to gather to round up the tribe. Chief Joseph then embarked upon the famous **Retreat of the Nez Percé**. Around 250 Niimíipu warriors (protecting twice as many women, children, and old people) outmaneuvered army columns many times their size, launching frequent guerrilla attacks in a series of narrow escapes. After four months and 1,700 miles (2,736km), the Niimíipu were cornered by Colonel Nelson Miles just 30 miles (48km) from the safety of the Canadian border. Following the five-day battle and siege at Bear Paw, the Niimíipu ceased fighting on October 5th, 1877. Chief Joseph then reportedly made his legendary speech of surrender, "My heart is sick and sad. From where the sun now stands I will fight no more forever".

Today some 1,500 Niimíipu live in a reservation between Lewiston and Grangeville – a minute fraction of their original territory. In addition to sites in Idaho (see above), the **Nez Perce National Historical Park** includes Big Hole National Battlefield and the Bear Paw Battlefield in Montana, Old Chief Joseph Gravesite in Oregon, Buffalo Eddy in Washington (Niimíipu petroglyphs), and Weippe Prairie (also in Idaho), where Lewis and Clark met the Niimíipu in 1805.

+1 208 843 7001; www.nps.gov/nepe Apr–Dec daily 8.30am–4pm; Jan–Mar Tue–Sat 8.30am–4pm), the museum focuses on tribal arts and crafts, while the **White Bird Battlefield** , 77 miles (124km) farther south on US-95, was where the tribe inflicted 34 deaths on the US Army, in the first major battle of the Retreat.

MOSCOW

The 30 miles (48km) of US-95 between Lewiston, at the north end of Hells Canyon, and **Moscow** ⑧, wind through the beautiful rolling hillsides of the fertile Palouse Valley. Moscow itself is a fun, friendly town that makes a good overnight stop, and is the site of the **University of Idaho** (www.uidaho.edu). Bookstores, galleries, bars and cafés line the tree-shaded Main Street, while theatre, music and independent cinema are on offer throughout the year, along with a sprinkling of arts festivals: the **Moscow Art-walk** (tel: +1 208 883 7036) brings together dozens of artists, galleries, and the public for diverting summertime exhibits, and the **Lionel**

Hydraulic mining drill demonstration in the Sierra Silver Mine.

Hampton Jazz Festival (tel: +1 208 885 6765; www.uidaho.edu/class/jazzfest) showcases big names new and old every February.

IDAHO PANHANDLE

The narrow, rugged, northern section of Idaho is known as the **Idaho Panhandle**, more easily accessed from Washington and Montana on I-90 – which follows the Coeur d'Alene River and its South Fork – than the southern part of the state. Though Wallace makes for an enticing historical attraction, this region really is all about the outdoors. In fact, the region has the highest concentration of lakes to be found anywhere in the western United States. The big three are Coeur d'Alene, Pend Oreille, and Priest Lake, and together they offer close to 150,000 acres (60,703 hectares) of water surface. Note that the Panhandle observes Pacific Time (1hr behind the rest of the state, which follows US Mountain Time).

Now a major resort and the capital of the Panhandle, **Coeur d'Alene** ⑨ ('core da lane') lies 50 miles (80km)

north of Moscow on the shores of lovely 25-mile-long (40km) Lake Coeur d'Alene, which stretches into the mountains. Poised on the lake is the expensive Coeur d'Alene Resort which dominates the unremarkable downtown, where cruises (late Apr–mid-Nov daily 1–3; www.cdacruises.com) give you a closer view.

Some 48 miles (77km) southeast of Coeur d'Alene lies the authentic Old West mining town of **Wallace ⑩**, established by one Colonel Wallace in 1884 and briefly the silver mining capital of the world. Those days are long gone, and the town has struggled to survive in recent years, despite being extremely picturesque; Its shabby, historic streets are some of the most memorable in the Rockies, and the 1997 movie *Dante's Peak* was filmed here. Get acquainted with the town's turbulent history on the **Sierra Silver Mine Tour**, a 75-minute trolley-car ride departing 420 North 5th Street (tel: +1 208 752 5151; www.silverminetour.org; daily June–Aug every 30min 10am–4pm, May, Sept and Oct 10am–2pm), which lets you descend 1000ft (305 meters) to appreciate the hard labor endured by miners a century ago.

To find out more, drop by the **Wallace District Mining Museum** (509 Bank Street; tel: +1 208 556 1592; https://wallaceminingmuseum.com; Thu and Fri 1–5pm, Sat 9am–5pm, with exceptions), which has replicas, photographs, and artifacts from the gold and silver heydays from the 1880s to the 1940s. To see what miners did on their days off, visit the **Oasis Bordello Museum** (605 Cedar Street; tel: +1 208 753 0801; May–Oct daily 10am–5pm), chronicling the colorful 100-year history of a certain local "institution."

Forty-four miles (71km) north of Coeur d'Alene, the pretty little town of **Sandpoint ⑪** lies at the northwestern end of 43-mile (69km) long **Lake Pend Oreille** (pronounced "PON-duh-ray"), with its downtown overlooking placid

Sandy Creek, but its main attractions are somewhat farther out. At the south end of the lake, **Farragut State Park ⑫** (13400 Ranger Road; tel: +1 208 683 2425; visitor center daily 9am–4pm), has 4,000 acres (1618 hectares) for boating, hiking, camping, and the like. To the northeast, the spiky Selkirk Mountains hold the **Schweitzer Mountain Resort ⑬** (tel: +1 208 263 9555, www.schweitzer.com), northern Idaho's best ski resort, with plenty of spacious, comfortable lodging.

Farther north still, **Priest Lake** is actually two lakes connected by a short river. The area's remote location makes it a good bet for travelers trying to avoid crowds, though even Priest Lake gets its share of traffic in the summer. Head to the east side for primitive camping and boating or to the western shores for family-style resorts, including **Hill's** (www.hillsresort.com) and **Elkins** (www.elkinsresort.com).

SUN VALLEY

Around 155 miles (250km) east from Boise, the Wood River Valley was where

Hells Canyon National Recreation Area.

Averell Harriman, convinced that the American West needed a grand ski resort in the European tradition, built **Sun Valley**  (www.sunvalley.com) in 1936. Now as popular in summer as it is in winter, Sun Valley and its neighboring town of **Ketchum** offer a smorgasbord of recreational options from the usual (golf and tennis) to the offbeat (llama trekking and paragliding). Today it becomes the center of the media world every July during the enormously influential Allen & Company Sun Valley Conference, held at the Sun Valley Lodge. The area is also one of Idaho's strongest in the arts, boasting such offerings as a professional theater troupe, several summer music series, and an active gallery scene.

THE SAWTOOTH MOUNTAINS

North of Ketchum and Sun Valley, Hwy-75 climbs through rising tracts of forests and mountains to top out after 20 miles (32km) at the spectacular panorama of **Galena Summit** (8,701ft/2652 meters). Spreading out far below, the meadows of the Sawtooth Valley stretch

A kayaker paddles though the mist and fog in early December on Coeur d'Alene Lake.

northward. The winding road – dubbed the **Sawtooth Scenic Byway** – meanders beside the Salmon River, whose headwaters rise in the forbidding icy peaks to the south, as the serrated ridge of the Sawtooth Mountains forms an impenetrable barrier along the western horizon. The main highlight along this stretch is **Red Fish Lake** (just off the highway, 60 miles/97km north of Ketchum), beautifully framed by Mount Heyburn and Grand Mogul peaks, home to sockeye salmon and plenty of hiking and camping opportunities in the area of alpine lakes known as Shangri-La. Visit **Redfish Center & Gallery** (tel: +1 208 774 3376; June to mid-Sept daily 9.30am–5pm) by the lake for information, wildlife talks, and boat trips.

A tiny collection of attractive wooden buildings, **Stanley** lies seven miles (11km) north of the lake – the main activity here in summer is organizing rafting trips (May–Sept). Operators include the River Company (tel: +1 208 788 5775; www.therivercompany. com), which operates three- to four-hour trips.

⊘ HEMINGWAY

Ernest Hemingway completed *For Whom the Bell Tolls* as a guest of the Sun Valley Lodge in 1939, and lived in Ketchum for the last two years of his life before his shotgun suicide in 1961. His simple, flat gravestone can be found in Ketchum Cemetery (1026 North Main Street/Hwy-75; www.ketchum-cemetery.org), next to those of his wife and son. The Hemingway Memorial (a bronze bust of the writer erected in 1966) is just off Trail Creek Road, one mile (1.6km) east from Sun Valley Lodge; it's inscribed with Hemingway's own words, ending "...Now he will be a part of them forever."

The Ketchum Community Library actually owns Hemingway's last home in the valley, on a private drive off East Canyon Run Boulevard and where Mary Hemingway lived until 1986, but it remains closed to the public.

Taking a five-day rafting trip down the Middle Fork of the Salmon River is perhaps the most exhilarating and unforgettable experience in Idaho; by the time you've finished you'll feel like one of Lewis and Clark's team. The river drops 3000ft (914 meters) during its 105-mile (169km) journey through the isolated and spectacular River of No Return Wilderness. Trips usually begin in Stanley, end in Salmon, Idaho, and cost from $2000 and up (June–Sept only; www.rowadventures.com).

SALMON RIVER SCENIC BYWAY

East of Stanley, the **Salmon River Scenic Byway** (still Hwy-75) follows the Salmon River through the Salmon-Challis National Forest, a gorgeous route that snakes through wooded gorges and soaring mountains. At the town of **Sunbeam** ⓱ (13 miles/21km from Stanley), it's worth branching left onto the Custer Motorway (also known as Forest Road 070), a mostly gravel road that curves northwest up the Yankee Fork creek. You'll pass the **Yankee Fork Gold Dredge** (eight miles/13km from Sunbeam) a 112ft (34 meter), a nearly thousand-ton barge that once mined gold from the stream (https://yankeeforkdredge.com; summer daily 10am–4.30pm), and a few miles farther on, the preserved ghost town of **Custer** ⓲, a gold-mining camp that flourished from 1879 to 1910; you can also visit the less developed site of Bonanza. The old schoolhouse operates as a small museum (summer daily 10am–4pm).

Beyond Custer the road is much rougher – unless you have a 4WD it's best to head back to Sunbeam. The two routes come together near Challis, where the landscape becomes much more arid and treeless. **Land of the Yankee Fork Interpretive Center** (summer daily 9am–5pm; rest of year Tue–Fri 10am–4pm; tel: +1 208 879 5244) near **Challis** ⓳ at the intersection of highways 75 and 93, chronicles the

history of the region's Gold Rush from 1870. From Challis US-93 runs 60 miles (97km) north through a series of stunning gorges to **Salmon** ⓴, where the **Sacajawea Center** (2700 Main Street, Hwy-28; tel: +1 208 756 1188; www.sacajaweacenter.org; summer Mon–Sat 9am–5pm, Sun 12.30–5pm) contains a small exhibit on the Lewis and Clark expedition in Idaho as seen through the eyes of their Shoshone translator.

For a good scenic drive off the beaten path, try taking Highway 28 southeast 22 miles (35km) to **Tendoy**, the place where you can retrace Meriwether Lewis' steps over Lemhi Pass on the **Lewis and Clark Backcountry Byway**.

CRATERS OF THE MOON NATIONAL MONUMENT

From Sun Valley south, Idaho's landscape changes dramatically. At **Craters of the Moon National Monument** ㉑ near Arco (tel: + 1208 527 1300; www.nps.gov/crmo; daily 24hr), visitors can survey the results of thousands of years of intense geological activity. Scientists

Spattercone Trail in Craters of the Moon National Monument and Preserve, Idaho.

believe that the monument's vast lava fields were created over a series of eruptions that began about 15,000 years ago, with the most recent commotion taking place 2,000 years ago and another one due any century now. A seven-mile (11km) loop road (open late Apr to mid-Nov) provides access to the monument's main features, and the lava-strewn campground makes an interesting place to spend a night.

POCATELLO AND IDAHO FALLS

Pocatello ㉒ and Idaho Falls, the region's two largest cities, are close geographically and similar in size. Culturally, however, the towns are farther apart. Pocatello's two main touchstones are its railroad heritage and its college-town setting, and is a bit scruffier than its neighbor to the north. Idaho Falls, meanwhile, has a strong Mormon influence and a decidedly scientific bent. Despite, or maybe because of, their differences, both cities are well worth exploring. Pocatello's highlights include Ross Park, with a replica of Fort Hall

(3002 Avenue of the Chiefs; tel: +1 208 233 0434; May to early Sept) a major fur trading post and stopping point along the Oregon Trail in the 19th century. Adjacent to the replica is the small (but fun for kids) Zoo Idaho (2900 South 2nd Avenue; tel: +1 208 234 6264; https://zooidaho.org; see website for latest hours), and Bannock County Historical Museum (3000 Avenue of the Chiefs; tel: +1 208 233 0434; Mon–Sat 10am–4pm) that houses railroad memorabilia and Shoshone-Bannock exhibits.

In Idaho Falls ㉓, the best thing to do is plan a picnic on the Greenbelt and a walk through the architecturally rich Ridge Avenue Historic District; sadly, there's not much left of the original falls on the Snake River after a damming project.

The Fort Hall Reservation, home to Native Americans from the Shoshone and Bannock tribes, takes up much of the land between Pocatello and Idaho Falls. The very fine Shoshone-Bannock Indian Festival, held the second week of August, ranks among the biggest events of its kind in Idaho.

Bruneau Dunes State Park, Idaho.

THE SNAKE RIVER PLAIN

I-84 roughly follows the Snake River across much of south-central Idaho, its once-wild water now dammed to serve some of the most productive soil in North America. This is the land of Idaho's "famous potatoes" and of sugar beets, beans, barley, and a cornucopia of other crops. Irrigation is the life-blood of dry Idaho, and several dams in the region – notably Minidoka Dam northeast of Rupert via Highway 24 – have interpretive exhibits telling how the river is harnessed.

Yet the Snake still runs high for a time each year, generally before spring planting season and again in fall after the canals shut down. In these seasons, plan a detour to Caldron Linn, a small but savage chasm on the river near Murtaugh, or **Shoshone Falls** ㉔. The latter cascade, often called the "Niagara of the West," is just a few miles east of the city of **Twin Falls** ㉕ via Falls Avenue or Addison Avenue East. While in Twin Falls, consider a stop at the **Herrett Center** (315 Falls Avenue; tel: +1 208 732 6655; https://herrett.csi.edu; Tue and Fri 9.30am–9pm; Wed and Thu 9.30am–4.30pm; Sat 1–9pm). This handsome facility on the College of Southern Idaho campus includes a state-of-the-art planetarium and houses impressive collections of stone tools and Native American artifacts.

US-30 west of Twin Falls is known as the **Thousand Springs Scenic Route**. The name came after Oregon Trail pioneers spotted countless streams of foaming water crashing from the black canyon walls; there are no longer anywhere near a thousand springs, but those that remain still make for an enchanting sight. These days, this area is best known as the trout-farming capital of the world, producing between 85 and 90 percent of the world's commercially raised trout catch (along with some more exotic species like sturgeon and tilapia). Area restaurants often feature fish that have been caught just hours earlier.

US-30 continues through the little Hagerman Valley, where pastimes include fishing, boating, rafting, bicycling, and soaking in hot pools. Another area attraction, the **Hagerman Fossil Beds National Monument** ㉖ (221 North State Street; tel: +1 208 933 4100; www.nps.gov/hafo) came to prominence after Smithsonian Institution archeologists unearthed fossils of a zebra-like animal here during expeditions in the 1930s. The Thousand Springs Scenic Route returns to I-84 at Bliss.

From here, it's a straight shot back to Boise, unless you happen to get waylaid by such sights as **Three Island Crossing State Park** ㉗ in Glenns Ferry (tel: +1 208 366 2394; visitor center Tue–Sat 9am–4pm), where the Oregon-bound emigrants made their toughest river crossing (a feat reenacted on the first Saturday of August); or the **Bruneau Dunes State Park** ㉘ (tel: +1 208 366 7919; daily 7am–10pm), the tallest single-structured sand dunes in North America.

Clearing fog at the Sawtooth Mountains.

The moon rising above the Teton Mountain Range.

USA: THE ROCKIES

TRAVEL TIPS

TRANSPORT

GETTING THERE

By Air

Many people choose to fly into the Rockies region, then continue their trip by bus, train, plane, or rented car. Several international airlines connect Denver and Salt Lake City airports with parts of North America, Mexico/Central America, Europe, and Asia.

From Canada to Denver, Air Canada connects with Montréal, Toronto, and Vancouver, United flies from Toronto and Vancouver, and WestJet flies from Calgary. To Salt Lake City, Delta flies from Calgary, Toronto, and Vancouver.

From Europe to Denver, British Airways and United fly from London, while Air France operates seasonal flights from Paris; other services are operated by Icelandair (Reykjavík–Keflavík) and Lufthansa (Frankfurt,

Munich). To Salt Lake City, Delta flies from London and Paris.

From Asia, United flies to Denver from Tokyo–Narita.

From other parts of the world, you'll have to change planes in Chicago, Dallas/Fort Worth, on the West Coast (typically LA), or East Coast (typically New York or Atlanta).

Other major destinations in the Rockies that have direct airports with connections to other US cities include: Aspen, Billings, Boise, Bozeman, Colorado Springs, Durango (CO), Eagle/Vail, Glacier Park (Kalispell), Grand Junction, Hailey/Sun Valley, Helena, Idaho Falls, Jackson Hole (for Grand Teton National Park), and Missoula. Yellowstone National Park is served by a handful of domestic flights to Yellowstone Airport (West Yellowstone, MT), Yellowstone Regional Airport (Cody, WY), and Yellowstone International Airport in Bozeman, MT (though the latter is

Frontier Airlines planes.

still 88 miles/142km from the park entrance).

By Road

From Canada or Mexico, passing through customs and immigration at the US border can be a lengthy process, with lines of an hour or two not uncommon on weekends, though the crossings between Montana and the Canadian provinces of Alberta and Saskatchewan tend to be lowkey. If possible, avoid the border, traveling in either direction, on Friday or Sunday late afternoons and evenings.

The major bus company with routes into the US is Greyhound Lines. Some routes end or begin at a Canadian or Mexican city just over the border, where you can subsequently transfer to a local carrier, but there are also special direct services to cities like Denver. For further details, contact Greyhound at tel: +1 214 849 8100, or www.greyhound.com.

⊘ Airlines

Air Canada
Tel: +1-888-247 2262
www.aircanada.com
Air France
Tel: +1-800-237 2747
www.airfrance.com
Alaska Airlines
Tel: +1-800-252 7522
www.alaskaair.com
Allegiant Air
Tel: +1-702-505 8888
www.allegiantair.com
American Airlines
Tel: +1-800-433 7300
www.aa.com
British Airways
Tel: +1-800-247 9297
www.britishairways.com
Delta Air Lines
Tel: +1-800-221 1212
www.delta.com

Frontier Airlines
Tel: +1-801-401 9000
www.flyfrontier.com
Icelandair
Tel: +1-800-223 5500
www.icelandair.com
JetBlue
Tel: +1-800-538 2583
www.jetblue.com
Lufthansa
Tel: +1-800-645 3880
www.lufthansa.com
Southwest Airlines
Tel: +1-800-435 9792
www.southwest.com
United Airlines
Tel: +1-800-864 8331
www.united.com
WestJet
Tel: +1-888-937 8538
www.westjet.com

By Rail

Amtrak offers two direct passenger train routes into the Rockies: the California Zephyr which runs between Chicago and Emeryville (San Francisco), via Denver, Glenwood Springs, and Grand Junction in Colorado, and Provo and Salt Lake City in Utah; and the Empire Builder between Chicago and Portland/Seattle via Glacier National Park and Whitefish in Montana, and Sandpoint in Idaho.

Amtrak's USA Rail Pass allows you to hop-on/hop-off between 10 segments over 30 days.

Both first-class and coach accommodation is available, each with dining cars.

For further information, telephone the nearest train station or contact Amtrak at 1-800-USA-RAIL or www.amtrak.com.

GETTING AROUND

Though it is possible to travel around the Rockies by bus, renting a car is far more convenient, and will allow exploration of national parks and isolated towns and destinations not covered by public transportation. Once you've arrived in the region, air travel is of limited use; most flights simply shuttle back and forth between the major hubs in Denver and Salt Lake City.

By Air

Domestic air services can be useful if you aim to focus on one area, since driving can be very time-consuming; a straightforward drive between Yellowstone and Denver will take over 10 hours non-stop, for example. A number of no-frills and discount

---

⊘ Heritage railroads

While the Rockies is served by few regular passenger trains, the region does boast several "heritage railroads," restored railways that offer rides on old trains (sometimes steam) on often very scenic stretches of track – most only operate in the summer months. Most of these railways can be found in Colorado, where the **Cripple Creek and Victor Narrow Gauge Railroad** (https://cripplecreekrailroad.com) operates 45-minute rides on early 20th-century steam trains.

The **Royal Gorge Route Railroad** (www.royalgorgeroute. com) runs longer trips (via diesel train) from Cañon City to scenic Royal Gorge, while the **Broadmoor Manitou & Pikes Peak Cog Railway** (www.cograilway. com) is the world's highest and longest cog railroad, traversing the summit of Pike's Peak. The incredibly picturesque **Durango and Silverton Narrow Gauge Railroad** (www.durangotrain.com) and **Georgetown Loop Railroad** (www.georgetownlooprr.com) also use steam trains, while the **Leadville, Colorado and Southern Railroad** (www.leadville-train. com) runs a 1955 diesel engine. In Utah, **Heber Valley Railroad** (www.hebervalleyrr.org) also runs steam trains, and the **Golden Spike National Historical Park** (www.nps.gov/gosp) operates replicas of the original steam trains that met at Promontory Summit on May 10th, 1869.

---

airlines compete with United and Delta on the most traveled routes, and offer services to smaller towns; Denver-based Frontier Airlines and Southwest Airlines are the most common.

By Rail

Railways are a comfortable way to travel for both short and long distances, although trains are few and far between in the Rockies: the Amtrak service between Denver and Salt Lake City cuts through the heart of Colorado to Grand Junction, and the Empire Builder runs across the far north of Montana and Idaho, but as far as trains go, that's about it. In Utah, the FrontRunner commuter rail system runs from Ogden to Provo along an 82-mile (132km) corridor serving Salt Lake City and the Utah Valley.

By Road

Buses

Buses are inexpensive and good for shorter distances or for getting to small towns for those not driving, though coverage is limited. Greyhound Lines is the main operator; buses run across Montana between Billings, Bozeman, Butte, Missoula, and on to Coeur d'Alene in Idaho; Salt Lake City to Ogden, Twin Falls, and Boise in Idaho; from Denver to Fort Collins, Cheyenne (WY), Laramie (WY), Rawlins (WY), and Salt Lake City; and Denver to Grand Junction via Vail and Glenwood Springs. For Yellowstone National Park, the best route is Bozeman to West Yellowstone, but there are also buses between Idaho Falls and Jackson, and West Yellowstone (summer only). There is no public transportation between Denver and Rocky Mountain National Park.

Budget carrier Flixbus (www. flixbus.com) now operates services between Salt Lake City, Provo, Ogden, Pocatello, and Idaho Falls, and as far as Las Vegas.

Driving

To really appreciate the Rockies, you'll need a car. Renting is usually straightforward: foreign drivers' licenses are valid in the USA. Driving is on the right and seat belts are mandatory, as are child seats.

Highway speed limits and other laws differ slightly from state to

Greyhounds are famous intercity buses serving over 3,800 locations.

state; in Colorado top limits range 65–75 mph (105–121km/h), but in Idaho its 70–80 mph (113–129km/h) and Montana, Utah and Wyoming a zippy 75–80 mph (121–129 km/h). The American Automobile Association (AAA) is a good source for information and driving regulations (www.aaa.com).

If you are traveling from Canada, check with your insurer before you depart to make sure it covers you during your stay in the US.

Car Rentals

All the major international car rental companies have offices throughout the Rockies and rentals can be easily arranged before arriving in the US. Call the following firms, toll-free, for information:

Alamo
Tel: 1-888-233 8749
www.alamo.com
Avis
Tel: 1-800-352 7900
www.avis.com
Budget
Tel: 1-800-214 6094
www.budget.com
Enterprise
Tel: 1-855 266 9565
www.enterprise.com
Hertz
Tel: 1-800-654 4173
www.hertz.com
National
Tel: 1-844-393 9989
www.nationalcar.com
Sixt
Tel: 1-888-749 8227
www.sixt.com

Thrifty
Tel: 1-800-334 1705
www.thrifty.com

Motor Homes

If you plan to rent a camper/recreational vehicle (RV) in July and August, you should book 3–4 months in advance. Both companies listed below offer pick-up and drop-off at numerous locations across the country.
El Monte RV
Tel: 1-888-337-2214
www.elmonterv.com
Cruise America
Tel: 1-800-671-8042
www.cruiseamerica.com

Cycling

Though the altitude (and the ups and downs) can make cycling in the Rockies a challenge, plenty of visitors do travel the region by bike. Popular routes include Salt Lake City through Colorado to Denver or Pueblo, but it is crucial to avoid major highways. For information about dedicated bike trails see "The Outdoors Experience", page 95.

State by State

Colorado

By Air

Denver International Airport (www.flydenver.com) is the region's biggest aviation hub, served by numerous airlines from all over North America and several cities in Europe. It also offers connections to destinations

all over the Rockies, including Bozeman, Durango, Glacier Park/Kalispell, Grand Junction, Jackson Hole, and Missoula with Frontier Airlines; Boise, Bozeman, Colorado Springs, and Salt Lake City with Southwest; and Aspen, Billings, Boise, Bozeman, Butte, Cheyenne, Cody, Colorado Springs, Eagle/Vail, Glacier Park/Kalispell, Grand Junction, Gunnison/Crested Butte, Helena, Idaho Falls, Jackson Hole, and Missoula with United.

Airport Transfer: The airport is 24 miles (39km) northeast of downtown. Taxis charge a flat rate to downtown and to Boulder (elsewhere is on the meter). The University of Colorado A Line (light rail) links the airport with Union Station, downtown (37min), every 15–30min (daily 3am–1am). RTD buses (www.rtd-denver.com) serve various locations downtown every 15–30min (daily 3.30am–midnight). Shared-ride shuttles, such as Denver Best Rides (http://denverbestrides.com), drop passengers at downtown hotels, and also serve the ski resorts further afield.

By Rail

Amtrak trains arrive on the northwest edge of downtown Denver at Union Station, 1701 Wynkoop Street. There's usually just one departure daily to Chicago, Glenwood Springs (5hr 40min); Grand Junction (52min); and Salt Lake City (15hr).

By Bus

The Denver Greyhound terminal is close to downtown at 1055 19th Street. There are usually several daily departures for Colorado Springs (1hr 30min–1hr 45min); Glenwood Springs (3hr 35min); Grand Junction (5hr 5min–5hr 45min); and Vail (2hr 20min–3hr). Whilst cutting west across the state on I-70, buses stop at the Frisco Transfer Center in Summit County (10 miles/16km north of Breckenridge), from where free buses radiate to the surrounding ski resorts.

By Car

I-70 is the major east-west artery running across central Colorado, between Denver and Grand Junction, providing fast and convenient access to all the major ski resorts, Aspen and Leadville. From Denver highways also fan out north (to Cheyenne, Wyoming), south

---

⊘ Rules of the Road

Besides remembering to drive on the right, there are few other safety considerations to keep in mind. As some traffic rules vary from state to state, ask your car rental company if you have any queries of this nature. While the USA has an extensive and modern system of highways, most of which are well numbered and clearly marked, at times it is very helpful to know your north from south and your east from west.

Speed limits are posted in miles per hour (mph) and they vary from 20–35 mph (32–56km/h) in built-up areas to between 75–80 mph (121–129km/h) on highways.

Headlight rules also differ between states. In Colorado, Utah, and Wyoming, headlights must be turned on when you cannot see at least 1,000ft (305 meters) in front of you; in Idaho and Montana it's 500ft (153 meters).

In all US states you may turn right at a red traffic light (except where prohibited by a sign), after coming to a full stop and making sure that the way is clear before you do so.

School buses display flashing lights before stopping and after leaving a stop; by law you must stop (from either direction), until everyone is clear of the road and the bus is moving.

(to Colorado Springs) and east to Kansas and Nebraska. Though the state is laced by an excellent road network, beyond the interstates allow extra time for twists and turns, and potential snow closures in winter.

In the following sections, telephone area codes are given in brackets after the place name.

Denver (303, 720 and 983)
Free buses run up and down 16th Street Mall, while RTD also run pay-to-ride buses throughout the city (www.rtd-denver.com); frequent services to local sports venues and the airport leave from the Market Street Station at Market and 16th. Buy a MyRide reloadable fare card to get up to $0.20 off each ride (accepted on light rail also). Denver's multi-line light rail system (daily, 24hr) links downtown, the 16th Street Mall, the Denver Broncos stadium, the Pepsi Center, and the airport.

Denver's RTD also runs the regular FF1 and FF2 buses (45–50min) from downtown Denver to the Downtown Boulder Station, at 1800 14th Street.

Aspen (970)
Tiny Aspen/Pitkin County Airport (www.aspenairport.com) lies four miles (6km) north of Aspen; free buses run into Aspen and Snowmass. Most flights to Aspen originate in Denver, Dallas/Fort Worth, or Chicago-O'Hare. The nearest Amtrak (and Greyhound) station to Aspen is in Glenwood Springs, 40 miles (64km) away. RFTA buses run every 12–30min to Aspen (1hr). Free RFTA buses (www.rfta.com) connect Aspen's four ski mountains with each other in winter, plus the airport and outlying areas (Aspen to Snowmass Village is free and runs all year).

Vail (970)
Limited flights (mostly from Denver or Dallas/Fort Worth) are also available to Eagle County Regional Airport (www.flyvail.com), 35 miles (56km) west of Vail. Ground transportation from the airport to ski resorts is provided by Eagle County Regional Transportation Authority (aka ECO Transit; www.eaglecounty.us/transit). Vail Transit Department provides free year-round bus service to and from Vail Mountain and throughout Vail town.

Many skiers also fly from Denver to Gunnison Airport (www.flygunnisonairport.com), a 40min trip from Crested Butte via the Alpine Express (www.letsride.co/locations/crested-butte).

Idaho

By Air
Boise Airport (www.iflyboise.com) is three miles (5km) south of downtown Boise, just off I-84; get into town by taxi or Valley Regional Transit bus (Mon–Fri 6.15am–9.15pm; every 15–30min, Sat every hour; www.valleyregionaltransit.org).

Friedman Memorial Airport (https://iflysun.com) in Hailey serves Sun Valley and Ketchum, with most flights from Salt Lake City (Delta) and Seattle (via Alaska Airlines). Mountain Rides (www.mountainrides.org) provides bus service into Hailey and to other destinations, otherwise taxis are always available (tel: +1 208 481 2119).

By Rail
Amtrak's Empire Builder train runs across the Idaho Panhandle, stopping at Sandpoint (only), on its journey from Chicago to the Pacific Northwest – incredibly scenic, but of limited use in terms of traveling around the state.

By Bus
Greyhound buses link Boise with Moscow, ID (1 daily; 6hr 45min), Portland, OR (1 daily; 9hr 35min); Salt Lake City (1 daily; 6hr 50min) and Spokane, WA (1 daily; 8hr 30min).

Sun Valley Express (tel: + 1 208 576 7381, www.ctcbus.com) runs once-daily shuttles from Boise airport to Sun Valley and back (around 3hr). Mountain Rides buses link Sun Valley resort with Ketchum and other locations in the valley (tel: +1 208 788 7433; www.mountainrides.org)

By Car
I-84 slices across southern Idaho, east to west, from Twin Falls to Boise and Oregon, with I-86 and I-15 providing equally swift connections to Pocatello and Idaho Falls, and on to Montana and Utah. Heading further north is much slower; scenic byways snake across the mountains, while US-95 links Boise with the Panhandle, but it's crucial to allow plenty of time: Boise to Sandpoint

will take at least 9 hours without factoring in rest stops.

Montana

By Air
Bozeman Yellowstone International Airport (https://bozemanairport.com) is actually Montana's busiest airport; it lies seven miles (11km) northwest of downtown Bozeman, with taxis meeting flights (Big Sky Shuttle operates taxis to Big Sky ski resort: https://bigskyshuttle.net). Public transportation is limited; you're better off renting a car. Flights run to numerous US cities, but these tend to be summer only; Denver is by far the biggest destination (Frontier, Southwest, United), with Minneapolis and Salt Lake City also major feeder airports.

Billings Logan International Airport (www.flybillings.com) is just two miles (3.2km) northwest of downtown Billings. Taxis meet most flights and local MET Transit bus #1 (ww.ci.billings.mt.us/259/MET-Transit) runs into downtown every 30min or so.

Missoula Montana Airport (https://flymissoula.com) is four miles (6km) northwest of downtown Missoula on West Broadway; taxis and free Mountain Line public buses (Mon–Fri 11 daily; https://mountainline.com) serve the airport.

Park International Airport (http://www.iflyglacier.com) is six miles (10km) northeast of Kalispell, served primarily by flights from Denver, Salt Lake City and Seattle. Rent a car or contact Mountain Shuttle (www.mountainshuttlemt.com).

Helena Regional Airport (https://helenaairport.com) is two miles (3.2km) northeast of downtown Helena; you'll need to call a taxi (tel: +1 406 449 5525) or arrange a hotel shuttle.

By Rail
Amtrak's Empire Builder train runs across northern Montana on its journey between Chicago and Seattle/Portland, stopping at West Glacier, which is a short walk from the west gate of Glacier National Park; East Glacier Park, 30 miles (48km) south of St Mary (1hr 40min by train from West Glacier); and Essex (summer only), in between the two (40min from West Glacier). Other than that, there are no train services in Montana.

By Bus

The Greyhound/Jefferson Lines bus station in Billings is downtown at 1830 4th Avenue North. The main destinations are Bismarck, ND (1 daily; 6hr 55min); Bozeman (2 daily; 2hr 20min); Butte (2 daily; 3hr 35min–4hr); and Missoula (2 daily; 5hr 45min–6hr).

In Bozeman, the Greyhound/Jefferson Lines stop is at the Walmart at 1500 North 7th Avenue (just off I-90, junction 306), 1.5 miles (2.4km) from the city center, with usually two buses daily to Billings, Butte, and Missoula. In Missoula itself, Greyhound/Jefferson Lines pull in at 1660 West Broadway, on the edge of downtown. From here, there's usually two daily services to Billings (5hr 45min), Bozeman (3hr 25min–3hr 40min), Butte (2hr); Coeur D'Alene, ID (3hr); and Spokane, WA (4hr).

By Car

At a risk of stating the obvious, Montana is big: driving across it east to west takes around 12 hours, and that is without any stops. I-94 (from North Dakota to Billings) combined with I-90 (from Billings to Bozeman, Butte, Missoula and Idaho) makes a relatively swift passage across the southern side of the state, while I-15 shoots south to north from Idaho Falls to Butte, Helena, Great Falls, and on to the Canadian border. Allow plenty of time while traversing the rest of the state, on mainly traffic-free, but much slower two-lane highways.

Utah

By Air

Salt Lake City International Airport, four miles (6km) west of downtown, is connected with the city center by trams on the TRAX Green Line ($2.50; tel: +1 801 743 3882; www.rideuta.com). Alternatively, taxis and shuttles also run into town via Xpress Shuttles (tel: +1 801 596 1600, https://expressshuttleutah.com), while Canyon Transportation (tel: +1 801 255 1841, https://canyontransport.com) serves the skiing areas.

By Rail

Amtrak's Californian Zephyr serves Salt Lake City, Provo, Green River and Helper, linking them once daily with Denver (14hr) to the east and Nevada and California to the West; other than the ride over to Denver, it's not an especially useful way to get around the area. Salt Lake station is downtown at 320 South Rio Grande Avenue. The more convenient FrontRunner train service ($2.50 base fare, with $0.60 per additional stop) makes frequent trips between Ogden, Salt Lake City and Provo.

By Bus

Greyhound provides limited services in Utah, with buses from Salt Lake City (300 South 600 West) to Boise via Ogden and Twin Falls (1 daily; 7hr 5min), to Denver via Cheyenne, WY (2–3 daily; 10hr 30min), to Las Vegas via Provo and St George (2 daily; 8hr), and to San Francisco (2 daily; 15hr).

A free comprehensive bus system operates daily in Park City between 6am and 2.30am (www.parkcity.org). The six routes are color-coded (download the Park City mobile bus app for convenience).

By Car

Salt Lake City sits at the heart of Utah's interstate network, with I-80 running west to Nevada and east into Wyoming, and I-15 running north into Idaho and south to Las Vegas in Nevada. I-70 cuts across Colorado from Denver into central Utah. Other than those relatively swift connectors, driving long-distance can be very slow, though the roads are rarely busy beyond the congested Utah Valley.

Salt Lake City (385 and 801)

Local buses and TRAX trams (trolleys) are operated by the Utah Transit Authority (tel: +1 801 743 3882, www.rideuta.com); journeys within the downtown area are free (it's a good idea to tell the driver you intend to stay in the free zone when you board).

Regular UTA buses run every day between 6.30am and 7.30pm from Salt Lake City to the Cottonwood canyons resorts during winter (services are less frequent in summer); from downtown, take the Blue TRAX line to Midvale Fort Union Station, then transfer to the Ski Bus for Brighton and Solitude, or the one for Alta and Snowbird. The trip takes around one hour.

Salt Lake's bike share program is called Greenhike (www.greenbikeutah.org), with stations all over downtown; 24/hr passes are $7 (unlimited 30min trips; $5 for each 30min thereafter).

Wyoming

By Air

Wyoming's busiest airport is Jackson Hole Airport (www.jacksonholeairport.com), eight miles (13km) north of Jackson in Grand Teton National Park. The main flights here are from Denver (United) and Salt Lake City (Delta). You can rent cars here, or take a taxi (tel: +1 307 699 7221) to your hotel – there is no public transport. Casper–Natrona County International Airport (www.iflycasper.com) also offers services to Salt Lake City and Denver, while Cody's Yellowstone Regional Airport (www.flyyra.com) has flights to Denver and Chicago. Flying into Wyoming it's best to arrange car rentals from the airport in advance.

By Bus

Greyhound provides limited bus services in Wyoming, with Cheyenne connected to Laramie (55min) and Salt Lake City (8hr 35min) once a day; Denver (1hr 35min–2hr 30min) twice daily; and Billings, Montana (1 daily; 10hr) via Casper (3hr 30min) and Buffalo (5hr 30min).

Salt Lake Express (https://saltlakeexpress.com) runs the only regular public transport to Jackson, from Idaho Falls (2 daily; 2hr), with connections to Salt Lake City, Boise and Butte. Within Jackson itself, START buses (daily 6.30am–10pm, every 30min; http://jacksonwy.gov/587/START-Bus), provide free transport within the town, and charge for trips to Teton Village.

By Car

Driving across Wyoming can be long and tedious, with some 430 miles/692km (7 hours non-stop) between Cheyenne and Jackson. I-80 cuts along the southern side of the state to Salt Lake City, while I-25 provides a fast link between Cheyenne, Casper, Buffalo, and on into Montana via I-90, but travel across the mostly empty western and central parts of the state is on two-way roads.

A

Accommodation

Accommodation options in the Rockies are much the same as in the rest of the US, albeit with a bigger choice of cabins and campgrounds in the national parks. Reservations are essential in the busy summer months. Almost all hotels, motels, and resorts accept major credit cards, but it's a good idea to check in advance, especially if you travel in remote areas. Most hotels are now completely smoke-free, so if you require a smoking room, make sure to ask.

Hotels and motels

Motels, or "motor hotels", tend to be found beside the main roads away from city centers, and are thus much more accessible to drivers. Budget hotels or motels can be pretty basic, but in general standards of comfort are uniform – each room comes with a double bed (often two), a TV, phone, and usually a coffeemaker, plus an attached bathroom. For places with higher rates, the room and its fittings simply get bigger and include more amenities, and there may be a swimming pool and extras such as irons and ironing boards, or premium cable TV (HBO, Showtime, etc). Almost all hotels and motels now offer free wi-fi, albeit sometimes in the lobby only.

The least expensive properties tend to be family-run, independent "mom 'n' pop" motels, but these are rarer nowadays. When you're driving along the main interstates there's a lot to be said for paying a few dollars more to stay in motels belonging to the national chains. These range from the ever-reliable and cheap Super 8 and Motel 6 through to the mid-range Days Inn and La Quinta,

up to the more commodious Holiday Inn Express and Hampton Inn.

Few budget hotels or motels bother to compete with the ubiquitous diners by offering full breakfasts, although most will provide free self-service coffee, pastries, and, if you are lucky, fruit or cereal, collectively referred to as "continental breakfast."

B&Bs

Staying in a B&B is a popular, often luxurious, alternative to conventional hotels in the Rockies. Some B&Bs consist of no more than a couple of furnished rooms in someone's home, and even the larger establishments tend to have fewer than 10 rooms, sometimes without TV or phone, but often laden with potpourri, chintzy cushions, and an assertively precious Victorian atmosphere. If this cozy, twee setting appeals to you, there's a range of choices throughout the region, but keep a few things in mind: for one, you may not be an anonymous guest, as you would be in a chain hotel, but may be expected to chat with the host and other guests, especially during breakfast. Also, some B&Bs enforce curfews, and take a dim view of guests stumbling in after midnight after an evening's partying. The only way to know the policy for certain is to check each B&B's policy online – there's often a lengthy list of dos and don'ts.

The price you pay for a B&B always includes breakfast (sometimes a buffet on a sideboard, but more often a full-blown cooked meal). The crucial determining factor is whether each room has an en-suite bathroom; most B&Bs provide private bath facilities, although that can damage the authenticity of a fine old house. At the top end of the spectrum, the distinction between a "boutique hotel" and a "bed-and-breakfast inn" may amount to no

more than that the B&B is owned by a private individual rather than a chain.

Historic hotels and lodges

Throughout the Rockies, many towns still contain historic hotels, whether dating from the arrival of the railroads or from the heyday of Route 66 in the 1940s and 1950s. So long as you accept that not all will have up-to-date facilities to match their period charm, these can make wonderfully atmospheric places to spend a night or two.

In addition, several national parks feature long-established and architecturally distinguished hotels, traditionally known as lodges, that can be real bargains thanks to their federally controlled rates. The only drawback is that all rooms tend to be reserved far in advance. Among the best are the Jackson Lake Lodge in Grand Teton, the Old Faithful Inn in Yellowstone, and Glacier Park Lodge and Many Glacier Hotel in Glacier National Park.

Hostels

Hostel-type accommodation is not as plentiful in the USA as it is in Europe, but provision for backpackers and low-budget travelers does exist in the Rockies. Unless you're traveling alone, most hostels cost about the same as motels; stay in them only if you prefer their youthful ambience, energy, and sociability. These days, many hostels are independent, with no affiliation to the HI-AYH (Hostelling-International-American Youth Hostels; http://hiusa.org) network. Those few hostels that do belong to HI-AYH tend to impose curfews, limit daytime access hours, and segregate dormitories by sex. A dorm bed in a hostel usually costs $20–45 per night. Alternative methods of finding a cheap room online are through www.

airbnb.com and the free hosting site www.couchsurfing.org.

National parks and camping

The ideal way to see the Rockies – especially if you're on a low budget – is to camp in state and federal campgrounds. While hotel-style lodges are found only in major parks, every park or monument tends to have at least one well-organized campground. Often, a cluster of motels can also be found not far outside the park boundaries. National parks and monuments are often surrounded by tracts of national forest – also federally administered but much less protected. These too usually hold appealing rural campgrounds. Public campgrounds range in price from free (usually when there's no water available, which may be seasonal) to around $35 per night. If you're camping in high season, either reserve in advance or avoid the most popular areas.

With appropriate permits – subject to restrictions in popular parks – backpackers can also usually camp in the backcountry (a general term for areas inaccessible by road). Backcountry camping in the national parks is usually free. Before you set off on anything more than a half-day hike, and whenever you're headed for anywhere at all isolated, be sure to inform a ranger of your plans, and ask about weather conditions, specific local tips and potentially dangerous wildlife (especially if you are carrying food with you). Carry sufficient food and drink to cover emergencies, as well as all the necessary equipment and maps. Check whether fires are permitted; even if they are, try to use a camp stove in preference to local materials. In wilderness areas, try to camp on previously used sites. Where there are no toilets, bury human waste at least six inches into the ground and 100ft (30 meters) from the nearest water supply and campground.

Admission charges

Most museums and art galleries in the Rockies charge admission, but discounts are generally available for children, students, and senior citizens. Most adult charges are in the range of around $10–25, with museums in the bigger cities such as Denver tending to charge the higher rates.

National Parks and most state parks also charge admission (usually per vehicle), and these can add up fast: Rocky Mountain National Park, Glacier National Park, and Yellowstone for example, all cost $35 each, though this covers seven days of entry in each park. It you intend to visit more than two national parks, consider buying an Annual Pass for $80, from any federal site or via the USGS store (https://store.usgs.gov/pass/index.html).

Age restrictions

You must be at least 21 years of age or older to purchase alcohol or tobacco products in the USA. In most Rockies states you can drive a car from the age of 16 or 17, but rental companies will not rent cars to anyone under 21.

B

Budgeting for Your Trip

The daily costs for an average traveler in the Rockies vary considerably across the region. In a large city like Denver, or staying in one of the bigger lodges in the national parks, the comfortable daily cost per person (assuming two people sharing a room) should be about $250 ($150 for hotel, $20 for breakfast, $25 for lunch, $50 for dinner, and $10 for transport/gas). Staying in smaller towns and parks, especially if camping, your costs will fall dramatically: to around $30 (camping) or $90 (motel), $10 on transport, and $40 (or much less self-catering) for food for the day. In most places a beer will cost $6–8, and a glass of wine a bit more.

C

Children

Overall, the Rockies – like the rest of the US – is very child- and family-friendly, with reduced admission fees at most attractions and kid-friendly activities, menus, and more, but western towns may be quite small and remote; supplies may be limited. If you need baby formula, special foods, diapers, or

medication, carry them with you. It's also a good idea to bring a general first-aid kit for minor scrapes and bruises. Games, books, and crayons help kids pass the time in the car. Carrying snacks and drinks in a day pack will come in handy when kids (or adults) get hungry and there are no restaurants nearby.

Inquire about special children's programs at parks, museums, and other attractions. Be sure that wilderness areas, ghost towns, and other back-country places are suitable for children. Are there abandoned mine shafts, steep stairways, cliffs, other hazards? Are there special precautions regarding wildlife? Is a lot of walking necessary? If so, will it be too strenuous for a child? Are strollers permitted? Are food, water, shelter, bathrooms, and other essentials available at the site?

Avoid dehydration by having children drink plenty of water before and during outdoor activities, even if they don't seem particularly thirsty. Put a wide brimmed hat and sunblock (at least 30 SPF) on children to protect them from the sun. Don't push children beyond their limits: rest often, provide plenty of snacks, and allow for extra napping.

Climate

Peak season across the Rockies is generally between early June and early September, when you can expect temperatures in the high sixties all the way up to 100°Fahrenheit (20–37° Celsius), depending on whether you are in the high desert of Wyoming, the plains of Idaho or the

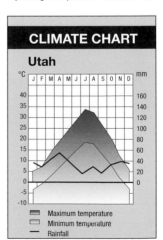

CLIMATE CHART

Utah

mountains of Colorado. Be prepared for wild variations in the mountains – and, of course, the higher you go the colder it gets, especially at night. The altitude is high enough to warrant a period of acclimatization, while the sun at these elevations can be uncomfortably fierce.

Spring, when the snow melts, is the least attractive time to visit, and while the delicate golds and reds of aspen trees light up the mountainsides in early fall, by October the weather is generally a bit cold for enjoyable hiking or sports. Most ski runs are open by late November and operate well into March – or even June, depending on snow conditions. The coldest month is January, when temperatures below 0°F (-17° Celsius) are common.

For visitors, one of the biggest factors to take into consideration when planning a Rockies trip is access to national parks – arguably the region's biggest attraction. Unless you've come to ski (or snowmobile), most parks remain inaccessible to cars for large parts of year (typically Oct–April) because of snow. All of Yellowstone's roads (aside from the Mammoth Springs entrance) start closing in October, and start opening again only on the third Friday in April – but don't expect everything to be open until the end of May.

Note that the Great Plains just to the east of the Rockies experience dramatically different weather conditions. Alternately exposed to seasonal icy Arctic winds and humid tropical airflows from the Gulf of Mexico, winters can be abjectly cold, and it can freeze or even snow in winter as far south as Texas, though spring and fall get progressively longer and milder farther south through the Plains. Tornadoes (or "twisters") are a frequent local phenomenon, tending to cut a narrow swath of destruction in the wake of violent spring or summer thunderstorms. Eastern Montana is affected by tornados, but they are generally small and infrequent. Colorado typically sees a lot more tornadoes annually, but primarily in the eastern plains region. Tornadoes in Idaho and Wyoming are very rare.

Black Hills

Temperatures usually range from 20°F–75°F (-7°C to 24°C). Annual average precipitation is about 17 inches (43cm), with heavy snowfall at high elevations.

Colorado

Temperatures usually range from 30°F (-1°C) in winter to 75°F (24°C) in summer, cooler at high elevations. Annual rainfall averages 14 inches (36cm) in Denver; but only eight inches (20cm) in Grand Junction; expect extremely heavy snowfall at high elevations.

Idaho

Temperatures usually range from 25°F to 75°F (-4°C to 24°C), cooler at high elevations. Annual average rainfall is between eight inches (20cm) and 14 inches (36cm); expect heavy snowfall in winter, especially in the mountains.

Montana

Temperatures usually range between 10°F (-12°C) in winter to 80°F (27°C) in summer; extreme lows in winter dip well below 0°F (-18°C). Heavy snow accumulation, especially at high elevations. Annual average rainfall is 13 to 14 inches (33–36cm).

Utah

Average temperatures range from 25°F (-4°C) in winter to 78°F (26°C) in summer. Annual average precipitation is 14 inches (36cm). Snowfall is heavier and temperatures cooler at high elevations.

Wyoming

Average temperatures usually range from 20°F (-7°C) in winter to 70°F (21°C) in summer; extreme heat and cold are common. Snowfall may be heavy in winter, especially at high elevations. Annual average precipitation is 14–17 inches (36–43cm).

What to Wear

Weather can change unpredictably in any season, so be prepared for just about anything. The best plan is to dress in layers that can be peeled off or put on as conditions dictate. Bringing rain gear is always a good idea. A high-SPF sunblock, wide-brimmed hat, and sunglasses are a good idea, too, even if the day starts out cloudy. The high-altitude sun can be merciless, especially when reflected off snow or water.

If you plan on doing a lot of walking or hiking, it's worthwhile to invest in a sturdy pair of hiking shoes or boots. Consider buying them a half or full size larger than usual and be sure to break them in properly before arriving. A thin, inner polypropylene sock and a thick, outer sock will help keep your feet dry and comfortable. If blisters or sore spots develop, quickly cover them with moleskin, available at just about any pharmacy or camping supply store.

With few exceptions, western dress is informal. A nice pair of jeans or slacks, a polo or button-down shirt, and boots or shoes are appropriate at all but the fanciest places and events. In the summer you will need shorts, T-shirts, lightweight dresses, and slacks for the mornings and sometimes a light sweater or jacket in the evenings. In the winter you will need a warm jacket, scarf, mittens, sweaters, hat, jeans, and warm footwear. For the slopes you will need at least one warm ski outfit, ski gloves, ski hat, and sunglasses or goggles. You can find these things in the many ski shops at the resorts.

Remember to bring along your swimsuit so you can enjoy the hot springs found throughout the Rockies. Many large hotels and resorts have swimming pools, spas, saunas, and workout equipment.

Crime and safety

Many areas of the Rockies are best enjoyed on foot and it is generally very safe to walk the streets or hike in the national parks. Crime rates across the region have been falling for many years and are generally very low. However, some general safety rules do still apply: you should be careful when sightseeing, shopping, and moving about, especially after dark. Whenever possible, it is best to travel or hike with another person and to avoid deserted areas. Never leave your luggage unattended, especially at the airport.

After parking, always lock your car and don't leave luggage, cameras, and other valuables in view; lock them in the trunk. At night, try to park in well-lit areas.

Never leave money, jewelry, or other valuables in your hotel room, even if only for a short time. Don't carry around more cash than you need and use credit cards whenever possible. When making purchases, avoid making a display of large amounts of cash.

A grizzly bear on his hind legs.

Wildlife safety

Realistically, traveling in the Rockies is far safer than wandering around most cities; your biggest irritations while hiking are likely to be mosquitoes, flies, and blackflies – but make no mistake, bears (see page 250) are potentially very dangerous, and most people blow a whistle while walking in bear country to warn them off. If confronted don't run, make loud noises, or sudden movements, all of which are likely to provoke an attack.

Cougars pose a somewhat lesser threat – they usually avoid groups of people, but unlike with bears, the best strategy with cougars is to try and fight them off. Fatalities from snakebites are also rare – wear proper boots and if you do disturb a snake, back away so that it has room to move freely. Even the most venomous bites can be treated successfully if you receive immediate medical attention: call 911 or notify park staff.

Ironically, more tourists get hurt by otherwise fairly harmless animals, almost always because they get too close when taking a photo. On average, bison injure one or two people in Yellowstone every year in this way. Never ever approach wildlife; stay at least 100 yards (91 meters) away from bears and wolves, and at least 25 yards (23 meters) away from all other animals, including bison and elk.

Ghost towns

Travelers in the Rockies should exercise caution around old buildings and abandoned mines. Structures may be unstable and the ground may be littered with broken glass, nails and other debris. Mine shafts are particularly dangerous. Never attempt to enter a mine shaft or cave unless accompanied by a park ranger or other professional.

Customs regulations

All people entering the United States must go through Customs. Be prepared to have your luggage inspected and keep the following guidelines in mind:

1. There is no limit to the amount of money you can bring into the US. If the amount exceeds $10,000 (in cash and other negotiable instruments), however, you must file a special report.

2. Any objects brought for personal use may enter duty-free.

3. Adults may enter with a maximum of 200 cigarettes or 50 cigars or 2 kilograms of tobacco and/or 1 liter of alcohol duty-free.

4. Gifts valued at less than $400 can enter duty-free.

5. Agricultural products, meat, and animals are subject to complex restrictions; to avoid delays, leave these items at home unless absolutely necessary.

6. Illicit drugs and drug paraphernalia are strictly prohibited. If you must bring narcotic or habit-forming medicines for health reasons, be sure that all products are properly identified, carry only the quantity you will need while traveling, and have either a prescription or a letter from your doctor.

E

Eating out

In Denver and Salt Lake City, you can pretty much eat whatever you want, whenever you want, thanks to the ubiquity of restaurants, 24-hour diners, and bars and street carts selling food well into the night. Also, along all the major highways and on virtually every town's main street, restaurants, fast-food joints, and cafés try to outdo one another with bargains and special offers. Whatever you eat and wherever you eat it, service is usually prompt, friendly, and attentive – thanks in large part to the American institution of tipping. Waiters depend on tips for the bulk of their earnings; fifteen to twenty percent is the standard rate, with anything less sure to be seen as an insult.

Broadly, steaks and other cuts of beef are prominent in the Rockies, over items such as fresh seafood (with the exception of Denver), though local trout and salmon are ubiquitous throughout the mountains. Wild game, including bison and elk, is also popular (often served as burgers). There are some local differences. In Colorado, lamb is also very popular, with some critics claiming the area produces the best in the world, usually served as lamb chops, often with a warm cheese fondue. Mexican food (or at least the Tex-Mex version) is also incredibly popular, with even small towns serving up nachos, tacos, cheese enchiladas, and burritos from one or two holes-in-the-wall. Other more exotic Colorado dishes include "Rocky Mountain oysters," which are not oysters at all but bull or bison testes, served breaded and fried.

Wyoming is serious cowboy country, and chuck wagon-style dinners are wildly popular here – communal meals of baked beans, steak, chicken, and buffalo sausages cooked on a pitchfork, with deep-fried onions and homemade brownies. Other popular meaty dishes include chicken-fried steaks, prime rib, Native American-style fry bread, buffalo steaks, elk sausage, and biscuits and gravy for breakfast.

In Montana, desserts made from local huckleberries appear on menus everywhere, while "beans & sheepherders" is a legendary pinto bean and ham soup invented in Ingomar's Jersey Lilly Saloon in 1948. Ice cream (especially Wilcoxson's and Big Dipper), flathead cherries, chokecherries, Hutterite chicken, lentils, morels, and even Cornish pasties are other Montana specialties.

Idaho, in addition to the Basque food served up in the capital of Boise, is of course known for potatoes, best served with local "fry sauce;" there's even ice cream potatoes! Other dishes not to miss are Idaho white sturgeon caviar, habanero pizza, fresh trout, and lamb.

Finally, there are also regional variations on American staples. You can get plain old burgers and hot dogs anywhere, but for a truly American experience, grab a green chili burger, or a piping-hot "Double Johnny Burger," gooey with cheese, and thin-sliced beef from My Brother's Bar in Denver, or one of the city's signature "Elk-Jalapeno Dogs" at Biker Jim's Gourmet Dogs. Mountain pie pizzas were invented in Idaho Springs, Colorado. Almost every state has at least one spot claiming to have invented the hamburger, and regardless of where you go, you can find a good range of authentic diners where the buns are fresh, the patties are large, handcrafted, and tasty, and the dressings and condiments are inspired.

Electricity

Most wall outlets have 110-volt, 60-cycle, alternating current. A transformer is necessary if you are using European or 220-volt equipment; most smartphones and computers accept both currents these days, so hair dryers tend to be the biggest problem for travelers.

Embassies and consulates

In the USA:

Australia: 1145 17th Street NW, Washington DC, 20036, tel: 202-797-3000, https://usa.embassy.gov.au; Honorary Consul for Australia, 1664 Platte Street, 4th Floor Denver, CO 80202, tel: 720-366-7500.
Canada: 501 Pennsylvania Avenue NW, Washington, DC 20001, tel: 202-682 1740, https://www.international. gc.ca; Consulate General of Canada, 1625 Broadway, Suite 2600, Denver, CO 80202, tel: 844-880-6519.
Ireland: 2234 Massachusetts Avenue NW, Washington DC 20008, tel: 202-462-3939, https://www.dfa.ie/irish-embassy/usa.
New Zealand: 37 Observatory Circle NW, Washington, DC 20008, tel: 202-328-4800, https://www.mfat.govt.nz.
South Africa: 3051 Massachusetts Avenue NW, Washington, DC 20008, tel: 202-232-4400, https://www. saembassy.org.
UK: 3100 Massachusetts Avenue NW, Washington, DC 20008, tel: 202-462-1340, https://www.gov.uk.

US Embassies overseas:

Australia: Moonah Place, Yarralumla, Canberra, ACT 2600, tel: 02-6214-5600.
Canada: 490 Sussex Drive, Ottawa, Ontario K1N 1G8, tel: 613-688-5335.
Ireland: 42 Elgin Road, Ballsbridge, Dublin 4 tel: 01-668-8777.
New Zealand: 29 Fitzherbert Terrace, Thorndon, Wellington 6011, tel: 04-462-6000.

South Africa: 877 Pretorius Street, Arcadia, Pretoria, tel: 012-431-4000.
UK: 33 Nine Elms Lane, London, SW11 7US, tel: 020-7499-9000.

Emergencies

In case of an emergency dial 911 for police, fire, ambulance, or any other emergency. If you dial the operator "0" and state the nature of the emergency, you can receive some assistance.

Etiquette

Good manners are valued in the Rocky Mountain states: hold doors open for people following you, don't jump the line, let people get off public transportation before you get on, offer your seat to older passengers or pregnant women. Show respect when visiting churches – keep your voice down and ask before taking photos.

F

Festivals

On July 4, America's Independence Day, the entire region takes time out to picnic, drink, salute the flag, and watch or participate in fireworks displays, marches, beauty pageants, eating contests and more, all to commemorate the signing of the Declaration of Independence in 1776.

January *(Denver, CO)*
National Western Stock Show (https://nationalwestern.com)
One of the region's biggest rodeos takes place alongside family entertainments, horse shows, parades, livestock exhibitions, craft stalls and all sorts of food stalls. It's been held here since 1906 and is now the world's largest livestock show.

January *(Park City, UT)*
Sundance Film Festival (https://festival.sundance.org)
Established in 1978, America's premier event for indie movie-makers features dramatic and documentary features and short films, as well as showcasing multimedia installations and performances. The festival began as the Utah/US Film Festival but was renamed in 1991 after Robert Redford's character the Sundance Kid from the film

Butch Cassidy and the Sundance Kid (Redford was one of the early sponsors of the festival).

Late January *(Ogden, UT)*
Hof German Fest (www.hofgermanfest.com)
This annual German-themed festival is held in honor of Ogden's twin city of Hof, Germany. It usually encompasses two to three days of authentic German food (wiener schnitzel, bratwurst and knockwurst), German-style dances, polka bands and craft booths.

Late January *(Lewistown, MT)*
Montana Winter Fair (www.montanawinterfair.com)
This winter celebration of Montana's agriculture and Western way of life goes back to 1946, and today features a vast spread of events, from chili cook-offs, dog shows and a fiddle contest, to rodeos and "ski-joring", where a person on skis is pulled by a horse.

First weekend of February *(Whitefish, MT)*
Whitefish Winter Carnival (https://whitefishwintercarnival.com)
The gateway to Glacier National Park hosts this fun festival amidst the snow every year, with parties, parades, skijoring, a "penguin plunge" into the lake and the coronation of the "King and Queen of the Snows".

Late February *(Moscow, ID)*
Lionel Hampton Jazz Festival (www. uidaho.edu/class/jazzfest)
The campus of the University of Idaho in tiny Moscow, Idaho, is the unlikely location of the largest annual jazz festival west of the Mississippi. It runs over four days and features concerts from global jazz greats as well as student performances and workshops.

March *(Jackson, WY)*
Winter Fest (www.jhfoodandwine. com/winter-fest)
Jackson Hole Food & Wine hosts this annual three-day series of events in Teton Village, highlighting the rich food and beverage culture of the valley.

Saturday before March 17 *(Denver, CO)*
St Patrick's Day Parade (www.denverstpatricksdayparade.com)

St Patrick's Day has become virtually national holiday in the USA, not just celebrated by Irish-Americans, but by all. Parades and parties take place all over the Rockies, but Denver hosts the biggest bash, a four-hour parade starting at Coors Field and involving multiple bands, dancers and floats.

Late May (Jackson, WY)
Old West Days (www.jacksonholewy.com)
This annual celebration of local Western history and culture includes live music, theater, arts and crafts, food stalls, rodeo events, and more. There's also an elk antler auction, chili cookoff, Teton Powwow, and Old West Brewfest.

Late May, Memorial Weekend
(Denver, CO)
Denver Arts Festival (https://denverartsfestival.com).
Fine arts and crafts festival that primarily showcases Colorado artists, as well as a select group of national artists, in Denver's Central Park neighborhood. There are also food and drink stalls, live music, and a special Kids Art Zone.

Late May, Memorial Weekend
(Telluride, CO)
Mountainfilm (www.mountainfilm.org)
Telluride's alternative film festival showcases documentaries that celebrate adventure, activism, social justice, culture, and the environment.

Late May to late September (Boise, ID)
Idaho Shakespeare Festival (https://idahoshakespeare.org)
Shakespeare plays feature all summer long at this popular festival, with performances held at the atmospheric outdoor amphitheater; bring blankets and low-backed lawn chairs for the general admission lawn seating. Most nights there are also live concerts on the Meadow Stage alongside the patio of Café Shakespeare.

June–early August (Boulder, CO)
Colorado Shakespeare Festival (https://cupresents.org/series/shakespeare-festival)
In association with the University of Colorado Boulder since 1958, this festival runs throughout June and July, serving up two or three Shakespeare productions every season. There's also at least one contemporary play with a Shakespearean theme.

Mid-June, the weekend closest to the Summer Solstice (Telluride, CO)
Telluride Bluegrass Festival (https://bluegrass.com/telluride)
Some the world's best Blues artists perform at this annual festival in the mountains, with what is probably the most beautiful backdrop anywhere. There's also lots of food, arts and crafts, and arts performances.

Mid-June (Fort Washakie, WY)
Eastern Shoshone Indian Days Powwow (https://windriver.org).
One of the region's biggest Native American celebrations takes place on the Wind River Reservation in Wyoming, a free festival that includes a rodeo, games, relay races, craft stalls, music and dancing.

Late June (Sturgis, SD)
Black Hills Bluegrass Festival (https://blackhillsbluegrass.com)
The Rush No More Resort & Campground (I 90, Exit 37) hosts this celebration of traditional bluegrass and acoustic music, with some the country's top performers in attendance.

July to late August (Aspen, CO)
Aspen Music Festival (www.aspenmusicfestival.com)
One of the most venerable festivals in the Rockies was established in 1949, and now arranges over 400 classical music events through the summer season, given by the Aspen Chamber Symphony and a host of globally famous performers.

Early July (Cody, WY)
Cody Stampede Rodeo (www.facebook.com/codystampede)
Taking place over four days at the start of July, this professional rodeo forms part of the Cody Nite Rodeo series, which runs June through August. It's one of the most competitive rodeos in the nation, with all the best riders taking part.

Early July (Butte, MT)
Montana Folk Festival (https://montanafolkfestival.com)
This three-day festival features some of the best folk music artists in the country, in one of Montana's most intriguing cities. Admission is free to all performances on the festival's six stages in Uptown Butte.

Late July (Cheyenne, WY)
Cheyenne Frontier Days (www.cfdrodeo.com)
The world's largest outdoor rodeo and celebration of all things Western takes place at Frontier Park outside Cheyenne, an incredibly enjoyable introduction to all the big rodeo events. There's also a big carnival with funfair rides, live music, dancing, chuckwagon cook-offs, an Indian Village and free pancake breakfast.

Late July to early August (Great Falls, MT)
Montana State Fair (www.cascadecountymt.gov).
Montana ExpoPark has hosted this classic state fair since 1931. Enjoy carnival rides, exhibitions, crazy food, live music, horse racing, rodeo, and comedy performances over nine days.

Late July to late August (Sun Valley-Ketchum, ID)
Sun Valley Music Festival (www.svmusicfestival.org)
One of the best classical music festivals in the country, offering three weeks of free concerts from world-famous pianists and cellists to performances from the Festival Orchestra. Held at a gorgeous mountain setting – the open-air Sun Valley Pavilion.

Mid-August (Douglas, WY)
Wyoming State Fair (https://wystatefair.com)
This very Western fair features all the usual exhibitors and vendors, but is primarily known for its WSF State Championship Ranch Rodeo and PRCA Rodeo held concurrently, as well as a crazy demolition derby.

Mid-August (Telluride, CO)
Telluride Jazz Festival (www.telluridejazz.org)
Top jazz artists have performed here since 1977, with that magical mountain backdrop and all the summer activities you can handle over three days. It's more intimate than other jazz festivals, though the quality of the performers is always high, with food vendors, craft brewers and the Jazz After Dark program adding to the allure.

Late August (Crow Agency, MT)
Crow Fair (www.crow-nsn.gov/crow-fair.html)

The Crow tribe's annual celebration is one of the largest Native American festivals, featuring various contests, craft stalls, parades, traditional dances, a daily rodeo, and thousands of teepees near the Little Big Horn River.

Late August *(Boise, ID)*
Western Idaho Fair (www.idahofair.com).

Idaho holds three state fairs in different parts of the state, but this is the biggest, with over 300 vendors (craft stalls and food), a massive carnival, rock and country concerts, competitions and all sorts of circus acts, from jugglers to hypnotists.

Late August to early September
(Pueblo, CO)
Colorado State Fair (https://coloradostatefair.com)
The region's biggest state fair boasts over 10,000 exhibitors, 60 live concerts, 45 thrill rides, 130 food stalls, and over 5,000 live animals. Held over 11 days, it's lots of fun for families, with admission around $14.

Early September *(Telluride, CO)*
Telluride Film Festival (www.telluridefilmfestival.org)
The National Film Preserve runs this increasingly high-profile festival, screening over 80 movies and short films representing numerous countries, along with special artist tributes, round tables, and student programs.

Mid-September *(Salt Lake City, UT)*
Utah State Fair (www.utahstatefair.com)
Utah's annual state fair at the dedicated Utah State Fairpark also includes an entertaining rodeo, a huge food fair, live concerts and a huge skatepark.

Late September or early October
(Denver, CO)
Great American Beer Festival (www.greatamericanbeerfestival.com)
Colorado is one of America's craft beer powerhouses, so it's fitting that it also hosts one of the nation's biggest beer festivals – it also features the world's largest commercial beer competition, at the Colorado Convention Center.

Late September *(Custer, SD)*
Custer State Park Buffalo Roundup (https://gfp.sd.gov/buffalo-roundup)
The main and most impressive event at this Buffalo Roundup and Arts Festival is when local cowboys and cowgirls roundup and drive Custer State Park's herd of approximately 1,300 buffalo for testing, branding and sorting.

Early December *(Vail, CO)*
Vail Snow Days (www.vailsnowdays.com)
This four-day festival in one of Colorado's ski capitals features free rock concerts at Ford Park, after dark parties, an expo village, and numerous craft stalls.

H

Health and Medical Care

Being ill in America is a very expensive affair; make sure you are covered by medical insurance while traveling in the Rockies. The US has an excellent, but private healthcare system. An ambulance can cost $1,000, emergency room treatment can rise from $300 to $15,000 incredibly fast (fees for drugs, appliances, supplies, and the attendant physician are all charged separately), and just seeing a local doctor or dentist will be at least $100. In most cases you'll have to pay up front and claim insurance later. For minor ailments it's not worth the expense of seeing a doctor, but you need insurance anyway, mainly to cover you in case of accident or serious illness (especially if skiing or mountain biking) – operations and emergency treatment can cost tens of thousands of dollars. Should you find yourself requiring a doctor or dentist, ask if your hotel has links to a local practice, or search online. In general, inoculations aren't required for entry to the USA, though you should check the latest Covid-19 regulations at https://travel.state.gov.

Altitude Sickness
Remember that the air is thinner at higher elevations. Unless properly acclimated, you may feel

Multiple World Champion Saddle Bronc rider, Dan Mortensen, at the Cheyenne Frontier Days rodeo.

uncharacteristically winded. If you experience nausea, headache, vomiting, extreme fatigue, light-headedness, or shortness of breath, you may be suffering from altitude sickness. Although the symptoms may be mild at first, they can develop into a serious illness. Return to a lower elevation and try to acclimate gradually.

Water

It's always a good idea to carry a little more water than you think you'll need when hiking. The rule of thumb is a gallon a day (4.5 liters) per person, more in extreme conditions. Drink at least a quart at the start of a hike (around a liter), and prevent dehydration by drinking at regular intervals while you're on the trail even if you don't feel particularly thirsty; don't wait until you've become dehydrated before you start drinking. All water taken from natural sources must be purified before drinking. Giardia is found in water (even crystal clear water) throughout the Rockies and can cause severe cramps and diarrhoea. The most popular methods of purifying water are using a water purification tablet, a water-purification filter (both available from camping supply stores) or by boiling water for at least 15 minutes.

Sunburn

The sun can be fierce, even on a cool day. Protect yourself by using a high-SPF sunscreen and wearing a wide-brimmed hat and sunglasses, even if the day starts out cloudy. Sunshine reflected off snow can cause serious burns even on the coldest days. Wear sunglasses or ski goggles at all times.

Pharmacies

Pharmacies are widely available throughout the Rockies – almost every town has one, though only big cities such as Denver and Salt Lake City tend to have 24hr branches.

I

Internet

Almost all hotels and many coffeeshops and restaurants in towns offer free wi-fi for guests, though some upscale hotels charge for access. The main exception is in national and state parks, and wilderness areas

throughout the Rockies – though things are gradually improving, wi-fi and often cellphone coverage can be spotty or non-existent. If you are going to require wi-fi access, always ask in advance of your stay – don't assume it's available.

L

LGBTQ+ travelers

The LGBTQ+ scene in America is huge, albeit heavily concentrated in the major cities – though Denver and even Salt Lake City boast active scenes, in rural areas of the Rockies things are a lot more conservative. Though active discrimination is unusual, LGBTQ+ travelers may need to be careful to avoid hassles and possible aggression. The Center in Missoula (www.gaymontana.org) is a good resource. Most of the Rocky Mountain states claim LGBTQ+ populations of under three percent, but it's worth noting that though just 3.3 percent of Wyoming's population identifies as LGBTQ+, Casper and Cheyenne held their first pride marches in 2017, and Mary Cheney, daughter of arch-conservative Dick Cheney (who supports same-sex marriage), also identifies as gay.

M

Media

The daily newspaper that is most widely read in Colorado is the Denver Post (www.denverpost.com). This and national newspapers are available at drug stores, grocery stores, bookstores, and coin operated newspaper stands. Weekly newspapers include the Aurora-based Sentinel Colorado (www.sentinelcolorado.com), and the Intermountain Jewish News (www.ijn.com). The 5280 (www.5280.com) monthly magazine focused on Denver, also covers a variety of material about Colorado; Denver Life (https://denverlifemagazine.com) is similar, while the 303 Magazine (https://303magazine.com) targets young professionals.

Other major Colorado newspapers include the Colorado Springs Gazette (https://gazette.com), the Pueblo Chieftain (www.chieftain.

com), and Boulder Daily Camera (https://www.dailycamera.com).

The two major newspapers in Salt Lake City are now both weeklies, albeit with daily online editions: the Salt Lake Tribune (www.sltrib.com) and the Deseret News (http://deseretnews.com). Most of the smaller towns in Utah have local newspapers. The Standard Examiner (https://www.standard.net) printed in Ogden has a wide circulation.

In Montana, some of the well-circulated newspapers are the Billings Gazette (http://billingsgazette.com), the Bozeman Daily Chronicle (www.bozemandailychronicle.com), Helena's Independent Record (https://helenair.com), Butte's Montana Standard (https://mtstandard.com), the Great Falls Tribune (www.greatfallstribune.com), and the Missoulian (https://missoulian.com).

The prominent daily newspapers in Wyoming are the Casper Star Tribune (https://trib.com) and Cheyenne-based Wyoming Tribune Eagle (www.wyomingnews.com).

In Idaho the main newspapers are the Idaho Statesman (www.idahostatesman.com) in Boise; the Lewiston Morning Tribune (https://lmtribune.com); and the Post Register (www.postregister.com) in Idaho Falls; the Idaho State Journal (www.idahostatejournal.com) in Pocatello; and the Times News in Twin Falls (www.magicvalley.com).

Television

Cities and many large towns have their own local TV stations in addition to the usual national networks and cable stations. Complete listings appear in daily newspapers or online.

Money

The US dollar comes in $1, $2, $5, $10, $20, $50, and $100 denominations. One dollar comprises one hundred cents, made up of combinations of one-cent pennies, five-cent nickels, ten-cent dimes, and 25-cent quarters.

The big bank names are Capital One, Chase, Bank of America, Citibank, Wells Fargo, and US Bank. With an ATM card, you'll be able to withdraw cash just about anywhere, though you'll be charged $2–5 per transaction for using a different bank's network. Foreign cash-dispensing cards linked to international networks, such as Plus or Cirrus, are also widely accepted – ask your home bank or credit card company which branches you can use.

Credit and debit cards are the most widely accepted form of payment at major hotels, restaurants, and retailers, even though a few smaller merchants still do not accept them. You'll be asked to show some plastic when renting a car, bike, or other such item, or to start a "tab" at hotels for incidental charges; in any case, you can always pay the bill in cash when you return the item or check out of your room. It's advisable to arrive with at least $100 in cash (in small bills) to pay for ground transportation and other incidentals.

Tipping

As in most parts of the United States, service personnel rely on tips for a large part of their income. Your gratitude in the form of a tip is not only appreciated but expected, especially in restaurants, where 15 to 20 percent is standard. When sitting at a bar, you should leave at least a dollar per round for the barkeeper; more if the round is more than two drinks. Hotel porters and bellhops should receive at least $2 per piece of luggage, more if it has been lugged up several flights of stairs. About fifteen percent should be added to taxi fares, rounded up to the nearest 50¢ or dollar. It is not necessary to tip chambermaids unless you have an extended stay in a small hotel or resort. Tipping is not always necessary in cafeterias and other self-service or fast-food restaurants, but do tip if you feel the service you have received is worth it.

O

Opening Hours

Standard business hours are Mon–Fri 9am–5pm. Many banks open a little earlier, usually 8.30am, and nearly all close by 3pm. A few have Saturday morning hours. Post offices tend to be open Mon–Fri 8am–5pm and Sat 8am–noon. Big city post offices may have extended hours. Most stores keep weekend hours and may stay open late one

or more nights a week. As a general rule, most museums are open Tue–Sun, 10am–5/6pm, though most have one night per week where they stay open at least a few hours later. On national public holidays banks and offices are likely to be closed all day, and some stores will be closed or have reduced hours.

P

Postal Services

Even the most remote towns are served by the US Postal Service (www.usps.com). Smaller post offices tend to be limited to business hours (Mon–Fri 9am–5pm,), although central, big-city branches may have extended weekday and weekend hours.

Stamps are sold at all post offices and at some convenience stores, filling stations, hotels, and transportation terminals, usually in vending machines.

In the USA, the last line of the address includes the city or town and an abbreviation denoting the state ("MT" for Montana; "CO" for Colorado, for example). The last line also includes a five-digit number – the zip code – denoting the local post office. It is very important to include this, though the additional four digits that you will sometimes see appended are not essential. You can check zip codes on the US Postal Service website (www.usps.com).

Public holidays

Government offices, banks, and post offices are closed on public holidays. Public transportation usually runs less frequently on these days.
January 1: New Year's Day
January 15: Martin Luther King, Jr's Birthday
Third Monday in February: Presidents Day
March/April: Easter Sunday
Last Monday in May: Memorial Day
July 4: Independence Day
First Monday in September: Labor Day
Second Monday in October: Columbus Day
November 11: Veterans Day
Fourth Thursday in November: Thanksgiving Day
December 25: Christmas Day

R

Religious Services

Freedom of religion in the US is guaranteed in the First Amendment to the United States Constitution; while there is no official religion, Christianity and specifically Protestantism dominates. In the Rockies over half the population identifies as practicing Christians (mostly Protestant). Mormons account for over 55 percent of residents in Utah, 23 percent in Idaho, 9 percent in Wyoming, and just 5 percent in Montana. There are also large Roman Catholic congregations and tiny communities of Jews, Muslims, Hindus, and other religious faiths.

S

Shopping

The Rockies offers plenty of shopping opportunities – from the malls and boutiques of Denver and Aspen to the arts and crafts stands of small towns across the plains and mountains. Shopping in Denver has always been an attraction. The 16th St Mall with its free shuttle bus offers a mile of excellent shopping, Larimer Square offers interesting and quaint stores in restored Victorian buildings, and antiques shops are abundant on South Broadway. Cherry Creek, two miles (4km) southeast of downtown, has many intimate shops, restaurants, and cafes. Denver's Tattered Cover is considered one of the finest bookstores in the country.

Outside Denver, travelers will find a surprising variety of galleries, Native American jewelry stores, clothing boutiques, and craft stands at ski resorts and mountain towns throughout the region. For almost all purchases, state taxes will be applied at checkout.

Smoking

Smoking in public is generally frowned upon in the US, though the slightly less invasive practice of vaping (e-cigarettes) has taken off in recent years. In most Rocky Mountain states, smoking is banned in workplaces, schools, childcare facilities, restaurants, bars, retail stores, and recreational/cultural facilities – Wyoming is the exception, where you can still find smoking areas in some bars and restaurants.

Marijuana and other drugs

Over recent years, the legalization of marijuana for recreational purposes has been introduced in a number of US states. The first to pass the measure in the Rockies was Colorado; it is now also legal in Montana, but still illegal in Idaho, Utah, South Dakota (where they narrowly declined to legalize it in 2021), and Wyoming, where even being under the influence of marijuana is a misdemeanour that can land you in jail. "Pot," as it is commonly referred to in America, is now on sale at licensed shops in Colorado and Montana, though there are no Amsterdam-style coffeeshops anywhere as of yet. Rules as to whether only local residents can buy it and how much vary from state to state; smoking in public is usually still illegal.

Paradoxically, the substance is still illegal at the federal level but this has not been creating problems in the above states. Many other states allow the usage of medical marijuana but only with a license. Note that in states where pot is still illegal like Idaho and Wyoming, you can be prosecuted even if you have bought it legally elsewhere, so it's wise not to take it across state lines in such cases. Also note that all other recreational drugs remain illegal at both state and federal level, and even possession of a tiny amount can get you into serious trouble.

T

Tax

Most items you buy will be subject to some form of state – not federal – sales tax, from six percent in Idaho, 4.7 percent in Utah and four percent in Wyoming, to less than three percent (in Colorado) and zero percent (in Montana). In addition, varying from state to state, some counties and cities may add another point or two to that rate. Though Montana has no state sales tax, for example, goods may be liable to some other form of tax from the local county (and in certain resorts). Hotel taxes are usually slightly different and also vary from state to state; Montana for example imposes a four percent lodging sales tax, plus another four percent "lodging facility use" tax.

Telephones

Public telephones are becoming rare thanks to the explosion of mobile phone use (more commonly called a cell phone in America), but you should still be able to find them at highway rest areas, service stations, motels, and restaurants. The quickest way to get assistance is to dial 0 for the operator; local calls usually cost 25 cents and can be dialed directly. Rates vary for long-distance calls, but they can also be dialed directly with the proper area and country code.

If you are planning to take your cell phone from outside the USA, you'll need to check with your service provider whether it will work within the country: you will need a tri-band or quad-band phone that is enabled for international calls (all iPhones and most smartphones should be OK). Using your phone from home will probably incur hefty roaming charges for making calls and charge you extra for incoming calls. Many travelers turn off voicemail and data roaming before they travel to avoid such charges. If you have a compatible (and unlocked) GSM phone and intend to use it a lot, it can be much cheaper to buy a US SIM card ($10 or less) to use during your stay. AT&T (www.att.com) is your best bet. Some networks also sell basic US flip phones (with minutes) for as little as $25 (no paperwork or ID required).

Calling home from the USA

For country codes not listed below, dial 0 for the operator, or log onto www.countrycallingcodes.com.
Australia 011 + 61 + area code minus its initial zero.
New Zealand 011 + 64 + area code minus its initial zero.
Republic of Ireland 011 + 353 + area code minus its initial zero.
South Africa 011 + 27 + area code.
UK 011 + 44 + area code minus its initial zero.

Time zone

Most of the Rockies fall within the Mountain Time Zone (MT), two hours behind the East Coast (10am in New York is 8am in Denver). However, the Idaho Panhandle (north of the Salmon River) in northern Idaho observes Pacific Time (PT); the Pacific zone also includes the three coastal US states and Nevada, and is three hours behind New York (10am in the Big Apple is 7am in the Idaho Panhandle). The Eastern zone is a further five hours behind Greenwich Mean Time (GMT), so 3pm London time is 10am in New York, and 8am in Denver. The USA puts its clocks forward one hour to daylight saving time on the second Sunday in March and turns them back on the first Sunday in November, though the US Senate has voted unanimously to make daylight saving time permanent from 2023.

Tourist information

Each state has its own tourist office. These offer prospective visitors a colossal range of free maps, leaflets, and brochures on attractions from overlooked wonders to the usual tourist traps. You can either contact the offices before you set off, or, as you travel around the country, look for the state-run "welcome centers," usually along main highways close to the state borders. In addition, visitor centers in most towns and cities – often known as the "Convention and Visitors Bureau," or CVB – provide details on the area, as do local Chambers of Commerce in almost any town of any size.

Black Hills

Black Hills & Badlands Tourism Association: tel: 605-355-3700; https://www.blackhillsbadlands.com
South Dakota Department of Tourism: www.travelsouthdakota.com

Colorado

Colorado Tourism Office: www.colorado.com
Aspen Chamber Resort Association: 590 North Mill Street, Aspen; tel: 970-925-1940; www.aspenchamber.org
Boulder Convention & Visitors Bureau: 2440 Pearl Street, Boulder; tel: 303-442-2911; www.bouldercoloradousa.com
Breckenridge Tourism Office: 111 Ski Hill Road, Breckenridge; tel: 970-453-5579; www.gobreck.com
Glenwood Springs Visitor Center: 802 Grand Avenue, Glenwood

Springs; tel: 970-945-6580; www.
visitglenwood.com

Gunnison Crested Butte Tourism
and Prosperity Partnership: 601 Elk
Avenue, Crested Butte; tel: 970-349-
6438; http://gunnisoncrestedbutte.
com

Ouray Chamber Resort Association:
1230 North Main Street, Ouray; tel:
970-325-4746; www.ouraycolorado.
com

Telluride Tourism Board: 236 West
Colorado Avenue, Telluride; tel: 970-
728-3041; www.telluride.com

Vail Valley Partnership: 97 Main
Street, Edwards; tel: 970-476-1000;
www.visitvailvalley.com

Visit Colorado Springs: 515 South
Cascade Avenue, Colorado Springs;
tel: 719-635-7506; www.visitcos.com

Visit Durango: 802 Main Avenue,
Durango; tel: 970-247-3500; www.
durango.org

Visit Fort Collins: 1 Old Town Square,
Fort Collins; tel: 970-232-3840;
www.visitftcollins.com

Visit Grand Junction: 740 Horizon
Drive, Grand Junction; tel: 970-256-
4060; www.visitgrandjunction.com

Idaho

Idaho Department of Commerce-
Tourism Development: https://vis-
itidaho.org

Boise Convention & Visitors
Bureau: 1101 West Front Street,
#100, Boise; tel: 208-344-7777;
www.boise.org

Coeur d'Alene Convention & Visitor
Bureau: 105 North 1st Street, #100
Coeur d'Alene; tel: 208-664-3194;
https://coeurdalene.org

Greater Sandpoint Chamber of
Commerce: 1202 Fifth Avenue,
Sandpoint; tel: 208-263-2161;
https://visitsandpoint.com

Visit North Idaho: https://visitnorthi-
daho.com

Visit Southern Idaho: 2015 Neilsen
Point Place, Suite 200, Twin Falls;
tel: 208-732-5569; https://visit-
southidaho.com

Montana

Montana Office of Tourism: www.
visitmt.com

Billings Chamber of Commerce: 815
South 27th Street, Billings; tel: 406-
245-4111; www.visitbillings.com

Bozeman Convention & Visitors
Bureau: 2000 Commerce Way,
Bozeman; tel: 406-586-5421; https://
visitbozeman.com

Butte Elevated: 1000 George Street,
Butte; tel: 406-723-3177; https://
butteelevated.com

Central Montana Tourism Office: tel:
406-761-5036; https://centralmon-
tana.com

Destination Missoula: 101 East Main
Street, Missoula; tel: 1-800-526-
3465; https://destinationmissoula.com

Glacier Country Tourism: 4852
Kendrick Place, Suite 101 Missoula;
tel: 1-800-338-5072; https://gla-
ciermt.com

Visit Helena: tel: 1-406-449-2107;
https://helenamt.com

Visit Southeast Montana: tel: 1-800-
346-1876; https://southeastmon-
tana.com

Visit Southwest Montana: tel: 1-800-
879-1159; http://southwestmt.com

Yellowstone Country: tel: 1-800-736-
5276; http://visityellowstonecountry.
com

Utah

Utah Office of Tourism: https://www.
visitutah.com

Park City Chamber of Commerce:
1850 Sidewinder Drive #320, Park
City; tel: 800-453-1360; https://www.
visitparkcity.com

Visit Salt Lake: 90 South West
Temple, Salt Lake City; tel: 801-534-
4900; https://www.visitsaltlake.com

Wyoming

Wyoming Office of Tourism: https://
travelwyoming.com

Casper Convention & Visitors
Bureau: National Historic Trails
Center, 139 West 2nd Street, Casper;
tel: 307-234-5362; www.visitcasper.
com

Visit Cheyenne: One Depot Square,
121 West 15th Street, Cheyenne; tel:
800-426-5009; www.cheyenne.org

Visit Laramie: 800 South 3rd Street,
Laramie; tel: 307-745-419; www.vis-
itlaramie.org

Tour operators and travel agents

The United States Tour Operators
Association has a comprehensive
listing of US tour operators; visit
their website at https://ustoa.com.
For hiking, biking, skiing, and kayaking in the Rocky Mountains:

Denver Adventures
Tel: 303-984-6151; https://denverad-
ventures.com

G Adventures
Tel: 212-228-6655/1-888-800-4100;
www.gadventures.com

**Green Jeep Tours (Rocky Mountain
National Park)**
Tel: 970-577-0034; www.greenjeep-
tour.com

Rocky Mountain Holiday Tours
Tel: 970-482-5813/1-800-237-7211;
https://rmhtours.com

Rocky Mountain Outdoor Center
Tel: 719-395-3335; https://rmoc.com

Rocky Mountain Tours (ski trips)
Tel: 800-525-7547; www.rockymoun-
taintours.com

Western Spirit Cycling Adventures
Tel: 435-259-8732; https://western-
spirit.com

Wildland Trekking
Tel: 928-223-4453/1-800-715- 4453;
https://wildlandtrekking.com

Committed anglers may want to
consider:

Montana Angler
Tel: 406-522-9854; www.montan-
aangler.com

UK
Contiki Holidays
Tel: +41 22 929 9216 from Europe;
www.contiki.com

Travelpack
Tel: 020-8585 4080; www.travelpack.
com

Ski trips to Vail, Aspen and Jackson
Hole are the focus of:
Frontier Ski
Tel: 020-8776 8709; https://frontier-
ski.co.uk

Eco-tours to Yellowstone National
Park are offered by:
Windows on the Wild
Tel: 020-8742 1556; www.window-
sonthewild.com

Travelers with disabilities

By international standards, the USA
is exceptionally accommodating for
travelers with mobility concerns or
other physical disabilities. By law,
all public buildings, including hotels
and restaurants, must be wheelchair
accessible and provide suitable toi-
let facilities. Most street corners
have dropped curbs (though less
so in rural areas), and most public transportation systems include
subway stations with elevators and
buses that "kneel" to let passengers
in wheelchairs board.

The Americans with Disabilities
Act (1990) obliges all air carriers to
make the majority of their services
accessible to travelers with disabilities, and airlines will usually let
attendants of disabled people who
need it accompany them at no extra
charge.

Almost every Amtrak train includes one or more coaches that have accommodation for passengers with accessibility needs. Guide dogs travel free and may accompany blind, deaf, or disabled passengers. Be sure to give 24 hours' notice. Hearing-impaired passengers can get information on tel: 800-523-6590 (TTY/TDD).

Greyhound, however, has its challenges. Buses are not equipped with lifts for wheelchairs, though staff will assist with boarding (intercity carriers are required by law to do this), and the "Helping Hand" policy offers two-for-the-price-of-one tickets to passengers unable to travel alone (remember to carry a doctor's certificate). The American Public Transportation Association, in Washington DC (www.apta.com), provides information about the accessibility of public transportation in cities.

The American Automobile Association (http://aaa.com) produces the Handicapped Driver's Mobility Guide, while the larger car-rental companies provide cars with hand controls at no extra charge, though only on their full-sized (i.e. most expensive) models; reserve well in advance.

Resources

Most state tourism offices provide information for travelers with disabilities. In addition, the Society for Accessible Travel and Hospitality (SATH), in New York (https://sath. org), is a not-for-profit travel-industry group of travel agents, tour operators, hotel and airline management, and people with disabilities. They pass on any enquiry to the appropriate member, though you should allow plenty of time for a response. Mobility International USA (www.miusa.org) offers travel tips and operates exchange programs for people with disabilities; it also serves as a national information center on disability.

The "America the Beautiful Access Pass" (www.nps.gov/plan-yourvisit/passes.htm), issued without charge to permanently disabled or blind US citizens, gives free lifetime admission to all US national parks. It can only be obtained in person at a federal area where an entrance fee is charged; you'll have to show proof of permanent disability, or that you are eligible for receiving benefits under federal law

Visas and passports

Under the Visa Waiver Program, citizens of Australia, Ireland, New Zealand, and the UK do not require visas for visits to the US of 90 days or less. You will, however, need to obtain Electronic System for Travel Authorization (ESTA) online before you fly, which involves completing a basic immigration form in advance. Do this only on the official US Customs and Border Protection website: at the time of research the website was https://esta.cbp.dhs.gov/esta, but note that similar sites that might seem official will charge you more and are a scam. There is an official processing fee of $4, and a further $10 authorization fee once the ESTA has been approved (all paid via credit card online). Once given, authorizations are valid for multiple entries into the US for around two years – it's recommended that you submit an ESTA application as soon as you begin making travel plans; in most cases the ESTA will be granted immediately, but it can sometimes take up to 72hr to get a response. You'll need to present a machine-readable passport to Immigration upon arrival. Note that ESTA currently only applies to visitors arriving by air or cruise ship: crossing the land border from Canada, those qualifying for the Visa Waiver Program do not need to apply for ESTA – instead you must fill in an I-94W form, though this is liable to change so check the current requirements before you travel. Canadians now require a passport to cross the border, but can travel in the US for up to a year without a visa or visa waiver.

At the time of writing, most foreign citizens can enter the USA provided they are fully vaccinated against Covid-19; the US authorities currently accept any Covid-19 vaccine approved for emergency use by the World Health Organisation or approved by the US Food and Drug Administration (FDA). You may, regardless of vaccination status have to provide proof of a negative Covid test taken within 24 hours of your departure time before you are allowed to board a flight. However, the situation may remain subject to specific restrictions for some time, and vaccination or proof of a negative Covid test may be required. For the latest information, consult

https://travel.state.gov/content/travel/en/international-travel.html.

Websites and apps

Airbnb: airbnb.com
America's premier site for apartment, individual rooms or mansion rentals.
Colorado Dude & Guest Ranch Association: www.coloradoranch.com
Comprehensive introduction to the state's all-inclusive dude and guest ranches, which often include whitewater rafting, fishing, overnight pack trips, cattle round ups and more.
Colorado River Outfitters Association: www.croa.org
Get the lowdown on over 50 licensed professional river rafting outfitters in Colorado.
Gasbuddy: www.gasbuddy.com
Useful for long-distance drives in the Rockies: operates apps and websites that list real-time fuel prices at thousands of gas stations across the United States.
Incident Information System: https://inciweb.nwcg.gov
This site provides instant updates on extreme weather that affects the whole US.
National Park Service: https://www.nps.gov/index.htm
The Park Service website details the main attractions of the national parks, plus opening hours, the best times to visit, admission fees, hiking trails and visitor facilities.
Visit The USA: www.visittheusa.com
The USA's official tourist website has useful tips and travel information on the Rockies region.

Weights and measures

Despite efforts to convert to metric, the US still uses the Imperial System – in areas near the Canadian border you will occasionally see miles converted to kilometers.
1 foot = 30.48 centimeters
1 yard = 0.9144 meter
1 mile = 1.609 kilometers
1 pint = 0.473 liter
1 quart = 0.946 liter
1 ounce = 28.4 grams
1 pound = 0.453 kilogram
1 acre = 0.405 hectare
1 sq. mile = 259 hectares

It would be hard to argue for the Rocky Mountains as a literary hotbed, though to be sure the rugged lands and postcard images have fired the imaginations of many, from the first Native Americans to Lewis and Clark and more. Prolific novelist Annie Proulx lived in Wyoming for many years, Ivan Doig set most of his books in his native Montana, and in 1961, while camping in southern Idaho, irascible author Richard Brautigan wrote *Trout Fishing in America*. Writer Peter Heller currently lives in Denver, setting most of his novels in the Rockies.

The books below include those most evocative of the Rockies backdrop, as well as ones that should prove most entertaining and useful during your trip. The majority should be easy to find on the internet or can be ordered by your favorite bookstore.

HISTORY AND SOCIETY

Ancient North America by Brian Fagan. Archeological history of America's Native peoples, from the first hunters to cross the Bering Strait up to initial contact with Europeans.
Bury My Heart at Wounded Knee by Dee Brown. Still the best narrative of the impact of white settlement and expansion on Native Americans across the continent.
The Indian Creek Chronicles by Pete Fromm. An engaging and rousing tale of seven winter months spent alone in a tent in the Selway-Bitterroot Wilderness guarding salmon eggs. There are some marvelous descriptions of the author discovering nature in the mountains.
Made in America by Bill Bryson. A compulsively readable history of the American language, packed with bizarre snippets and facts.
Mormon Country by Wallace Stegner. A collection of 28 essays focusing on Mormon life and the wide range of non-believers who lived in Mormon country in the late 19th and early 20th centuries. There are some great tales here, and Stegner tells them superbly.
Pioneer Women by Joanna L. Stratton. Original memoirs of women – mothers, teachers, homesteaders, and circuit riders – who ventured across the plains from 1854 to 1890. Lively, superbly detailed accounts, with chapters on journeys, homebuilding, daily domestic life, the church, the cowtown, temperance, and suffrage.
The Last Stand: Custer, Sitting Bull and the Battle of the Little Big Horn by Nathaniel Philbrick. Meticulous and highly entertaining account of the build-up to the Battle of the Little Big Horn, with insights into the lives of all the main players.
The Life of Hon. William F. Cody, Known as Buffalo Bill by William F. Cody. Larger-than-life autobiography of one of the Wild West's greatest characters, treasurable for the moment when he refers to himself more formally as "Bison William."

☉ Send us your thoughts

We do our best to ensure the information in our books is as accurate and up-to-date as possible. The books are updated on a regular basis using destination experts, who painstakingly add, amend and correct as required. However, some details (such as opening times or travel pass costs) are particularly liable to change, and we are ultimately reliant on our readers to put us in the picture.

We welcome your feed back, especially your experience of using the book "on the road", and if you came across a great new attraction we missed.

We will acknowledge all contributions and offer an Insight Guide to the best messages received.

Please write to us at:
Insight Guides
PO Box 7910
London SE1 1WE

Or email us at:
hello@insightguides.com

Undaunted Courage by Stephen E. Ambrose. Perhaps the most accessible account of Lewis and Clark's pioneering journey of discovery from St Louis, over the Montana and Idaho Rockies, to the Pacific coast in 1806.

FICTION

A River Runs Through It by Norman MacLean. Unputdownable – the best-ever novel about fly-fishing, set in beautiful Montana lake country.
Big Sky by A.B. Guthrie Jr. When published in the 1930s it shattered the image of the mythical West. Realistic historical fiction at its very best, following desperate mountain man and fugitive Boone Caudill, whose idyllic life in Montana was ended by the arrival of white settlers.
Centennial by James A. Michener. Michener's easy-to-read saga is based on the fictional town of Centennial, but is set amidst the real history of northeast Colorado.
Close Range: Wyoming Stories by E. Annie Proulx. Proulx's masterly Wyoming-set short stories include *Brokeback Mountain*.
Dog Stars by Peter Heller. Enigmatic tale set in post-apocalyptic Colorado, part love story, with shades of Mad Max.
Housekeeping by Marilynne Robinson. The award-winning author is thought to have based the fictional town of Fingerbone in her haunting 1980 novel following the lives of women, on her hometown of Sandpoint, Idaho.
The Miseducation of Cameron Post by Emily M. Danforth. Compelling LGBTQ+ coming-of-age story set in Miles City, Montana, tackling the controversial issue of gay "conversion therapy."
The Virginian by Owen Wister. Wister's most famous Western novel is still a good read, set in 1880s Wyoming.

CREDITS

PHOTO CREDITS

All images **Shutterstock**

COVER CREDITS

Front cover: Maroon Bells & Lake,
Aspen, Colorado *Sean Xu/Shutterstock*
Back cover: Garden of the Gods,
Colorado *Shutterstock*
Front flap: (from top) The Wrangler
Building, Cheyenne Wyoming
Shutterstock; American Indian woman
Shutterstock; Skiier at the Big Sky
Resort, Montana *Shutterstock*; Pikes
Peak *Shutterstock*
Back flap: Moose in Grand Teton
National Park, Wyoming *Shutterstock*

INSIGHT GUIDE CREDITS

Distribution
UK, Ireland and Europe
Apa Publications (UK) Ltd;
sales@insightguides.com
United States and Canada
Ingram Publisher Services;
ips@ingramcontent.com
Australia and New Zealand
Booktopia;
retailer@booktopia.com.au
Worldwide
Apa Publications (UK) Ltd;
sales@insightguides.com
Special Sales, Content Licensing and CoPublishing
Insight Guides can be purchased in bulk quantities at discounted prices. We can create special editions, personalised jackets and corporate imprints tailored to your needs.
sales@insightguides.com
www.insightguides.biz

Printed in China

All Rights Reserved
© 2022 Apa Digital AG
License edition © Apa Publications Ltd UK

First Edition 2022

www.insightguides.com

Editor: Annie Warren
Author: Stephen Keeling
Picture Editor: Piotr Kala
Cartography: Carte
Layout: Greg Madejak
Head of DTP and Pre-Press: Katie Bennett
Picture Manager: Tom Smyth
Indexer and proofreader: Penny Phenix
Head of Publishing: Kate Drynan

CONTRIBUTORS

Stephen Keeling has written numerous guidebooks about North America since his first visit to the USA in 1991, when he traveled across the Rockies on Greyhound buses, fueled by 50-cent coffee and cheeseburgers.

He lives in New York City, but loves Idaho's scenic byways, the buffalo herds in the Black Hills and just about all of Colorado. This first edition was edited by **Annie Warren** and proofread and indexed by **Penny Phenix**.

ABOUT INSIGHT GUIDES

Insight Guides have more than 45 years' experience of publishing high-quality, visual travel guides. We produce 400 full-colour titles, in both print and digital form, covering more than 200 destinations across the globe, in a variety of formats to meet your different needs.

Insight Guides are written by local authors, whose expertise is evident in the extensive historical and cultural

background features. Each destination is carefully researched by regional experts to ensure our guides provide the very latest information. All the reviews in **Insight Guides** are independent; we strive to maintain an impartial view. Our reviews are carefully selected to guide you to the best places to eat, go out and shop, so you can be confident that when we say a place is special, we really mean it.

Legend

City maps

	Freeway/Highway/Motorway
	Divided Highway
	Main Roads
	Minor Roads
	Pedestrian Roads
	Steps
	Footpath
	Railway
	Funicular Railway
	Cable Car
	Tunnel
	City Wall
	Important Building
	Built Up Area
	Other Land
	Transport Hub
	Park
	Pedestrian Area
	Bus Station
	Tourist Information
	Main Post Office
	Cathedral/Church
	Mosque
	Synagogue
	Statue/Monument
	Beach
	Airport

Regional maps

	Freeway/Highway/Motorway (with junction)
	Freeway/Highway/Motorway (under construction)
	Divided Highway
	Main Road
	Secondary Road
	Minor Road
	Track
	Footpath
	International Boundary
	State/Province Boundary
	National Park/Reserve
	Marine Park
	Ferry Route
	Marshland/Swamp
	Glacier Salt Lake
	Airport/Airfield
	Ancient Site
	Border Control
	Cable Car
	Castle/Castle Ruins
	Cave
	Chateau/Stately Home
	Church/Church Ruins
	Crater
	Lighthouse
	Mountain Peak
	Place of Interest
	Viewpoint

INDEX

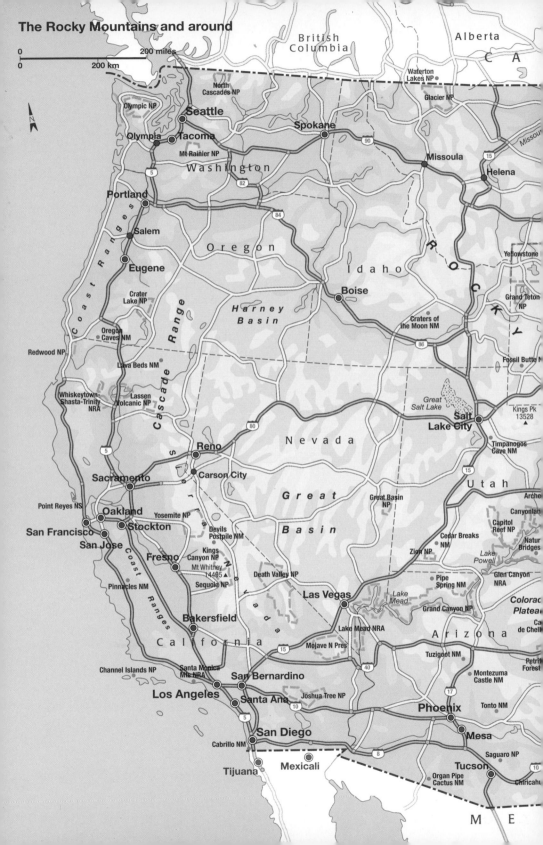